Slavery in Brazil

Brazil was the American society that received the largest contingent of African slaves in the Americas and the longest-lasting slave regime in the Western Hemisphere. This is the first complete modern survey of the institution of slavery in Brazil and how it affected the lives of enslaved Africans. It is based on major new research on the institution of slavery and the role of Africans and their descendants in Brazil. Although Brazilians have incorporated many of the North American debates about slavery, they have also developed a new set of questions about slaveholding: the nature of marriage, family, religion, and culture among the slaves and free colored; the process of manumission; and the rise of the free colored class during slavery. It is the aim of this book to introduce the reader to this latest research, both to elucidate the Brazilian experience and to provide a basis for comparisons with all other American slave systems.

Herbert S. Klein is Director of the Center for Latin American Studies, Professor of History, and Senior Fellow at the Hoover Institution at Stanford University, as well as Gouverneur Morris Professor Emeritus of History at Columbia University. Klein is the author of some 20 books and 155 articles in several languages on Latin America and on comparative themes in social and economic history. Among these books are four comparative studies of slavery, the most recent of which are *African Slavery in Latin America and the Caribbean* (coauthor), *The Atlantic Slave Trade*, and *Slavery and the Economy of São Paulo, 1750–1850* (coauthor). He has also published on such diverse themes as *The American Finances of the Spanish Empire, 1680–1809* and *A Population History of the United States* and is coauthor of *Brazil since 1980* and *Mexico since 1980*.

Francisco Vidal Luna was Professor of Economics at the Universidade de São Paulo until his retirement in 1997. Aside from his academic career, he was Chief da Assessoria Econômica da Secretaria da Fazenda do Estado de São Paulo (1983–1985), Head of IPLAN-IPEA (1985–1986), and Secretário de Planejamento of the Secretaria do Planejamento of the Presidência da República (1986–1987). Luna was also socio gerente, vice president, and president of the Banco Inter-American Express (1987–2002). In 2005, he became the Secretary of Planning and Budget of the Municipality of São Paulo, and in 2008, he took on the role of Secretary of Economy and Planning of the state government of São Paulo. Luna is the author of some fifty articles and papers and eleven books on Brazilian economic history and the Brazilian economy, among which are *Minas Gerais: Escravos e Senhores*, *Minas Colonial: Economia e Sociedade* (coauthor), *Slavery and the Economy of São Paulo, 1750–1850* (coauthor), and *Brazil since 1980* (coauthor).

Slavery in Brazil

HERBERT S. KLEIN
Stanford University

FRANCISCO VIDAL LUNA
University of São Paulo

CAMBRIDGE UNIVERSITY PRESS
Cambridge, New York, Melbourne, Madrid, Cape Town, Singapore,
São Paulo, Delhi, Dubai, Tokyo

Cambridge University Press
32 Avenue of the Americas, New York, NY 10013-2473, USA

www.cambridge.org
Information on this title: www.cambridge.org/9780521141925

First published 2010

Printed in the United States of America

A catalog record for this publication is available from the British Library.

Library of Congress Cataloging in Publication data

Klein, Herbert S.
Slavery in Brazil / Herbert S. Klein, Francisco Vidal Luna. – 1st ed.
p.   cm.
Includes bibliographical references and index.
ISBN 978-0-521-19398-6 (hardback) – ISBN 978-0-521-14192-5 (pbk.)
1. Slavery – Brazil – History.   2. Slaves – Brazil – History.   3. Freedmen – Brazil –
History.   4. Blacks – Brazil – History.   5. Brazil – Civilization-African influences.
I. Luna, Francisco Vidal.   II. Title.
HT1126.K54   2009
306.3′620981 – dc22   2009022572

ISBN 978-0-521-19398-6 Hardback
ISBN 978-0-521-14192-5 Paperback

To
Samantha Olivia Klein

Contents

vii

Preface

In recent years, there has been an outpouring of studies on the institution of slavery and the role of Africans and their descendants in Brazil. The earliest work on slavery in Brazil and the Afro-Brazilian experience was much influenced by anthropologists, whereas the more recent studies have seen an impressive participation of economists and sociologists along with the ongoing work of historians. Just as U.S. scholars were much influenced by the work of Brazilians in the 1950s and 1960s, for example, today Brazilian scholars are very aware of the new work done in the United States in the past four decades. Although the Brazilians have incorporated many of the North American debates about slavery in the United States, they have also developed a new set of questions about slaveholding and its distribution in the population as well as the nature of marriage and family among slaves. In fact, one could argue that the Brazilian historians and economists are doing more studies on their institution of slavery than is now occurring in the United States, despite the imbalance in the size of the historical profession in the two countries.

Ever since 1988, the centenary of abolition in Brazil, there has been an outpouring of new studies in theses, articles, and books. This has been the work of several distinct regional Brazilian schools of historical analysis. Along with the traditional political and social studies of the Bahian school, there has now emerged the original quantitative work of the São Paulo school of economic historians, the demographic historians of Minas Gerais, and the social historians of Rio de Janeiro. Although sometimes local historians have worked in isolation on given themes, more and more there is cross-fertilization, with Bahian historians using Paulista models and Paulistas replicating *Carioca* studies. All of these investigators have created an extensive new literature on the functioning of slavery and the role of free colored in eighteenth- and early-nineteenth-century Brazil. Finally, thanks to the efforts of CAPES of the Ministry of Education, almost all recent theses and dissertations are now online and can be accessed at two different websites.[1]

It is the aim of this study to introduce the reader to this latest research, to elucidate the Brazilian experience, and to provide a basis of comparisons for all other American slave systems. The organization of the book is somewhat unusual, as we have tried to provide both a chronological framework and a structural analysis at the same time. To understand slave life in Brazil, it is essential first to understand how and why the Portuguese used slaves as a primary labor force within this Portuguese colony and independent nation. Thus, Part I provides a chronological analysis of the political economy of slavery in Brazil from its founding until the late-nineteenth century. Our emphasis in these chapters is to provide an understanding of the timing and evolution of the various economic sectors that used slave labor. The concern here is with the macroeconomic changes and developments. Part II deals with the slaves themselves in their daily lives. The second half of the book is synchronic in nature, emphasizing the demographic, social, and political aspects of slave and free colored life and culture. Even here, however, we are concerned with relating underlying economic patterns with these structural changes and delineating regional and temporal variations. The last chapter returns to a more strictly chronological approach but tries to provide as broad a model as possible to incorporate the multiple experiences that made up the long process of transition from slave to free labor in Brazil.

Certain qualifications should be made at the outset about the limits of our study. Although American Indians were enslaved by the Portuguese and used in commercial export industries in the first century of the colonization, we will only concentrate on the enslaved Africans and Afro-Brazilians. Amerindian slavery lasted a short time and has been only moderately studied, and it was the Africans and their descendants who were the primary servile labor force that dominated and defined Brazilian slavery for most of its history. Next, because of varying terminology applied in the several languages to Afro-Americans, readers should be

---

[1] The first gives full access to some 606 master's theses and 127 doctoral dissertations (as of August 30, 2008) at http://www.dominiopublico.gov.br/pesquisa/PesquisaPeriodico Form.jsp. The second website is maintained by CAPES directly with complete search facilities and is found at http://bdtd2.ibict.br.

aware of our definitions. We use the term *pretos* or "blacks" to refer to persons defined by the society as having only African ancestry. In contrast, the term *pardos* or "mulattoes" refers to persons of mixed African and European or even African and Amerindian or Asian background. *Afro-Brazilian* is the term used to designate persons born in America who are defined as blacks and mulattoes. *African* is used here only to define persons born in Africa, and the term *Creole* is used to designate a person born in the Americas. We use the term *colored*, as in free colored, as inclusive of both blacks and mulattoes regardless of their place of birth. Finally, the *free colored* sometimes can be divided into those born free (*livres*) or those who were emancipated in their own lifetime (called either *forros* or *libertos*), a distinction of importance made by Brazilians in the slave period.

In writing this book we have had the support of many colleagues. Iraci Nero da Costa, Stanley Engerman, Stuart Schwartz, Mariza Soares, and João Reis kindly critiqued the manuscript for us. As ever, we owe a special debt to our editor, Frank Smith, who encouraged us to write this work in the first place.

Menlo Park, California
São Paulo, Brazil
August 2008

PART ONE

THE POLITICAL ECONOMY OF SLAVE LABOR

I

Origins of the African Slavery in Brazil

Slavery was well-known in most complex societies centuries before the establishment of the Brazilian colony by the Portuguese. Slaves were usually a small part of any labor force in most preindustrial societies and were most commonly tied to the household economy. In a few societies, they were used in agriculture, mining, or other productive enterprises beyond the household economy. No ethnic group escaped enslavement, and all societies treated their slaves as outsiders, rootless and ahistorical individuals ultimately held against their will by the threat of force. Because of their legal position, slaves were also the most mobile labor force available in any society.

In the work they performed and in their lack of control over their own lives, slaves were not unique from other subordinate members of their respective societies. Peasants were often in a temporary condition of servitude, some being tied to the land on a permanent basis. Children, women, and prisoners often lived lives indistinguishable from those of slaves in terms of the labor they performed or the rights immediately available to them. But it was the lack of ties to family, kin, and the community that finally distinguished slaves from all other workers. True slaves were persons without the bindings and linkages common to even the lowest free persons and who were thus completely dependent on the will of their masters. Masters could use their slaves at far less cost in reciprocal obligations than any other labor group in their societies.[1]

---

[1] The best model for distinguishing slaves from forced or dependent laborers is provided by Orlando Patterson, *Slavery and Social Death: A Comparative Study* (Cambridge: Harvard University Press, 1982). A discussion of these same issues for the classical period

Slavery as a system of industrial or market production was a much more limited phenomenon. Most scholars now date its origins for Western society in the centuries immediately prior to the Christian era in the Greek city-states and the emerging Roman Empire of the period. Recent studies have suggested that for slavery as an "industrial" system to exist, there needed to be an important market economy emerging with a limited supply of peasant labor and with abundant sources of slaves – usually via conquest or purchase.

The Roman case is unusual among known preindustrial societies because of the size and importance of both its slave population and their economic role in the economy. It was one of the most urban premodern societies and had important international trade. Slaves were used in food production and other agricultural activities as well as in the urban crafts. It has been estimated that at the height of the Roman Empire, the population of Italy contained some two to three million slaves, who represented a very high 35 to 40 percent of the total population.[2]

Although slaves did not disappear from Europe until well into the modern period, slavery as a major economic institution collapsed with the barbarian invasions of the fifth to the eighth centuries A.D. The decline of urban markets, the breakdown of long-distance trade, and the increasing self-sufficiency of agriculture created a situation in which slave labor was no longer viable, and peasant agricultural labor again predominated. Slavery was reduced to household and domestic tasks, and the early Middle Ages' stress on defense and security led to the rise of serfs, were peasants who sacrificed part of their freedom in return for protection by the local elite, and serfs and free peasants became the dominant labor force in Europe.[3]

is found in M. I. Finley, "Between Slavery and Freedom," *Comparative Studies in Society and History*, 6, no. 3 (April 1964).

[2] For the most recent survey of slavery in the classical world with the latest bibliography, see Jean Andreau and Raymond Descat, *Esclave en Grèce et à Rome* (Paris: Hachette, 2006). On slavery in the classical Greek period, see Yvon Garlan, *Slavery in Ancient Greece* (rev. ed.; Ithaca, NY: Cornell University Press, 1982). On Roman slavery, see Keith Bradley, *Slavery and Society at Rome* (Cambridge: Cambridge University Press, 1994); Keith Hopkins, *Conquerors and Slaves* (Cambridge: Cambridge University Press, 1978); and the excellent recent study of Walter Scheidel, "Quantifying the Sources of Slaves in the Early Roman Empire," *The Journal of Roman Studies*, vol. 87 (1997) as well as the older collection of essays edited by M. I. Finley, *Classical Slavery* (London: F. Cass, 1987).

[3] On slavery in Europe in the post-Roman times, the classic work based on primary sources is Charles Verlinden, *L'esclavage dans l'Europe médiévale* (2 vols.; Brugge: De Tempel, 1955–1977), and the survey of William D. Phillips, *Slavery from Roman Times to the*

At no time during this period of retrenchment did slavery itself disappear from Europe. Among the Germanic peoples on the northern frontiers, it remained important because of constant warfare, and in the non-Christian world of the Mediterranean, slavery experienced a renaissance from the eighth to the thirteenth centuries. The Muslim invasions of the Mediterranean islands and Spain brought the increasing use of slaves in agriculture and industry.

Despite this revival of slavery in the peripheries, slavery in mainland Christian Europe was confined to domestic activities and a few other limited activities. Only in the more advanced Islamic Mediterranean world were slaves used in large numbers. But the subsequent conquest of these states by the northern Iberian Christians resulted more in enserfment than slavery for the captured Muslims. By the end of the Middle Ages, the emerging power of the European economy was fed by an expanding peasant labor force. Although the legal structures originating in Roman law were still intact in Christian Europe, the institution of slavery was not a major force by the time the first Portuguese caravels sighted the Guinean coastline at the beginning of the fifteenth century.

Slavery also existed in the African continent from the beginning of recorded times. As in medieval Christian Europe, it was also a relatively minor institution in the period before the opening up of the Atlantic slave trade. Slavery could be found as a domestic institution in most of the region's more complex societies, and a few exceptional states influenced by Islam may have developed more industrial forms of slave production. In these societies, moreover, the status of slaves was not as precisely defined as in regimes in which slaves played a more vital role in production. Children of free fathers and slave mothers would often become free members of the kin group; second-generation acculturated slaves would become less subject to sale and assumed far more rights and privileges.[4]

Early Transatlantic Trade (Minneapolis: University of Minnesota Press, 1985). The basic relations between serfdom and slavery are examined in Marc Bloch, *Slavery and Serfdom in the Middle Ages, Selected Essays* (Berkeley: University of California Press, 1975) and discussed in Pierre Dockès, *Medieval Slavery and Liberation* (London: Methuen, 1982). Recent discussions on medieval slavery and its decline are found in Pierre Bonnaissie, *From Slavery to Feudalism in South-Western Europe* (Cambridge: Cambridge University Press, 1991) and Susan M. Stuard, "Ancillary Evidence for the Decline of Medieval Slavery," *Past & Present* 149 (November 1995).

[4] Slavery in Africa has been the subject of wide interest and controversy in recent years. A good introduction to this debate can be found in Walter Rodney, *How Europe Underdeveloped Africa* (London: Bogle-L'Ouverture Publications, 1972). The most recent and the best attempt at classification and historical analysis is Paul E. Lovejoy, *Transformations in*

African slaves were also to be found outside the continent as well. With no all-embracing religious or political unity, the numerous states of Africa were free to buy and sell slaves or even to export them to non-African areas. Caravan routes across the Sahara predated the opening up of the African Atlantic coast, and slaves formed a part of Africa's export trade to the Mediterranean from pre-Roman to modern times. Given the widespread use of slaves within Africa, there was also an internal slave trade well before the opening of the West African-Atlantic routes.

Africans were being shipped outside the continent in steady numbers for at least some six centuries prior to the arrival of the Portuguese, with an estimated 3.5 to 10 million Africans being sent to Asia, Europe, and the Middle East. These forced African migrations contained more women and children than would the emigrants later participating in the Atlantic slave trade, and they also came from regions that would be only moderately affected by the Atlantic movements. The internal slave trade also was biased toward women. To supply these two slave markets, the whole complex of enslavement practices from full-scale warfare and raiding of enemies to judicial enslavement and taxation of dependent peoples had come into use and would also be the source of slaves for the Atlantic slave trade when this came into existence in the early fifteenth century. These pre-Atlantic slave trades were less intense and had less of an impact on local conditions than the Atlantic trade. Their annual volume was lower and was spread over more years than the Atlantic trade.[5]

The arrival of the Portuguese explorers on the sub-Saharan African coast in the early 1400s represents a major new development in the history

---

Slavery: A History of Slavery in Africa (Cambridge: Cambridge University Press, 1983). For detailed case studies, see the essays in Jean Claude Meillassoux, *L'Esclavage en Afrique précoloniale* (Paris: Presses Universitaires de France, 1975); Suzanne Miers and Igor Kopytoff, eds., *Slavery in Africa: Historical and Anthropological Perspectives* (Madison: University of Wisconsin Press, 1977); James Watson, ed., *Asian and African Systems of Slavery* (Berkeley: University of California Press, 1980); and finally Claire C. Robertson and Martin A. Klein, eds., *Women and Slavery in Africa* (Madison: University of Wisconsin Press, 1983).

5 On the North African and East African trades, see Patrick Manning, *Slavery and African Life: Occidental, Oriental, and African Slave Trades* (Cambridge: Cambridge University Press, 1990); François Renault and Serge Daget, *Les traites négrières en Afrique* (Paris: Karthala, 1985); and the essays of Ralph A. Austen, "The Trans-Saharan Slave Trade: A Tentative Census," in Henry A. Gemery and Jan S. Hogendorn, eds., *The Uncommon Market: Essays in the Economic History of the Atlantic Slave Trade* (New York: Academic Press, 1979); "The 19th Century Islamic Slave Trade from East Africa (Swahili and Red Sea Coasts): A Tentative Census," *Slavery & Abolition*, IX (1988), and "The Mediterranean Islamic Slave Trade Out of Africa: A Tentative Census," *Slavery & Abolition*, XIII (1992).

of the slave trade from Africa in terms of its intensity, the sources of its slaves, and the usage made of these slaves in America. Initially, however, there was little to distinguish the Portuguese from the Muslim traders of North Africa. The Portuguese aimed at bypassing North African Saharan routes via a route from the sea. Their prime interest was gold, with slaves, pepper, ivory, and other products as secondary concerns. They purchased slaves as early as 1444, but sent them primarily to Europe to serve as domestic servants. Thus, the new sea trade started as an extension of the older overland trades. The Portuguese even carried out extensive slave trading along the African coast to supply the internal African slave market in exchange for gold, which they then exported to Europe. Their concentration on gold as opposed to slaves was based on the growing scarcity of precious metals in Europe. An expanding European economy was running an increasingly negative balance of trade with Asia, and the direct European access to the sub-Saharan gold fields helped pay for that trade.[6]

It was only with the introduction of sugar production to the eastern Atlantic islands and the opening up of the Western Hemisphere to European conquest at the end of the fifteenth century that a new and important use was found for these slaves. As slaves once again became a major factor in agricultural production within the European context, Portuguese interest in its African trade slowly shifted from a concern with gold and ivory to one primarily stressing slaves.

The first of the Crusades marked the revival of international markets for Christian Europeans and brought them actively into the slave trade. From the tenth to the thirteenth century, Genoese and Venetians expanded into Palestine, Syria, the Black Sea, and the Balkans, adding to their possessions in the eastern Mediterranean islands of Crete and Cyprus. These colonies created a new impetus to slavery. A market in Slavic peoples developed in this period, which gave rise to the use of the

---

[6] The standard analysis of Portuguese world trade in the first three centuries of exploration is Vitorino Magalhães Godinho, *Os descobrimentos e a economia mundial* (2nd ed. rev.; 4 vols.; Lisbon: Editorial Presença, 1981–1983). The best single interpretation of the early Portuguese slave trade is found in Ivana Elbl, "Volume of the Early Atlantic Slave Trade, 1450–1521," *Journal of African History*, XXXVIII (1997). Elbl (p. 75) estimates that "Europeans exported approximately 156,000 slaves from Atlantic Africa between 1450 and 1521." In turn, Godinho estimated a total of 140,000 to 150,000 slaves were taken from Africa by 1505. Godinho, *Os descobrimentos*, IV, p. 161. These figures are higher than the current estimate for Europe found in the new Atlantic slave trade database. Also see Luis Felipe de Alencastro, *O trato dos viventes: Formação do Brasil no Atlântico Sul, séculos XVI e XVII* (São Paulo: Companhia das Letras, 2000).

term *slave* to define this status. Slavs, of course, were not the only peoples to be enslaved. On the islands of the eastern Mediterranean, for example, Africans could be found in the early fourteenth century, along with Muslims from North Africa and Asia Minor and Christians from Greece, the Balkans, and northern Europe.

Sugar was introduced from Asia to Europe during the Islamic invasions, but it was the First Crusade at the end of the eleventh century that gave the Christians a chance to become sugar producers in their own right. In the twelfth and thirteenth centuries, Christian estates in Palestine produced sugar with a mixed labor force made up of slaves, *villeins*, and free workers. After the fall of these lands to the Turks at the end of the thirteenth century, the center of sugar production moved to Cyprus. Here Italian merchants and local rulers used slave and free labor to produce sugar. Cyprus in turn was soon replaced by the Venetian colony of Crete and then by Sicily, which had been producing sugar for the European market since the late eleventh century. With the fall of Palestine and Syrian centers to the Turks, Sicilian production temporarily became preeminent. The Mediterranean coast of Islamic Spain in the late thirteenth and early fourteenth centuries became another important production center for Northern and Western Europe. The westernmost advance of European sugar production reached the southern Portuguese province of the Algarve at the beginning of the fifteenth century. In not all of these cases was sugar produced by slaves, nor were they the exclusive labor force in any particular area. But the identification of slavery with sugar was well established long before the conquest of America. The techniques of sugar production and slave plantation agriculture that developed on the eastern Atlantic islands and later in the New World had their origins in the eastern Mediterranean in the early Middle Ages.[7]

As long as the Portuguese concentrated their efforts in the regions of Senegambia and the Gold Coast, they integrated themselves into the existing network of Muslim traders. The Muslims had brought these coasts into their own trade networks, and the Portuguese tapped into them through navigable Senegal and Gambia rivers. Even their establishment of São Jorge da Mina (Elmina) on the Gold Coast fit into these developments. But the settlement of the island depot and plantation center of São Tomé in the Gulf of Guinea and the beginning of trade relations with the

---

[7] The history of sugar production in Mediterranean Europe is discussed in J. H. Galloway, *The Sugar Cane Industry: An Historical Geography from Its Origins to 1914* (Cambridge: Cambridge University Press, 1989), chapter 3; and Noel Deerr, *The History of Sugar* (2 vols.; London: Chapman and Hall, 1949–1950).

Kingdom of the Kongo after 1500 substantially changed the nature of the Atlantic slave trade.

The Kongolese were located by the Zaire River (also known as the Congo River) and were unconnected to the Muslim trade before the arrival of the Portuguese. The Portuguese sent priests and advisers to the court of the Kongolese king, and the Kongolese king's representatives were placed on São Tomé. These changes occurred just as the Spanish conquest of the Caribbean islands and the Portuguese settlement of the Brazilian subcontinent were beginning and thus opened the new American market for African slaves. The decimation of the native Arawak and Carib peoples in the Caribbean islands and of the Tupi-Guarani speakers along the Brazilian coast encouraged the early experimentation with African slave labor.

The opening up of the Iberian American colonies initially involved the reexport of acculturated and Christianized blacks from the Iberian Peninsula who were brought in the households of the conquistadores. But after the opening up of Brazil on the one hand and Congo and São Tomé regions to Portuguese trade, a direct Africa-to-America movement began to Spanish America as well. After 1500, the volume of this Atlantic trade slowly rose from an annual few hundred slaves in the first half of the century to more than a thousand per annum by the 1550s and to more than three thousand per annum by the 1580s.[8] Non-Christian and non-Romance-language speakers taken directly from Africa, whom the Portuguese called *boçais*, now made up the overwhelming majority of slaves coming to America.

Another major change came about in the 1560s as a result of internal African developments. Hostile African invasions of the Kingdom of the Kongo led to direct Portuguese military support for the regime and finally,

---

[8] This and all subsequent estimated numbers on the Atlantic slave trade come from the latest version of the project on the trade that is under the direction of David Eltis. This project began with David Eltis, Stephen D. Behrendt, David Richardson, and Herbert S. Klein, *The Transatlantic Slave Trade: 1562–1867: A Database* (New York, Cambridge: Cambridge University Press, 2000); was revised by David Eltis, "The Volume and Structure of the Transatlantic Slave Trade: A Reassessment," *The William & Mary Quarterly*, 3rd series, 58, no. 1 (January 2001), which supplements the original estimates given by Philip Curtin in *The Atlantic Slave Trade: A Census* (Madison: University of Wisconsin Press, 1969) with the new Cambridge data set, plus further additions. For the most recent revisions and additions to the old Cambridge slave voyage data set of 2000, see The Trans-Atlantic Slave Trade Database, Voyages (Emory University) available at http://www.slavevoyages.org/tast/index.faces. The "estimates" are under a separate heading and are the numbers used throughout this volume. These can be found at http://www.slavevoyages.org/tast/assessment/estimates.faces. I have accessed the material as of August 2008 when this website was finally open to the public.

in 1576, to their establishment of a full-time settlement at the southern edge of the kingdom at the port of Luanda. With the development of Luanda came a decline in São Tomé as an entrepôt, for now slaves were shipped directly to America from the mainland coast and from a region that was to provide America with the most slaves of any area of Africa during the next three centuries. By 1600, the Atlantic slave trade was to pass the north and east African export trades in total volume, although it was not until after 1700 that slaves finally surpassed all other exports from Africa in value.[9]

Just as the beginnings of the Portuguese slave trade had complemented a traditional trading system, the first use of Atlantic slave-trade Africans by Europeans was in traditional activities. For the first half-century, the European slave ships that cruised the Atlantic shoreline of Africa carried their slaves to the Iberian Peninsula. The ports of Lisbon and Seville were the centers for a thriving trade in African slaves, and from these centers slaves were distributed rather widely through the western Mediterranean. Although Africans quickly became a significant group within the polyglot slave communities in the major cities of the region, they never became the dominant labor force in the local economies. Even in the southern coastal cities of Portugal, where they were most numerous, they never represented more than 15 percent of the population whereas in other Portuguese and Castilian port cities they usually numbered less than 10 percent. Africans were used no differently than the Moorish slaves who preceded and coexisted with them. African slaves and freedmen were to be found primarily in urban centers and worked mostly in domestic service. The city with the largest number of these African slaves was probably Lisbon, which by the 1550s already had some ten thousand slaves, which rose to some fifteen thousand by the 1630s. In other areas of the Iberian Peninsular, the impact of this first generation of Africans was also significant. About two-thirds of the slaves imported from 1489 to 1516 were African, and an average of about 250 Africans were imported annually.[10] By the sixteenth century, such central areas as Portugal and Andalucia already had large slave populations. By 1573, the whole of

[9] David Eltis, "The Relative Importance of Slaves and Commodities in the Atlantic Trade of Seventeenth-Century Africa," *The Journal of African History*, 35, no. 2 (1994).

[10] Vicenta Cortes Alonso, *La esclavitud en Valencia durante el reinado de los reyes católicos (1479–1516)* (Valencia: Ayuntamiento, 1964), pp. 57–60; and Alfonso Franco Silva, *La esclavitud en Sevilla y su tierra a fines de la edad media* (Sevilla: Diputación Provincial de Sevilla, 1979). For the latest survey of the different groups enslaved in the Iberian

Portugal was said to contain more than 40,000 slaves, a large number of whom were sub-Saharan Africans.[11] But in general, African slaves even in Mediterranean Europe were few in numbers and mostly to be found in urban households. Even the wealthiest European masters owned only a few slaves, and an owner who held fifteen African slaves in sixteenth-century Portugal was considered very unusual. Although slave owners were wealthy aristocrats, institutions, and professionals – many of whom were also major landowners – they infrequently used their slaves in agriculture. Slaves were sometimes to be found in rural occupations but never as a significant element in the local agricultural labor force because of their high costs and the availability of cheap peasant labor.[12]

Despite the important role these acculturated European-African slaves initially played in establishing the legal, social, and cultural norms in Europe and then again in America for the Africans who followed them, the Christian and Portuguese-speaking African slaves were not the basis for the new European slave labor system being established by the Portuguese in the Atlantic World. It was the Africans brought directly to the previously unpopulated eastern Atlantic islands beginning in the first half of the fifteenth century who were to define the new plantation model of Afro-American slave labor. The use by Europeans of African slaves in plantations evolved not in continental Europe with its acculturated slaves but in these Atlantic islands.

Just as Portugal was opening up the African coast to European penetration, its explorers and sailors were competing with the Spaniards in colonizing the eastern Atlantic islands. By the 1450s, the Portuguese were developing the unpopulated Azores, Madeira, the Cape Verde Islands, and São Tomé while the Spaniards were conquering the inhabited Canary Islands by the last decade of the century. Some of these islands proved ideal for sugar cultivation, so Italian merchants were not slow in introducing the latest in Mediterranean sugar-production techniques. After much experimentation, the most important sugar-producing islands turned out

Peninsular, see Alessandro Stella, *Historie d'esclaves dans la peninsula Ibérique* (Paris: École des Hautes Études en Sciences Sociales, 2000).

[11] Frédéric Mauro, *Le Portugal et l'Atlantique au XVIIe siècle, 1570–1670; étude économique* (Paris: SEVPEN, 1960), p. 147; Verlinden, *L'esclavage dans l'Europe médiévale* I, p. 837.

[12] A. C. de C. M. Saunders, *A Social History of Black Slaves and Freedmen in Portugal, 1441–1555* (Cambridge: Cambridge University Press, 1982) provides the most complete study of Africans in Portugal, with chapter 3 covering their demography and chapter 4 their occupations. The Lisbon population estimates are given in ibid., pp. 54–5. Also see the recent survey by Stella, *Historie d'esclaves dans la peninsula Ibérique*.

to be Madeira, the Canaries, and São Tomé. Sugar became the prime
output on Madeira by the middle of the century, and by the end of the
fifteenth century, Madeira had become Europe's largest producer. The
Portuguese imported *Guanches*, the native Canarians, as slaves along
with Africans, and by the end of the 1450s, Madeira sugar was being
sold on the London market. By 1493, there were eighty sugar mills (or
engenhos) on the island refining an average of 18 tons of sugar per annum.
Given the terraced nature of the sugar estates, production units were relatively small, however, and the largest plantation held only some eighty
slaves, a size that would be considered moderate by Brazilian standards
in the next century.

Madeira had a particularly sharp rise and fall in its sugar evolution,
and by the 1530s, it was well outdistanced by competition from the other
islands. The Canary Islands were the next big entrant into the sugar-
production race, and by the first decades of the sixteenth century, the
local coastal estates were milling on average of 50 tons per annum. Here,
as in Madeira, *Guanche* natives were first used as slaves, along with
Islamic slaves imported from Spain, but very quickly Africans became
the dominant slave labor force on the estates. As on Madeira, there were
more masters and sugar producers than mill-owners, and an intermediate group of small-scale, slave-owning planters evolved who worked for
larger and richer mill-owners who could afford the extremely high costs
of establishing sugar refineries.

The final Atlantic island to develop a major sugar plantation slave system was the African coastal island of São Tomé, which, like the Azores,
Cape Verde Islands, and Madeira, had been uninhabited prior to Portuguese penetration. By the 1550s, there were some sixty mills in operation on the island and some two thousand plantation slaves, all of whom
were Africans. There were also on average at any one time some five to
six thousand slaves in slave pens on this entrepôt island being held for
transport to Europe and America. Eventually, American competition and
its increasingly important role as a transfer and slave-trade provisioning
center led to the decline of the São Tomé sugar industry.

Thus, all the Eastern Atlantic sugar islands went through a boom-and-
bust cycle that rarely lasted more than a century. But all the major sugar-
producing islands established functioning plantation slave regimes, which
became the models of such institutions transported to the New World.
Non-Christian and non-Portuguese-speaking Africans directly imported
from the African coast were brought to work the rural estates on these
islands. Urban slavery and domestic slavery were minor occupations,

and slaves were held in extremely large numbers by the standards of European slaveholdings of the period. All the trappings of the New World plantation system were well established, with the small number of wealthy mill-owners at the top of the hierarchy holding the most land and the most slaves, followed by an intermediate layer of European planters who owned slaves and sugar fields but were too poor to be mill-owners in their own right. A poor European peasant population hardly existed, with only skilled administrative and mill operations opened to non-slave-owning whites. The lowest layer consisted of the mass of black slaves who made up the majority of the labor force as well as of the population as a whole. Thus, well before the massive transplantation of Africans across the Atlantic, the American slave plantation system had already been born.[13]

It was the establishment of the Portuguese colony of Brazil after 1500 that was to mark the beginnings of the modern slave plantation economy of the Americas, which so influenced hemispheric developments for the next four centuries. Although large slave plantations producing sugar had temporarily appeared in the first decades of the sixteenth century in Santo Domingo, by the middle decades of the century, when Brazilians began to establish their own slave plantations, those of the Spanish Caribbean were in decline and would not revive again until the late eighteenth century.[14] It was thus the successful Brazilian system that would influence the pattern of all future commercial agricultural slave regimes. What distinguished this American slave society from most previous slave societies was in fact the domination of slaves as agricultural workers, their vital importance in the production of goods for the international market, and their importance within the local societies. The French, the

---

[13] The Portuguese Atlantic experience is analyzed in John L. Vogt, *Portuguese Rule on the Gold Coast, 1469–1682* (Athens: University of Georgia Press, 1979). The background chapters in Stuart B. Schwartz, *Sugar Plantations in the Formation of Brazilian Society (Bahia, 1550–1835)* (Cambridge: Cambridge University Press, 1985) provide a good general survey of the Madeira and Azorian experience; and a detailed study of the Madeira sugar industry is found in Alberto Vieira, "Sugar Islands: The Sugar Economy of Madeira and the Canaries, 1450–1650," in Stuart B. Schwartz, ed., *Tropical Babylons: Sugar and the Making of the Atlantic World, 1450–1680* (Chapel Hill: University of North Carolina Press, 2004). The standard studies of slavery on these islands are found in Alberto Vieira, *Os escravos no arquipélago da Madeira: séculos XV a XVII* (Funchal: Centro de Estudos de História do Atlântico, 1991); and Manuel Lobo Cabrera, *La esclavitud en las Canarias orientales en el siglo XVI (negros, moros y moriscos)* (Las Palmas: Cabildo Insular de Gran Canaria, 1982).

[14] Genaro Rodríguez Morel, "The Sugar Economy of Española in the Sixteenth Century," in Schwartz, ed., *Tropical Babylons*.

English, and the late-eighteenth-century Spanish colonies would adopt
the Portuguese American slave system as their own, and so the study of
African slavery in Brazil is fundamental to the study of the Afro-Brazilian
experience of the 4.8 million Africans who arrived on its shores. This
history is also crucial if one is to understand the experience of the overwhelming majority of Afro-Americans even in the Northern Hemisphere.

There has been an intense recent debate in the literature about why
Africans became the primary group enslaved in the Americas, which
would eventually cause Americans to equate skin color with slave status for the next four centuries. Some have suggested a special cultural or
racial bias of the Europeans that allowed them to enslave Africans. Yet
this seems a very strange argument given the long and intimate contact
that Europeans had with Africans from preclassical times to the early
modern period and the integration of these African slaves into a multi-
ethnic, multireligious, and multicolored slave population in continental
Europe and the Eastern Atlantic islands well before the opening of the
Americas to European conquest and colonization. But the increasing cost
of non-African slaves does offer a possible explanation. The rise of the
Ottoman Empire in the eastern Mediterranean and the consolidation of a
powerful independent Moroccan state in North Africa closed off or made
more costly traditional sources of slaves from these regions. At the same
time, the opening up of water transport to sub-Saharan markets made
African slaves considerably cheaper than they had been via the Saharan
caravan routes. Enslavement of non-Africans did not end, as the famous
existence of Christian slaves in North Africa well into the eighteenth
century demonstrated, but it was no longer significant in the European
slave markets by the middle of the sixteenth century. Given the steady
export of West African gold and ivories and the development of Portugal's
enormous Asiatic trading empire, the commercial relations between Western Africa and Europe now became common and cheap. Western Africans
brought by sea had already replaced most other ethnic and religious
groups in the European slave markets by the middle of the sixteenth century. Although Iberians initially enslaved Canary Islanders, these were
later freed, as were the few Indians who were brought from America.
The Muslims who had been enslaved for centuries were no longer significant as they disappeared from the Iberian Peninsula itself due to these
powerful Muslim states in the Maghreb region, which closed the trade in
Muslims to easy Christian European exploitation. In turn, the expansion
of the Turks in the eastern Mediterranean closed off traditional Slavic
and Balkan sources for slaves to Western Europeans, a move supported

by the Roman Catholic Church that sought an end to Christians enslaving other Christians. On the other hand, the growing efficiency of the Atlantic slave traders, the dependability of African slave supply, and the decline of prices explain why Africans would became the major available source of slave labor for sixteenth-century Europe.

Thus, the increasing costs of slaves coming from Europe and the declining costs of African slaves are powerful factors in determining why Africans became the major source of slaves for America. Even then, they were not the only racial and ethnic groups enslaved. Until the late sixteenth century, American Indians were an important part of the slave population, and they were dominant in Brazil until 1600. In fact, there were even well-known cases of Moorish slaves residing in the Americas.[15] Thus, one can sufficiently explain the turn toward African slaves by standard economic criteria of supply constraints and need not seek cultural explanations to understand this decision to use Africans.

But why was there a demand for slaves in the first place? This is a more difficult question to answer. It is evident that the classic equation in all of America was that for the European conquerors, land was cheap and labor was costly.[16] Yet the existence of at least some twenty to twenty-five million American Indians in 1492 would seem to suggest that the Europeans would have an abundant supply of labor available for the exploitation of their new colonies.[17] Moreover, Europe itself was experiencing major

---

[15] On the Morisco and Central American Indian slaves found in sixteenth-century Peru, see James Lockhart, *Spanish Peru, 1532–1560: A Social History* (2nd ed.; Madison: University of Wisconsin Press, 1994), pp. 222–4, 228–31.

[16] On whether slavery or some other form of forced labor might result from a cheap land and costly labor situation, see Evsey D. Domar, "The Causes of Slavery or Serfdom: A Hypothesis," *Journal of Economic History*, 30, no.1 (March 1970).

[17] For determining the population movements of Indians, Africans, and Europeans in America in this first century, the best overall assessment will be found in Nicolás Sánchez-Albornoz, *La población de America Latina: Desde los tiempos precolombianos al año 2025* (2nd rev. ed.; Madrid: Alianza Editorial, 1994); and his more recent "The Population of Colonial Spanish America," in Leslie Bethell, ed., *Cambridge History of Latin America*, vol. II (Cambridge: Cambridge University Press, 1984). Reliable numbers on the Indian population of Mexico are found in William T. Saunders, "The Population of the Central Mexican Symbiotic Region, the Basin of Mexico, and the Teotihuacán Valley in the Sixteenth Century," in William M. Denevan, ed., *The Native Population of the Americas in 1492* (Madison: The University of Wisconsin Press, 1976); and for Peru, in David Nobel Cook, *Demographic Collapse, Indian Peru 1520–1620* (Cambridge: Cambridge University Press, 1981). For the Portuguese American territories in the same period, see Maria Luiza Marcílio, "The Population of Colonial Brazil," *The Cambridge History of Latin America* (11 vols.; Cambridge: Cambridge University Press, 1984), II.

population growth in the sixteenth century and seemingly might have provided the manpower needed to develop these American colonies. Yet despite these alternative labor supplies, America became the great market for an estimated 10.5 million African slaves who arrived in the course of the next five centuries, and it was in the New World that African slavery most flourished under European rule. Until the 1830s, more Africans than Europeans crossed the Atlantic annually and, as late as 1750, it was estimated that more than three-quarters of the emigrants to America were African slaves.[18]

Why did Europeans turn to Africans to populate their mines, factories, and farms in such numbers if they had access to conquered Indians and large numbers of poor within their own borders? Initially, it appeared as though the few thousand Iberian conquistadors would turn toward Indian slavery as the major form of labor in America. Already using the enslaved labor of Africans, Muslims, and *Guanches* in Europe and the Atlantic islands, the first Spaniards and Portuguese immediately went about enslaving all the American Indians they could find and keep. However, for a series of political, cultural, and religious reasons, the governments of both Spain and Portugal eventually decided against permanently enslaving the American Indians. Both governments had just banned enserfment and other forms of semifree labor arrangements within Europe and were committed to the principle of free wage labor, at least in terms of their own metropolitan populations. For the Spaniards, it would also prove more profitable to exploit the major imperial systems created by the advanced Amerindian empires through their hierarchies of nobles governing major peasant populations than to enslave all workers through force. Although African slaves would be brought to the Spanish American possessions in the centuries after the conquest, they never formed the labor base of these societies and rather resembled in their use of domestic and of urban slavery the patterns then prevalent in Europe.

The situation of the Portuguese, however, was entirely different. Their American possessions initially held no silver or precious metals to be exploited or any other easily extracted resource that could pay for the high costs of full-scale colonization of these vast lands. They would thus be forced to produce agricultural products for the European market and

[18] David Eltis, "Slavery and Freedom in the Early Modern World," in Stanley L. Engerman, ed., *Terms of Labor, Slavery, Serfdom, and Free Labor* (Stanford: Stanford University Press, 1999), pp. 28–9, table 1.

would need large stocks of labor to produce these goods. In contrast to the Amerindians of the central valley of Mexico or the highlands of Peru, the coastal Indians of Brazil were less easy to exploit through indirect rule. The Brazilian Indians were not accustomed to major agricultural activity or taxation. Although the various Tupi-Guarani Indians were willing to cut Brazil wood in exchange for European products, they were unwilling to change their semi-nomadic ways or abandon their simple village organizations for such imported goods. Although the Portuguese initially had a large pool of Indians to exploit and wholeheartedly enslaved them, this Indian slave labor would eventually prove too unreliable and costly to guarantee the necessary agricultural labor force needed to maintain the economic viability of their American colony. High levels of disease, constant conflict on the frontier with noncaptive Indians, and an ever declining pool of Indians to capture, all made this an ever more expensive and unreliable source of workers. Finally, the unification of Portugal with Spain after 1580 made the metropolitan government less sympathetic to Indian slave labor than the independent Portuguese state had been, and the Spanish Crown consistently pushed the Portuguese planters to abandon this labor source.

Thus, for a multiplicity of economic, political, and even religious reasons, the Iberians eventually abandoned the possibility of Indian slavery. But what was to prevent them from exploiting their own peasantry and urban poor? Given the demands of both the metropolitan and imperial labor markets, wages for Portuguese workers in Europe were too high to make mass migration to America a cost-effective operation. With just over one million in population,[19] Portugal was straining its resources to staff the vast African and Asian trading empire it was establishing from the early 1400s to the beginning of the sixteenth century. Demand for labor was so high that there was no pool of cheap Iberian labor that could be tapped for the initially quite poor lands of Brazil. With dyewoods – a product easily worked by free Indian labor – as the only important export from its American possession, compared with the gold, slaves, ivory, and spices from Africa and Asia, Portuguese America was a very uninteresting proposition for European laborers.

---

[19] The first official census of Portugal in 1527–32 estimated a population of between 1 and 1.5 million persons. João José Alves Dias, "A População," in Joel Serrão and A. H. de Oliveira Marques, eds., *Nova Historia de Portugal* (12 vols.; Lisbon: Editorial Presença, 1998), V, p. 13.

Given these constraints, and the history of sugar and slave production in their eastern Atlantic islands, it was inevitable that the Portuguese settlers in Brazil would use American Indians and then African slaves to create the first modern slave plantation system in the Americas. Brazil soon became the dominant sugar producer in the Western world, and its organization of African slave labor became the model that all other Europeans would follow in subsequent centuries.

2

The Establishment of African Slavery in Brazil in the Sixteenth and Seventeenth Centuries

Why did the Portuguese decide massively to import Africans into Brazil, when this was a minor part of their world empire and when the dominant overseas institutions it developed were trading factories and not colonies? In fact, the first thirty years of colonial contact in Brazil fit the African and Asian patterns more than the colonization of Madeira and the Azores.

The initial conquest and contact with Brazil was marginal to the great Portuguese international imperial expansion of the fifteenth and sixteenth centuries. Claiming the region through expeditions that found Brazil on the road to the East Indies, the Portuguese were little interested in its immediate development. With the riches of Asia available to them as the Portuguese opened up a water route to the islands of Indonesia and then to India, Japan, and China, there was little demand for the development of Brazil beyond an emporium for tropical products unavailable in Europe.[1] The first commercial exports in fact were woods, from which were extracted dyes. These so-called Brazil wood trees were usually cut by local Indian groups and then shipped by the Portuguese to Europe

---

[1] A good survey of the expansion of Portugal in the fifteenth century is found in A. H. de Oliveira Marques, *A expansão quatrocentista* (vol. 2 of the *Nova História da Expansão Portuguesa*, edited by Joel Serrão and A. H. de Oliveira Marques; Lisbon: Editorial Estampa, 1998). On the products of this new world trade of the Portuguese, the best source remains Vitorino Magalhães Godinho, *Os descobrimentos e a economia mundial* (2nd ed. rev.; 4 vols.; Lisbon: Editorial Presença, 1981–1983). For the impact of Portugal on Indian Ocean trade, see K. N. Chaudhuri, *Trade and Civilization in the Indian Ocean: An Economic History from the Rise of Islam to 1750* (Cambridge: Cambridge University Press, 1985), chapter 3. Still worth consulting is the classic work of Charles R. Boxer, *The Portuguese Seaborne Empire, 1415–1825* (London: Hutchinson, 1969).

on a seasonal basis, with no permanent Portuguese settlers residing in America.[2] Castaways and other marginal Portuguese began living with local Tupi–Guarani-speaking Indian communities along the coast and became the crucial cultural brokers who kept the contact with the mother country alive.[3] For some twenty years after its exploration and official integration into the Portuguese Empire, Brazil remained a backwater with seasonal trade with independent Indian groups being the only dominant form of contact, a pattern of colonization that reduced Indian-Portuguese conflict to a minimum.[4]

This situation changed rapidly, however, when Portugal was suddenly confronted by European rivals willing to contest this transitory control over its American territories. French and British merchants began to send their own ships into Brazilian waters to pick up the profitable dyewoods, and they soon used the coast as a base for attacking the Portuguese East Indies fleets that cruised the South Atlantic. The French and British even went so far as to set up more than temporary logging camps at both the Amazonian estuary in the Northeast and in Guanabara Bay in the south. The establishment of this latter settlement – the so-called French Antarctica colony – finally convinced the Portuguese that full-scale exploitation of Brazil was imperative for the safety of their entire overseas

---

[2] The most detailed discussion of this trade is found in Frédéric Mauro, *Le Portugal et l'Atlantique au XVIIe siècle (1570–1670), étude économique* (Paris: SEVPEN, 1960), pp. 118–45. It is estimated that the pau brasil trade, which was a royal monopoly, saw an estimated 150,000 tons exported between 1502 and 1625, and the returns to the Crown represented between 1 and 2 percent of total imperial income in any given year. Harold Johnson, "Desenvolvimiento e espansão da economia brasileira," in Harold Johnson and Maria Beatriz Nizza da Silva, eds., *O império luso-brasileiro, 1500–1620* (vol. 6 of the *Nova História da Expansão Portuguesa*, edited by Joel Serrão and A. H. de Oliveira Marques; Lisbon: Editorial Estampa, 1998), pp. 222–3.

[3] On the various Indians in contact with the Portuguese in the sixteenth and seventeenth centuries, see Manuela Carneiro da Cunha, ed., *História dos índios no Brasil* (São Paulo: Companhia das Letras, 1992). On the Indian-Portuguese trade relations to 1533, see Filipe Nunes de Carvalho, "Do descobrimento a União Ibérica," in Harold Johnson and Maria Beatriz Nizza da Silva, eds., *O império luso-brasileiro, 1500–1620* (vol. 6 of the *Nova História da Expansão Portuguesa*, edited by Joel Serrão and A. H. de Oliveira Marques; Lisbon: Editorial Estampa, 1998), pp. 111–13. A discussion of the intermediary *mamelucos* or Portuguese-Indian population who acted as cultural brokers between the Indian and Portuguese worlds is found in Alida C. Metcalf, *Go-betweens and the Colonization of Brazil* (Austin: University of Texas Press, 2005).

[4] A good survey of this period is found in Harold Johnson, "Portuguese Settlement, 1500–1580," in Leslie Bethell, ed., *The Cambridge History of Latin America* (11 vols.; Cambridge: Cambridge University Press, 1984), vol. I, pp. 249–86.

empire. Thus, despite their limited population resources, the Portuguese decided to commit themselves to full-scale colonization.[5]

Because the Portuguese already had extensive experience with African slaves in their Atlantic islands and had ready access to African labor markets, once the decision was made to exploit their American colony, then the turn toward African workers was only conditioned by the availability of capital for importation of African slaves. In turn, that capital became available from the proceeds of sugar exported to Europe. Thus, by 1600, Indian slaves were being replaced by African slaves everywhere in the coastal plantation regions, and the pattern of African slave labor plantations producing crops for the European market had been firmly established.[6]

African slavery had already developed in the Spanish colonies in Mexico, Peru, Central America, and the remainder of South America before the evolution of the Brazilian slave plantation model. Nevertheless, it would represent a distinct slave system differing in many ways from the system that would evolve in Portuguese America. In cases where the native population was large and integrated into complex social systems, African slavery filled specialized roles in colonial economic development, mostly working in domestic households and urban occupations.[7] In zones where the native population was scattered and minimally organized or where severe demographic decline had occurred, African slavery enjoyed a more prominent role in the labor force. Although African slaves in Spanish America occasionally dominated certain individual economic sectors (such as gold or copper mining),[8] they were mostly a minor element in the Indian- and mestizo-peasant-dominated labor force. This explains why

---

5 For a history of French Antartica, see Vasco Mariz and Lucien Provençal, *Villegagnon e a França Antártica* (Rio de Janeiro: Nova Fronteira, 2000) and Frank Lestringant, *L'expérience Huguenote au nouveau monde (XVIe siècle)* (Geneva: Librairie Droz, 1996).

6 The standard study on the shift from Indian to African slave labor is Stuart B. Schwartz, *Sugar Plantations in the Formation of Brazilian Society, Bahia, 1550–1835* (Cambridge: Cambridge University Press, 1985), chapter 2.

7 An excellent study of the style of slavery typical in the major urban centers of colonial Spanish America is Frederick P. Bowser, *The African Slave in Colonial Peru, 1524–1650* (Stanford: Stanford University Press, 1974).

8 On such atypical mining role of slaves in Spanish America, see William F. Sharp, *Slavery in the Spanish Frontier: The Colombian Chocó, 1680–1810* (Norman: University of Oklahoma Press, 1976) and María Elena Díaz, *The Virgin, the King, and the Royal Slaves of El Cobre: Negotiating Freedom in Colonial Cuba, 1670–1780* (Stanford: Stanford University Press, 2000).

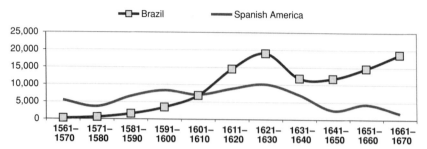

GRAPH 2.1. Estimated annual African slave arrivals to Spanish America and Brazil, 1561–1570 to 1661–1670. *Source:* Emory voyage data set, August 28, 2008, available at http://www.slavevoyages.org/tast/assessment/estimates.faces.

the African slave trade, which was significant to these Spanish mainland colonies until the mid-seventeenth century, declined rapidly afterward as the Amerindian and mestizo populations began to expand and fill the labor needs of the Spanish elite.[9] Even though African arrivals to Brazil would slow in the mid-seventeenth century due to the Dutch invasions, the long-term trend was rising, and these African arrivals never fell to the level of Spanish American imports after 1611 (see Graph 2.1).

The northern Europeans who followed the Iberians to America within a few decades of the discovery had even fewer Indians to exploit than the Spanish and the Portuguese. They were unable to develop an extensive Indian slave labor force, let alone the complex free Indian labor arrangements developed by the Spaniards. Nor did they have access to precious metals to pay for imported slave labor. But, unlike the Iberians of the sixteenth century, they did have a cheaper and more willing pool of European laborers to exploit, especially in the crisis period of the seventeenth century. Even with this labor available, peasants and the urban poor could not afford the passage to America. Subsidizing that passage through selling of one's labor to American employers in indentured contracts became the major source of colonial workers in the first half-century of northern European settlement in America. The English and the French were the primary users of indentured labor, and they exploited a significant pool of workers faced by low wages and poor opportunities within the European economy. They were also not above transporting convicts to the colonies. In fact, a significant part of the labor

---

[9] On the evolution of the Spanish American colonial population in this period, see Nicolás Sánchez-Albornoz, *La población de América Latina: Desde los tiempos precolombinos al año 2025* (2nd rev. ed.; Madrid: Alianza Editorial, 1994), chapters 4 and 5.

migration to English America was transported convicts, whereas the rest were overwhelmingly indentured servants.[10] But the end of the seventeenth-century crisis in Europe and especially the rapid growth of the English economy in the last quarter of the century created a thriving labor market in Europe and resulted in a consequent increase in the costs of indentured laborers.[11]

With their European indentured laborers becoming too costly and with no access to American Indian workers or Indian slaves, it was inevitable that the English and the French would turn to African slaves, especially after developing sugar or other plantation-produced crops that could profitably be exported to the European market on a mass scale and pay for this expensive labor force. In this evolution, the Brazilian slave plantation model became the norm in many parts of the English, French, and Dutch colonies of America. Even those regions such as New England that had no such plantations depended on trade with the Caribbean slave plantations for their own survival.

After 1650, the previously marginal and neglected areas of the Caribbean quickly developed as slave plantation colonies and were destined to become great slave centers of the eighteenth and nineteenth centuries. For all of these new emerging European colonies, the mature Portuguese model of commercial agricultural plantations and African slave labor would be the model used to sustain growth. The only difference was in the initial pre-African labor force employed. Whereas the Portuguese quickly came to rely on Indian slave labor to initiate their plantation systems, the European colonies of the West Indies had few Indians to enslave and were forced to rely on indentured European workers. They, like the Portuguese in Brazil in their first century, also lacked precious metals, so they too looked for American or imported plants that could find

---

[10] It has been estimated that "approximately 50,000 British convicts were sentenced to servitude and forcibly transported to America between 1718 and 1775 [and] they represented roughly a quarter of all British arrivals and half of all English arrivals in this period." Farley Grubb, "The Transatlantic Market for British Convict Labor," *Journal of Economic History*, 60, no. 1 (March 2000), p. 94.

[11] For the indentured servant trade and its rise and fall in British America, see David W. Galenson, *White Servitude in Colonial America: An Economic Analysis* (Cambridge: Cambridge University Press, 1981), and his two essays on this subject, "White Servitude and the Growth of Black Slavery in Colonial America," *Journal of Economic History*, 41, no. 1 (March 1981), and "The Rise and Fall of Indentured Servitude in the Americas: An Economic Analysis," *Journal of Economic History*, 44, no. 1 (March 1984); and Farley Grubb, "The End of European Immigrant Servitude in the United States: An Economic Analysis of Market Collapse, 1772–1835," *Journal of Economic History*, 54, no. 4 (December 1994).

a European market. Once that market was established, they too would turn away from these alternative forms of labor and begin to base their export industries on African slave labor. The experience of the Portuguese American colonial development became the standard for all of these later colonies, even to the point of the direct transference of Brazilian slaves and Brazilian sugar technology to the Caribbean in the mid-seventeenth century.

With Portugal's decision to colonize Brazil came the need to find an export product more reliable and profitable than dyewood. In this context, its pre-American experiences in the Azores, Madeira, and São Tomé showed that sugar was the ideal crop to guarantee the existence of a profitable colony. This decision was greatly aided by the fact that the Portuguese still dominated the Atlantic slave trade at this time and could easily and more cheaply deliver slaves to America than any other European maritime power. The Crown was forced to offer extraordinary privileges to wealthy Portuguese entrepreneurs in an effort to generate the capital needed to open up this American frontier. The resulting captaincies looked more like feudal states than colonies and relatively few of them were economically successful. The new leaders of the colony were mostly men who had generated their initial wealth in the East Indies trade and could provide the crucial capital and credit needed to import the machines and the technicians who would get the sugar plantation regime going on a profitable basis. Although most of these feudal-style proprietary captains failed to establish viable settlements, a few succeeded admirably, and the key element was the production of cane sugar for the European market. Thus, by the 1550s was born the first plantation system in the New World, a system that very rapidly dominated the sugar markets of Europe and effectively ended the importance of the eastern Atlantic island producers.[12]

---

[12] On the use of private contracts and temporary government grants in the establishment of overseas Portuguese settlements and the subsequent establishment of full royal control, see Francisco Bethencourt, "Political Configurations and Local Powers," in Francisco Bethencourt and Diogo Ramada Curto, *Portuguese Oceanic Expansion, 1400–1800* (Cambridge: Cambridge University Press, 2007). For the evolution of these captaincies in Brazil, see the survey by Johnson, "Portuguese Settlement, 1500–1580," pp. 249–86; and most recently, the various essays in Johnson and Silva, eds., *O império luso-brasileiro, 1500–1620*. For the evolution of sugar production in this period, see Stuart B. Schwartz, "A Commonwealth within Itself: The Early Brazilian Sugar Industry, 1550–1670," in Stuart B. Schwartz, ed., *Tropical Babylons: Sugar and the Making of the Atlantic World, 1450–1680* (Chapel Hill: University of North Carolina Press, 2004), pp. 158–200.

Brazil was not the first American region to produce sugar, as Columbus had already brought sugar to Santo Domingo as early as 1493.[13] But the initially large sugar estates in that island eventually declined into small farms producing for just local and regional markets. The headlong rush of Spanish colonists to the mainland eliminated the incentives to develop these islands into full-scale production zones despite the quality of their soils. Even in Brazil, enterprising colonists had begun to plant sugar as early as the 1510s.[14] It was not until the formal establishment of the Proprietary Captaincies into which Brazil was divided that systematic production began. The Portuguese fleet of 1532 carried along sugar experts from the Madeira plantations, and the new governors who took over their regions all brought plantings from Madeira or São Tomé. After many trials and problems with Indian raiding, two areas stood out initially as the most profitable centers of colonization and sugar production. These were the two northeast provinces of Pernambuco and Bahia. By the 1580s, Pernambuco already had more than sixty *engenhos* producing sugar for the European market,[15] and by the last decades of the century, it was intimately connected to the Antwerp market. Given the initially marginal interest of the Portuguese in this zone, it was Dutch shipping that played a vital role in linking Brazil to the northern European sugar markets, the site of Europe's fastest-growing economies.[16] By the 1580s, Bahia had emerged as the second-largest producer with some forty mills, and the two areas produced about three-quarters of all the sugar on the continent.[17] By 1600, Brazil was producing an estimated 8,000 to 9,000 metric tons of sugar per annum from approximately two hundred sugar mills and had become Europe's single most important source for this rapidly expanding product.[18]

---

[13] Genaro Rodríguez Morel, "The Sugar Economy of Española in the Sixteenth Century," in Schwartz, ed., *Tropical Babylons*, p. 87.

[14] J. H. Galloway, *The Sugar Cane Industry: An Historical Geography from its Origins to 1914* (Cambridge: Cambridge University Press, 1989), pp. 61–70.

[15] On the Atlantic background and early sugar industry in Brazil, see Galloway, *The Sugar Cane Industry*, chapter 4; and the sources cited in note 18.

[16] On the evolution of the Dutch sugar trade with Brazil, see Christopher Ebert, "Dutch Trade with Brazil before the Dutch West India Company, 1587–1621," in Johannes Postma and Victor Enthoven, eds., *Riches from Atlantic Commerce: Dutch Transatlantic Trade and Shipping, 1585–1817* (Leiden: Brill, 2003).

[17] Schwartz, *Sugar Plantations*, p. 19.

[18] The most detailed estimate of Brazilian production in the sixteenth and seventeenth centuries is found in Mauro, *Le Portugal et l'Atlantique au XVIIe siècle (1570–1670)*, pp. 192–257; also see Schwartz, *Sugar Plantations*, chapter 7.

The sugar mills of Brazil's Northeast soon evolved into far larger operations than their Atlantic islands predecessor. By the end of the sixteenth
century, Brazilian mills were producing six times the output per annum
of the Atlantic islands *engenhos*.[19] Much of this increase was due to the
greater size of American sugar plantings, which involved not only the
lands of the mill-owners but those of the smaller dependent planters tied
to the mills (known as *lavradores da cana*). This allowed many owners to
construct expensive, large, water-driven mills with capacities far greater
than their own field production. At the end of the century, Brazilians also
worked out a new type of milling process that effectively increased the
percentage of juice extracted from the canes. This was the introduction
of the three-roller vertical mill to Brazil in 1617, which greatly increased
output at a reduced cost.[20] With excellent soils, the most advanced milling
technology, and close contact with the booming Dutch commercial network, Brazil dominated sugar production in the Western world by 1600.
What had been a colony settled in a marginal way and with little interest
from the Crown now began to take on more and more of a central role
in Portugal's vast empire, with sugar being the crucial link connecting
Portugal, Africa, and Brazil.[21]

Given the insatiable demand of the mills for unskilled agricultural
labor, the Brazilians would experiment with many forms of labor organization that later colonists would attempt, excluding only indentured
European workers. They imported African slaves from the very beginning, but they also sought to enslave the local American Indian populations and turn them into a stable agricultural labor force. The Tupi
speakers who occupied the northeast coastal region were settled in large
villages of several hundred persons and engaged in agricultural production. They were thus not the seminomadic and primarily hunting groups
encountered further in the interior, although they were largely subsistence
agricultural producers and nothing like the Andean or Mexican peasants
with their complex markets and long-distance trade. Their constant warfare and putative ritual cannibalistic practices gave the Portuguese an
excuse to conquer and enslave them, and initially, their agricultural experience promised the potential of making them into an effective labor
force.

---

[19] Based on the estimates in Mauro, *Le Portugal et l'Atlantique au XVIIe siècle*, chapter 3.
[20] Schwartz, *Sugar Plantations*, pp. 127–8.
[21] On the evolution of the sugar industry in the northeastern region, see Mauro, *Le Portugal et l'Atlantique au XVIIe siècle*, pp. 192–201; and Schwartz, *Sugar Plantations*,
chapter 7.

The Portuguese tried converting the Indians and paying them wages, but the primary means of extracting their labor was to turn them into chattel slaves. From 1540 to 1570, Indian slaves were the primary producers of sugar in Brazil and accounted for more than four-fifths of the labor force in the Northeast and almost all of the labor component in the southern sugar mills developing in the Rio de Janeiro region. Owners obtained these slaves through purchase from other Indian tribes or direct raiding on their own. They also encouraged free Indians to work for wages, which quickly tied them to the estates, so that thereafter little distinction could be made between enslaved and debt-peon Indian laborers.[22]

Although Portuguese efforts in this area showed that an enslaved and indebted Indian labor force could be created from the Tupi-Guarani Indians of the coast despite an open frontier and constant warfare with Indian groups, the institution of Indian slavery, which now claimed tens of thousands of Indians, was doomed to failure. The most important factor undermining its importance was the endemic diseases the Europeans brought with them, which became epidemic when they affected the Indians. In the 1560s, at the height of Indian slavery, a major smallpox epidemic broke out among these previously unexposed populations of Indians. It was estimated that thirty thousand Indians under Portuguese control, either on plantations or in Christian mission villages, died of the disease. This susceptibility to disease along with their shorter life expectancy resulted in lower prices for Indian slaves than for African slaves. When combined with increasing Crown hostility toward Indian enslavement, especially after the unification of the Portuguese Crown with that of Spain after 1580, Indian slavery was made less secure and more difficult to maintain.

This decline in the utility of Indian slave labor combined with the increasing wealth of the Brazilian planters led to the beginnings of mass importations of African slave labor after 1570. Whereas the Northeast had few Africans before 1570, by the mid-1580s, Pernambuco alone reported two thousand African slaves, now comprising one-third of the captaincy's sugar labor force. With each succeeding decade, the percentage of Africans in the slave population increased. By 1600, probably just under half of all slaves were now Africans, with some fifty thousand

---

[22] The standard source on the use of enslaved Indians in the northeastern sugar industry is Stuart B. Schwartz, "Indian Labor and New World Plantations: European Demands and Indian Responses in Northeastern Brazil," *American Historical Review*, 83, no. 3 (June 1978).

Africans having arrived in the colony up to that time. In the next two decades, the Indian slaves progressively disappeared from the sugar fields, and by the 1620s, most sugar estate workers were black.[23]

In the 1570–1620 transition period shift to African labor, Africans first moved into the most skilled slave positions in the *engenhos*, working more in the sugar-making processes than in field cultivation. Because many West Africans came from advanced agricultural and iron-working cultures, they were far more skilled in many of these activities than were the native American Indians. They also came from the same disease environment as the Europeans, and most of the epidemic diseases for the Indians were endemic ones for the Africans. Thus, in terms of skills, health, and involvement in more routinized agricultural labor, the Africans were perceived as far superior to their Indian fellow slaves, and the three-to-one price differential paid by planters reflected this perception. As capital was built up from sugar sales, there was a progressive move toward Africans on the part of all Brazilian sugar planters.

That the sugar economy was expanding rapidly can be seen from the numbers. By 1600, Brazil had close to two hundred *engenhos* producing a total of between 8,000 and 9,000 metric tons of sugar per annum, and by the mid 1620s, Brazilian output rose to 14,000 tons per annum. All of this occurred during a period when European sugar prices were constantly rising. Moreover, the introduction of the three-roller vertical mills in the second decade of the seventeenth century both reduced considerably the costs of mill construction and increased the juice extracted from the cane. While there appears to have been a price drop in the 1620s, prices firmed up in the next two decades as Brazilian sugar dominated European markets. Thus, slave importations began to rise dramatically, and by the 1630s and 1640s, Africans were arriving in Brazil in much greater numbers than to Spanish America, a trend that would maintain itself into the nineteenth century.

The middle decades of the seventeenth century would prove to be the peak years of Brazil's dominance of the European sugar market. No other sugar-producing area rivaled Brazil at this point, and Brazilian sugar eliminated the eastern Atlantic islands as major producers. It was this very sugar production monopoly that excited the envy of other European powers and led to the rise of alternative production centers. Crucial to this

---

[23] On the movements of slaves to Brazil, see Herbert S. Klein, *The Atlantic Slave Trade* (2nd printing; Cambridge: Cambridge University Press, 2002); and Schwartz, *Sugar Plantations*, chapter 13.

new American plantation movement would be the Dutch, who from the beginnings of the American sugar trade in the sixteenth century had been firm partners of the Brazilian planters, providing them with the crucial transport and marketing of their sugars in European markets.

But the rise of other non-Iberian modern states in sixteenth-century Europe created a group of rivals who wished to reproduce the Portuguese success in the Asian trade and challenge their monopoly of American sugar production. This movement would lead to systematic attacks on the Portuguese Empire. At the same time, changes in metropolitan governments would have a profound impact on Brazil. In 1580, the last of the kings of the royal Portuguese House of Avis died with no heirs to assume the throne, and Portugal and its empire were taken over by the Spanish Hapsburgs. Thus began the period of "captivity" in Portuguese history, or the unification of Portugal with Spain under Philip II, which would last until the Portuguese rebellion of 1640.

Initially this unification brought strength to Portugal and its empire, as Castile was the most powerful and richest state in Europe during the second half of the sixteenth century. But that power eventually was the undoing of the Portuguese colonial world, as it exposed Portugal to the enemies of the Spanish Crown. It would also involve Portugal in a war with Spain's Dutch rebels, who had been Portugal's long-term trading partners. Given the close relationship between Portugal and the Dutch in the sugar trade, every effort was made to maintain the intimate trading relations, even though the northern Dutch provinces were in active revolt from the late 1560s and especially after the mid-1570s. But eventually the long Dutch wars of independence had their impact on this traditional trading relationship. Not only did Spain eventually seize Dutch ships involved in this trade, but also the Dutch themselves decided to end all direct trade with Brazil after 1621. This was the year that the Dutch founded the Dutch West Indies Company to exploit both African and American resources and use force to conquer these regions.

Although northern European pirates systematically attacked the Portuguese trade with Asia and Africa, it was the Dutch who emerged in the late sixteenth century as the most aggressive, competent, and powerful of Iberia's rivals. A part of the Spanish Empire since the ascension to the Spanish throne of the Hapsburg Charles V, the seven northern and largely Protestant provinces of the Low Countries had gone into a final phase of their wars of independence against Spain in the 1590s. For the Spaniards, these Dutch wars of independence proved to be a long and disastrous affair and probably one of their costliest imperial conflicts.

By 1609, the Dutch had secured de facto independence and were able to use their advanced commercial system and their dominance in European overseas trade to carry the war deep into the Iberian Empire. Whereas the Spanish American possessions were too powerful to conquer despite several assaults, the Asian, African, and eventually American empire of Portugal was less well defended.

Because the Dutch had become deeply involved in the Brazilian sugar industry, Portuguese America was initially protected from Dutch imperial pretensions. As long as the Spaniards did not attempt to interfere with this international trading, all was well. But the war with the Dutch proved to be a long and bloody affair, and the Spanish finally attacked Dutch shipping to Brazil in the first decade of the seventeenth century. This ended the neutrality of Brazil and of Portuguese Africa in the great imperial conflict, and in the last round of fighting after the end of the so-called twelve-year truce in 1621, the Dutch assaulted both Portugal's African settlements and the Brazilian plantations.

As early as 1602, the Dutch had established their East Indies Company to seize control of Portugal's Asian spice trade. That competition was not peaceful and involved constant attacks by the Dutch on Portuguese shipping and its Pacific commercial networks. With the foundation of the West Indies Company in 1621, the Dutch decided to compete directly in Africa and America with the Portuguese. In a systematic campaign to capture both Brazilian and African possessions, the Dutch West Indies Company sent the first of many war fleets into the South Atlantic in 1624. They temporarily captured the town of Salvador and with it Brazil's second-largest sugar-producing province of Bahia. But a year later, a combined Spanish-Portuguese armada succeeded in recapturing the province. In 1627, a second Dutch West Indies Company fleet attempted to take Recife, Brazil's premier sugar port and center of the province of Pernambuco, the colony's richest sugar plantation region. Although repulsed by the Portuguese, the Dutch fleet succeeded in capturing the annual Spanish silver armada on its return to Europe, thus enormously enriching the Company's coffers.

Another major fleet and army was outfitted by the Company in 1630, and after bitter fighting, the Dutch captured Recife and most of the province of Pernambuco. With this base in sugar production, the Dutch were now direct competitors of their former Brazilian partners. The next step in this competition was to deny Brazil access to its sources of African slaves. Thus, new expeditions were mounted by the Company to seize Portuguese African possessions, which also resulted in the Dutch themselves becoming a dominant power in the Atlantic slave-trading system. First the fortress of São Jorge de Mina on the Gold Coast was captured in 1638, and then came the fall of Luanda and the whole Angolan coastal region in 1641.[24]

The seizure of Pernambuco and the Portuguese African settlements by the Dutch affected sugar production and the slave system in both Brazil and the rest of America. For Brazil, the Dutch occupation resulted in Bahia replacing Pernambuco as the leading slave and sugar province, it led to the reemergence of Indian slavery, and the ensuing interior slave trade opened up the interior regions of Brazil to exploitation and settlement. For the rest of America, Dutch Brazil would become the source for the tools, techniques, credit, and slaves that would carry the sugar revolution into the West Indies, thereby terminating Brazil's monopoly position in European markets and leading to the creation of wealthy new American colonies for France and England.

For the first fifteen years, Pernambuco proved to be a source of great wealth for the West Indies Company, and the city of Olinda (Recife), under the governorship of the Prince of Nassau, became an unusual multiracial and multireligious community of considerable culture. However, the long, drawn-out war for the interior *engenhos* of Pernambuco led to a decline in production and the emergence of Bahia as the premier site of Brazilian production (see Graph 2.2), especially after the planters' revolt in 1645. At the same time that the Dutch stranglehold over African slave sources reduced supplies and increased prices, Brazilian planters once more resorted to Indian slave labor, which the Crown temporarily permitted. The source of slaves was now no longer the Tupi speakers of the coast, but distant interior tribes of various linguistic families. These tribes were captured in slave-raiding expeditions by the special bands

---

[24] On the expansion of the Dutch in the seventeenth century and their conflict with Portugal, see Charles R. Boxer, *The Dutch Seaborne Empire, 1600–1800* (New York: A. A. Knopf, 1965); Chaudhuri, *Trade and Civilization in the Indian Ocean*, chapter 4; Jonathan I. Israel, *Dutch Primacy in World Trade, 1585–1740* (Oxford: Clarendon Press, 1989); and the important new collection of essays edited by Postma and Enthoven, *Riches from Atlantic Commerce*, which includes studies on the Dutch West Indies Company. On the Dutch colony in Brazil, there are numerous studies, including the classic work of José Antônio Gonçalves de Mello, *Tempo dos Flamengos: Influência da ocupação holandesa na vida e na cultura do norte do Brasil* (3rd ed. rev.; Recife: Fundação Joaquim Nabuco, Editora Massangana, 1987); and Evaldo Cabral de Mello, *O Negócio do Brasil: Portugal os Países Baixos e o Nordeste 1641–1669* (Rio de Janeiro: Topbooks, 1998). A recent survey is that of Leonardo Dantas Silva, *Holandeses em Pernambuco: 1630–1654* (Recife: Instituto Ricardo Brennand, 2005).

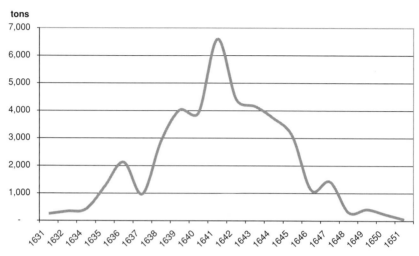

GRAPH 2.2. Dutch sugar exports from Pernambuco, 1631–1651. *Source:* Henk Den Heijer, "The Dutch West India Company, 1621–1791," p. 88.

of hunters (or *bandeirantes*) coming from the interior settlement of São Paulo. These *paulista bandeirantes* roamed the whole interior of Brazil and into the upper reaches of the Rio de la Plata basin, seeking slaves and shipping them to the coast. As a result, much of the interior of Brazil was explored for the first time, and São Paulo itself expanded from its very crude beginnings into a thriving settlement. All of this would lead to new uses of slave labor being developed in the Brazilian interior by the end of the century.

In terms of the rest of America, the Dutch control in Pernambuco led to their active intervention in the overseas West Indies settlements of the French and English. Although the fighting between the Dutch and Portuguese in the interior reduced Pernambuco's role as the region's leading sugar producer, the province still sent a large quantity of sugar into the European market and revived Dutch sugar commercialization networks that had been badly disrupted by the previous closure of the Dutch trade to Brazil. In need of furnishing their Amsterdam refineries with American sugar, especially after the precipitous post-1645 drop in Pernambuco production, the Dutch began to bring slaves and the latest milling equipment to the British and French settlers in the Caribbean and carried their sugar into the European market. In the 1640s, Dutch planters with experience in Pernambuco arrived in Barbados as well as Martinique and Guadeloupe to introduce modern milling and production techniques. Dutch slavers provided the credit to the local planters to buy African slaves, while Dutch West Indian freighters hauled the finished sugar to the refineries in Amsterdam.

Even more dramatic was the actual migration of Dutch planters and their slaves to these islands in 1654 when Pernambuco and Olinda finally fell to the Portuguese troops. In Guadeloupe, some six hundred Dutchmen and three hundred slaves arrived in this period, and an equal number landed in Martinique. To Barbados came another thousand or so. Although many of these new colonists eventually returned to the Netherlands, enough remained in America to give a major boost to the Caribbean sugar industry in the 1650s. It was these transplanted Dutchmen who proved decisive in effectively implementing the sugar plantation system on the islands.[25]

But the rise of the French and British West Indies slave plantation economy ended the importance of the Netherlands as a major American factor in the production and marketing of plantation staples. Also, several English-Dutch wars from the 1650s onward and the various tariff and navigation acts that the British and French issued in this period eventually denied the Dutch access to their imperial markets. This growth of the French and British American empires was also at the expense of Brazilian sugar production and the role of Brazilian sugar in the markets of Europe. Not only were the French and British islands both equaling Brazilian sugar output by the first quarter of the eighteenth century, but the trade restrictions imposed by these two powers to end the Dutch influence over their new colonies also had a direct impact on Brazilian sugar markets. By the first half of the eighteenth century, England and France were satisfying their own needs as well as the demands for sugar of practically all of northern and eastern Europe. France, which had been a heavy consumer of Brazilian sugars until the 1690s, put up tariffs in that decade that eliminated Brazilian sugar from the French market. By the eighteenth century, only the top grades of Brazilian clayed sugar could still be found in any of the northern markets, and most Brazilian output was confined to southern Europe and the Mediterranean. So efficient were the French West Indies producers that they soon dominated even these

---

[25] Gabriel Debien, *Les esclaves aux antillais françaises (XVIIe–XVIIIe siècles)* (Basse-Terre: Société d'Historie de la Guadeloupe, 1974), p. 178. For the crucial role the Dutch played in the origins of the Barbados sugar revolution of the 1640s and 1650s, see William A. Green, "Supply versus Demand in the Barbadian Sugar Revolution," *Journal of Interdisciplinary History*, 18, no. 3 (Winter 1988), pp. 409ff.

southern markets and also eliminated the more expensive British West Indies producers from the European continent.[26]

This severe restriction of Brazil's international markets and its relative stagnation in production, however, did not eliminate Brazil as an important world sugar producer. Its monopoly position was overturned, but the continued growth of European consumption, the excellent quality of its best grades of clayed white sugar, and the growth of demand in the home and imperial markets guaranteed that the Brazilian plantations would remain a major force in the world market. In 1760, Brazil was still ranked as the world's third-largest producer behind the British and French West Indies and accounted for 17 percent of world production.[27] At the same time, the colonial economy would be revitalized and transformed by the opening up of new slave industries at the very end of the seventeenth and beginning of the eighteenth century. Thus, the volume of the traffic of African slaves would continue at an ever-increasing rate into the new century.

---

[26] The best survey of the Brazilian sugar trade throughout the colonial period is found in Schwartz, *Sugar Plantations*, chapters 7 and 15; and on the rise of competition from the British and French West Indies, see Galloway, *The Sugar Cane Industry*, chapters 4 and 5.

[27] Manuel Moreno Fraginals, *El Ingenio: Complejo económico social cubano del azúcar* (3 vols.; Havana: Editorial de Ciencias Sociales, 1978), vol. I , p. 42. Although Brazil's relative position would decline in the last half of the eighteenth century, by 1815–1819 it had doubled production to some 79,000 tons per annum and now accounted for 20 percent of world sugar cane production. Fraginals, *El Ingenio*, vol. II, p. 173.

3

Slavery and the Economy in the Eighteenth Century

The growth of the West Indies plantation system in the seventeenth and the early eighteenth centuries did not put an end either to the Brazilian sugar industry or to the thriving slave system upon which the Brazilian economy rested. The Dutch occupation and the subsequent growth of the West Indies sugar industry did, however, seriously affect the colonial economy. Not only was a large part of the Pernambuco sugar industry destroyed, taking a long time to recover, but Brazilian export markets were also reduced and production stagnated for most of the late seventeenth and the early eighteenth centuries. Bahia did continue to grow, but the golden age of profitability had passed. Competition from the West Indies sent sugar prices into a decline relative to the first half of the century, and West Indian demand for slaves meant rising African slave prices, thus squeezing planter profits. By the last two decades of the century, the Brazilian economy was in a relatively depressed state, and an anxious Crown began seeking new markets and products to revive the colonial economy.

Among the many attempts to develop new resources, the Crown began to explore the interior with hopes of finding mineral wealth. The success of the *paulista bandeirantes* in supplying Indian slaves at mid-century had led to government subsidization of systematic surveys of the interior.[1]

---

[1] During the last thirty years of the seventeenth century, the Crown directly involved itself in the question of gold production. There is abundant documentation with respect to this theme in the correspondence between the Court and the *paulistas*. The Crown furnished some resources, sending some mining specialists, offering prizes to the discoverers, and establishing the legal norms in mining, but it aimed to have the *paulistas* invest most of

After numerous discoveries of minor deposits of gold and precious stones throughout the second half of the seventeenth century, a major expedition in 1689–90 discovered substantial alluvial deposits of gold in the region of what is today Minas Gerais, some 200 miles inland from the port of Rio de Janeiro. Thus, at the end of the century, an entirely new type of slave economy would emerge on Brazilian soil, that of slave mining. Gold and then diamonds would be the basis for this eighteenth-century phenomenon, and Brazil would again be the initiator of a system of production that would soon be replicated in Spanish America. Although silver mining would still be based on Indian free wage and forced contract labor in the Andes and Mexico, gold mining in the isolated regions of the interior of Spanish America would often be worked by African slave labor, much as it was in Brazil.[2]

The rush to these gold deposits by the coastal whites with their slaves was immediate. Before the 1690s, the interior region of Minas Gerais in the heartland of the gold region had been populated by only unconquered Indians. As early as 1710 there were probably some 20,000 whites and an equal number of blacks there; by 1717, the slaves had increased to 35,000, and by the early 1720s, passed 50,000. The 100,000-slave population figure was probably reached in the 1730s, and by the 1760s, there were 249,000 free and slave colored and only 71,000 whites in the province. At the time of the census of 1776, there were 266,000 colored, of

the capital and effort. See Pedro Taques de Almeida Paes Leme, *Notícias das Minas de São Paulo e dos sertões da mesma capitania* (São Paulo: Prefeitura do Município de São Paulo, 1954). For the contract written by Bartolomeu Bueno da Silva with the Crown to discover gold in Goiás in 1720, see Alida C. Metcalf, *Families of Planters, Peasants, and Slaves: Strategies for Survival in Santana de Parnaíba, Brazil, 1720–1820* (Austin: University of Texas Press, 1983), p. 57.

[2] For a good introduction to the evolution of the mining economy in Minas in this period, see Charles R. Boxer, *The Golden Age of Brazil, 1695–1750: Growing Pains of a Colonial Society* (Berkeley: University of California Press, 1962); Virgílio Noya Pinto, *O ouro brasileiro e o comércio anglo-português* (São Paulo: Companhia Editora Nacional, 1979); and Sérgio Buarque de Holanda, "Metais e pedras preciosas," in Sérgio Buarque de Holanda, ed., *História geral da civilização brasileira* (10 vols.; São Paulo: Difusão Européia do Livro, 1960), tomo I, vol. 2, chapter 6, pp. 259–310; and Francisco Vidal Luna, *Minas Gerais: Escravos e senhores* (São Paulo: FEA-USP, 1980); Francisco Vidal Luna and Iraci del Nero da Costa, *Minas Colonial: Economia e Sociedade* (São Paulo: FIPE/PIONEIRA, 1982); João Pandiá Calógeras, *As Minas do Brasil e sua legislação* (Rio de Janeiro: Imprensa Oficial, 1905); W. L. von Eschwege, *Pluto Brasiliensis* (São Paulo: Ed. Nacional, 1944, 2 vols.); Alice P. Canabrava, "João Antonio Andreoni e sua obra," in André João Antonil, *Cultura e Opulência do Brasil*. Introdução e vocabulário por A. P. Canabrava (São Paulo: Ed. Nacional, s/d).

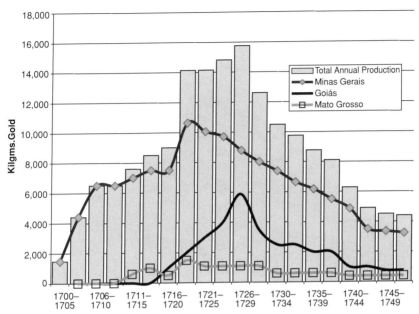

GRAPH 3.1. Average annual Brazilian gold production, 1700–1799. *Source:* Pinto, *O ouro brasileiro e o comércio anglo-português*, p. 114.

whom 157,000 were slaves and an extraordinary 109,000 were free.[3] By 1808, the free colored had passed the slave population in total numbers, and although the slave population continued to grow – eventually reaching some 383,000 by 1872 – the free colored remained the dominant population in the province until the end of slavery.[4] The rapidity of the growth of the slave population, its size, and its makeup marked Minas Gerais as an unusual zone of slave labor in Brazil. In turn, this gold-mining boom lasted into the second half of the eighteenth century (see Graph 3.1) and was also sustained by a boom in diamond exports in the

[3] A good survey of the available census data for Minas Gerais in the eighteenth and early nineteenth centuries is found in Eduardo França Paiva, *Escravos e libertos nas Minas Gerais do século XVIII* (São Paulo: Annablume, 1995), pp. 67–78. For a rather detailed census of Minas Gerais in 1814 with birth and death listings, see ANRJ, cod. 808, 1, fols. 130–2.

[4] Laird W. Bergad, *Slavery and the Demographic and Economic History of Minas Gerais, Brazil, 1720–1888* (Cambridge: Cambridge University Press, 1999), table 3.2, p. 91.

later eighteenth century.[5] Although the first six decades were a true gold rush, by the last quarter of the eighteenth century there was an increasing diversification in the regional economy, which would also be reflected in changes in the structure of the slave labor force. Finally, all of this growth led to the emergence of major urban centers in this interior province by midcentury, with Ouro Preto alone reaching twenty thousand persons, only about ten thousand fewer than in the key port cities of Salvador de Bahia and Rio de Janeiro in this period.[6]

In the first half of the eighteenth century, during the great gold rush period, the rapidly expanding slave population of Minas Gerais primarily came directly from Africa. In a sample of early eighteenth-century censuses from the principal districts of the Minas Gerais, Africans consistently made up more than 95 percent of the total Afro-Brazilian slave population. There were also a significant number of Indian slaves, who made up 2 percent of the total slave labor force, compared to Creole colored, who were 5 percent, and Africans, who in this total made up 93 percent of all the slaves (see Table 3.1). Even as late as 1738, in a census of some eight thousand slaves in the diamond district of Serro do Frio, the ratio of African born among the slaves was 95 percent, and the Indian slaves had disappeared from the census.[7] But as time went on, the ratio of Africans declined even as the total provincial slave population continued to grow. In Congonhas do Sabará in 1771, the percentage of Africans declined to 68 percent and by the census of 1804, among the slaves whose origin was known, only 41 percent were Africans, and the rest were born in Brazil (see Table 3.2).[8] This rise in importance of a native-born slave population is a theme we will return to in discussing the developments of Minas in the nineteenth century. However, it is clear

---

[5] According to Carlos Leonardo Kelmer Mathias, already by the period 1711–1717, Minas Gerais exhibited a higher value of slave sales than occurred in Rio de Janeiro in the same period (1711–1720), which shows the intense nature of economic activity in Minas in these first twenty years of its colonization. Mathias, "O perfil econômico da Capitania de Minas Gerais na segunda década do século XVIII, notas de pesquisa, 1711–1720," in *Anais do XII Seminário sobre a Economia Mineira* (2006), pp. 6–8.

[6] Dauril Alden, "Late Colonial Brazil, 1750–1808," in Leslie Bethell, ed., *The Cambridge History of Latin America* (11 vols.; Cambridge: Cambridge University Press, 1984), II, table 3, p. 605.

[7] Luna, *Minas Gerais: Escravos e senhores*, p. 82, tabela 9.

[8] Francisco Vidal Luna, "Estrutura da Posse de Escravos em Minas Gerais (1804)," in Iraci del Nero da Costa, ed., *Brasil: História Econômica e Demográfica* (São Paulo: IPE/USP, 1986), tabela 7.

TABLE 3.1. *Origin of the Slave Population in Selected Minas Gerais Districts,
1718–1738*

		Slaves					
		Africans		Creoles		Colored	Indians
Districts	Year	Number	%	Number	%	Subtotal %	Number
Vila de Pitangui	1718	245	91	25	9	100	28
Vila de Pitangui	1719	342	91	33	9	100	37
Vila de Pitangui	1720	346	91	33	9	100	37
Vila de Pitangui	1722	731	89	90	11	100	54
Vila de Pitangui	1723	695	90	80	10	100	45
Vila Rica	1718	3,862	96	157	4	100	59
Vila do Carmo	1718	7,694	96	318	4	100	187
Vila de São João del Rei	1718	1,041	91	97	9	100	140
Serro do Frio	1738	7,491	95	399	5	100	0
Total		22,447	95	1232	5	100	587

Source: Luna, "Estrutura da Posse de Escravos em Minas Gerais (1718)," tabela 7, and
Minas Gerais: Escravos e senhores, tabelas 2, 7, 9, and 13.

that already by the end of the eighteenth and beginning of the nineteenth
century, the growth of the slave population was no longer being sustained
by just the incorporation of new African arrivals.

The African origins among these first two or three generations of
Mineiro slaves shifted over time and place. Of the African-born slaves

TABLE 3.2. *Division of Slaves by Origin in Selected Minas
Districts in 1804*

District	Africans	Creoles	% Africans
Abre Campo	25	33	43
Capela do Barreto	61	131	32
Furquim	372	582	39
Gama	132	83	61
Inficionado	252	174	59
Itacolomi	75	62	55
Mariana	131	116	53
Nossa Senhora dos Remédios	36	97	27
Nossa Senhora das Dores	74	122	38
São Caetano	262	380	41
Vila Rica	1,151	1,688	41
Total Known as to Origin	2,571	3,468	43

Source: Luna, "Estrutura da Posse de Escravos em Minas (1804)," tabela 7.

listed in the 3 district sample of 1718, some 42 percent were from the Cape Verde, Senegal, or West African regions (the majority being Nagos and Minas from the Bight of Benin), and 58 percent were from the southern African regions of Congo-Angola, who were mostly Bantu speakers.[9] This ratio between Western and Central Africans fluctuated among different districts of the province over time, with the available data for the whole eighteenth and early nineteenth centuries showing a progressive domination in all towns and districts of Southern Africans.

The dominance of these Africans had a profound impact on the demographic characteristics of the local slave population, and initially the miners and other slave owners made no attempt to alter these developments. The gold fever initially did not encourage masters to think about long-term population concerns or family structural arrangements for their slaves, and they primarily purchased adult African males. The fact that the Crown granted out mining concessions on the size of slaveholdings and the immediate need for adult slave workers also encouraged this trend. The granting of tracks of land along gold-producing riverbanks – except for the discoverer – was based on the number of slaves owned by the miner. To obtain a grant of 66 meters (called a *data*) required a minimum of twelve slaves, the assumption being that they were all adult workers.[10] Moreover, the Crown finally resolved on a tax on mining based not on gold production, which was difficult to calculate and register, but on the basis of a head tax on slaves.[11] Thus, the early sexual balance in the gold fields and towns of Minas Gerais was heavily biased toward adult males,

---

[9] Francisco Vidal Luna and Iraci del Nero da Costa, "Algumas características do contingente de cativos em Minas Gerais," in *Anais do Museu Paulista* (São Paulo: USP) (1979) tomo XXIX, tabelas 5, 7.

[10] Luna, *Minas Gerais: Escravos e senhores*, p. 39 and footnote 9, p. 60.

[11] According to the "Regimento de 1702, artigo 5°," which announces the discovery of an area of potential gold mines, it was required that the Superintendente das Minas and his representative the Guarda-Mor were to divide any new mining region by lottery among interested wealthy miners: "regulando-se pelos escravos que cada um tiver que em chegando a doze escravos e daí para cima, fará repartição de uma data de trinta braças [corresponde a 66 metros] conforme o estilo e àquelas pessoas que não chegarem a ter doze escravos lhes serão repartidas duas braças e meia por cada escravo para que igualmente fiquem todos lucrando da mercê que lhes faço (. . .)," which corresponds to 5.5 meters per slave. The original discoverer of the gold deposit was to get first choice of mine along with one mine reserved for the Crown before the lottery began and none could participate if they did not have the twelve slave miners. For the details of the law, see Leme, *Notícias das Minas de São Paulo e dos sertões da mesma capitania*, p. 190; also see Luna, *Minas Gerais: Escravos e senhores*, p. 39.

TABLE 3.3. *Distribution of Slaves by Sex in Selected Districts of Minas Gerais in 1718*

	Men	Women	Sex Ratio
Vila Rica	3,870	363	1,066
Vila do Carmo	8,003	596	1,343
Vila de São João del Rei	1,291	48	2,690
Vila de Pitangui	255	43	593
TOTAL	13,419	1,050	1,278

Source: Luna, "Estrutura da Posse de Escravos em Minas Gerais (1718)," tabela 7, and *Minas Gerais: Escravos e senhores*, tabelas 2, 7, 9, and 13.

often reaching an extraordinary ten or more males for every female slave (see Table 3.3). In fact, males represented 93 percent of all slaves in this year. Such a ratio meant that the only way to maintain the slave population at the more than 100,000 population range was through heavy and constant migration of slaves from the coastal ports.[12]

In a census of four districts of Minas in 1718, the ratio of African born among the 12,842 slaves whose origin was known was 88 percent, and an extraordinary 92 percent of the male slaves were Africans.[13] Another study found that among the 402 adult slaves appearing in inventories in Sabará between 1725 and 1759, 88 percent were Africans and their sex ratio was 532 males per 100 females. These ratios remained the same for such inventories for Sabará written in the period of 1760 to 1808. Although the importance of adult Africans declined to 76 percent of all adult slaves listed, their sex ratio remained extraordinary at 844 males per 100 females. This compared to a rate of 166 Creole slave males per Creole female adult slaves in the first period and a sex ratio for adult Creoles of 115 in this second period.[14] But this pattern began to change quickly in the second half of the eighteenth century. By the census of 1804, the majority of slaves were already Creoles (or native born) and thus the

---

[12] For censuses up to 1759, the sex ratio among slaves was usually in the 500+ males to 100 females ratio; see Francisco Vidal Luna, "Estrutura da Posse de Escravos," in Francisco Vidal Luna and Iraci del Nero da Costa, *Minas Colonial: Economia e Sociedade*, p. 51, tabela 11.

[13] Francisco Vidal Luna, "Estrutura da Posse de Escravos em Minas Gerais (1718)," in A.E.M. Barreto et al., *História Econômica: Ensaios* (São Paulo: IPE/USP, 1983), tabelas 7 and 9.

[14] Kathleen J. Higgins, *"Licentious Liberty" in a Brazilian Gold-Mining Region: Slavery, Gender, and Social Control in Eighteenth-Century Sabará, Minas Gerais* (University Park: Pennsylvania State University Press, 1999), pp. 74–5, tables 2.7 and 2.8.

TABLE 3.4. *Division of Slaves by Sex in Selected Minas Districts in 1804*

District	Men	Women	Sex Ratio
Abre Campo	45	13	346
Bacalhau	747	281	266
Capela do Barreto	110	82	134
Furquim	691	330	209
Gama	186	36	517
Guarapiranga	203	97	209
Inficionado	1,112	358	311
Itacolomi	219	78	281
Mariana	167	89	188
Morro de Santa Ana	140	66	212
Nossa Senhora das Dores	127	83	153
Nossa Senhora dos Remédios	159	94	169
Passagem	274	144	190
São Caetano	454	227	200
Vila Rica	1,649	1,190	139
Total	6,283	3,168	198

Source: Luna, "Estrutura da Posse de Escravos em Minas Gerais (1804)," tabela 6.

sex ratio had become far more balanced, although the 40 percent or so who were Africans guaranteed that there were still significantly more men than women among the slaves (see Table 3.4). The overall ratio for the entire slave population whose sex was known now stood at 198 males per 100 females, a major change from the figures for the early eighteenth century.[15]

Not only were the Africans predominantly male, but they were also overwhelmingly adults. Thus, all studies of age among the African slaves in the eighteenth century show a ratio of fewer than 10 children (0–15 years of age) per 100 Africans, a ratio unlike the 40 to 50 children per 100 Creoles, or native-born slaves.[16] Given the adult nature of the African migration, this extremely low incidence of children is not surprising, but along with the sex ratio it is another indicator showing that growth of the slave population could not come from natural growth of the African population itself. As long as Africans dominated the local labor force,

---

[15] Luna, "Estrutura da Posse de Escravos em Minas Gerais (1804)," tabela 6.
[16] Francisco Vidal Luna and Iraci del Nero da Costa, "Estrutura da Massa Escrava de Algumas Localidades Mineiras (1804)," in *Revista do Instituto de Estudos Brasileiros* (1981), tabela 2.

importation of more Africans was necessary to keep the servile population growing despite the probably positive natural growth rates of the Creole slave population.

Slowly this distortion in the age structure of the resident slave population also began to change in the second half of the eighteenth century. In a census of slaves in Sabará in 1776, children ages 0 to 15 years made up approximately 28 percent of the total 21,268 slaves who were registered. Moreover, the overall sex ratio of the children was 117 males per 100 females compared to double that rate for adults.[17] Clearly then, the first half of the eighteenth century was one dominated by Africans who greatly influenced the age and sex ratios of the resident slave population. This would change slowly over the course of the century in Minas Gerais as native-born slaves began to become ever more important in the labor force. Given this rise in importance of Creole slaves, the ratio of children in the total slave population increased, along with the ratio of women. In the census of Vila Rica of 1804, for example, children now represented 22 percent of the total slave population of the 2,763 slaves whose age was known.[18]

The distribution of slave ownership became increasingly concentrated over time. The Crown reserved the well-defined mine sites for their discoverers and for miners who held twelve or more slaves; those with fewer slaves were allowed to get smaller claims proportional to the number of slaves they possessed if any areas were left unclaimed, but the majority of these small slaveowning miners tended to concentrate on itinerant prospecting, which meant extraordinary freedom for their few slave miners who in fact were paid in gold for any minerals discovered.[19] Slaves

---

[17] Mariana L. R. Dantas, "Black Townsmen: A Comparative Study of Persons of African Origin and Descent in Slavery and Freedom: Baltimore, Maryland and Sabará, Minas Gerais, 1750–1810," (Ph.D. diss.; Baltimore: Johns Hopkins University, 2003), p. 132, table 2.4.

[18] Iraci del Nero da Costa, *Vila Rica: População (1719–1826)* (São Paulo: IPE/FEA-USP, 1979), p. 245, tabela 5.

[19] On the organization of the mining industry and government policy, see Francisco Vidal Luna, "Mineração: Métodos extrativos e legislação," *Estudos Econômicos*, vol. 13 (1983), pp. 845–59; and "Economia e Sociedade em Minas Gerais (Período Colonial)," in *Revista do Instituto de Estudos Brasileiros*, vol. 24 (1982), pp. 33–44. On the technology used to extract gold in Minas in this period, see the detailed study by Flávia Maria da Mata Reis, "Entre faisqueiras, catas e galerias: Explorações do ouro, leis e cotidiano das Minas do Século XVIII (1702–1762)," (Dissertação de mestrado, Belo Horizonte: FFCH-UFMG, 2007). The Crown even went so far as to declare in 1752 that all miners who owned thirty or more slaves – a distinct minority – were exempted from their slaves or mining equipment being seized for debt. Boxer, *The Golden Age of Brazil*, p. 184.

were worked in gangs and were carefully supervised by white or free colored overseers, but this was only on the large scale and fixed works called *lavras*. Thus, in certain clearly delineated gold fields, such as those in the environs of the cities of Vila Rica and Vila do Carmo, heavy concentration of slaves guaranteed a certain stability on a par with the discipline found in a controlled plantation environment.[20] Here and at other well-defined alluvial gold fields, heavy investment was carried out in the construction of the *lavras*, which had elaborate sluice constructions or dredging operations, and that required major hydraulic works that in their more elaborate development led to channeling of rivers, excavation of riverbanks, or alternatively, the construction of hillside terraces and the setting up of sluices and other water-diverting projects. All these activities required a high ratio of more skilled slaves who were carpenters, masons, and smiths, but also a great deal of physical labor.[21] These tightly controlled and well-developed mining camps probably absorbed the majority of the mining slaves in the province. In a year of mining decadence, that of 1814, it was estimated that there were still 6,662 workers (of whom 6,493 were slaves) in some 555 *lavras* or hydraulic mine works, and 5,747 individual prospectors of whom 1,871 were slaves in Minas.[22] These 8,364 slaves made up only about 6 percent of the estimated 149,000 slaves in the province at this time.[23]

Probably half the miners and a quarter of the slaves were the itinerant prospectors, even in the earlier period. Many of these itinerant miners were in fact unsupervised slaves in scattered river sites throughout the province of Minas Gerais, and then further west into the provinces of Goiás and Mato Grosso. Already by 1735, Goiás had 10,263 mine workers, the majority of whom were slaves and *forros* working in both gold

---

[20] There were already almost 21,000 slaves in Vila Rica by 1735. See Alda Maria Palhares Campolina, Cláudia Alves Melo, and Mariza Guerra de Andrade, *Escravidão em Minas Gerais: Cadernos do Arquivo* (Belo Horizonte: Arquivo Público Mineiro/COPASA MG, 1988), p. 31.

[21] A.J.R. Russell-Wood, "Colonial Brazil: The Gold Cycle, c. 1690–1750," in Leslie Bethell, ed., *The Cambridge History of Latin America* (11 vols.; Cambridge: Cambridge University Press, 1984), II, p. 573. Detailed distraction of the extractive methods can be found in Francisco Vidal Luna, *Minas Gerais: Escravos e senhores*; João Pandiá Calógeras, *As Minas do Brasil e sua legislação*; Eschwege, *Pluto Brasiliensis*; André João Antonil, *Cultura e Opulência do Brasil*, Introdução e vocabulário por A. P. Canabrava (São Paulo: Ed. Nacional, s/d).

[22] Eschwege, *Pluto Brasiliensis*, vol. II, pp. 20–49.

[23] Bergad, *Slavery and the Demographic and Economic History of Minas Gerais*, table 3.2, p. 91.

and diamond mining in both fixed mines and in prospecting[24]; whereas Mato Grosso had 11,910 slaves by 1797.[25] In these cases, slave owners late on the scene and initially with little capital to develop elaborate works or with enough slaves to obtain a royal grant relied exclusively on itinerant slave miners and prospectors known as *faiscadores*. These *faiscadores* usually spent considerable time away from their masters prospecting for gold, eventually returning a fixed amount of gold dust to their owners, otherwise paying for all their own expenses and even receiving a wage in gold for their efforts or sometimes their freedom.[26] Although local governments attacked this itinerant style of mining as dangerous for social control, it was simply too widespread to destroy. In contrast, the formal mine works, the *lavras*, employed large groups of slaves under very close supervision.[27]

Even though slave ownership was restricted to a minority of the *mineiro* population, the ratio of slave-owning households was relatively high, accounting for a third or more of the households in the towns of Minas Gerais in the eighteenth century.[28] As can be seen from the census of 1718, the majority of 2,120 slave owners (60 percent) held five or fewer slaves (of the total of 14,665 slaves) and controlled just under a quarter of all slaves (see Table 3.5). This pattern was repeated in a larger sample of owners and slaves in three zones of Minas in the early 1720s, that of Vila Rica, Sabará, and São José del Rei, which encompassed some 3,163 owners and 19,820 slaves (see Table 3.6). In the 1717 and 1718

---

[24] Gilka V. F. Salles, *Economia e escravidão na Capitania de Goiás* (Goiânia: CEGRAF/UFG, 1992), p. 231. On the gold mining developments in this province in the eighteenth century, see Eschwege, *Pluto Brasiliensis*, I, pp. 88–118. Interestingly, the overwhelming majority of the slaves in early eighteenth-century Goiás were Africans from the Bight of Benin, the so-called Mina slaves, almost all of whom were brought into the province from the port of Salvador. Maria Lemke Loiola, "Trajetórias Atlânticas, percursos para a Liberdade: Africanos e Descendentes na Capitania dos Guayazes" (Dissertação de mestrado, FCHF, Universidade Federal de Goiás, Goiânia, 2008), tabela 1, p. 35 and figura 4, p. 46.

[25] Lucia Helena Gaeta Aleixo, "Mato Grosso: Trabalho escravo e trabalho livre (1850– 1888)" (Dissertação de mestrado, PUC São Paulo, 1984), p. 63, tabela 13. On the gold mining developments in this province in the eighteenth century, see Eschwege, *Pluto Brasiliensis*, I, pp. 119–36.

[26] On "wages" for slave miners and other positive incentives, see Boxer, *The Golden Age of Brazil*, pp. 162–203.

[27] Russell-Wood, "Colonial Brazil," II, pp. 581–2; Eschwege, *Pluto Brasiliensis*, II, p. 126.

[28] Francisco Vidal Luna and Iraci del Nero da Costa, "Demografia Histórica de Minas Gerais no Período Colonial," *Revista Brasileira de Assuntos Políticos* (Belo Horizonte, UFMG), vol. 58 (1984), tabela 5.

TABLE 3.5. *Distribution of Slaves and Owners by Size of Holdings, in
Fourteen Districts in 1715–1717 and Seventeen Districts in 1718*

	1715–1717		1718	
Size of Holding	Owners	Slaves	Owners	Slaves
1	18%	3%	25%	5%
2	16%	5%	17%	6%
3	14%	6%	12%	7%
4	7%	4%	9%	6%
5	8%	6%	7%	7%
1–5	62%	24%	60%	22%
6–10	22%	25%	21%	23%
11–20	12%	28%	13%	27%
21–40	4%	15%	5%	18%
41+	1%	7%	1%	9%
Total	100%	100%	100%	100%
(n)	539	3,503	2,071	14,365

Source: Seção Provincial, Arquivo Público Mineiro; for 1718, Luna, "Estrutura da Posse
de Escravos em Minas Gerais (1718)," tabela 7.

samples, more than 60 percent of the owners held four or fewer slaves,
and the figures for the three zones of 1721–22 were quite similar with
close to 60 percent of the owners holding five or fewer slaves, and in
both cases these small slave owners controlled about a fifth of the slave
labor force. In both cases, the next largest group owners in terms of
slaveholdings – those who held 6 to 10 slaves in the 1710s or 5 to 9
slaves in the 1720s – were one-quarter of the owners and roughly owned
a quarter of the slaves. For those who owned more than ten slaves, there

TABLE 3.6. *Distribution of Owners and Slaves by Size of Holding; Selected
Towns, Minas Gerais in the 1720s*

Size of Slaveholdings	Vila Rica 1721		Sabará 1721		São José del Rei 1722	
	Owners	Slaves	Owners	Slaves	Owners	Slaves
1–4	57%	20%	57%	20%	56%	19%
5–9	25%	27%	22%	22%	24%	24%
10–19	13%	28%	16%	31%	12%	24%
20–49	5%	22%	5%	21%	7%	27%
50+	0%	3%	1%	6%	1%	7%
	100%	100%	100%	100%	100%	100%
(N)	1,757	10,471	912	5,992	494	3,357

Source: Tarcísio Rodrigues Botelho, "População e escravidão nas Minas Gerais, c. 1720."

was more variation among the communities studied, and there were very few owners with more than fifty slaves. In a 1718 sample of *comarcas*, the average slaveholding consisted of seven slaves and the average in the three communities in 1721–22 was between six and seven slaves as well.[29]

These distributions show a surprising lower level of inequality in terms of slaveholdings among the slave-owning class compared to later slave distributions. The GINI index of inequality in the distribution of slaves among owners shows relatively low inequality levels from the mid-.40s to the mid-.50s, but also a very high mid-.60s for two *mineiro* districts. These high variations in the GINI suggest that there were some significant variations in the holding of slaves that were related to local economic conditions (see Table 3.7). Nevertheless, most of the GINI indexes generated for most of these eighteenth-century districts suggest that in general, these distributions of slaves among owners were probably less unequal than would be the case in nineteenth-century Brazil. As we shall see in the next chapter, an almost complete census carried out in Minas between 1831 and 1832 found a GINI of .57 among slave owners, a figure on the higher end compared to most of the GINIs so far calculated for eighteenth-century Minas Gerais. Finally, it is worth noting that these *mineiro* slave owners were surprisingly literate. A study of 263 male and female slave owners in Vila Rica in 1718 found that an extraordinary 87 percent of them were literate, and for Vila do Carmo in the same year, the figure was 85 percent for the 176 slave owners of both sexes whose literacy was known.[30]

A study of postmortem inventories for the Minas zones of Rio das Mortes and Rio das Velhas during the eighteenth century also showed a pronounced unequal distribution of slaves (see Table 3.8), which probably reflected the undercounting of poorer slave owners who may not have made out wills. What is interesting is that when the owners are broken down by sex, women tended to be found among the smaller slaveholders, with 70 percent holding ten or fewer slaves, compared to

---

[29] These ratios were roughly the same as was found for a census of Sabará in 1720 for 894 masters and 5,908 slaves. Some 78 percent of the masters owned nine or fewer slaves, but their slaves made up only 42 percent of all slaves. Higgins, "*Licentious Liberty*," p. 49, table 2.2.

[30] In both cases, the number of owners whose literacy was not known was quite small, only thirty-two in Vila Rica and sixteen in Vila do Carmo. Rodrigo Castro Rezende, Mariângela Porto Gonçalves, Regina Mendes Araújo, and Karina Paranhos da Mata, "Os proprietários de escravos nas Minas Gerais em 1718–1719: Um estudo comparativo dos distritos de Vila do Carmo e Vila Rica," *XIII Encontro da Associação Brasileira de Estudos Populacionais*, ABEP (2002), tabelas 7–10, pp. 19–21.

TABLE 3.7. *Slave Owners and Their Slaves with Indices of Ownership and Distribution*

District	Years	Total of Owners	Total Slaves Owned	Median Slaveholding	Modal Slaveholding	GINI Index of Inequality among Owners
Vila de Pitanguy	1718	49	300	6.1	2	0.403
Vila de Pitanguy	1719	62	415	6.7	4	0.397
Vila de Pitanguy	1720	62	419	6.8	2	0.480
Vila de Pitanguy	1722	124	893	7.2	2	0.508
Vila de Pitanguy	1723	135	867	6.4	2	0.532
Serro do Frio	1738	1744	7937	4.6	1	0.573
Santa Ana das Lavras	1764	95	471	5.0	1	0.484
Engenho do Mato	1764	27	289	10.7	1	0.498
São João del Rei	1764	30	243	8.1	3	0.524
Carrancas	1764	74	655	8.9	1	0.643
Congonhas do Sabará	1771	235	1350	5.7	1	0.549
São João Baptista	1778	12	35	2.9	1	0.388
Sepurihu	1789	122	513	4.2	1	0.542
São Domingos	1789	99	729	7.4	1	0.645
Agua Suja	1789	175	1093	6.2	1	0.583
Congonhas do Sabará	1790	124	556	4.5	1	0.537
Santa Ana do Sapucai	1790	85	342	4.0	1	0.498
Santa Luzia	1790	917	5931	6.5	1	0.647
São João da Barra Longa	1792	175	1407	8.0	1	0.558
Inficionado	1792	367	2248	6.1	1	0.618

Sources: Luna, "Estrutura da Posse de Escravos em Minas Gerais (1718)," tabela 7, and *Minas Gerais: Escravos e senhores*, tabelas 5, 30, and 34.

65 percent of the males in this category, a finding probably due to the overrepresentation of *forras* (free colored women) among the female slave owners in Minas.[31]

The sexual divisions are more pronounced for the *forros* who owned slaves and made out their wills in these two districts of Minas Gerais in

[31] This differed from the important sugar zone of Itu in São Paulo, where the value and size of estates for women and men were roughly equal; see Joseph Cesar Ferreira de Almeida, "Entre engenhos e canaviais: Senhoras do açúcar em Itu (1780–1830)" (Dissertação mestrado, FFLCH-USP, 2007), tabela 5, p. 55.

TABLE 3.8. *Structure of Slave Ownership in Postmortem Inventories in the Comarcas of Rio de Velhas (1720–1784) and of Rio das Mortes (1716–1789)*

Slaveholdings	Slave Owners		% of All Owners	% of Slaves
	Men	Women		
1	42	16	9	1
2	45	17	10	2
3	49	20	11	3
4	43	19	10	4
5	27	17	7	3
1–5	206	89	46	13
6–10	108	51	25	19
11–20	78	23	16	22
21–40	49	14	10	26
41+	14	5	3	21
Total (n)	480	200	100	100
(n)				6,656

Source: Eduardo França Paiva, "Por meu trabalho, serviço e indústria: Histórias de africanos, crioulos e mestiços na Colônia – Minas Gerais, 1716–1789" (São Paulo: Tese de doutorado, FFLCH-USP, 1999).

this period. Clearly, their average size of slaveholdings were smaller – just half of the ten-slave average among the non-*forro* owners. Nevertheless, it is interesting to note that among the *forros*, women held on average more slaves than the males and were more likely to be slave owners than were the *forro* men, playing a much more prominent role than females in the non-*forro* population (see Table 3.9). This same pattern could be found among some forty-nine *forro* slave owners in Sabará in 1720, where the thirty-seven women slave owners among the *forro* population controlled more than two-thirds of the ninety-nine slaves that this group owned, but again, the average holding of the freed women slave owners was less than the male owners.[32]

In the breakdown of ownership by occupation, which exists only for the district of Carmo in 1718, the largest slave owners were officials, who most probably were miners. Clearly defined miners held on average nine slaves, whereas *faiscadores* held on average half that number.[33] It is evident from this distribution that only a few held large numbers of slaves, and these appear to have been concentrated in the mining sector. Of course, the very largest slave owners in the province in the first half of the eighteenth century were the miners. In São Caetano in 1804, for

---

[32] Higgins, *"Licentious Liberty,"* p. 81, table 2.11.
[33] Luna, "Estrutura da Posse de Escravos em Minas Gerais (1718)," tabelas 1–5.

TABLE 3.9. *Structure of Slave Ownership among Forros in Postmortem Inventories in the Comarcas of Rio de Velhas (1720–1784) and of Rio das Mortes (1716–1789)*

Slaveholdings	Forro Slave Owners			% of Slaves Owned	
	Men	Women	% of All Owners	Male Owners	Female Owners
1	6	10	14	4	2
2	2	9	10	3	4
3	7	14	18	16	10
4	6	9	13	18	8
5	0	12	10	0	14
1–5	21	54	65	41	38
6–10	6	26	28	33	45
11–20	3	4	6	26	12
21–40	0	1	1	0	5
41+	0	0	0	0	0
Total			100	100	100
(n)	33	95		135	434
No slaves	3	10			

Source: Paiva, "Por meu trabalho, serviço e indústria," *loc. cit.*

example, miners averaged twenty-three slaves, compared to just three on average for the *faiscadores*.

The availability of all the data on slaves in eighteenth-century Minas has a lot to do with the Crown's attempt to control gold smuggling and to tax this resource. Unable to control the illegal extraction of gold, the desperate Crown in 1735 gave up attempting to tax smelted gold (the usual Iberian manner of determining output and extracting taxes) and resorted to charging a slave head-tax for all masters in the mining zones and collecting tolls on all goods moving in and out of the province. Although there were variations of this taxing system over time, it was also initially adopted – although at a higher rate – for the slaves in the diamond districts as well, although here a full royal monopoly was established with strict control on exports.[34] Even this was insufficient, and in 1719, all goldsmiths were ordered to leave the province and all working goldsmiths in Brazil were banned from working in 1766.[35]

---

[34] For a detailed analysis of the evolution of the taxing structure in gold, see Luna, "Mineração," pp. 845–59; and for the gold and diamond taxing and monopoly arrangements, see Boxer, *The Golden Age of Brazil*, chapters 7 and 8.

[35] Boxer, *The Golden Age of Brazil*, pp. 317–18.

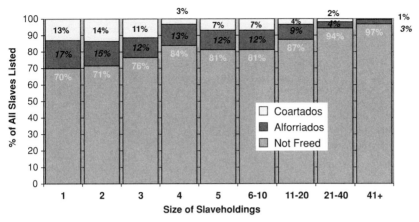

GRAPH 3.2. Slaves freed, self-purchased, or remaining slaves in postmortem inventories in the Comarcas of Rio das Velhas (1720–1784) and Rio das Mortes (1716–1789) by size of slaveholding *Note:* (n = 10,600 slaves). *Source:* Eduardo França Paiva, *Escravidão e universo cultural na colônia, Minas Gerais, 1716–1789* (Belo Horizonte: UFMG, 2001).

The Crown's attempt to control mining was more successful than its halfhearted attempt to control the rise of a mixed population of free colored. Although the Crown opposed the emergence of this class of person, the normal patterns of settlement, rewards for labor, and general miscegenation that became the norm for social relations in the province all led to the extraordinarily rapid rise, through manumission, self-purchase, and reproduction, of a large free colored population in the mining camps. Probably in no other slave region of America did the population of free colored grow as rapidly or become as important an element so early in the settlement process as in Minas Gerais, with this growth coming from very high rates of natural reproduction as well as a relatively steady movement of slaves into free status. Although it is difficult to estimate the annual flow of manumitted slaves (known as *forros*, or free persons who were born slaves) into the total free colored class, one study of inventories of two *comarcas* (districts) in Minas Gerais in the eighteenth century showed that 14 percent of all slaves were either gratuitously manumitted or purchased their freedom over the course of the century. Of these 932 ex-slaves (out of 6,656 listed), some 36 percent purchased their own freedom. Interestingly, as can be seen in Graph 3.2, the smaller the holding, the more likely that manumission and self-purchase were to occur.

We also have some census data from individual towns and districts that list *forros* as a separate group. In these estimates for some six regions in Minas Gerais in the period 1735–1749, the average ratio of *forros* was only 1 to 1.5 percent of the total population in these districts. But these numbers are based on tax records, which essentially taxed both slaves and *forros*, with the class of *forro* slave owners excluded because they already paid taxes on the slaves they owned and thus were excluded from the *forro* censuses. As early as 1714 in the district of Sabará, there were ninety-one black and mulatto slave owners who represented 7 percent of the total group of slave owners listed in that year. In Serro do Frio in 1738, there were 387 *forros* (244 of them women) who owned slaves, and they represented 22 percent of the slave owners and held 10 percent of all slaves.[36] That *forros* made up a significant part of the population is evident in a household census of the Minas parish of Freguesia de Congonhas do Sabará in 1771. Of the 393 households in the parish, 112 were headed by a *forro* and 72 percent of these *forro* household heads were women. This compared to the much lower ratio of only 16 percent of the households that were headed by a woman in the non-*forros* households.[37]

By 1786, when there were some 174,000 slaves in the province, the number of free colored, both those freed in their lifetime and those born free, had already passed the 123,000 level. Their growth now continued even more dramatically than that of the slave population. By the first decade of the nineteenth century, freedmen outnumbered slaves and had become the largest single group in this fast-growing provincial population. That growth would continue into the nineteenth century despite the continued expansion of the slave population. Although the Portuguese government protested the growth of this class and charged that it was based on theft of gold and other minerals, there was little that it could do to stop its expansion. One perceptive Royal judge, Teixeira Coelho, noted in a 1780 "Instruction for Governing Minas Gerais" that the rules against vagabonds (*vadios*) should be suspended with regard to Minas:

> ... although these vagabonds are prejudicial in other places, here they are useful. Negro *forros* and *mestiços* – in the majority made up of mulattoes, *caboclos,* and *carijós* [Indians] perform a service by populating distant locals such as Cuiete, Abre Campo, and Pecanha, where they establish frontier forts, they make up the bands who enter the forest and destroy the *quilombos* and fugitive slaves, they

---

[36] Luna, *Minas Gerais: Escravos e senhores*, p. 133, tabela 38.
[37] Arquivo Nacional, Rio de Janeiro, "Rol das Pessoas que Confessam e Comungam na Freguesia de Congonhas do Sabará, 1771," Caixa 202, pacote único.

cultivate subsistence farms, in short, they carry out a series of tasks which could not be carried out by the slave labor force.[38]

Free blacks and mulattoes played an important part of colonial *mineira* society and by the end of the century became the dominant group within the region. The elite always despised them and attempted to prevent their social mobility in every way possible, but to little avail.[39]

The Brazilian gold-mining economy also gave rise to an important regional urban culture. By the second half of the century, Minas Gerais had numerous urban centers in the ten- to twenty-thousand range that supported a highly developed urban lifestyle based heavily on both skilled and unskilled slave labor. The restriction of clergymen in the province also led to the massive organization of a complex group of confraternities or lay religious brotherhoods that were responsible for most of the church constructions and the elaborate celebration of religious holidays. These organizations served both religious functions and as mutual aid and burial societies and were vital centers of social activity for its participants. Most of these *Irmandades*, or brotherhoods, were for the poorer elements of the society and most were organized along color lines, with the most famous one for blacks being dedicated to the Nossa Senhora do Rosário (Our Lady of the Rosary), which was organized by both slaves and free persons of color. The elite tended instead to congregate in tertiary order confraternities sanctioned by the provincials of the various missionary orders.[40]

---

[38] "[P]orque estes vadios, que em outra parte seriam prejudiciais, são ali úteis. Negros forros e mestiços na sua maior parte – mulatos, caboclos, carijós – , serviam para povoar locais distantes como Cuieté, Abre Campo e Peçanha, onde se iam estabelecendo presídios; engrossavam os contingentes que entravam mato adentro destruindo quilombos e prendendo foragidos; cultivam plantações de subsistência, enfim, realizavam uma série de tarefas que não podiam ser cumpridas pela mão-de-obra escrava." Reproduced in Laura de Mello e Souza, *Desclassificados do Ouro: A Probreza Mineira No Século XVIII* (4th ed.; Rio de Janeiro: Graal, 2004), p. 104.

[39] On royal officials and their expressed opposition and/or ambivalence to the free colored population, the standard work is that of Mello e Souza, *Desclassificados do Ouro*, see especially pp. 144ff. Also see Boxer, *The Golden Age of Brazil*, pp. 164ff. As the royal Governor Lourenço de Almeida declared, "even the so-called great ones [of the province of Minas Gerais] being bred in the milk of servitude" (p. 164). The Crown went so far as to prohibit free persons of color from being members of the municipal council, tried passing sumptuary laws against black and brown women, and even tried to prevent free colored from having arms, although permitting *capitães do mato* to organize armed bands and of course putting free persons of color into militias organized on color grounds.

[40] Caio César Boschi, *Os Leigos e o Poder (Irmandade Leigas e Política Colonizadora em Minas Gerais)* (São Paulo: Editora Ática, 1986), pp. 19–20. As he noted, "ser admitido numa ordem terceira significava pertencer à 'elite social' e ser de 'origem racial branca

The Nossa Senhora do Rosário black brotherhoods were established in all the towns in Minas by the 1720s and the records of some 62 of them have survived (out of 322 *irmandades* scattered throughout colonial Minas), making them the largest single such organization among the 52 types of brotherhoods established in colonial Minas Gerais.[41] Much of colonial town life revolved around these confraternities and they were fundamental in patronizing the arts and music as well as being responsible for major church construction.[42] So vibrant was this religious activity – much of which involved African and Afro-Brazilian artists, architects, and musicians – that the whole movement has been defined as a distinct *barroco mineiro* culture. In towns like Vila Rica, which reached a population of twenty thousand by the 1740s, the mining elite as well as artisans and even the poor supported a surprisingly rich local cultural development, which was expressed in a rather sumptuous display of architecture, the plastic arts, and music along with public ceremonials.[43] There is little question that the numerous black and brown religious brotherhoods were extremely important in the creation of this *mineiro* culture. In Minas Gerais, the most famous sculptors and architects were free colored. Antônio Francisco Lisboa, known as Aleijadinho, was the son of a slave woman and a white Portuguese-born architect father. His sculptures and decorations of eighteenth-century churches of Minas earned him the reputation as Brazil's leading artist of the Rococo period, and he, like his father, also worked as an architect.[44] Another was the slave-born Manuel

e católica incontestável.'" Moreover, the tertiary order of Nossa Senhora do Carmo attracted the miners and elite merchants, whereas the order of S. Francisco de Assis was the preferred association of military men and bureaucrats. Boschi, *Os Leigos e o Poder*, pp. 162, 164. This social division between *irmandades* and *ordem terceiras* associations explains the domination of the former organization and the relative lack of the latter ones in colonial Minas.

[41] Boschi, *Os Leigos e o Poder*, pp. 187–8. Also see Elizabeth W. Kiddy, *Blacks of the Rosary: Memory, and History in Minas Gerais, Brazil* (University Park: Pennsylvania State University Press, 2005); Célia Maria Borges, *Escravos e libertos nas irmandades do Rosário: Devoção e solidaridade em Minas Gerais, séculos XVIII e XIX* (Juiz de Fora: Editora da UFJF, 2005); and Julita Scarano, *Devoção e escravidão – a Irmandade de Nossa Senhora do Rosário dos Pretos no Distrito Diamantino no século XVIII* (São Paulo: Ed. Nacional, 1976).

[42] Boschi notes that the precarious nature of the official church presence in Minas meant that the *irmandades* were in fact the ones solely responsible for the erection of churches in the local towns. Boschi, *Os Leigos e o Poder*, p. 23.

[43] For an introduction to the urban architecture of this culture, see Suzy de Mello, *Barroco mineiro* (São Paulo: Editora Brasiliense, 1985).

[44] For a recent review of his life and times, see Ana Helena Curti, ed., *Aleijadinho e seu tempo: Fé, engenho e arte* (Rio de Janeiro: Banco Central do Brasil, 2006), and for the latest catalog of his religious sculptures, Myriam Andrade Robeiro de Oliveira, et. al,

da Cunha, who was the leading portraitist of the age and also painted many walls and altars of Brazil's leading churches. He was trained in both Brazil and Portugal and had already achieved an outstanding career before his manumission. In music, the composers of Minas were almost all mulattoes. The most outstanding was Emerico Lobo de Mesquita, who was organist to a major white brotherhood, a member of the mulatto brotherhood, and a composer totally current with the latest in European Baroque composition. A more prominent if less skilled composer was the Jesuit Padre José Mauricio Nunes Garcia, whose mother was a *forra* (slave woman freed in her lifetime) and whose father was a *mestiço* and who himself was appointed court composer when the imperial family moved to Brazil in 1808.[45]

Although gold was the initial metal exported first from Minas Gerais, then from Goiás in the 1720s and Mato Grosso in the 1730s, it was not the only mineral produced. In 1729, in the northern end of Minas Gerais, it was announced that diamonds had been discovered in Brazil.[46] Like gold, diamonds were found in alluvial deposits, on the beds or banks of rivers, or in wadis left by seasonally active rivers. Slave labor was used to obtain these precious stones in the same manner as for gold, through panning, hydraulic works, and active washing of soils. The impact on the European market of the diamond finds in Minas Gerais and Goiás was immediate, and international prices dropped by two-thirds as a result of the discoveries. The Crown tried to create a royal monopoly on the extraction of these stones, but it was only partially successful. In fact, diamonds would prove harder to control than gold, because the latter required smelting. The eighteenth-century diamond boom, which started and peaked later than gold, tended to use fewer slaves in far more scattered holdings than in the gold-washing operations.[47]

O Aleijadinho e sua oficina: Catálogo das esculturas devocionais (São Paulo: Editora Capivara Ltda., 2002).

[45] On the musicians, see Daniela Miranda, "Músicos de Sabará: A prática musical religiosa a serviço da Câmara (1749–1822)," (Tese de doutorado; Belo Horizonte: FFCH/UFMG, 2002), and Francisco Kurt Lang, "A musica barroca," in Sergío Buarque de Holanda, ed., *História geral da civilização brasileira*, II, pp. 121–44.

[46] It has been pointed out that diamonds had probably been known and exploited before this date, but that this was the official date of announcement of the discovery to the Crown. Buarque de Holanda, "Metais e pedras preciosas," pp. 241–2. A good survey of the establishment of the exclusive diamond district and the far greater royal control exercised over this mining activity compared to that of gold is found in Boxer, *The Golden Age of Brazil*, chapter 8.

[47] The Crown initially limited those renting the annual royal diamond monopoly from using more than six hundred slave miners – a policy designed to keep production low and prices high. Eschwege, *Pluto Brasiliensis*, II, p. 120. In fact, in the key diamond mining

The rise of mining centers in the central interior zone of Minas Gerais would also have a profound impact on the subsequent growth of slavery and black populations in other parts of Brazil. The gold-mining boom of Minas Gerais powerfully shifted the center of gravity of the Brazilian economy and population from the north to the center and south. The logistics of interior transport guaranteed that the balance of trade to and from the interior provinces would be directed both to Bahia and to the southern cities.[48] Thus, the mines of Minas Gerais, Goiás, and Mato Grosso became the crucial hinterland of the southern port of Rio de Janeiro as well as the entire southeastern region. Rio de Janeiro soon outpaced Bahia in international shipping and trade and quickly approached the 50,000-population size of the imperial capital. The Crown recognized this new geographic reality by shifting the capital of the colony from Salvador, in Bahia, to Rio de Janeiro in 1763. This only furthered the city's dynamic expansion, and by the end of the century, Rio de Janeiro was not only Brazil's leading slave-trading port and the major port for Minas trade, but it was also Brazil's leading urban center with more than one hundred thousand persons. That made Rio de Janeiro, along with Mexico City, one of the two largest cities in America.[49]

Other southeastern regions also benefited tremendously from the growth of this new interior market. Although the gold rush fever initially disrupted coastal production by attracting large numbers of speculators and coastal planters with their slaves, it soon created dynamic new markets that only the coastal zones were equipped to supply. In the first few years, the gold fever absorbed the workforce in Minas to such an extent that few interior workers, free or slave, were able to systematically engage in agriculture or stock breeding. Although this quickly changed and farming and ranching became established, especially along the major trade routes (the so-called *caminhos*), demand still outstripped

district of Serro do Frio, the average slaveholding in 1734 was five slaves (Arquivo da Casa dos Contos, "Serro do Frio: Escravos, Livro de Matrícula." Codice no. 1068). This compared to an average of seven slaves in four gold mining districts in 1718. Luna, "Estrutura da Posse de Escravos em Minas Gerais (1718)," p. 6, tabela 7.

[48] The standard source on the provisioning of the mines of Minas Gerais is Mafalda P. Zemella, *O abastecimento da Capitania das Minas Gerais no século XVIII* (São Paulo: Hucitec-Edusp, 1990) and recently, for a case study of individual merchants, Cláudia Maria das Graças Chaves, *Perfeitos negociantes, mercadores das minas setecentistas* (São Paulo: Annablume, 1999).

[49] On the population of Mexico City in this period, see Herbert S. Klein, "The Demographic Structure of Mexico City in 1811," *Journal of Urban History*, 23, no. 1 (November 1996), pp. 66–93.

local supply.[50] Thus, many of the food and animal needs for this growing interior province were supplied by the coastal provinces. The central
and southern highlands around São Paulo began producing animals and
foodstuffs for the *mineiro* market, but these quickly proved incapable of
satisfying demand. To supply beef, hides, and the crucial mules for the
great inland shipping caravans, a whole grazing industry was fostered
in the open plains of Rio Grande do Sul and as far south as the eastern
bank of the Plata River (in modern Uruguay). A major series of interior
trails were now opened between these southern zones and São Paulo in
the 1730s.

São Paulo would ultimately be the region most affected by the opening
up of the interior mines. Until the late eighteenth century, the province of
São Paulo at the southern limit of the Portuguese colony of Brazil was,
like much of North America at the time, a lightly settled, forested frontier. However, it was home to a rather unusual combination of Indians,
mestiços, and whites. By the standards of the rest of Brazil, it was a backward region, peopled by the marginal elements of Portuguese society.
Probably in no other region of the Americas had Indian slaves and Indian
and *mestiço* free workers been so fully integrated into a white-dominated
colonial regime. As allies, dependents, and slaves, the local Indians were
tightly woven into the fabric of *paulista* society and formed the base of its
armies, farm laborers, and even its urban workers. This gave local society
an unusual *mestiço* aspect and created a frontier population famous for
its military prowess, its exploring ability, and its extraordinary mobility,
attributes that carried *paulista* bands over all of Eastern South America
from the Amazon to the Rio de la Plata.[51]

---

[50] Zemella, *O abastecimento da Capitania das Minas Gerais*, chapter 8.

[51] On the settlement and social and economic evolution of the colony of São Paulo, see
the fundamental works of Sérgio Buarque de Holanda, *Caminhos e Fronteiras* (2nd ed.;
São Paulo: Cia. das Letras, 1995); *Monções* (2nd ed.; São Paulo: Alfa Omêga, 1976);
Visão do Paraíso (São Paulo: Editora Brasiliense, 1994); "Movimentos de população em
São Paulo no Século XVIII," *Revista do Instituto de Estudos Brasileiros*, 1 (1966), pp.
55–111; and *Raízes do Brasil* (Rio de Janeiro: José Olympio Editora, 1956); those of
Alfredo Ellis Jr., "Ouro e a Paulistania," *Boletim de História da Civilização Brasileira*,
8, (1948); "O Ciclo do Muar," *Revista de História*, vol. I (São Paulo, 1950) and with
Miriam Ellis, "A economia paulista no século XVIII," *Boletim de História da Civilização
Brasileira*, 11, 1950; Leme, *Notícias das Minas de São Paulo e dos sertões da mesma
capitania*; the studies of Caio Prado Junior, *Evolução Política do Brasil e Outros Estudos* (8th ed.; São Paulo: Brasiliense, 1972) and those of Alcântara Machado, *Vida
e Morte do Bandeirante* (São Paulo: Livraria Martins, 1965) and Cassiano Ricardo,
Marcha para Oeste (Rio de Janeiro: José Olympio, 1942). Along with these classic
works, there are the studies of Alice P. Canabrava, "Uma economia de decadência: Os

Although some sugar and its derivative *aguardente* (brandy made from sugar) were produced in the province of São Paulo from the beginning, these industries only satisfied local needs. Because of the difficulties of transport from the interior highlands, they did not become important exporters of these products until the second half of the eighteenth century. Far from the seat of colonial authority, this region was characterized by slash-and-burn agriculture, small coastal settlements, modest highland villages, and scattered peasant farms producing subsistence food crops in a densely forested interior. São Paulo was the province slowest to develop and the shift to African slave labor here took the longest time, only getting fully underway in the second half of the eighteenth century. Although a few Africans were to be found in the province from its earliest settlement, it was the local Indian population, either as slaves or as settled villagers under the control of the white and *mestiço* colonists, who were the fundamental labor force until well into the eighteenth century.[52] Large numbers of Indians had been reduced to subservient, pacified villages (called *aldeamentos*) that were exploited for labor,[53] even as the local colonists continued to enslave Indians. Given the comparative poverty of the region, free and enslaved Indians remained the core of the labor force available to the small white and mestiço population. Although the extent of this Indian slave trade is debated,[54] there is no question that it was crucial in the evolution of the *paulista* economy because it provided one

---

níveis de riqueza na Capitania de São Paulo, 1765–67," *Revista Brasileira de Economia* (Rio de Janeiro), 26, no. 4 (Out./Dez. 1972), pp. 95–123; and "A repartição da terra na capitania de São Paulo, 1818," *Estudos Econômicos*, 2, no. 6 (Dez. 1972), pp. 112–15.

[52] Only at the beginning of the eighteenth century did Africans become numerically important in São Paulo. Alcântara Machado, who did an elaborate study of the wills and testaments in the first centuries of Paulista colonization, found approximately 100 Africans in these documents in the seventeenth century. Interestingly, their values were always superior to those for the Indian slaves. Machado, *Vida e Morte*, p. 181. Ellis Jr., "O Ouro e a Paulistania," p. 4, analyzed two thousand inventories in the sixteenth and seventeenth centuries and found fewer than three hundred Africans. Queiroz, from a study of alternative sources, found Africans in the earliest period but concluded that they were of little importance in the first two centuries of Portuguese occupation. Suely Robles Reis de Queiroz, *Escravidão Negra em São Paulo* (Rio de Janeiro: Livraria José Olympio Editora, 1977), p. 12.

[53] Several aldeamentos became vilas or districts (bairros) of the city of São Paulo. On this theme, see Pasquale Petrone, *Aldeamentos Paulistas* (São Paulo: EDUSP, 1995), pp. 84–351.

[54] There exist disagreements in the literature with respect to the magnitude of these transactions, but not to their occurrence. Ellis Jr., "O Ouro e a Paulistania," p. 53; Roberto C. Simonsen, *História Econômica do Brasil* (São Paulo: Companhia Nacional 1977),

of the few sources of export income for a province that was still largely oriented toward subsistence agriculture.[55] But increasing government and church opposition to Indian enslavement – together with the growth of economic activities that permitted the *paulistas* to buy expensive African slaves – gradually led to the substitution of African slaves for Indian slaves after 1700, resulting in the end of Amerindian enslavement by the middle of the eighteenth century. In turn, the Indians settled in the *aldeias* did not survive as an autonomous culture after the middle of the nineteenth century.[56] In the early development of Minas Gerais, the original *paulista* explorers brought their Indian slaves with them, and such slaves remained important for the first twenty years of the colonies' development, after which they were totally replaced by African slaves.

By the time of the first available census of São Paulo in the 1760s and 1770s, the African and Afro-Brazilian slaves were well distributed in the province, with a very high ratio of slaves to free in the coastal communities, in the capital region, and in the west *paulista* zone (see Table 3.10). Moreover, there was clearly a progressive increase of the importance of

---

p. 218; and Buarque de Holanda, "Movimentos de população," among others, emphasize the importance of the Indian enslavement. On the other side are scholars like Monteiro (*Negros da Terra*, pp. 76–81) who admit the existence of this traffic in Indians to other *capitanias*, but refute its importance.

[55] For a more detailed analysis of the *paulista* economy in the sixteenth and seventeenth centuries, see Francisco Vidal Luna and Herbert S. Klein, *Slavery and the Economy of São Paulo, 1750–1850* (Stanford: Stanford University Press, 2003), chapter 1.

[56] Indian slavery was systematically attacked by the Crown in the second half of the eighteenth century, but the continued persistence of the aldeamentos allowed forced labor to continue in a disguised form. In 1802, the aldeamentos were supposedly abolished, but the use of Indian forced labor continued, however precariously, until the middle of the nineteenth century. In 1846, there was a final attempt to resurrect these villages, but they had disappeared by then. Among the abundant literature on this subject, see Agostinho Marques Perdigão Malheiro, *A escravidão no Brasil: Ensaio Histórico-Juridico-Social* (2 vols.; Rio de Janeiro: Typografhia Nacional, 1866); Georg Thomas, *Política indigenista dos portugueses no Brasil, 1500–1640* (São Paulo: Edições Loyola, 1982); Rodrigo Otávio, *Os selvagens americanos perante o direito* (São Paulo: Companhia Editora Nacional , 1946); Warren Dean, "Indigenous populations of the São Paulo-Rio de Janeiro coast: Trade aldeamento, slavery and extinction," *Revista de História*, 117 (1984), pp. 3–26; Alexander Marchant, *Do escambo à Escravidão: As relações econômicas de portugueses e índios na colonização do Brasil, 1500–1580* (São Paulo: Companhia Editora Nacional, 1980); John Manuel Monteiro, *Negros da Terra: Índios e Bandeirantes nas Origens de São Paulo* (São Paulo: Companhia das Letras, 1994) and his essay "From Indian to Slave: Forced Native Labour and Colonial Society in São Paulo during the 17th Century," *Slavery & Abolition*, 9, no. 2 (September 1988), pp. 105–27; Petrone, *Aldeamentos Paulistas*; and Manuela Carneiro da Cunha, ed., *História dos Índios no Brasil* (São Paulo: Companhia das Letras, 1992).

TABLE 3.10. *Census of Free and Slave Population of São Paulo in 1765/68 and 1777*

Regions	Free	Slaves	Total	Sex Ratio of Slaves	Slaves: As % of Total Population
Population – 1765/1768					
Paraíba Valley	11,185	3,727	14,912	137	25
Capital region	19,439	8,868	28,307	117	31
West Paulista	6,000	2,734	8,734	130	31
Southern Road	14,325	3,910	18,235	143	21
Coast	9,598	4,094	13,692	149	30
Total	60,547	23,333	83,880	131	28
Population – 1777					
Paraíba Valley	18,102	4,901	23,003	123	21
Capital region	32,315	9,054	41,369	110	22
West Paulista	8,352	2,634	10,986	111	24
Southern Road (1)	19,146	4,355	23,501	124	19
Coast	10,261	4,304	14,565	127	30
Total	88,176	25,248	113,424	117	22

Source: Luna and Klein, *Slavery and the Economy of São Paulo*, table 1.1, p. 25.

the native-born Afro-Brazilian slaves, as shown by the relative low and declining sex ratios of the slave population in the two census periods.

Also, when the *paulistas* began to import Africans in significant numbers, their distribution among slave owners was more weighted to the smaller slave owners than those of Minas Gerais in this same period. In contrast to Minas districts in this period, the São Paulo slave owners tended to be more evenly distributed and the more than two-thirds of the owners who owned fewer than six slaves accounted for a very significant third of all slaves, as can be seen in a census of 1777–1778 (see Table 3.11). This difference was due to the greater poverty of the *paulistas* slave owners and to their concentration in agriculture, with little significant mining.

The Paulista's discovery of the Minas gold fields initially created a boom in local foodstuff production and finally provided the capital to get local sugar production up to international standards and encouraged the beginnings of an important local sugar industry. But the opening of more direct routes from Rio de Janeiro to the Minas gold fields (the so-called *caminho novo* that was opened in stages from 1707 to 1720), and the fact that only eighteen thousand persons occupied the *paulista* plains

TABLE 3.11. *Distribution of Slaves and Owners by Size of Slaveholdings in Seven Districts in São Paulo, 1777–1778*

Slaveholding	Owners	Slaves
1	25%	5%
2	17%	6%
3	12%	7%
4	9%	6%
5	7%	7%
1–5	70%	31%
6–10	18%	25%
11–20	9%	23%
21–40	2%	12%
41+	1%	9%
Total	100%	100%
(n)	3,465	18,723

Source: Arquivo Público do Estado de São Paulo, Mapas de População.

meant that São Paulo could not respond fast enough to the demands of the mining markets, so it was replaced by the provincial producers in Rio de Janeiro. This involved Rio de Janeiro producers in everything from supplying foodstuffs and locally produced sugar to Rio becoming the chief port for all of the interior mining provinces' imports (slaves included) and exports. In turn, São Paulo's economy also became more dependent on the far larger Rio de Janeiro market for its capital and markets.

Given the slower growth of the *paulista* African slave population with relatively lower levels of African immigration compared to that of Minas, it is not surprising to find a more balanced sex ratio among the provincial slaves in the eighteenth century. Although knowledge about the specific origin and/or color is limited for the slaves in the census of 1777–78, the overall sex ratio of the 22,607 whose age was known was 143 male slaves per 100 female slaves, and the overall age of the 21,602 slaves whose age was known was a relatively high average of 26.5 years. Although these age and sex ratios were less biased than the comparable age and sex ratios of the slave population of Minas in the first half of the eighteenth century, these numbers still show that slaves arriving directly from Africa were having an important influence on the local population. The few data we have from this census on the origin and color of the slaves (for fewer than two thousand of these slaves) suggest a sex ratio for the

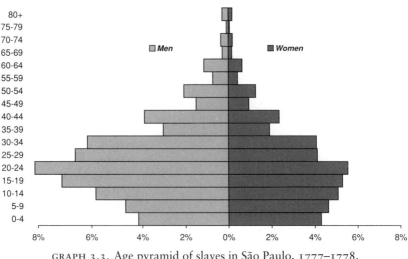

GRAPH 3.3. Age pyramid of slaves in São Paulo, 1777–1778.

African-born slaves of 155 males per 100 females, compared to 99 males per 100 females among the Creole or native-born slaves, with their average age being 36 years for Africans compared to 21 years for the native-born ones. The total slave population showed this African influence in terms not only of the sex distribution, but also the bunching of the population in the most important economically active ages – and the relatively low percentage of children among these Paulista slaves – only 29 percent were children of either sex under 15 years of age (see Graph 3.3).

Although Rio de Janeiro profited most from the opening of the interior gold mines, the backward linkages of the mining sector resulted in a more even distribution of population within Brazil and the spread of slavery to all sectors of the colonial economy. Slaves now reached the frontier working in food producing farms, and they also joined the burgeoning cattle industry in both the central northern coastal region as well as in the new cattle zones of the southern pasturelands.

The case of the southern province of Rio Grande do Sul was typical of these developments. The early part of the century brought an active opening up of the southern grasslands of the region, for both political reasons to prevent Spanish expansion northward and as a response to the demands from Minas Gerais. By the end of the century, there were some 21,000 slaves and 5,000 free persons of color, both *forros* and those born free in a population of 71,000. The slaves were linked into the export sector of the economy. Whereas the cowboys on the cattle ranches were mostly Indians or free peon *gauchos*, the salting and beef-drying establishments were run with slave labor. Jerked or dried beef (called *charque*) was produced in special factories (*charqueadas*), which usually used from sixty to ninety slaves. By the early nineteenth century, these *charqueadas* of the Rio Grande do Sul region were in full production and were employing some five thousand slaves. The market for the dried beef was domestic, because Brazilian products did poorly in competition with Spanish output from the Rio de la Plata region. The consumers of Brazilian jerked beef were almost always slaves, the dried beef of Rio Grande do Sul being a major source of protein in the diets of plantation and mining slaves in central and northern Brazil.[57]

Whereas the *gauchos* of the cattle ranches of the Rio Grande do Sul region were mostly free and Indian laborers, those further to the north in the so-called Campos Gerais area – the area around the city of Curitiba – employed both free and slave labor in the ranches where both mules and horses as well as cattle were kept. Slaves would also be employed in various crafts needed on the ranch and transporting products to and from the *fazendas*.[58] In this entire region of southern São Paulo known as Paraná, the overall ratio of slaves to total population was 20 percent by the first available census of 1798, whereas in the local ranching districts of Castro and Palmeira, the rates of slave ownership were a high 52 percent and 39 percent, respectively, of all households.[59] On these and on the ranches further south, there were also a large number of free colored servants, employees, and dependents who worked on the estates, usually in less export-oriented capacities. Finally, in all the southern towns, some

---

[57] By the early nineteenth century, there are good data on several *charqueadas*. The one owned by João Nunes Batista had sixty-six slaves on his estate, of which thirty-one worked as *carneadores*, *charqueadores*, and sailors in the production and transport of jerked beef. Ester J. B. Gutierrez, *Negros, Charqueadas, e Olarias: Um estudo sobre o espaço pelotense* (2nd ed.; Pelotas: Editora e Gráfica Universitária – UFPel, 2001), pp. 61–62. A survey of numerous *charqueadas* at mid-century found an average of eighty-four slaves per estate, with most of these slaves being skilled workers directly employed in the processing and transportation of meat products. Gutierrez, *Negros, Charqueadas, e Olarias*, p. 91. By the mid-nineteenth century, a typical *charqueador* employed 80 slaves and 10 free workers and slaughtered some 200 to 250 cows per day. Mário José Maestri Filho, *O escravo no Rio Grande do Sul: A Chaqueada e a gênese do escravismo gaúcho* (Porto Alegre: Escola Superior de Teologia São Lourenço de Brindes, 1984), p. 89.

[58] The largest ranching estates in this region, centered in the Castro district, on average owned seventeen slaves. Horácio Gutiérrez, "Escravidão e pequena propriedade no Paraná" (unpublished manuscript).

[59] Horácio Gutiérrez, "Donos de terras e escravos no Paraná: Padrões e hierarquias nas primeiras décadas do século XIX," *História*, 25, no. 1 (2006), pp. 102–3.

TABLE 3.12. *Distribution of Slaves and Slave Owners in Paraná, 1804*

	Ranchers		All Slave Owners	
	Owners	Slaves	Owners	Slaves
1	18%	2%	28%	5%
2	11%	3%	15%	5%
3	15%	5%	12%	7%
4	5%	2%	7%	5%
5	8%	5%	7%	6%
1–5	56%	17%	70%	29%
6–10	22%	21%	17%	24%
11–15	9%	13%	6%	14%
16–20	3%	7%	2%	7%
21–40	7%	24%	4%	19%
41+	3%	18%	1%	7%
Total	100%	100%	100%	100%
(n)	151	1,246	909	4,976

Source: Arquivo Público do Estado de São Paulo, Mapas de População.

of which were reaching the ten-thousand level by late in the century, slaves formed the largest single element in the workforce and were the majority of skilled craftsmen. The three southern provinces of Santa Catarina, Rio Grande do Sul, and Paraná had a combined slave population of some 27,000 slaves and some 13,000 free persons of color by 1811.[60]

A census of Paraná in 1804 provides a more complete view of this frontier ranching economy. With a relatively small population of slaves, it was evident that the cattle breeders and fatteners – the ranchers – were the elite of the society and concentrated a large group of local slaves. They were mostly middle-sized slaveholders with an average of eight slaves per unit, and although they made up just 17 percent of all slave owners in the province, they controlled a quarter of the provincial slave population in this year (see Table 3.12).

By this period, the ratio of Africans in the labor force of this region was relatively small, accounting for only 13 percent of the local slave force. Moreover, this was an aging population whose average age was nineteen years older than the average Creole slave, who was just twenty-one

---

[60] Herbert S. Klein, "Os homens livres de côr na sociedade escravista brasileria," *Dados* (Rio de Janeiro), no. 17 (1978), tabela 1.

years of age. By this time, the Creole slaves had a sex ratio of 97 males to 100 females, compared to the still highly imbalanced ratio of the Africans (who had 147 males to 100 females). Without more massive imports of Africans, it appears that the expanding local slave population was progressively being supplied by children born to the local Creole population.

The southern grasslands provided a new area for slave labor to supply mules and other animals to the mining economy and the rest of the society. But once settlement got underway to the south, local industries could be developed, which created a new labor market for slaves. With strong settlements now established along the coast of Rio Grande do Sul and Santa Catarina to support the grazing industry, Brazilians began to engage in commercial fishing activities with important slave participation. Although offshore coastal whaling had been practiced in Brazil from the beginnings of colonization, the industry became a major factor only when the southern provinces were successfully opened to colonization in the eighteenth century. From Cabo Frio in the province of Rio de Janeiro south to Laguna in Santa Catarina, whaling became a major industry from the second half of the eighteenth century until the first decades of the next century. The center of the industry was the island of Santa Catarina in the province of the same name, which had a commercial whale oil-producing factory (or *armação*) as early as 1746. By the 1770s, the region of Santa Catarina alone was taking over one thousand whales per annum. During the June to September whaling season, free colored, poor white, and slave fishermen in open boats did the harpooning and bringing of the whales inshore. Once beached, they were then cut down and boiled for their oil, which was sold both nationally and internationally for use in illumination. These very costly and elaborate cutting and boiling factories were run mostly with slave labor. A typical *armação* was a major operation, on average employing between fifty and one hundred slave workers. One of the biggest in the early nineteenth century was the Armação de Nossa Senhora da Piedade on the island of Santa Catarina, which owned 125 slaves, of whom 107 were working adults.[61] Along with unskilled laborers, the slave workforce included free

---

[61] Myriam Ellis, *A Baleia no Brasil Colonial* (São Paulo: Edições Melhoramentos, EDUSP, 1969), p. 100. On the extensive use made of slaves in the oil-producing factories on shore, see Fernando Henrique Cardoso and Octavio Ianni, *Côr e mobilidade social em Florianópolis* (São Paulo: Companhia Editora Nacional, 1960), pp. 23–6. The Santa Catarina whaling factories were the most important ones in the mid- to late eighteenth century, but there were also major factories in the ports of Salvador de Bahia and Rio de Janeiro going back to the seventeenth century – all of them being shore-based

colored and white carpenters, blacksmiths, and coopers, as well as the specialized skills relating to the cutting of the whale and the production of the spermaceti. The seven leading whaling companies on the island in 1817 held a total of 329 slaves.[62] Although a highly seasonal occupation, the factories could employ as many as two to three thousand slaves in a good season.

The opening up of the Brazilian interior stretched Brazilian settlement both southward and westward and also encouraged the creation of major transportation networks to tie these vast markets together. Slaves were vital in the large canoe fleets and mule trains made up by the coastal and southern merchants to supply the enormous import needs of the interior mining provinces. Given the poor records of these activities, it is difficult to estimate the number of slaves involved. But another major area of transport fostered by the interior and southern markets was coastwise shipping. In this case, there is a basis of estimating the relative role of the African- and American-born slaves. Contemporary reports list high rates of participation of slaves as sailors in all types of coastal shipping. A rough estimate of interregional coastwise shipping at the end of the eighteenth century would suggest the number of vessels employed at approximately two thousand ships. Assuming a minimum of five slaves per crew on these ships (or one-third of the average coastal trader's complement of sailors), then something like ten thousand slaves were sailors involved in *cabotagem* trade in the late eighteenth century.[63]

Brazil was also rather unusual in its use of slave sailors in international shipping as well, especially so in its Atlantic slave-trade routes. Because of its direct trading relations with Africa, in which no triangular linkages existed with Portugal, Brazil developed a very powerful merchant marine early on. Hundreds of Brazilian-owned ships plied the South Atlantic, taking Brazilian *aguardente*, gunpowder, tobacco, and European and American manufactured goods to Angolan and Mozambican ports and exchanging them for slaves, who were then brought to

whaling companies; see Dauril Alden, "Yankee Sperm Whalers in Brazilian Waters, and the Decline of the Portuguese Whale Fishery (1773–1801)," *The Americas*, 20, no. 3 (January 1964), pp. 270ff.

[62] Ellis, *A Baleia no Brasil Colonial*, p. 190. For a full discussion of the different employments of slaves and free colored in the industry, see Ellis, *A Baleia no Brasil colonial*, chapter 3.

[63] This is a rough figure suggested by early-nineteenth-century shipping data. In the 1830s, for example, there was an average of 1,807 ships (averaging per annum 123,733 tons) listed as being *cabotagem* or coastal vessels arriving just into the port of Rio de Janeiro. *Jornal do Comércio* (Rio de Janeiro), 4 Janeiro 1840, for all the 1830s.

Brazil. Brazilian-owned vessels also controlled most of the carrying trade to Europe, in sharp contrast to the Spanish American areas. Given the crucial role slaves played in all aspects of the Brazilian economy, it was no accident that even on slavers there were typically slaves listed as members of the crew. In 147 of the 350 slave ships that arrived in the port of Rio de Janeiro between 1795 and 1811, Brazilian-owned slaves were listed as crew members. These slaves numbered 2,058 out of the 12,250 sailors engaged in the trade. On average, there were fourteen slave sailors per ship, or just under half the total crew on a typical slaver. Because the registers always justified the need to use slaves due to the lack of free sailors, this would suggest that slaves were even more important in the other international routes of the period.[64] Nor was Rio de Janeiro unique in this respect. The governor of Bahia in 1775 reported to the Crown that the port of Salvador only had 678 sailors who were free persons, and although the majority of these were white, they were insufficient to man the slave ships leaving for Africa, so that "the *navios* and *corvetas* which carry out our commerce with Africa, usually equip themselves with a small crew of four to seven white sailors and make up the rest of the crew with black slaves."[65]

The growth of mining was matched by the development of new agricultural products coming from newer production zones as well as the revival of the northeastern sugar industry and the growth of a major new center of sugar production in the south. All this growth of traditional and new exports led to a major expansion of the colonial economy of Brazil in the second half of the eighteenth century. The emergence of a dynamic administration in Portugal under the Marques de Pombal from 1750 to 1777 also brought about the further development of the Brazilian economy and a new slave-based industry in the north of the country. A typical Enlightenment regime, the Pombal administration used classic mercantilist procedures to encourage the growth of previously neglected regions of Brazil. With the interior and the south booming, it turned its attention to the major northeastern regions of Pará and Maranhão, which until the

---

[64] Herbert S. Klein, *The Middle Passage: Comparative Studies in the Atlantic Slave Trade* (Princeton: Princeton University Press, 1978), pp. 58–9.

[65] " . . . esta falta faz que os navios e corvetas que trilham o comércio d'Africa, costumam equiparse com uma pequena equipagem de quatro ou seis marinheiros brancos, suprindo os pretos captivos para o resto da mareação de que carecem." IHGB/CU, Arq. 1-1-19, "Correspondência do Governador da Bahia, 1751–1782" folios 228v-230, 3 Julho 1775, Bahia. The governor reported that slaves made up 64 percent of the 1,905 sailors registered in the province of Bahia and were 39 percent of its 2,069 fishermen.

second half of the eighteenth century were backward and sparsely settled areas. In 1755 and 1759, respectively, he created two major monopoly trading companies: the Grão-Pará e Maranhão Company and the Companhia Geral de Pernambuco e Paraíba. Both were given economic support by being allowed monopoly rights to slave importation into these two regions – the only break in the usual free-trade policy that Portugal allowed. In turn, these companies were required to invest in the commercial development of the northeastern regions. All told, these companies imported some eighty-five thousand Africans to the four northeastern regions of Pará, Maranhão, Pernambuco, and Paraíba in the period 1756–1787.[66]

After much experimentation, a major new export crop was developed under Pombaline company initiatives in both Maranhão and Pernambuco. This was cotton, which was produced on plantations using slave labor. At approximately the same time cotton was developing in the British colonies with the aid of slave labor, it was also becoming a major staple export of Brazil. Beginning in the 1760s, Maranhão cotton plantations began to export to Europe. Production rose steadily in the next decades and quickly spread to the neighboring province of Pernambuco. The typical cotton plantation in these two states contained fifty slaves per unit, not too different from what the average size of a cotton plantation in the southern states of the United States would be in the nineteenth century. With the steady increase in European prices came a continuous increase in production. So aggressive was the Brazilian response that by the early 1790s it accounted for 30 percent of British raw cotton imports.[67] By the first decade of the nineteenth century, more than thirty thousand slaves were involved in cotton production in the northeastern states. The cotton plantation system continued to expand

---

[66] António Carreira, *As companhias pombalinas de Grão-Pará e Maranhão e Pernambuco e Paraíba* (2nd ed.; Lisbon: Editorial Presença, 1982), p. 249.

[67] Serious exports of cotton began from Maranhão in the 1760s, by the 1770s Pará became an important but minor producer, and finally in the 1790s, Pernambuco replaced Maranhão as the leading producer. Alden, "Late Colonial Brazil, 1750–1808," II, table 8, pp. 636–7. By 1796–1800, cotton exports reached 4,443 tons and were worth almost the same as sugar exports in that quinquenium, and now represented some 30 percent of British cotton imports. Jorge M. Pedreira, "From Growth to Collapse: Portugal, Brazil, and the Breakdown of the Old Colonial System (1760–1830)," *Hispanic American Historical Review*, 80, no. 4 (2000), p. 843. Cotton even temporarily surpassed the value of sugar in the first decade of the nineteenth century and was then Brazil's leading export. José Jobson de Andrade Arruda, *Brasil no comércio colonial* (São Paulo: Editora Ática, 1980), pp. 353–4.

for two decades more until ginned U.S. cotton production wiped out its comparative advantage and brought a long-term decline to the industry.

The efforts of the Pombaline companies were also important in finally reviving the sugar plantation economy in Pernambuco in the 1770s and 1780s. Although Pernambuco never regained its dominant position in the industry, it became the second-largest northeastern producer after Bahia. In turn, Bahia had grown not only from the expansion of its sugar industry but also from its close ties with Minas Gerais. Its location near the São Francisco River, the only major inland river route to the mines, guaranteed steady contact with the mines. At first, the Crown tried to prevent trade with the mines and feared for the loss of crucial slave labor from the plantations. However, the rise of sugar prices after 1711 eased the pressure on the Bahian sugar industry, so the Crown lifted its ban on the sale of Bahian slaves to the interior. Trade with the mines also encouraged the expansion of the interior northeastern manioc and foodstuffs frontier and promoted the growth of an important livestock industry, which now supplied both the coastal plantations and the interior mines.

But the major change in sugar in the late eighteenth century was not so much the revival of the older northeastern region as the growth of new sugar products and new sugar production regions. Rio de Janeiro and São Paulo became the centers of production of both *mascavo* (brown sugar) and of *aguardente* (brandy made from sugar). Although sugar had been cultivated in the Campos dos Goitacases region of Rio de Janeiro for well over a century, there began a major expansion of the sugar estates in the second half of the eighteenth century. By 1779, Campos already had five sugar estates that contained more than 100 slaves each, with an average of 15 slaves per unit in 159 large and small sugar-producing *engenhos*. Moreover, slaves represented more than half of the estimated thirty thousand local population.[68] At the end of the colonial period, Rio de Janeiro would rank third in Brazilian production and account for two-thirds of *mascavo* sugar output. It was also Brazil's major producer of *aguardente*, which was exported to Africa as well as supplying the internal market. By this time, Rio de Janeiro had some eighty-four thousand slaves,[69] of whom possibly a quarter were employed in all aspects of its sugar industry. Neighboring São Paulo, although only a moderate sugar

[68] Silvia Hunold Lara, *Campos da Violência. Escravos e senhores na Capitania do Rio de Janeiro, 1750–1808* (Rio de Janeiro: Paz e Terra, 1988), pp. 138–9.
[69] Lara, *Campos da Violência*, p. 136.

producer and slave zone at the end of the century, finally began exporting from both its coastal enclaves and highlands to the west of the city of São Paulo into the international market in this late eighteenth-century period, and this evolution marked the beginning of what would prove to be the most important slave and plantation region of Brazil in the nineteenth century.

Despite the growth of new sugar production areas and the fact that sugar still accounted for one-third of the value of all Brazilian exports, the industry was relatively depressed through most of the eighteenth century. Whereas colonial production was still averaging some 36,000 tons per annum in the 1730s, by the 1770s it was down to 20,000 tons and probably accounted for less than 10 percent of total American sugar output. Nevertheless, volume and importance fluctuated during the eighteenth and early nineteenth centuries. In the middle of the eighteenth century, Brazil's 27,000 tons per annum output placed it in third place behind Saint Domingue (at 61,000 tons) and Jamaica (at 36,000 tons). It also became an important alternative source for northern European markets in the frequent imperial wars that France and England fought in the eighteenth century, which temporarily would halt the West Indian trade to Europe. Thus, in the 1760s, Brazilian sugar captured about 8 percent of Europe's market for sugar and in the warfare of the 1790s, took a 15 percent share of the market. This continued vitality of the Bahian and Rio de Janeiro sugar plantations guaranteed that even with the massive growth of mineral exports in the eighteenth century, when Brazil became the world's greatest single source for gold, sugar still represented the single most valuable Brazilian export and alone accounted for half the value of its total exports. At this time, the number of slaves involved in all forms of sugar production, which involved both the exporting of finished white sugar and the semi-processed brown sugar, as well as the production of *aguardente* for both national consumption and export to Africa, was probably fewer than 100,000 persons. By the early 1780s, European tensions and the disruptions of trade were beginning to affect prices and to encourage national production, and in the 1790s, the profound impact of the French Revolution and the subsequent Haitian revolution would create a new era of expansion for Brazilian sugar.[70]

---

[70] A good overview of the sugar trade in this period is found in Galloway, *The Sugar Cane Industry*, chapters 4 and 5; Schwartz, *Sugar Plantations in the Formation of Brazilian Society*, chapter 15; and Noel Deerr, *The History of Sugar* (2 vols.; London: Chapman and Hall, 1949–1950).

The final major development in the colonial economy of Brazil related to slave labor was the surprising diversification that was taking place in the province of Minas Gerais by the end of the eighteenth century. As first gold output and then diamond production declined after the middle decades of the century, the *mineiro* economy was faced with a serious economic crisis. By the first decade of the nineteenth century, mining for both gold and diamond production was in full decline, yet the slave population of the province at this time stood at more than 150,000 persons and would continue to grow for the rest of the century. Urban decay had set in with the decline in mineral extraction and diminished even further the opportunities for slave use. The free colored population, moreover, was now employed everywhere and was greater in number than the slaves. Yet the slave population continued to grow at a steady pace through the nineteenth century, and by the time of abolition at the end of the century, it had more than doubled, which meant that at both the beginning and the end of the nineteenth century, Minas Gerais had the largest slave population of any province in Brazil.[71]

The major developments that accounted for Minas retaining and expanding its slave labor force seem to have been a combination of diversification in agricultural production, which supplied the internal market, and then, several decades later, an expansion into coffee for international export. In the southern and eastern regions of the province, a diversified agriculture developed in the late eighteenth and early nineteenth centuries based on slave production. Sugar, coffee, staples, and cattle were produced in Minas on farms using slave labor.[72] The total number of slave owners in the free population was higher and the number of slaves held per owner was lower in Minas than in the coastal provinces, and under the impact of agricultural diversification, this pattern was

---

[71] The best single source on the nineteenth-century slave population by province is Joaquim Norberto de Souza e Silva, *Investigações sobre os recenseamentos da população geral do Império e de cada província de per si tentados desde os tempos coloniais até hoje* ([1870]; reprint, São Paulo: Instituto de Pesquisas Econômicas, 1986).

[72] For an analysis of the regional economies within Minas Gerais, see Clotilde Andrade Paiva, "População e economia nas Minas Gerais do século XIX" (Tese de doutorado, São Paulo: FFLCH/USP, 1996); Marcelo Magalhães Godoy, "Espaços canavieiros regionais e mercado interno subsídios para o estudo da distribuição espacial da produção e comércio de derivados da cana-de-açúcar da província de Minas Gerais," *X Seminário sobre a Economia Mineira* (2002) and Marcelo Magalhães Godoy, Mario Marcos Sampaio Rodarte, and Clotilde Andrade Paiva, "Negociantes e tropeiros em um território de contrastes, o setor comercial de Minas Gerais no século XIX," *Anais V Congresso Brasileiro de História Econômica*, ABPHE (2003).

accentuated even further. What this diversification meant for the development of slavery in Minas Gerais in the nineteenth century has created a very important debate within Brazilian historiography, a theme that will be treated in the next chapter.

Although much of *mineiro* economic history is still poorly understood, the vitality of slavery in its borders in the late eighteenth and early nineteenth centuries made for a nontraditional and highly unusual slave economy by American standards. Some have even argued that slavery was essentially dedicated to subsistence agriculture from the late eighteenth-century decline of mining to the mid-nineteenth century rise of commercial coffee production, but this seems too extreme a position.[73] More likely, it would appear that local output was being successfully exported into a national market and that Minas Gerais had reversed the direction of its relations with the coastal economy, for it now became a major supplier of the foodstuffs needed to run the coastal plantation regimes, but these are themes that will be explored in the next chapter.[74]

In all of Brazil by 1800, there were now close to one million slaves. Brazil thus held the largest single concentration of African and Creole slaves in any one colony in America and also accounted for probably one of the most diverse economic usage of slaves to be found in the Western Hemisphere. Although a detailed breakdown of the slave population by economic activity is always difficult, it is evident that no more than one-quarter of all the slaves were to be found in plantations or mines. The rest were spread widely through the cities and rural areas of the nation, engaged in every possible type of economic activity. As many as 10 percent of the total slave population may have had an urban residence, but the rest were involved in rural activities, employed in farming, fishing, transportation, and every conceivable type of occupation. Brazil, with its half a million free colored, was also the largest center of the new class of black and mulatto freedmen in America. Although sugar, gold, diamonds, and other export products went through the classic colonial boom-bust cycles, the vitality of the Brazilian economy was such that new products were developed, new regions opened up, and a lively internal market

---

[73] Roberto Borges Martins, "Growing in Silence: The Slave Economy of Nineteenth-century Minas Gerais, Brazil," (Ph.D. diss., economics, Vanderbilt University, 1980); and Amílcar V. Martins Filho and Roberto B. Martins, "Slavery in a Non-Export Economy: Nineteenth-Century Minas Gerais Revisited." *Hispanic American Historical Review*, 63, no. 3 (1983), pp. 537–68.

[74] Francisco Vidal Luna and Wilson Cano, "Economia escravista em Minas Gerais," *Cadernos* IFCH/UNICAMP (Outubro 1983).

created. All this guaranteed that the flow of slaves would not cease. In the last decade of the century, an estimated 28,000 African slaves were arriving annually in the ports of Brazil, above all Rio de Janeiro and Salvador da Bahia. By the first decade of the new century, that number would rise to 34,000 per annum and would keep increasing every decade until the 1830s.[75] Brazil was also home to a thriving free colored population, which at this time numbered almost 500,000 persons. Without question, then, Brazil in 1800 had the largest population of Africans and Afro-Americans among the European colonies and was the largest slave system in the Americas.[76]

[75] The trade would fluctuate between fifteen and nineteen thousand African arrivals per annum until the 1780s, when it would begin a long, secular rise, reaching thirty thousand per annum by the 1790s. These figures are based on the latest estimates of volume of the trade in the Emory data set accessed on August 18, 2008.

[76] For comparative data on slave and free colored in the Americas, see Herbert S. Klein and Ben Vinson III, *African Slavery in Latin America and the Caribbean* (2nd rev. ed.; New York: Oxford University Press, 2007), appendix tables 1–3.

4

Slavery and the Economy in the Nineteenth Century

The evolution of Brazilian slave society in the nineteenth century is defined by several important developments. The first was the emergence of a new export crop, coffee, which would form the basis of a new slave plantation economy in the southeastern states. The second was the continued growth of the traditional colonial plantation crops. Sugar again became a world-competitive product with the decline of the sugar industries in both Saint Domingue and the British West Indies, and Brazilian cotton production, which, after suffering severe competition from the southern United States in the first half of the century, revived in the period of the world's cotton famine in the 1860s during the North American Civil War. Finally, there was also the continued growth of the slave population of Minas Gerais – the largest in Brazil – in a region that was primarily dedicated to production for the internal market and yet that retained and expanded its slave population even in the era of the internal slave trade.

The growth of all these traditional and newer export crops created an increasing demand for slaves, and the Atlantic slave trade reached its peak in the third decade of the nineteenth century. But the closing of the trade in 1850 led to both a secular rise in slave prices and the consequent expansion of the internal slave trade by both land and sea in the next two decades, until the interprovincial slave trade was finally abolished in the last decade before emancipation. All of these economic and social developments led to a progressive shift of the slave population within Brazil to the more dynamic regions from the less thriving centers and from the urban to the rural areas. With the ever-increasing expansion of free colored workers, the need for urban slaves declined. In fact, the very rapid growth of the free colored population in the nineteenth century meant that it became the largest single racial-legal group in the empire by the first census of 1872. Despite this growth of the free colored, plantation export agriculture in most regions remained primarily based on slave labor until the end of slavery.

The final major theme of the nineteenth century would of course be the slow abolition of slavery itself. Realizing that the institution could not survive in the world of the nineteenth century – especially after the Civil War eliminated African slavery in the United States – Brazil slowly moved toward emancipation of all slaves. In 1872, a law of free womb was declared and funds set up to purchase the freedom of slaves[1]; in 1885 all slaves older than 65 were freed[2] and final abolition came sixteen years later. In anticipation of eventual abolition, and because of a declining slave population after 1850, by the last quarter-century before abolition, Brazil was slowly shifting its labor base to a more complex mix of slave and free labor in most regions and industries and, except for Minas Gerais, the declining number of slaves was ever more concentrated in export agriculture. Although abolition would come as a shock to the sugar and coffee economy of the southeastern region in 1888, the transition to a new form of wage labor based on new immigrant groups would be relatively quick, with only a minimum of disruption in the export sector.

All these complex developments would see the shift of the slave population by region from their eighteenth-century distribution. The regions of the Northeast and of the South lost their relative importance as places of slave residence, and the three coffee provinces of Rio de Janeiro, Minas Gerais, and São Paulo took primacy as the slave centers of late nineteenth-century Brazil (see Table 4.1). Although the internal trade was not of the same size as the Atlantic slave trade, it was sufficient to shift the balance of slave population to the three states of Minas Gerais, Rio de Janeiro, and São Paulo. Traditional producers for the internal market as well as planters in regions with abundant sources of landless free workers were forced to slowly abandon their exclusive reliance on slave workers and adopt mixed slave and free labor or even based themselves exclusively on free wage workers. Although the internal trade would eventually be brought to a halt, by then the center of slavery had dramatically shifted

---

[1] On the debate about the law, see Martha Abreu, "Slave Mothers and Freed Children: Emancipation and Female Space in Debates on the 'Free Womb' Law, Rio de Janeiro, 1871," *Journal of Latin American Studies*, 28, no. 3 (October 1996), pp. 567–80.

[2] On the so-called Lei dos Sexagenários, see Joseli Maria Nunes Mendonça, *Entre a mão e os anéis: A Lei dos sexagenários e os caminhos da abolição no Brasil* (Campinas: Editora da UNICAMP, 1999).

TABLE 4.1. *Change in Relative Importance of the Slave Population by Province, 1819, 1872, 1886/87 (sorted by % importance in 1886/87)*

Province	1819	1872	1886/87
Minas Gerais	15.2	24.5	26.5
Rio de Janeiro*	13.2	22.6	23.5
São Paulo	7.0	10.4	14.8
Bahia	13.3	11.1	10.6
Pernambuco	8.8	5.9	5.7
Maranhão	12.0	5.0	4.6
Sergipe	2.4	1.5	2.3
Alagôas	6.2	2.4	2.1
Espírito Santo	1.8	1.5	1.8
Pará	3.0	1.8	1.5
Paraíba	1.5	1.4	1.3
Piauí	1.1	1.6	1.2
Rio Grande do Sul	2.6	4.5	1.2
Goiás	2.4	0.7	0.7
Santa Catarina	0.8	1.0	0.7
Paraná	0.9	0.7	0.5
Mato Grosso	1.3	0.4	0.4
Rio Grande do Norte	0.8	0.9	0.4
Ceará	5.0	2.1	0.0
Amazonas**	0.5	0.1	–
	100	100	100
(n)	1,107,389	1,510,806	723,419

Notes:
* Includes Imperial Court city of Rio de Janeiro.
** No data available for Amazonas in 1886–87.
Source: 1819: Norberto (1870), p. 152; Census of 1872; Ministério da Agricultura, *Relatório 1887*, p. 24.

toward the southeastern coffee and sugar plantations. Whereas Minas, Rio de Janeiro, and São Paulo accounted for only 35 percent of the total slave population in 1818, by 1872 they had increased their share to 58 percent and continued to increase to the end of slavery, arriving at 65 percent by 1886–87.

The Afro-Brazilian population would expand dramatically in the nineteenth century in terms of both slaves and free persons. The century began with the volume of African importations increasing from decade to decade until the 1840s (see Graph 4.1). At the same time, the growth of the native-born slaves, now all of African descent, kept increasing as well, so that the age and sex biases within the resident slave population became less distorted by the impact of the Atlantic migrants, although

GRAPH 4.1. Estimated average annual African slave arrivals in Brazil by decade, 1781–1850. *Source:* Emory data set, accessed August 18, 2008.

TABLE 4.2. *Population by Color and Status in 1872; Provinces Ranked by Total Colored Population Size*

	Free Colored	Slaves	Total Colored	Total Whites
Minas Gerais	805,967	370,459	1,176,426	830,987
Bahia	830,431	167,824	998,255	331,479
Pernambuco	449,547	89,028	538,575	291,159
Rio de Janeiro*	252,271	341,576	593,847	455,074
Ceará	368,100	31,913	400,013	268,836
São Paulo	207,845	156,612	364,457	433,432
Alagoas	217,106	35,741	252,847	88,798
Maranhão	169,645	74,939	244,584	103,513
Paraíba	200,412	21,526	221,938	144,721
R. G. do Sul	82,938	67,791	150,729	258,367
Piauí	121,527	23,795	145,322	43,447
Pará	110,556	27,458	138,014	92,634
Sergipe	100,755	22,623	123,378	49,778
R. G. do Norte	107,455	13,020	120,475	102,465
Goiás	103,564	10,652	114,216	41,929
Esp. Santo	27,367	22,659	50,026	26,582
Paraná	37,377	10,560	47,937	69,698
Mato Grosso	27,989	6,667	34,656	17,237
Santa Catarina	15,984	14,984	30,968	125,942
Amazonas	8,592	979	9,571	11,211
Total	4,245,428	1,510,806	5,756,234	3,787,289

Notes: * Includes the Município Neutro (city of Rio de Janeiro).
Source: Census of 1872.

the resident slave population still favored adults and males over women and children. Finally, the free colored population increased faster than the slave population, and by the time of the first national census in 1872, it had become the single largest group in Brazil (see Table 4.2).

The first major development in the Brazilian slave-based economy in the nineteenth century was the renewed expansion of the sugar plantation slave economy. The collapse of Haitian slave production and the mid-nineteenth century decline of British West Indian sugar production had an impact in reviving local production in the traditional northeastern region as well as in the newer centers of the Southeast. For Brazil, the Haitian collapse came at a time of a classic export crisis in Brazilian history. The last decades of the eighteenth century had seen a decline of both the gold and diamond mining industries in the central interior, while the sugar economy found itself in serious competition with the booming French and British producers of the West Indies.

Thus, the immediate impact of the decline of Saint Domingue – a powerhouse of multiple slave-produced products – was to give new life to old industries such as sugar and cotton, as well as open up the possibility of new slave-producing industries for the colony. Within a decade, sugar production surpassed its old 15,000 to 20,000 tons per annum limit as world prices and demand began a long upward secular trend and Brazilian production responded, reaching into the 100,000-ton range by the late 1840s.[3] The Haitian impact thus intensified the plantation system of the old Northeast by increasing the number of plantations and slaves in sugar production and by encouraging the expansion of the sugar fields in Rio de Janeiro and São Paulo. International demand was so intense that Brazil found itself once again competing on a world market. Confined mainly to Portugal and the Mediterranean for most of the eighteenth century because of restrictive tariffs on the part of Britain and France, Brazilian sugars again began to penetrate central and northern European markets, and above all, to supply the previously closed English market. Production also grew so steadily from decade to decade that Brazil once again moved into a leading position as a major world producer, accounting for 15 percent of world output by 1805, and until the 1830s, sugar remained Brazil's leading export in terms of value.[4] Although Cuban sugar had taken the lead early in the century, Brazil became America's second largest producer, especially after the crisis of emancipation disastrously affected British West Indian production in the 1830s. In the early 1840s, when its production was just half of Cuban output, Brazil accounted for more than one-fifth of American production and 13 percent of world cane exports (see Graph 4.2).[5]

The expansion of world sugar production throughout the nineteenth century, especially to new regions, meant that Brazil's ratio of total world cane sugar production declined in importance despite its increasing production. Several major American producers now entered the cane sugar market, including Cuba and Puerto Rico. Even Peru and Mexico began exporting sugar in the second half of the nineteenth century with the use

---

[3] For estimates of Brazilian sugar production in the eighteenth century, see Noel Deerr, *The History of Sugar* (2 vols.; London: Chapman and Hall, 1949–1950), II, p. 113.

[4] Peter Eisenberg, *The Sugar Industry in Pernambuco: Modernization without Change, 1840–1910* (Berkeley: University of California Press, 1974), p. 5, table 1.

[5] The data on American cane-sugar production come from Deerr, *The History of Sugar*, II, pp. 113, 131, 193–204. For an estimate of world output, see Manuel Moreno Fraginals, *El Ingenio: Complejo económico social cubano del azúcar* (3 vols.; Havana: Editorial de Ciencias Sociales, 1978), II, p. 173.

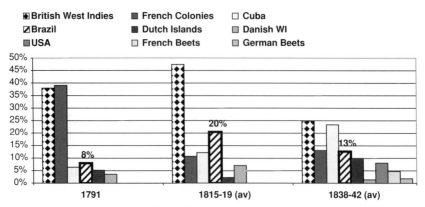

GRAPH 4.2. Relative share of Brazil in world sugar production. *Source:* Fraginals, *El Ingenio*, I, pp. 40–2; II:173.

of free Indian and Chinese indentured labor. Cuban competition especially had a profound impact on both prices and shares of the European markets attained by the Brazilians. There was also the growth of sugar production in Asia, which began to be a serious competitor to American cane production. African slaves were used by the French and British to produce large quantities of sugar in their Indian Ocean island possessions, but free labor was also used in India, Java, and later in the Philippines for sugar production. Even more important was the growth of the European beet-sugar industry, which fully came into its own in the 1850s. The beet-sugar industry, which accounted for roughly 15 percent of the world sugar market in mid-century, took half of the world sugar market by the 1880s. Nor could Brazil find an alternative market in the United States, as Louisiana production also expanded to meet national needs, with the shortfalls in U.S. consumption supplied by Cuba and Puerto Rico.[6] Nevertheless, production remained a relatively stable one-tenth of world production until the end of the century. Thus, despite the major increase in the value and volume of Brazilian sugar production, its relative share of the international sugar market declined, and by the end of the century, Brazil accounted for only 3 percent of total world sugar output.[7] This relative decline continued until well into the following decades, and Brazil would not recover its primary role as the world's leading cane-sugar producer for the world market until the late twentieth century (see Graph 4.3).[8]

[6] Galloway, *The Sugar Cane Industry*, chapter 7.
[7] Eisenberg, *The Sugar Industry in Pernambuco*, table 7, p. 20.
[8] Today, of course, Brazil is both the world's largest producer and exporter of cane sugar.

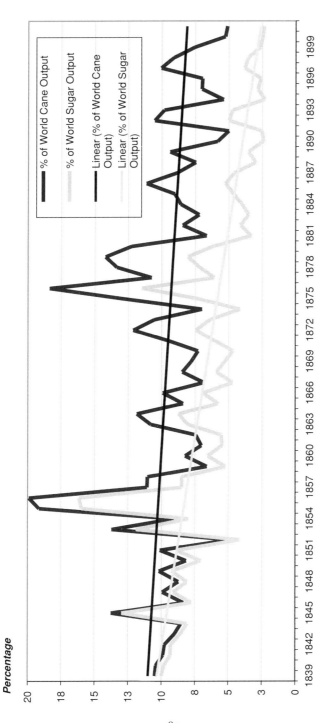

GRAPH 4.3. Brazilian sugar cane production as a percentage (with linear trends) of world cane production and world sugar (cane + beet) production, 1839–1909. *Source: Deerr, The History of Sugar*, II, pp. 113, 490.

Despite its relative decline in world markets, Brazilian sugar production expanded for most of the century. By the 1820s, national output was up to 40,000 tons and climbed to 70,000 tons by the next decade. A decade later, it was up to the 100,000-ton range, at which point it would remain for the next two decades as world prices were buffeted by the entrance of beet sugar into the European market (see Graph 4.4). But expansion got under way again with favorable world prices so that by the 1870s, Brazilian production averaged 168,000 tons and by the last decade of slavery output had climbed to more than 200,000 tons.[9]

Although the relative importance of Brazilian sugar on the world market and in the mix of Brazilian exports declined, the total value of sugar exports increased along with output until the early 1880s (see Graph 4.5). This meant that the sugar plantation slave economy actually increased throughout most of the nineteenth century, although there was a slow shift in production zones as southeastern producers became even more important in the total production picture.

The most intensive growth of the sugar industry in the nineteenth century initially occurred in the older regions of the Brazilian Northeast, with Bahia and Pernambuco leading all other regions. Although the *otahiti* variety of sugar cane was introduced into Brazil at this time, just as it had been into Cuba, there were no other major technological inventions in the industry. Mills were not changed in structure, nor were steam engines or railroads introduced until late into the nineteenth century.[10] Average output per mill in the northeastern sugar heartlands remained the same as it had been in the colonial period until the late nineteenth-century conversion to steam-driven mills. Thus, increased output in the key northeastern states was not based on major new technology for most of the nineteenth century, but rather on the expansion of the sugar zone into new lands beyond the traditional Recôncavo district and the increase in the number of mills. The existence of a growing national market successfully cushioned the local industry from severe world price shocks.

There was also a major shift in northeastern zones of production in this period. Between 1790 and 1820, Bahia doubled its mills to more than five hundred and increased its slave population to nearly 150,000 persons, with an important part of this population dedicated to nonsugar

---

[9] Deerr, *The History of Sugar*, II, p. 113.
[10] Eisenberg, *The Sugar Industry in Pernambuco*, chapter 3.

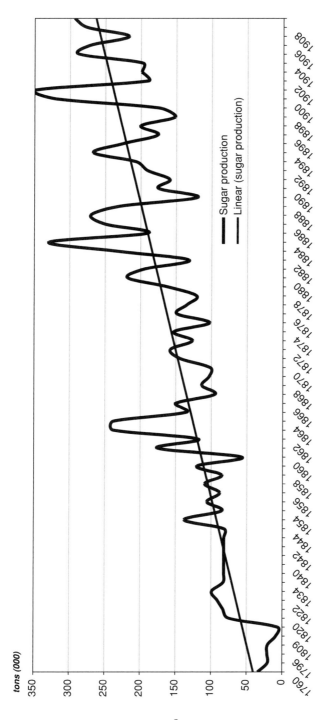

GRAPH 4.4. Estimate of Brazilian sugar production output and linear trend, 1760 to 1909. *Source:* Deerr, *The History of Sugar*, II, p. 113.

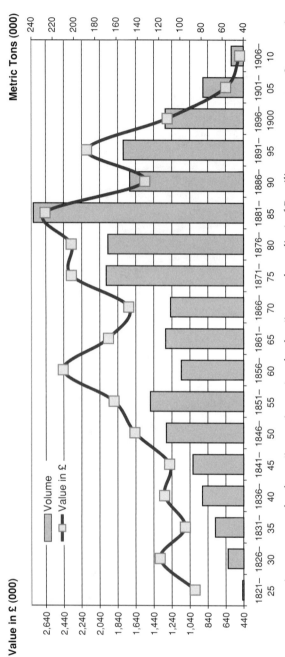

Value in £ (000)

Metric Tons (000)

GRAPH 4.5. Average annual volume (in metric tons) and value (in pounds sterling) of Brazilian sugar exports, 1821–1906.

production as the economy diversified and expanded.[11] It also contained the largest of the sugar *engenhos* in Brazil. A unique census of the district of Santiago do Iguape in Bahia in 1835 showed that this famous sugar production center contained 22 plantations with an average of 123 slaves per plantation, probably the largest such sugar estates in Brazil.[12] By this date, Bahia alone was exporting close to half of the Brazilian output. Thereafter production slowed, and by the late 1840s, Pernambuco production surpassed Bahian output. The Bahian sugar industry revived in the last quarter of the century, with major capital inputs finally bringing steam mills to more than three-quarters of the province's *engenhos*. It is estimated that by 1877 there were 802 *engenhos* in Bahia and about 800 in Pernambuco.[13]

The impressive growth of Pernambuco in the nineteenth century had its origins in the revitalization of the local economy carried out in the late eighteenth century. The work of the Pombaline monopoly company in Pernambuco had been effective and placed the province in an advantageous position to respond to the post-1791 boom in sugar prices. There was an expansion of mills in both the traditional and frontier areas; at the same time, the slave trade became quite intense, and the local slave population increased to almost 100,000 by the second decade of the nineteenth century. Sugar production expanded with each passing decade, and at mid-century, Pernambuco had passed Bahian levels. By the mid-1880s, it was producing more than 100,000 tons of sugar and accounted for almost half of Brazilian exports. This growth was achieved with a declining slave population. In the 1850s, at the closing of the slave trade, Pernambuco had 145,000 slaves; by the census of 1872, this dropped to 106,000, and it declined further to 85,000 in the next decade. [14] The growth of the free colored population more than made up for this decline, some of which was due to the post-1850 expansion of the internal slave trade that resulted in an estimated 23,000 to 38,000 Pernambucan slaves being shipped south into the southeastern coffee plantations between 1850 and the beginning of the 1880s.[15] Already by the 1850s, the plantations in the richest of Pernambuco's sugar zone were averaging seventy slaves

[11] Schwartz, *Sugar Plantations in the Formation of Brazilian Society*, pp. 423ff.
[12] B. J. Barickman, "Revisiting the Casa-grande: Plantation and Cane-Farming Households in Early Nineteenth-Century Bahia," *Hispanic American Historical Review*, 84, no. 4 (2004), p. 626.
[13] Deerr, *The History of Sugar*, I, p. 111.
[14] Eisenberg, *The Sugar Industry in Pernambuco*, table 22, p. 147.
[15] Eisenberg, *The Sugar Industry in Pernambuco*, p. 157.

and forty-nine free-wage workers in their labor force.[16] This ratio of free workers increased just as the introduction of steam increased sugar output per worker, and northeastern planters had little difficulty replacing slaves with poorly paid and often seasonal wage laborers. Moreover, in Pernambuco, as in Bahia and throughout the northeastern sugar zone, the increasing complexity of milling led to the greater importance of independent planters (*lavradores de cana*) with their own slaves who supplied cane to the mills as well as the increasing use of free-wage workers, seasonal labor, and even squatters.[17] Although few statistics exist on the *lavradores*, many of them were clearly poorer farmers. In a census of the Recôncavo parishes in 1816–1817, there were listed 165 *senhores de engenhos*, or mill owners, and 478 *lavradores de cana*, or cane farmers without mills. The *lavradores* averaged just ten slaves each, and a census of 1835 of one Bahian district suggests that almost a quarter of these cane producers held no slaves and that some 44 percent were free colored.[18]

A most impressive growth in the sugar industry in the post-1791 period was also registered in the province of Rio de Janeiro. Around Guanabara Bay and in the interior lowlands of Campos, a major industry developed. By the early 1820s, there were more than 170,000 slaves in the province, and in Campos alone, there were some 400 or so sugar estates with an average slave labor force of 36 slaves, or just under less than the contemporary Bahian rate of 66 slaves per *engenho*.[19] Sugar *engenhos* in this south central region in general used the same technology as in the Northeast but were on average smaller than those of the Northeast. In the middle decades of the century, however, there was considerable growth in the sugar industry. Finally, in the last quarter of the nineteenth century, there occurred an important change in the sugar-producing areas with the creation of the first steam-driven mills (*engenhos centrais*), a revolution in technology that had already occurred in other countries. With the support of the government, which guaranteed loans to construct these steam-driven mills, this new technology permitted Brazil to again become

---

[16] Eisenberg, *The Sugar Industry in Pernambuco*, p. 146.

[17] See Schwartz, *Sugar Plantations in the Formation of Brazilian Society*, chapter 15; and Eisenberg, *The Sugar Industry in Pernambuco*, chapter 8.

[18] Schwartz, *Sugar Plantations in the Formation of Brazilian Society*, p. 454, table 16–6; and Barickman, "Revisiting the Casa-grande," p. 627.

[19] Schwartz, *Sugar Plantations in the Formation of Brazilian Society*, pp. 428, 446, table 16–3. On the early evolution of sugar *engenhos* in Campos, see Arthur Cézar Ferreira Reis, "A provincial do Rio de Janeiro e o Município Neutro," in Sérgio Buarque de Holanda, ed., *História Geral da Civilização Brasileira* (11 vols.; São Paulo: Difusão Européia do Livro, 1960), tomo II, vol. 2, p. 317.

a player on the international sugar market. It also led to profound changes in the organization of labor. The new and very expensive industrial central mills, which were eventually established in the more advanced areas, were operated by free wage labor, and this led to the complete concentration of slaves in cane production. Numerous central mills were created not only in the Northeast and in Rio de Janeiro, but even in São Paulo. However, the initial transformation was only partial, as the steam technology was often applied to old mills without a complete transformation in the technology into what were called central mills, with all their technical innovation in processing. There also seems to have been problems with a sufficient supply of cane to these new steam mills, because in contrast to the traditional mills, they depended heavily on others to furnish cane. But this supply of cane from the older *engenhos* did not occur as expected, in part because of transport problems, but also because of the boycott of the traditional and powerful *senhores de engenhos* who saw themselves being transformed into simple suppliers of cane and owners of modest mills that could no longer produce sugar. Thus, the central mills, despite the support of the government, did not have the success expected, but they did represent the beginnings of the process of destruction of the old social order that was based on the traditional mills. Eventually there would be the rise of the *usinas*, or large-scale industries based on modern technology, that produced almost all of the cane it processed, thus being immune to the boycott of the old planters. With the *usinas* and their larger scale of production came new social groups in command of the sugar industry. This slow transformation would also represent a rupture in the structure of existing power relations even before the end of slavery in the sugar-producing regions.[20]

The final region to become a significant producer in this period was the captaincy of São Paulo. Along the coast near the port of Santos and in the previously mixed farming region around the city of São Paulo, sugar now began to be produced for world export. Although São Paulo always ranked a poor fourth in national output and accounted for no more than

---

[20] Deerr, *The History of Sugar*, I, p. 111; and Alice P. Canabrava. "A grande Lavoura," in Sérgio Buarque de Holanda (org.), *História Geral da Civilização Brasileira*, vol. 6 (Rio de Janeiro: Bertrand Brasil, 1997). Recent analysis of the government promotion of these central mills in the period from 1875–1889 is found in the works of Roberta Barros Meira, "O processo de modernização da agroindústria canavieira e os engenhos centrais na Província de São Paulo," *História e Economia Revista Interdisciplinar* (São Paulo), 3, no. 1 (2° semestre 2007), pp. 39–54; and Roberta Barros Meira, *Bangüês, engenhos centrais e usinas: O desenvolvimento da economia açucareira em São Paulo e a sua correlação com as políticas estatais (1875–1941)* (Dissertação de mestrado, Faculdade de Filosofia, Letras e Ciências Humanas, da Universidade de São Paulo, 2007).

5 percent of national production, sugar proved vital to the *paulista* economy. Sugar immediately became São Paulo's most valuable export, and
even though output barely climbed into the 1,000-ton figure in this early
period, it already accounted for well over half the value of all provincial exports. By the 1820s, sugar was the province's primary export and
was then in the 5,000- to 10,000-ton range. Sugar exports continued to
expand into the late 1840s, along with a major production of *aguardente*
for which both São Paulo and Rio de Janeiro became known, especially in
the trade to Africa for slaves.[21] Wherever sugar was established it eventually developed as plantation crop, and it also had the highest number of
slave workers per agricultural unit (see Table 4.4). Usually because of high
start-up costs and the quick maturation of the plants, planters concentrated primarily on growing sugar cane in most regions of the world. But
in southeastern Brazil, such sugar estates were fairly unusual by American standards in that they often continued to produce food crops as well.
During the course of the nineteenth century, the introduction of new technology from the more advanced Caribbean producers greatly increased
the investments and output of the sugar mills, all of which increased the
need for even more sugar cane. As can be seen in early nineteenth-century
data (see Table 4.3), the northeast still had the largest sugar estates in
terms of average number slaves per unit – almost double that of even the
premier sugar-producing center of Campinas in São Paulo, although as
can be seen in the changes from 1804 to 1829, the southeastern producers were beginning to approach these traditional northeastern big estate
levels. But none of these zones approached the average of more than two
hundred slaves per unit, which was the norm in Jamaica.[22]

[21] The best overall survey on the *paulista* sugar industry is Maria Thereza Schorer Petrone,
A lavoura canavieira em São Paulo. Expansão e declínio (1765–1851) (São Paulo:
Difusão Européia do Livro, 1968). Other studies of this period include Suely Robles
Reis de Queiroz, "Algumas notas sobre a lavoura de açúcar em São Paulo no período
colonial," *Anais do Museu Paulista*, vol. 21 (1967), pp. 109–277; and the several regional
studies that treat sugar in this period. Among these are the outstanding work of Lucila
Herrmann, *Evolução da estrutura social de Guaratinguetá num período de trezentos
anos* (São Paulo: Ed. Facsimilada. Instituto de Pesquisas Econômicas [IPE/USP], 1986);
as well as Carlos Almeida Prado Bacellar, *Os senhores da terra: Família e sistema
sucessório entre os senhores de engenho do oeste paulista (1765–1855)* (São Paulo:
UNICAMP, 1987) and Ramón Vicente Garcia Fernandéz, "Transformações econômicas
no litoral norte paulista (1778–1836)" (Tese de doutorado, FEA: Universidade de São
Paulo, 1992). On this theme, also see Meira, *Bangüês, engenhos centrais e usinas*.
[22] In 1832, Jamaica had 531 sugar estates, with an average of 223 slaves per estate, of
which only 4 produced another product in addition to sugar. B. W. Higman, *Slave
Populations of the British Caribbean, 1807–1834* (Baltimore: Johns Hopkins University
Press, 1984), p. 14.

TABLE 4.3. *Slaves on the Sugar Engenhos in Various Regions*

Years	Capitania de São Paulo in 1804	Capitania de São Paulo in 1829	West Paulista 1828	Campinas, SP 1829	Itu SP 1829	Rio de Janeiro 1778*	São Francisco Bahia 1816–17	Santo Amaro Bahia 1816–17
Number of *engenhos*	501	589	473	85	107	323	80	85
Slaves	8,387	18,224	15,142	3,521	2,897	11,623	5,560	5,253
Average slaves per unit	17	31	32	41	27	36	70	62
Mode	5	16	20		13	30		
Median	12	23	25	31	20			
			Percentage of slaves by size of slaveholding					
1–10 slaves	14.2	3.0	2.4	1.8	2.6	3.2		0.2
11–20 slaves	22.8	14.4	14.1	8.7	22.5	10.9		0.9
21–40 slaves	34.9	29.2	29.9	19.7	32.7	30.7	7.4	14.2
41–60 slaves	18.7	22.2	22.5	18.1	20.4	11.9	15.5	13.1
61–100 slaves	9.4	22.4	24.3	34.8	21.8	10.2	49.6	42.5
101+		8.8	6.8	16.9		33.1	27.5	29.1

* Just the *engenhos*.

Source: Arquivo Público do Estado de São Paulo, Mapas de população; Schwartz (1985), p. 364; and Costa (1982).

89

Although free persons were employed as specialized workers or as supervisors of slave labor on the typical sugar estates, the majority of the workers, either in the field or in the mills, were slaves. There was of course a difference in skills and in autonomy between slaves employed in agricultural tasks and those dedicated to the industrial process. In the fields, the work was heavy, little specialized, usually executed in gangs, and with a significant participation of women. The only specialized tasks in this area were supervision of the field workers. In the mills, the work was organized into specialized tasks categorized by skills and physical difficulties. Although some of these more specialized tasks involved free workers, the majority of work, even those jobs that were most complex and required greater training, were carried out by slaves who were of great value to their owners, which was reflected in their market prices. One of the best studies of these labor divisions on a northeastern sugar estate comes from the eighteenth century but was typical as well of those of the nineteenth century. There was a large group of specialized workers, and many of them were slaves.[23] In a sample of *engenhos* from the Bahian Recôncavo in the eighteenth century, among a group of 1,331 slaves, the majority worked in the fields (984), in the mills (126), and in transport (87); another 42 were artisans and 10 had supervisory functions, while 82 were employed as household domestic slaves.[24] A study of sugar *engenhos* in Minas Gerais in the 1830s found that among a sample of 589 slaves employed in sugar, 326 were field hands, 183 were artisans, 39 in domestic service, 28 in transport, and 13 in other occupations. In this case, an even higher percentage of slaves were to be found in skilled and semi-skilled labor beyond the unskilled field workers.[25]

Whereas the northeast remained concentrated in sugar and to a lesser extent in cotton during most the nineteenth century, the regions of Rio de Janeiro and São Paulo dramatically and rapidly opened up a new plantation crop that quickly competed with traditional sugar production. In terms of structural change and growth, it was not sugar production but

---

[23] For a description of these skilled positions, see Schwartz, *Segredos Internos*, chapter 12; and also André João Antonil, *Cultura e Opulência do Brasil*. Introdução e vocabulário por A. P. Canabrava (São Paulo: Ed. Nacional, s/d).

[24] Schwartz, *Segredos Internos*, p. 137, tabela 13.

[25] Marcelo Magalhães Godoy, "Fazendas diversificadas, escravos polivalentes – Caracterização sócio-demográfica e ocupacional dos trabalhadores cativos em unidades productivas com atividades agroaçucareiras de Minas Gerais no século XIX," *XIV Encontro Nacional de Estudos Populacionais, ABEP* (2004), p. 20, tabela 13.

rather coffee that was most affected by the Haitian experience. Although coffee had been produced in Brazil since the early eighteenth century and was already a minor but growing export at the end of the century, the halving of Haitian production in the new century and the growing demand for coffee in the North American and European markets created a major demand for new American production. It was coffee, greatly pushed by the collapse of Saint Domingue, that would be the slave crop par excellence in nineteenth-century Brazil.

Although coffee estates in the second half of the nineteenth century would finally rival the big sugar producers in terms of slave workers, they often started as mixed farming enterprises and for several decades were based on relatively small slaveholdings or were even produced by free wage laborers and family farmers. Given the long period of gestation for the coffee trees to mature, it was the norm for alternative food crops and other commercial products to be produced on the coffee estates. Even after these estates grew quite large and their trees were in full production, food crops were still planted in significant quantities even after the abolition of slavery.

The production of coffee in Brazil had initially been widely dispersed over the colony. But it was in the captaincy of Rio de Janeiro that the beans became a major product. What is impressive about this growth of coffee production in Brazil was how late it was in terms of American coffee development, how quickly Brazil came to dominate world production, and how concentrated the plantations were within Brazil itself. Thus, in a complete reversal from the experience of sugar, it was from the West Indies that Brazil learned to cultivate coffee. First from Saint Domingue and later from Cuba, Rio de Janeiro planters learned the techniques of producing coffee on a commercial scale. It was the combination of the crisis created by the elimination of Saint Domingue and the post-1815 rise in European and North American demand that sent prices rising, which finally got the industry into its mature phase.[26]

Before the end of the Napoleonic Wars, production was negligible, and even as late as 1821 the planters of Rio de Janeiro were exporting

---

[26] On the evolution of the coffee industry in Brazil, see Affonso de E. Taunay, *História do Café no Brasil* (20 vols.; Rio de Janeiro: Departamento Nacional do Café, 1939), especially vols. 1 and 2; and Stanley J. Stein, *Vassouras: A Brazilian Coffee County, 1850–1900* (Cambridge: Harvard University Press, 1957). The best study on coffee from the second half of the nineteenth century is the work by Antônio Delfim Netto, *O problema do café no Brasil* (São Paulo: IPE-USP, 1981).

Slavery in Brazil

no more than 7,000 tons. This was a third of Cuban and Puerto Rican output and was nowhere near the 42,000 tons that Saint Domingue had been producing in 1791. Even within the province itself, coffee did not replace sugar as the most valuable export until the 1820s. But in this decade the industry began its dramatic growth. In 1831 coffee exports finally surpassed sugar exports for the first time in Brazil, and they finally surpassed the tonnage record of Saint Domingue set in 1791. By the middle of the decade, Brazil was producing double the combined output of Cuba and Puerto Rico and was the world's largest producer. In the 1840s, output climbed to more than 100,000 tons per annum and doubled again to more than 200,000 by the 1850s (see Graph 4.6), by which time Brazil had become the world's largest producer and accounted for more than half of world production.[27] By the early 1830s, it had become the single most important export (see Graph 4.7) and had replaced sugar and cotton as the most valuable Brazilian commodity being exported, a position it would dominate for the rest of the century.

Although the costs of entrance into coffee production permitted participation of non-slave-owning farmers, coffee was produced by slave labor from the beginning. Moreover, as farmers increased their share of coffee production in their mix of outputs, slaves became an increasingly important part of the coffee labor force. Thus, the growth of coffee in the central provinces of Rio de Janeiro, Minas Gerais, and São Paulo, the top three producers, was closely associated with the growth and expansion of the Atlantic slave trade to Brazil, which reached its largest volume in the nineteenth century. The expansion of the coffee frontiers up from the coastal valleys and into the interior highlands was also typical of a slave plantation economy. Virgin lands were the crucial variable in determining productivity and, with no serious fertilization carried out, soil exhaustion made for a continuously expanding frontier. From the 1820s to the late 1860s, the central valleys of Rio de Janeiro were the core zones of exploitation, with the Paraíba Valley being the heartland of the new industry. From there it spread westward into the southeastern region of Minas Gerais, whose declining mining economy was revived first by sugar production and then by coffee. By the 1860s, local production expanded so rapidly that Minas Gerais temporarily replaced São Paulo as the nation's second-largest producer, with more than one-fifth

---

[27] Pedro Carvalho de Mello, "The Economics of Labor in Brazilian Coffee Plantations, 1850–1888" (Ph.D. dissertation, Department of Economics, University of Chicago, 1977), table 14b, p. 42.

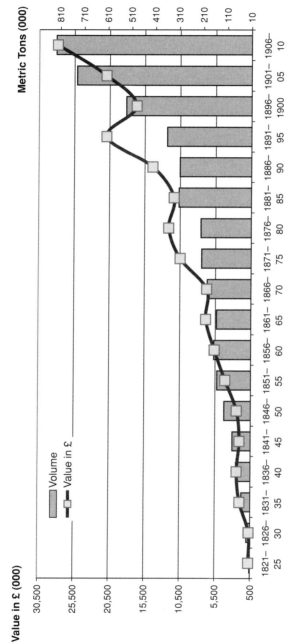

GRAPH 4.6. Average annual volume (in metric tons) and value (in pounds sterling) of Brazilian coffee exports, 1821–1910.

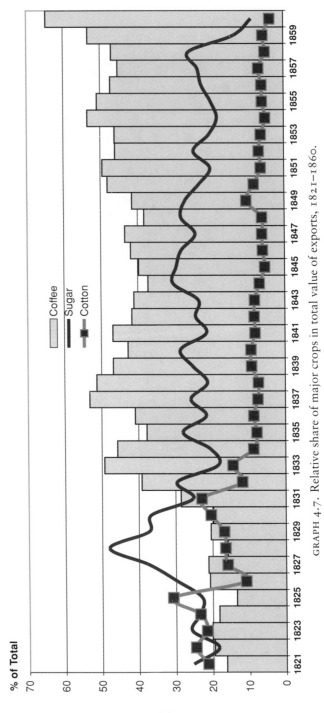

GRAPH 4.7. Relative share of major crops in total value of exports, 1821–1860.

of total coffee exports. For most of the 1860s and early 1870s it gained ground on Rio de Janeiro and maintained its lead over São Paulo.[28] It was only in the late 1870s and the 1880s, at the very end of the slave era, that the coffee frontier finally moved into the West Paulista plains area, and former sugar plantation regions like Campinas became the centers of coffee production. Even abolition and a shift to free labor did not stop the moving coffee frontier, which by the end of the nineteenth century had finally reached south of São Paulo into the province of Paraná.[29]

In its earliest days, coffee was produced on relatively small farms in the coastal region of Rio de Janeiro and in the interior Paraíba Valley. Initially coffee was produced on mixed crop farms and only slowly began to dominate local production. Given the long period for the trees to mature – coffee trees only began producing beans in the third or fourth year of growth – farmers reduced their risk by producing corn and other crops besides coffee. Even after major *fazendas* were created with hundreds of thousands of trees, intercropping of corn and other foodstuffs were common to all coffee plantations. There was wide variation in soil quality and in the ages of trees, which made annual production vary quite dramatically among plantations. In a study of representative São Paulo coffee municipalities, average production rose from 400 kilos per worker on the earliest farms of the 1820s to several thousand kilos per worker a decade or two later. In the mature phase of the industry in the last quarter of

---

[28] There were some 5,200 slaves on the coffee *fazendas* in Juiz de Fora, the largest coffee county in Minas Gerais, at the end of the slave era, with thirteen coffee estates holding more than 100 slaves. Luiz Fernando Saraiva, "Estrutura de terras e transição do trabalho em um grande centro cafeeiro, Juiz de Fora 1870–1900," *X Seminário sobre a Economia Mineira* (2002).

[29] For the evolution of coffee in the São Paulo province, see Warren Dean, *Rio Claro: A Brazilian Plantation System, 1820–1920* (Stanford: Stanford University Press, 1976); the dissertation of Carvalho de Mello, "The Economics of Labor in Brazilian Coffee Plantations, 1850–1888," and the Portuguese translation, "A economia da escravidão nas fazendas de café: 1850–1888," PNPE, 1984; mimeo; José Flávio Motta, "A família escrava e a penetração do café em Bananal (1801–1829)," *Revista Brasileira de Estudos Populacionais*, 5, no. 1 (1988), pp. 71–101; José Flávio Motta, *Corpos Escravos e Vontades Livres – Estrutura da Posse de Cativos e Família Escrava em um Núcleo Cafeeiro (Bananal, 1801–1829)* (São Paulo: Annablume/Fapesp, 1999). José Flávio Motta and Nelson Hideiki Nozoe, "Cafeicultura e acumulação," *Estudos Econômicos*, 24:2 (Maio/Ago. 1994), pp. 253–320; Armenio de Souza Rangel, "Escravismo e riqueza – Formação da economia cafeeira no município de Taubaté – 1765/1835" (Tese de doutorado, São Paulo: FEA-USP, 1990); and Renato Leite Marcondes, *A arte de acumular na economia Cafeeira* (Lorena, São Paulo: Editora Stiliano, 1998); and Francisco Vidal Luna and Herbert S. Klein, *Slavery and the Economy of São Paulo, 1750–1850* (Stanford: Stanford University Press, 2003), chapter 3.

the century, the average field hand produced just over 2,000 kilos of coffee per annum.[30] The number of slaves per coffee estate throughout Brazil slowly increased over the rest of the century, so that by the early 1880s, a survey of some 707 coffee *fazendas* in the leading producing province of Rio de Janeiro indicated an average of 43 slaves per unit.[31] This was a size of holding that was still lower than the average of 128 slaves per coffee estate achieved in Jamaica in 1832,[32] a figure approached only by a minority of Rio de Janeiro and São Paulo plantations even in the last decade of slavery.

The search for better and virgin soils was constantly drawing the coffee frontier inland. The interior valleys of the province were heavily forested and contained excellent soil. For this reason, initial output from the coffee trees was extremely high in the first fifteen or so years. However, denuded of forest and improperly planted, these steep valley lands were subject to soil erosion and rapid decline of productivity of their coffee groves. Thus, a boom–bust cycle accompanied coffee in these early centers. Typical of this first stage was the interior fluminense valley of Paraíba and its central district of Vassouras. Initially settled in the 1790s, Vassouras did not develop coffee *fazendas* until the 1820s. Yet the richness of the local soils, the high prices for coffee on European markets, and the availability of large amounts of capital and labor previously generated by the sugar plantation system allowed for the development of a new type of coffee plantation regime. It was in Vassouras that these first large coffee plantations made their appearance.[33]

During the course of the nineteenth century, the productivity of slaves increased as more stable virgin lands were opened in the highland plateaus and as more experience in planting was developed. It was estimated that an average output of a slave at the leading *fazendas* was close to thirty-four sacks of coffee per annum.[34] In the pre-railroad era – that is, in the period before the 1850s – transport costs were a large part of the final price of coffee, so a large percentage of the slave labor force was engaged

---

[30] This was expressed in an average of 33.6 bags of coffee at 60 kilos per bag. See Carvalho de Mello, "The Economics of Labor in Brazilian Coffee Plantations, 1850–1888," p. 18.

[31] C. F. Van Delden Laerne, *Brazil and Java: Report on Coffee-Culture in America, Asia, and Africa* (London: W. H. Allen, 1885), pp. 222–3.

[32] B. W. Higman, *Slave Population and Economy in Jamaica 1807–1834* (Cambridge: Cambridge University Press, 1976), p. 13, table 1.

[33] The classic study of the Vassouras coffee economy and society is Stein, *Vassouras*.

[34] See Carvalho de Mello, "The Economics of Labor in Brazilian Coffee Plantations, 1850–1888," p. 18.

in the moving of the coffee sacks to market on the backs of mules. A good one-third of the slave labor force on a coffee estate prior to the introduction of rail connections was off the plantation at any given time transporting goods to and from the distant port markets. The railroads eliminated these mule trains in the second half of the nineteenth century, which were replaced by ox-driven carts and feeder roads that led to the nearest railroad sidings.[35] This revolution in transport reduced costs considerably but did little to change the actual structure of the labor force on the coffee *fazendas*. In surveys from coffee plantations, the number of field hands never reached more than 58 percent of the total number of slaves on a given estate.[36] These field hands were divided into gangs and driven under supervision of local slave or white overseers. Just like the sugar estates of the Caribbean and the rest of Brazil, it turned out that the majority of workers on these field gangs were women. In coffee as in sugar, it was men who were exclusively given all the skilled occupations, and it was men who were underrepresented in the unskilled field tasks of planting, weeding, and harvesting. Given the large pool of free black and white labor available even in the most densely settled coffee zones, it was left to hired free laborers to do all the dangerous tasks of clearing virgin forests, a task usually reserved for male slaves in the British and French Caribbean.

The growth of the coffee *fazendas* and of the slave population devoted to them was not confined to the traditional areas but was constantly on the move throughout the Paraíba Valley complex. Older zones with aged trees and a low percentage of virgin forest lands, such as Vassouras, saw declining numbers of slaves in the working-age categories as these younger workers were exported to the newer production zones. Thus, although an intense African slave trade kept the *fazendas* supplied with slaves until the 1850s, reaching a high of fifty thousand African arrivals in all of Brazil per annum in the 1820s (see above Graph 4.1), most of the post-1850 plantation growth was accomplished through an intense internal slave trade migration of slaves at the intercounty, interprovincial, and interregional levels.[37] As older zones like Vassouras matured,

---

[35] For an analysis of the relative roles of mule, wagon, and rail in the transport of coffee, see Herbert S. Klein, "The Supply of Mules to Central Brazil: The Sorocaba Market, 1825–1880," *Agricultural History*, 64, no. 4 (Fall 1990), pp. 1–25.

[36] For Rio de Janeiro coffee plantations in the 1870s and 1880s, Carvalho de Melo estimates that field hands were 57 percent of the total labor force. See Carvalho de Mello, "The Economics of Labor in Brazilian Coffee Plantations, 1850–1888," p. 14.

[37] A detailed estimate of the internal slave trade is found in Chapter 6.

their ratio of Africans among the slaves declined, the average age of the slaves declined and ratio of men to women became more balanced as the population became more native born. Also, many of these older and less efficient producers began losing slaves to the expanding coffee producers in the interior.

The key new growth state for coffee was the province of São Paulo. A late exporter of any major products, São Paulo initially entered the sugar race as a minor producer but ranked fourth in total output by the early decades of the nineteenth century. By the late 1830s, the province held 79,000 slaves, most of whom were in rural occupations, and it was sugar that was the primary occupation. But in the 1840s, coffee finally passed sugar in importance. In that decade the number of slaves in sugar probably numbered twenty thousand, but those attached to coffee *fazendas* reached twenty-five thousand, while the province as a whole accounted for almost one-fourth of national production with its 53,000 tons of coffee. Shipping half of its coffee sacks through the port of Rio de Janeiro and the other half from its own coastal ports, São Paulo's provincial production finally passed *mineiro* levels by the late 1840s and began to approach Rio de Janeiro output by the 1880s. By 1854, São Paulo had more than 2,600 coffee *fazendas* worked by some 55,000 slaves, with the average estate holding just over 20 slaves (see Table 4.4).

Coffee not only moved southwest into São Paulo from Rio de Janeiro but also northwest into the southeastern region area of Minas Gerais known as the Zona de Mata. In the late 1820s, Minas was no longer a major mining center but was involved in a complex mix of farming and cattle ranching and was exporting everything from cotton and hides to sugar when coffee started to emerge as a major crop. By the 1850s, coffee finally became the major provincial export in terms of total value and boomed (except for the crisis with emancipation in the late 1880s) until the early twentieth century (see Graph 4.8). Although the quality of *mineiro* coffee was considered quite good, the average size and the total number of workers involved in coffee were somewhat smaller than in Rio de Janeiro and São Paulo.[38] Using the same techniques of planting, harvesting, and slave gang labor as Rio and *paulista* planters, the *mineiro*

---

[38] For a good overall survey of one of the principal coffee zone of Minas Gerais, see Rafael Rangel Giovanini, "Regiões em movimento: Um olhar sobre a Geografia Histórica do Sul de Minas e da Zona da Mata Mineira (1808–1897)" (Dissertação de mestrado, Geografia, Belo Horizonte: Universidade Federal de Minas Gerais, 2006), pp. 103ff; and Peter Louis Blasenheim, "A regional history of the Zona da Mata in Minas Gerais, Brazil, 1870–1906" (Ph.D. dissertation, Stanford University, 1982).

TABLE 4.4. *Fazendas, Workers, and Production in Coffee, Sugar, and Animals in São Paulo in 1854*

Products/Regions	Fazendas (number)	Agregados	Colonos	Slaves	Animals (mules)	Output (metric tons)	Value (mil réis)
Coffee							
Paraíba Valley	1,150	2,719	31	29,516	14,546	33,731	5,902,282
Capital region	230	349	11	4,372	2,952	2,947	556,965
West Paulista	556	723	2,042	13,519	4,992	11,222	2,311,576
Southern Road	43	199	2	1,262	479	220	45,700
Coast	633	233	73	7,165	373	4,488	818,450
Total	2,612	4,223	2,159	55,834	23,342	52,608	9,634,973
Average per *Fazenda*							
Paraíba	1,150	2	0	26	13	29	5,132
West Paulista	556	1	4	24	9	20	4,158
Province	2,612	2	1	21	9	20	3,689

Source: José J. Machado de Oliveira, "Quadro Estatístico de alguns Estabelecimentos Ruraes da Província de São Paulo," *Documento com que o Ilustríssimo e Excelentíssimo Senhor Dr. José Antonio Saraiva Presidente da Província de S.Paulo abrio a Assembléia Legislativa Provincial, no dia 15 de fevereiro de 1855* (São Paulo: Typ. 2 de Dezembro de Antonio Louzada Antunes: 1855).

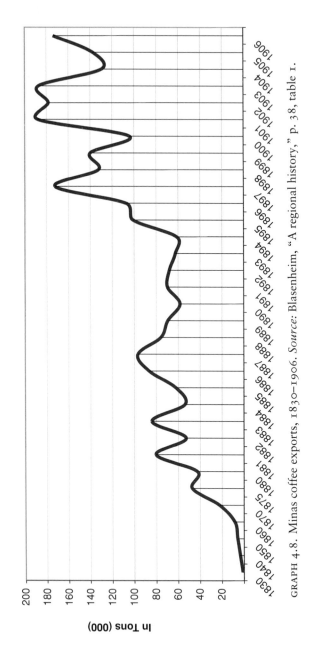

GRAPH 4.8. Minas coffee exports, 1830–1906. *Source:* Blasenheim, "A regional history," p. 38, table 1.

fazendas tended to be far more mixed crop endeavors, even with some cattle ranching, compared to the standard coffee *fazenda* in the other major coffee provinces. Like these other coffee regions, and in contrast to most other slave-based economies, their servile population expanded up to the day of total abolition itself. The slave population in the coffee *municípios* of Minas reached a maximum of 90,000 by the early 1870s and 96,000 by 1886–1887.[39]

As time went on, coffee increasingly absorbed more workers and finally became the largest single employer of Brazilian slaves in the last two decades of the slave era. After several failed experiments with imported European immigrant labor, the coffee planters, unlike their sugar compatriots in the northeast, abandoned all attempts to mix free and slave labor and concentrated exclusively on a slave labor force.[40] Thus, the end of the Atlantic slave trade in 1850, the consequent secular growth of coffee production, and the rise in slave prices all lead to a massive shift of slave laborers out of all parts of the empire into the coffee regions. This was most evident in the expansion of the internal slave trade after 1850. Although an internal slave trade had always existed, with the close of the African trade at mid-century there developed a significantly more important internal interprovincial and intraregional slave trade for the next two decades, which resulted in important shifts in the location of slaves within Brazil. It is estimated that the internal seaborne slave trade alone probably involved the migration of between 100,000 to 200,000 slaves from northeastern and far southern ports to Rio de Janeiro and Santos between 1850 and 1888.[41] There were also important shifts between poorer zones

---

[39] Giovanini, "Regiões em movimento," table 16, p. 149.

[40] On the pre-abolition attempts to incorporate free immigrant labor, see Dean, *Rio Claro*, chapter 4.

[41] One contemporary source reported that 26,622 slaves were imported into Rio de Janeiro from other states between 1852 and 1859, which would give an annual average of 3,327 slaves. Sebastião Ferreira Soares, *Notas estatísticas sôbre a producção agrícola e carestia dos generos alimenticios no Império do Brazil* (Rio de Janeiro: J. Villeneuve, 1860), pp. 135–6. The British Minister to Rio de Janeiro, W. D. Christie, reported that 34,688 slaves were imported by sea into Rio de Janeiro between January 1852 and July 1862, which would give a rate of 275 per month or 3,300 per annum. W. D. Christie, *Notes on Brazilian Questions* (London: Macmillan, 1865), p. 93. J. H. Galloway estimates the total loss of the Northeast at 90,000 slave migrants between 1850 and 1880, or 3,000 slaves per annum shipped by sea from the region to the port of Rio de Janeiro. See Galloway's "The Last Years of Slavery on the Sugar Plantations of Northeastern Brazil," *Hispanic American Historical Review*, LI, no. 4 (November 1971). His estimate may be considered the lower limit, because it excludes southern exports and any post-1880 figures. On the internal trade in one year to the port of Rio de Janeiro, see Herbert

within a given province and their richer neighboring districts.[42] It has been estimated that by the 1870s, the coffee counties of São Paulo contained some 81,000 slaves, and the coffee counties (municípios) of Rio de Janeiro another 148,000.[43] Together with the previously estimated population of coffee-based slaves for Minas Gerais, it would mean that coffee production absorbed something like 320,000 slaves. Of the 1.2 million economically active slaves listed in the first national census of 1872, some 808,000 were employed in agriculture, and they represented only a fifth of all slaves in the empire.

By the early 1880s, the coffee estates had reached their maximum size, but with significant regional variations. Clearly Rio de Janeiro still dominated with the largest estates and a significantly larger average size plantation labor force than was the norm in the other two major provinces of coffee production (see Table 4.5). In fact, the average Rio estate had twenty more slaves than the Minas and most of the *paulista* plantations, which meant that by the last decade of slavery, the *carioca* planters were approaching the size of the biggest sugar estates in the Northeast. As the well-known analysis of Van Delden Laerne showed, slaves were not only a fundamental part of the labor force, but their value also represented more than 40 percent of the total value of the estates and their coffee trees. Moreover, this number was close to the general value of almost all postmortem inventories for plantations of sugar or coffee for all regions

S. Klein, "The Internal Slave Trade in Nineteenth-Century Brazil: A Study of Slave Importations into Rio de Janeiro in 1852," *Hispanic American Historical Review*, LI, no. 4 (November 1971), pp. 567–8.

[42] See José Flávio Motta, "Escravos daqui, dali e de mais além: o tráfico interno de cativos em Constituição (Piracicaba), 1861–1880," *Anais do XXXIII Encontro Nacional de Economia ANPEC* (2005); "O tráfico de escravos na Província de São Paulo: Areias, Silveiras, Guaratinguetá e Casa Branca, 1861–1887" (Texto para Discussão. São Paulo: IPE/USP, 21, 2001); "Tráfico interno de cativos: o preço das mães escravas e sua prole," *XI Encontro Nacional de Estudos Populacionais*, ABEP (1998); and José Flávio Motta and Renato Leite Marcondes, "O Comércio de Escravos no Vale do Paraíba Paulista: Guaratinguetá e Silveiras na Década de 1870," *Estudos Econômicos*, 30, no. 2 (Abril–Junho 2000), pp. 267–99. Also see the several studies on Minas: Cláudio Heleno Machado, "O tráfico interno de escravos na região de Juiz de Fora na segunda metade do século XIX," *X Seminário de Economia Mineira* (2002); Rômulo, Andrade, "Havia um mercado de famílias escravas? (A propósito de uma hipótese recente na historiografia da escravidão)," *Revista de História* (Juiz de Fora), 4, no. 1 (1998), pp. 93–104; Camila Carolina Flausino, "Negócios da escravidão: Tráfico interno de escravos em Mariana: 1861–1886" (Dissertação de mestrado, História, Universidade Federal de Juiz de Fora, 2006).

[43] Carvalho de Mello, "The Economics of Labor in Brazilian Coffee Plantations, 1850–1888," tables 21 and 22, pp. 76–7.

TABLE 4.5. *Basic Statistics on Coffee Plantations in Rio de Janeiro, Minas Gerais, and São Paulo, 1881–1883*

Region**	Districts	Number of Fazendas	Size of Fazendas in Hectares	Number of Coffee Trees	Number of Slaves	Total Value of Fazendas, Including Slaves in Milreis	% of Total Value Due to Slaves	Slaves per Fazenda	Trees per Slave
Santos Zone–São Paulo	20	146	92,442	12,904,090	5,266	19,372,860	38.2	36	2,450
Rio Zone–Rio de Janeiro	13	191	119,945	37,638,543	10,712	26,651,098	47.0	56	3,514
Rio Zone–São Paulo	10	53	47,424	7,881,000	1,987	5,996,591	41.1	37	3,966
Rio Zone–Minas Gerais	11	153	90,453	20,633,000	5,568	15,122,308	44.0	36	3,706
	54	543	350,264	79,056,633	23,533	67,142,857	43.3	43	3,359

Notes:

* We have excluded all mixed coffee and other crop *fazendas*.

** The survey divided *fazendas* into those related to the port of Rio de Janeiro, no matter what the province; Santos includes only those *municípios* in central and southern São Paulo directly linked to the port of Santos.

Source: Van Delden Laerne, *Brazil and Java*, pp. 222–3.

of Brazil and was considerably more than the value of slaves in cattle ranching and mixed farming estates.[44]

But despite this ever-increasing concentration of slaves in coffee, the majority of Brazil's slaves still did not work in coffee or sugar *fazendas*,

[44] Among *senhores de engenho* in Salvador in the nineteenth century, the value of the slaves was 51 percent, and for those owning agricultural properties, it was 32 percent of total value. For most urban professionals, the figure was less than 10 percent. Katia M. de Queirós Mattoso, *Bahia, século XIX, Uma província no império* (Rio de Janeiro: Editora Nova Frontiera, 1992), tabela 116, p. 629. In the Agreste region of Pernambuco, slaves were worth 51 percent of all slave-owning estates (92) in the period of 1820–1849 – in this case much like the Bahian plantation owners – and in both cases, they represented the single most important wealth source. In a sample in the same period from the Sertão region of Pernambuco, which contained cattle ranches, slaves were second in importance to animals and represented 31 percent of the total wealth of these landowners. Flávio Rabelo Versiani and José Raimundo Oliveira Vergolino, "Posse de Escravos e Estrutura da Riqueza no Agreste e no Sertão de Pernambuco: 1777–1887." *Estudos Econômicos*, 33, no. 2 (Abr./Jun. 2003), tabelas 10 and 14, pp. 373, 375. In the cattle-growing and farming zone of Barbacena in Minas Gerais in some 302 postmortem inventories of leading planters and cattle ranchers from 1791–1822, slaves represented 35 percent of the total value of their estates. Adriano Braga Teixeira, "População, sistema econômico e poder na transição do século XVIII para o XIX em Minas Colonial – Barbacena – 1791/1822" (Dissertação de mestrado, Universidade Federal do Rio de Janeiro – UFRJ, 2007), tabela 14, p. 78; and in the São Paulo *município* of Mariana, which was dedicated to mixed farming production whose output went into the internal market, on the 227 farms that used slave labor, the slaves represented 39 percent of the total wealth of these farm families and were the most significant part of the family wealth by far. Heloisa Maria Teixeira, "Reprodução e famílias escravas, em Mariana, 1850–1888" (Dissertação do mestrado, USP-FFLCH, 2001), tabela 3, p. 32. In other cattle-growing regions, slaves were less important. Thus, slaves were of the same relative importance as animals and lands in the cattle regions of the Rio Grande de Sul province, and in the first half of the nineteenth century, they averaged about 20 percent of the value of all estates that contained slaves. Luiz Paulo Ferreira Nogueról, Diego Rodrigues, Ezequiel Giacomolli, and Marcos Smith Dias, "Elementos Comuns e Diferenças entre os Patrimônios Registrados na Pecuária Gaúcha e na Pernambucana no Início do Século XIX," *VIII Encontro de Economia da Região Sul – ANPEC SUL* (2005), tabela 9, which accounts for 326 postmortem inventories that listed slave ownership in the period from 1820–1849, for the districts of Pelotas, Rio Pardo, Rio Grande, and Porto Alegre. A study of Pelotas alone in the period of 1850–1871 found that slaves were still just second in importance to land and housing, but at 30 percent of the value of all slaveholding ranches, they were more important than cattle in this period. Luana Teixeira, "Trabalho escravo na produção pecuária: São Francisco de Paula de Cima da Serra (Rio Grande de São Pedro, 1850–1871)," *III Encontro Escravidão e liberdade no Brasil Meridional* (2007), tabela IV. Even in the far southern district of Lages in Santa Catarina, among the cattle ranchers, slaves were worth 18 percent of the total value of some 149 estates, with slaves being more valuable the wealthier the unit. Nilsen C. Oliveira Borges, "Terra, gado e trabalho: Sociedade e economia escravista em Lages, SC (1840–1865)" (Dissertação de mestrado, Universidade Federal de Santa Catarina, Florianópolis, 2005), tablea VIII, p. 86.

even in the central-south zone. For example, despite its dominant position in the total value of provincial exports, coffee absorbed only a small fraction of even the rural slaves within the province. Minas Gerais was unique in that its mixed farming sector, which exclusively produced for a local market, absorbed the majority of the slaves in this largest slave province in the empire. In the 1870s, there were 382,000 slaves in the province, of which 279,000 were listed as rural workers, and in the province as a whole, slaves on coffee *fazendas* represented fewer than a quarter of all the local slaves. Nor were the counties with the most slaves those most associated with coffee.[45] Cattle ranching, food processing, and the production of grains and root crops were all slave- as well as free-labor activities. There were even a significant number of slaves in skilled and semi-skilled occupations. In a detailed analysis of the unpublished census of 1831–32, some 14 percent of the 88,000 or so adult slaves were listed as skilled and semi-skilled nonagricultural workers, with the single largest area of activity being spinning and weaving of cotton. Moreover, slave artisans made up 20 percent of all workers in spinning and weaving and 28 percent of those in construction. It was estimated that almost one-quarter of all female adult slaves were in these nondomestic service occupations.[46] Thus, Minas Gerais represents the rare case within America of a large-scale employment of rural slaves for primarily local, regional, or national production. Minas Gerais was also unusual for a Center-South state in its distribution of slave ownership. As in the case of slaveholdings throughout mainland America, the average number of slaves held per slave owner was quite small, but, unlike most American slave zones, the number of slave owners was quite large, and they represented a much more sizable percentage of the free population. Big *fazendeiros* owning large numbers of slaves were few, and they controlled a relatively small share of the total provincial slave labor force.

However, Minas was not alone in this more complex distribution of slaves. It was found that even in Pernambuco, with its high concentration of slaves in sugar, between 30 to 40 percent of the rural slaves were found outside the plantation zones throughout the nineteenth century. These were engaged in cotton production, ranching, and food production. In

---

[45] Giovanini, "Regiões em movimento," tables 12 and 14, pp. 139, 144.

[46] Marcelo Magalhães Godoy, "Uma província artesã: O universo social, econômico e demográfico dos artífices da Minas do oitocentos," *Anais do XII Encontro Nacional da ABEP* (2004), tabelas 1, 6, and 7.

TABLE 4.6. *Distribution of Slave Holdings by Region, Pernambuco, 1800–1887*

Size of Slave	% Distribution of Slaves		
	Mata	Agreste	Sertão
1–5	12.2	16.8	23.7
6–10	10.7	24.7	27.3
11–20	10	19.0	32.7
21–50	38.8	19.8	11.8
More than 50	28.4	19.7	4.5
Total	100.1	100.0	100.0
Total estates	117	325	226
Total slaves	1,300	2,618	1,484

Notes: Distribution based on inventories that contained slaves.

Source: Versiani and Vergolino, "Slave holdings in nineteenth-century Brazilian northeast" (2002), table 3.

fact, cotton plantations in the interior *agreste* region actually produced a significant quantity of foodstuffs as well as cotton.[47] Moreover, as might be expected, these interior small farming, cattle, and cotton estates had much smaller holdings of slaves, and most slave owners had on average fewer slaves and there were far fewer larger units than found in the sugar-producing region (see Table 4.6).

As already noted, aside from producing sugar, which was still Brazil's second-most-valuable export, slaves were to be found producing rice,[48] cotton, poultry, pigs, and pork products as well as various grains and corn and general food production for the internal market. There was also a significant use of slaves along with free workers in the cattle industries of the traditional southern grazing lands, but also in the expanding cattle

---

[47] Versiani and Vergolino, "Posse de Escravos e Estrutura da Riqueza no Agreste e Sertão de Pernambuco," pp. 353–93; and by the same authors, "Slaveholdings in nineteenth-century Brazilian northeast: Sugar estates and the backlands" (paper presented at *XIII Congress of the International Economic History Association*, Buenos Aires, July 2002), which adds the sugar zones to their previous regional selections.

[48] A partial analysis of colonial slave-produced rice in Maranhão is found in Judith A. Carney, "'With Grains in Her Hair': Rice in Colonial Brazil," *Slavery & Abolition*, 25, no. 1 (April 2004), pp. 1–27. A more complete survey of an example of slaves working in rice production – this time in São Paulo in the nineteenth century – is found in Agnaldo Valentin, "Arroz no Vale do Ribeira (1800–1888)" (Tese de doutorado, FFLCH, Universidade de São Paulo, 2006).

ranches of the northeastern provinces. Brazilian cotton, which had been a vital colonial product and still supplied the European market with a major share of its raw cotton until the first decade of the nineteenth century, revived in the 1860–1880 period. The U.S. Civil War created a cotton famine for European mills, and the result was a revival both of the Maranhão cotton plantation sector as well as the growth of new cotton regions such as those of Minas Gerais, with even some production coming out of São Paulo. Although impressive in financial terms, this temporary growth in the value of cotton exports had no long-lasting or significant impact on local labor distribution. Production only doubled in the 1860–1880 period, whereas the value of these exports more than quintupled. The result was a temporary local shift of slaves into cotton, which had little long-term impact on slaves engaged in the other plantation crops.

The other 370,000 or so slaves in rural occupations could be found scattered throughout the empire in activities that went to feed the growing market of 9.9 million Brazilians. Slaves still remained important in the jerked beef industry in the southern provinces of Rio Grande do Sul, which successfully competed throughout the nineteenth century against the free-labor-based Uruguayan jerked beef industry. Although free workers were always present in this industry, the use of slaves remained important and profitable until the 1880s.[49] The same occurred in the expanding cattle ranches of the northeast where slave and free workers were the norm. They were also important in the manufacture of dairy and pork products for local and regional markets in Minas Gerais. Along with cotton, for example, northeastern farmers grew a host of crops, many of them for export. Bahia, for example, had a thriving tobacco and manioc flour production, a portion of which was produced by slave labor. Although the majority of tobacco and *cassava* producers were mostly small free farmers with a few *agregados*, or hired hands, a significant minority of these producers owned slaves and produced for export. In addition, the more successful of these farmers often began to purchase slaves as their profits increased. In the tobacco district of Cachoeira in the 1846–1860 period, two-thirds of the farmers owned nine or fewer slaves. And none held more than forty slaves. Even fewer slaves were used on the *cassava* farms, although these produced major quantities for sale in regional

---

[49] Leonardo M. Monasterio, "FHC errou? A economia da escravidão no Brasil meridional," *História e Economia Revista Interdisciplinar* (São Paulo, BBS), 1, no. 1 (2° semestre 2005), pp. 13–28.

TABLE 4.7. *Ratio of Slaves Owned by Size of Slaveholding (*Plantel) *in the 1870s by Region*

Slaveholding	Pernambuco and Pará	Maranhão, Pará, and Piauí	Sudeste	Bahia and Sergipe	Goiás	Rio Grande do Sul
1	768	2,343	3,386	1,012	881	420
2–4	1,957	5,657	9,571	1,908	2,376	1,297
5–9	2,088	5,365	9,747	1,798	2,173	1,750
10–19	1,956	4,621	9,322	1,974	1,371	1,220
20–39	1,850	2,623	7,775	1,621	384	255
40+	1,928	731	11,506	1,053	114	–
	10,547	21,340	51,307	9,366	7,299	4,942
Summary measures						
20+ slaves	36%	16%	38%	29%	7%	5%
Modal unit	5–9	2–4	5–9	2–4	2–4	5–9
Median unit	10–19	5–9	10–19	5–9	5–9	5–9
Mean no. of slaves	5.1	3.7	5.4	4.2	3.3	3.9

Source: Marcondes, "Desigualdades regionais brasileiras," (2005), tabelas 4–5, 5–5, 6–5, 7–5, 8–5, 9–5.

markets. However, even here a few individuals had more than ten slaves producing the flour.[50]

A recent attempt at a national evaluation of slave ownership throughout Brazil in the 1870s shows how widely but also how unevenly distributed were the slaves among the agricultural communities.[51] Sugar and coffee *municípios* had the highest average number of slaves per unit and the most unequal distribution of slaves, but everywhere else slaves were fairly widely distributed in small holdings in a host of agricultural, grazing, and other rural activities (see Table 4.7).

Finally, every major urban center was surrounded by truck gardens, many of which were run with small numbers of slaves often as independent units along with poor free farmers.

The 345,000 of the economically active slaves not directly engaged in agriculture in 1872 were often closely allied with plantation life. The most obvious example was the 95,000 slaves listed as day laborers, some of whom were probably employed in the *fazendas* alongside the resident

---

[50] B. J. Barickman, *A Bahian Counterpoint: Sugar, Tobacco, Cassava, and Slavery in the Recôncavo, 1780–1860* (Stanford: Stanford University Press, 1998), chapter 6.

[51] Renato Leite Marcondes, "Desigualidades regionais brasileiras: Comércio marítimo e posse de cativos na década de 1870" (Tese livre-docência, FEA, USP, Riberão Preto, 2005).

slave forces. Some of the seven thousand artisans listed as working in wood and metal crafts, especially carpenters and blacksmiths, may also have been employed on plantations. But as the example of Minas Gerais reveals, there was also within the slave labor force a significant proportion of slaves who were not directly related to export agriculture yet still played a significant economic role in the economy. Thus, slaves made up 10 percent of the 126,000 workers found in the textile factories, which were then coming into prominence as Brazil's first major industrial activity. The 175,000 slaves who were in domestic service accounted for 17 percent of all persons employed in that activity and made up 15 percent of the economically active slaves. Slaves also exceeded their 15 percent share of the laboring population in such activities as construction (4,000 of whom made up 19 percent of all such workers), masonry, stonework, and allied crafts (18 percent), just as they held more than their share of day laboring (23 percent). Finally, there were some occupations in which, even though slaves represented a small share of all workers, the absolute number of slaves was impressive. This was the case with seamstresses, in which the 41,000 slave women represented only 8 percent of the total workers in this occupation.

A great many slaves also lived in cities, in which, like the country at large, they formed a minority of the total colored population. A much higher percentage of the 4.2 million free colored than of the 1.5 million slaves lived in urban centers. Nevertheless, slaves were important in the labor force of every city. Of the 785,000 persons who lived in cities of 20,000 or more in 1872, a minimum of 118,000, or 15 percent, were slaves. This was probably not the highest number of urban slaves ever reached, as such urban-based slaves were in decline at this time, just as was the total slave population. Ever since the end of the slave trade at mid-century, the total number of slaves had declined from their peak of 1.7 million. As in most of the American slave states, the abolition of an intense Atlantic slave trade initially led to a negative growth rate of the resident slave population. The decline in total numbers also led to a shift in their distribution. The steep rise of slave prices as a result of the ending of the Atlantic slave trade, the increasing impact of manumission, and the continued expansion of coffee meant that ever more slaves would be sold from the city into the countryside. In 1849, for example, the city of Rio de Janeiro had 78,000 slaves, whereas in 1872 there were only 39,000. But slaves in Rio still represented more than one-fifth of the city's 183,000 people. Salvador, the second-largest center in 1872 with 108,000 residents, had 13,000 slaves, and Recife ranked third with

57,000 persons, of whom 10,000 were slaves. Even the still quite small city of São Paulo had 3,000 slaves out of a population of 28,000.[52] Urban slavery in Brazil had both the standard forms of rural master–slave relationship with direct ownership and resident employment along with direct ownership and rental to a third party. But there were also a fairly large number of slaves who were self-employed, or, as the Brazilians called them, *escravos de ganho*.[53] These slaves spanned the occupational spectrum from the least skilled and most dangerous of jobs to the most highly remunerative occupations. Such slaves even had multiple occupations. In the city of Salvador in the 1850s and 1870s, there were several cases noted of multiple skills or occupations occupied by one slave. Thus, the young slave boy André of the Nagô nation was both a sedan porter and an apprentice carpenter, while Ricardo, another young Nagô slave, worked both as a farmhand (*serviço de roça*) and as an *escravo de ganho*. Amália, a 20-year-old slave who was self-employed, worked as a cigar maker and as an ironer.[54] This same pattern of multiple occupations was found for the rental slaves of the city of Salvador in the mid-nineteenth century.[55] All information points out that these *escravos de ganho* porters, vendors, and semi-skilled and skilled artisans were not only self-employed and paid a fixed income to their owners, but they also took care of their own housing or lived as apprentices in the homes of master craftsmen who were not their owners. Studies of the major cities point out that local municipal records constantly show the existence of independent-slave households.[56] Such independent slaves even created complete families in these separate quarters, as occurred in the case of seven of the

---

[52] See Table 6.3 and its sources.

[53] On the self-renting slaves, see among others the works of Luiz Carlos Soares, "Os escravos de ganho no Rio de Janeiro do século XIX," *Revista Brasileira de História* V, no. 16 (1988), pp. 107–42; and Leila Mezan Algranti, "Os ofícios urbanos e os escravos de ganho no Rio de Janeiro Colonial (1808–1822)," in Tamás Szmrecsányi, ed., *História Econômica do Período Colonial* (São Paulo: Ed. HUCITEC/FAPESP, 1996), pp. 195–214.

[54] Maria Cristina Luz Pinheiro, "O trabalho de crianças escravas na cidade de Salvador, 1850–1888," *Afro-Ásia*, 32 (2005), p. 162.

[55] As Katia Mattoso noted, "...é difícil distinguir entre escravos de ganho, os que vão para as ruas mercadear, e escravos domésticos, pois seus proprietários utilizam seus serviços ou os alugam de acôrdo com suas necessidades do momento: um mesmo escravo pode, muito bem, ser ganhador e doméstico ao mesmo tempo." Katia M. de Queirós Mattoso, "Sociedade escravista e mercado de trabalho: Salvador–Bahia, 1850–1868," *Bahia Análise & Dados* (Salvador), 10, no. 1 (2000), p. 17.

[56] See, e.g., Leila Mezan Algranti, *O feitor ausente: Estudo sobre a escravidão urbana no Rio de Janeiro, 1808–1821* (Petrópolis: Vozes, 1988); and Ynaê Lopes dos Santos, "Além da senzala: Arranjos escravos de moradia no Rio de Janeiro (1808–1850)" (Dissertação de mestrado, Universidade de São Paulo, 2006).

eight slaves owned by widow Dona Catarina de Oliveira in the *paulista* district of Curitiba in 1776. Three of her slaves not only lived apart but also had their own families and independently farmed some lands, whereas the others simply lived apart and took care of their own household needs.[57] Such slaves were also let out in apprentice contracts to local free artisans. This was the case, for example, of four out of the five slaves owned by Antonio de Souza Ferreira, who died in Rio de Janeiro in 1824; two of these slaves were apprentices to a carpenter, one to a shoemaker, and one was already a journeyman carpenter. Artists and musicians were often self-employed slaves, although some of these resided with their masters. This was the case of the African-born Antonio José Dutra, a barber in Rio who on his death in 1849 owned thirteen slaves, mostly Africans, the majority of whom formed a band and brought him far greater income than either of his two rental properties or his barbering. These slave musicians also served as barbers in his shop.[58]

Many slaves were also rented to factory owners. In 1840, José Vieira Sarmento, for example, had a small tortoiseshell comb factory in the city that employed eleven of his own slaves (four journeymen and seven apprentices) and nine rented slaves.[59] In the Rio de Janeiro city of Niterói in 1855, for example, there were 130 slaves employed in the local factories, of which 85 were owned by the individual factory that employed them and 45 were rented. In the neighboring city of Rio de Janeiro, half (527) of the 1,039 workers employed in the local factories were slaves, although there is no corresponding breakdown into rented and owned. The largest textile firm in Brazil, the Companhia da Ponta D'Arêa, in late 1855 had a workforce of 622 workers, of whom 181 were slaves.[60] Moreover, despite the steady increase of foreign-born free workers in industry as late as 1872, the census listed 2,135 slave industrial workers compared to 9,458 foreign born in a total industrial workforce of 18,091.[61]

---

[57] Adriano Bernardo Moraes Lima, "Trajetórias de Crioulos: Um estudo das relações comunitárias de escravos e forros no têrmo da Vila de Curitiba (c. 1760 – c. 1830)," (Dissertação de mestrado, Universidade Federal de Paraná, Curitiba, 2001), p. 41.

[58] Zephyr Frank, *Dutra's World: Wealth and Family in Nineteenth-Century Rio de Janeiro* (Albuquerque: University of New Mexico Press, 2004).

[59] Luiz Carlos Soares, "A escravidão industrial no Rio de Janeiro do século XIX," *Anais do V Congresso Brasileiro de História Econômica ABPHE* (2003), p. 4.

[60] Artur José Renda Vitorino, "Operários livres e cativos nas manufaturas: Rio de Janeiro, segunda metade do século XIX," *I Jornada Nacional de História do Trabalho*, (Florianópolis: Laboratório de História Social do Trabalho e da Cultura, 2002), p. 7.

[61] Luiz Carlos Soares, "A manufatura na sociedade escravista: O surto manufatureiro no Rio de Janeiro e nas suas circunvizinhanças (1840–1870)," in F. Mauro, ed., *La préindustrialization du Brésil* (Paris: CNRS, 1984), p. 42.

In the detailed, unpublished census of Minas Gerais in 1831–1832, there were listed some 23,000 slaves who worked in such activities. These represented 17 percent of the provinces' slaves (compared to 41 percent of free persons who were working in manufacturing activities). Half of the slaves, like half of the free workers, were listed as working in manual and mechanical activities, but slaves were higher than their provincial average among metal workers, construction workers, and in textile activities, with 95 percent of the textile slave workers (or 9,998 of them) being women.[62]

All this flexibility made for a quite complex pattern of slave activity and for a much more pronounced intervention of the slave in the market economy as a consumer and earner of income. Although municipalities often complained about the relative freedom and lack of financial support for self-employed slaves, they proved so lucrative an investment for their masters that the practice was never abolished. Estimates from both urban and plantation slave rentals suggests that rented-out slaves – after paying for their own upkeep of housing and food (estimated at 20 percent of their gross income) – provided an annual profit of some 10 to 20 percent to their masters on their initial investment.[63] They were, however, only moderately used in the rural area and so were one of the major features that distinguished urban from rural slavery in Brazil. There was even a strike organized in Bahia in 1857 of the porters known as *ganhadores*. These haulers of objects, water, persons in sedan chairs, and innumerable other cargoes were organized into work groups usually along African nationalities. They also included both slave and free Africans, as well as Creoles both slave and free, although the dominant element was Nagôs or Yorubas. In that year, an attempt by the municipal government to tax their labor and create other forms of limitations on their freedom of contract led to a weeklong strike of all active workers, which effectively caused the urban government to abandon most of its tax and control efforts.[64]

Finally, slaves could be found in all parts of Brazil's complex transportation network, from muleteers in the mule trains that formed the

[62] Godoy, "Uma província artesã, p. 4.

[63] The best estimates of profitability of slave ownership in the nineteenth century comes from Carvalho de Mello, "The Economics of Labor in Brazilian Coffee Plantations," chapter 4.

[64] João José Reis, "The Revolution of the Ganhadores: Urban Labour, Ethnicity, and the African Strike of 1857 in Bahia, Brazil," *Journal of Latin American Studies*, 29, no. 2 (May 1997), 355–93.

basis of interior transport until well into the second half of the nineteenth century[65] to sailors in the shipping in both long-distance, coastal trade and among local fishermen. As we previously noted, slaves were to be found aboard slave ships bound for Africa as members of the regular crew and were vitally important in the coastal trade in the late eighteenth and early nineteenth centuries.[66] Even in the nineteenth century, slave sailors remained a fundamental part of the shipping industry. For example, in the port of Rio de Janeiro in the period of 1815 to 1826, officials issued passports for 2,463 slave sailors engaged in the coastal trade with southern ports.[67] In the southern Brazilian port town of Porto Alegre in 1857, there were 3,193 sailors listed as working from the port involved in either coastal trading, fishing, or local rowboat transport, 1,157 of whom were slaves. These slave sailors represented 49 percent of the sailors engaged in coastal trade, their most significant participation, and they accounted for 30 percent of the sailors engaged in long-distance oceanic trade, 27 percent of the river and port sailors, and only 10 percent of the fishermen.[68] More than a decade later in 1869, there was only a modest decline in the ratio if not the number of slave sailors. In that year the government listed 3,638 sailors as working from the port involved in oceanic and coastal trading, fishing, and local rowboat transport, of whom 1,168 – or almost a third – were slaves.[69] They were also a significant part of the boatyard workers in the same year of 1869, accounting for 72 of the 247 workers making and repairing ships in the port's naval yards.[70]

[65] African-born slaves seem to have been overrepresented among the *tropeiros*, and slaves made up a third of the labor force raising pack animals. See Marcelo Magalhães Godoy, Mario Marcos Sampaio Rodarte, and Clotilde Andrade Paiva, "Negociantes e tropeiros em um território de contrastes; o setor comercial de Minas Gerais no século XIX," *Anais do V Congresso Brasileiro de História Econômica*, ABHPE (2003).

[66] Also see Jaime Rodrigues, "Cultura marítima: Marinheiros e escravos no tráfico negreiro para o Brasil (sécs. XVIII E XIX)," *Revista Brasileira de História*, 19, no. 38 (1999), pp. 15–53. There are even cases of fugitive slaves claiming to be free and enlisting in the Brazilian Navy and serving aboard warships for many months. Álvaro Pereira do Nascimento, "Do cativeiro ao mar: Escravos na Marinha de Guerra," *Estudos Afro-Asiáticos*, no. 38 (Dez. 2000), pp. 1–25.

[67] Fábio W. A. Pinheiro, "Tráfico atlântico de escravos na formação dos plantéis mineiros, Zona da Mata, c. 1809–c. 1830" (Dissertação de mestrado, UFRJ, Rio de Janeiro, 2007), tabela 6, p. 75.

[68] Vinicius Pereira de Oliveira, "Sobre o convés: Marinheiros, marítimos e pescadores negros no mundo atlântico do Porto de Rio Grande/RS (século XIX)," *IX Encontro Estadual de História – ANPUH-RS* (Porto Alegre, 2008), pp. 3–5

[69] Paulo Roberto Staudt Moreira, *Os cativos e os homens de bem: Experiências negras no espaço urbano, Porto Alegre 1858–1888* (Porto Alegre: EST edições, 2003), p. 74.

[70] Moreira, *Os cativos e os homens de bem*, p. 75.

The relative decline in urban slavery, if not of the urban colored population, was part of a larger process of geographic redistribution of slaves that occurred in the post-Atlantic slave trade period. Not only were a higher proportion of slaves found in the most productive industries such as coffee but also in those regions in which those industries were concentrated. At mid-century, fewer than half of the slaves were to be found in three major coffee provinces, but by 1872 more than half were located there. An active post-1850 internal slave trade helped to concentrate slaves in the center-south district, with both the Northeast and the far southern provinces shipping their slaves to Rio de Janeiro, Minas Gerais, and, above all, to São Paulo. On the eve of abolition in 1887, almost three-quarters of the remaining 751,000 slaves could be found in these three provinces. Thus slavery, as in Cuba, was most heavily concentrated in the most dynamic regions of their respective societies on the eve of emancipation. With the cost of slaves rising and the growth rates of the slave populations still negative, ever more slaves were shifted into the export sectors of the two largest slave states in Latin America.

5

The Economics of Slavery

Slaves are the hands and feet of the *senhor do engenho* for without them
Brazil could not make, conserve, or expand its resources, nor have a viable
plantation system.[1]

This famous affirmation of Padre Antonil made at the beginning of the
eighteenth century could not be more true and need not be restricted to the
senhores de engenho (or sugar mill planters). They were the basic labor
for the majority, even of the free population, which depended on their
services. In all the economic activities developed in Brazil until the last
quarter of the nineteenth century, slaves were the essential labor force.
At the same time that the importance of slaves was recognized, there
was also a biased vision created of that contemporaneous society in Brazil.
This famous phrase, despite its obvious truth, perhaps lead to a distortion
of the Brazilian society of the period. The idea of a slave mass and a
planter elite to the exclusion of all other classes dominated Brazilian
historiography until the first half of the twentieth century. Plantations,
monoculture, and slave labor were considered the essence of Brazilian
society. This society was segmented between just slave owners and slaves,
with the latter seen as "things," culturally backward, morally perverted,
without any contribution to Brazilian culture. Fortunately, this vision of
Brazilian society began to change beginning in the 1930s, particularly
with the pioneer work of Gilberto Freyre, who gave life to the slaves and

---

[1] "Os escravos são as mãos e os pés do senhor do engenho, porque sem eles no Brasil não
é possível fazer, conservar e aumentar fazenda, nem ter engenho corrente." André João
Antonil, *Cultura e Opulência do Brasil*, Introdução e vocabulário por A. P. Canabrava
(São Paulo: Ed. Nacional, s/d), p. 159.

showed their important contribution to the formation of this culturally mixed society.

But if Freyre and his predecessors in the Bahian Afro-Brazilian movement finally changed the relative weight of Africans and their descendants in the formation of modern Brazil, they still maintained the older idea of a society filled with just planters and slaves. However, when we talk of masters, we should qualify what masters we are talking about. Usually the *senhor* was equated with slave owner. But who were Brazil's slave owners? What were the characteristics of the slave owners and in what activities did they use their slaves? We can give dozens of types of slave owners with social positions and economic interests completely different from one another. When we speak of a *senhor de engenho*, we are speaking of an economic and social elite, with dozens or even hundreds of slaves, located in the sugar cane agriculture in the northeast, in Rio de Janeiro, or in São Paulo. This type of elite was also crucial in the large coffee plantations (*fazendas*) in the Paraíba Valley in the last century of slavery. Perhaps large-scale mining in Minas Gerais in the so-called *lavras* presents similar characteristics. These are activities on a large scale with groups of slave workers organized in gangs with little specialization but with great physical labor. The rigid control and the physical violence needed to be productive perhaps are the factors that mark this form of economic exploitation. Nevertheless, one asks, how representative were these activities in Brazilian society? They were, obviously, economically very important, because they represented the principal economic activities in various periods of Brazilian history and were the reason for its occupation and colonization and the form of its insertion into the international market, within the rules of the colonial system or as an independent nation. But we cannot characterize slavery in Brazil only by the standards of these activities. At least from 1700, at no time in the history of slavery in Brazil were the slaves of the *engenhos*, the mining camps, or the extensive coffee fields the majority of the slaves then residing in Brazil. They were mostly in fact owned by slave owners quite different from the big planters and miners. Can we classify in the same economic and social category the priest who possessed on aged female slave who aided him in his parish work? Or the freed black woman who declared that she was poor in eighteenth-century Minas Gerais, but possessed seven slaves? Or the thousands of farmers who developed an agriculture directed toward the internal market and also produced subsistence crops who had one or two slaves to assist the farmer's family in their small plots? How do we define the *senhor* who used his slaves in commerce in the towns, or the itinerant miner (*faiscador*) who owned some slaves who were given complete freedom of movement and paid a daily wage in gold? How do we characterize the owners of *coartado* slaves (self-purchasing slaves) who had achieved an effective autonomy and who gradually paid for their own freedom? How do we characterize a farmer who possessed one slave and practiced family farming, working on a small plot with his slave? How do we characterize the master who liberated his slave, but conditions his manumission on the continued service to the master until his death? How does one classify the relations of the slave owner with his illegitimate child still maintained in slavery? Finally, how to place the *agregado* (servant) who resides in the home of others, has no identifiable activity, and owns slaves? These suggest a far more complex stratification and social organization than was originally suggested by the discussion of slavery in Brazil. The abundant current historiography on slavery shows everyday situations more complex, although equally frequent, which defined slavery in Brazil.

On the other hand, the category of *slave* is well determined, both legally and in practice, in Brazil and needs not be questioned. However, when we study the effective social space of slaves in Brazil, we find a variety of situations that need to be clarified in order to understand the organization and functioning of slavery in Brazil. Let us give some examples. How do we compare the social role, opportunities, and freedom of action for slaves in production compared to the enormous number of slaves in domestic service? How does one compare these three factors for slaves in the urban or rural area; for slaves in agricultural production and skilled slaves who transformed cane into sugar or were skilled artisans? How does one classify a slave married to a free person, or a slave whose children are free? Or, on the contrary, what is the relationship of a slave to his owner when the owner is a *forro* (or liberated slave) or is a master who lives from alms? How does one classify a household composed just of slaves; where does one put the *coartado* slave? What is the social position of a slave who was a child of his owner, and was recognized and freed in the owner's will? How does one compare the slaves who sweated in the gangs of the large agricultural estates with the slaves involved in the management of the mule trains or who raised cattle? These are just a few examples that suggest the complexity of slave society in Brazil and the varieties of social space that the slaves could possess within the system. The recent studies on Brazilian slavery show such extensive diversity among slaves and their masters and permit one to better understand the complex social relations prevalent in Brazil during the time when slavery existed in the colonial and independence periods.

The studies on slavery in Brazil, which have been carried out in the
last thirty years, have revealed a very complex society from the social
and economic perspective. We find manumitted slaves everywhere, and
even some who owned slaves. In the diamond district of Serro do Frio
at the height of the mining boom, they represented an extraordinary
20 percent of the slave owners. Would it be possible to classify them as
senhores? Would they have the social status of a *senhor*? We have also
found slaves in all kinds of activity. They are the labor force in all the
large mines and plantations, but they are also in foodstuff production,
artisanal activities, in commerce, in transport, in fishing, in art, and of
course, in domestic labor. They are more restricted in the rural areas
and freer in the cities. Meanwhile, miscegenation continues nonstop and
soon the *mestiços*, *mulatos*, and *pardos* are the majority of society –
as slaves, liberated slaves, and free persons of color. In spite of these
qualifications, it is important to stress that the slave regime in Brazil,
despite its complexities and differences in time and space, was based on
violence, apparent or not, which was the only way such a system of
labor could survive in any society. To show its more complex nature than
previously understood, does not soften the violence of the slave regime but
is rather to better understand that society. As one famous 1839 *Brazilian
Manual for Agriculturalists* warned its readers, given that slavery was a
violation of natural rights, the only way to force slaves to work was to
instill "fear, and only fear, but employed with system and art, because
excessive fear will be counterproductive...."[2]

The analysis of an interpretive model of slavery in Brazil is not an
easy task. Our interest is to find better means to classify these economic
and social relations, without preoccupying ourselves with a theoretical
analysis of the modes of production, which was a major theme in the
middle of the twentieth century.[3] We thus have examined the available

[2] "[M]edo, e somente o medo, aliás empregado com muito sistema e arte, porque o excesso
obraria contra o fim que se tem em vista." The quote is from Carlos Augusto Taunay,
Manual do agricultor brasileiro (reprint of the 1839 edition; São Paulo: Companhia das
Letras, 2001), p. 54. Schwartz quotes a Portuguese oberver who declared, "quem quiser
tirar proveito de seus negros, há de mantê-los, fazê-los trabalhar bem e surrá-los melhor;
sem isso não se consegue serviço nem vantagem alguma." Stuart B. Schwartz, *Segredos
internos, engenhos e escravos na sociedade colonial* (São Paulo: Companhia das Letras,
1995), pp. 122–3.

[3] See, for example, Fernando Henrique Cardoso, *Capitalismo e escravidão no Brasil
meridional: O negro na sociedade escravocrata do Rio Grande do Sul* (São Paulo:
Difusão Européia do Livro, 1962); Ciro Flamarion Cardoso, *Escravo ou camponês?
O protocampesinato negro nas Américas* (São Paulo: Brasiliense, 1987); Ciro Flamarion Cardoso et al., *Escravidão e abolição no Brasil: Novas perspectivas* (Rio de

literature for models to help us understand in general what was occurring without losing the specificity of the Brazilian experience or oversimplifying the Brazilian reality. The economist Stefano Fenoaltea has developed an explicit model of a slave economy based on both classical and modern slavery.[4] He affirms that in tasks that required greater physical effort, little skill, and little need for careful work, physical violence and the need for close supervision are the defining characteristics. In these cases, better output could be obtained from slaves by the effective or potential threat of violence. The costs of use of violence and strong supervision are compensated for by greater output. This was characteristic of the forms of labor usage in the great mines and plantations. On the other hand, when the work demands careful attention, dedication, and skill, the use of force is not as efficacious. In these cases, various forms of positive incentives have to be adopted. The Fenoltea model can be used to define the different labor systems used in Brazilian slavery. Routinized gang labor with actual and potential use of violence as the dominant form of labor control clearly prevailed on the large plantations and mines. In all of the other extraordinarily varied activities in Brazil, there was in fact a mix of both positive and negative incentives. It was these positive incentives that gave raise to the manumitted slaves, both voluntary and self-purchased. Everyone from slaves in households through itinerant venders and miners and day laborers had access to income or other positive forms of incentive to encourage their labor. In some activities, it was the most efficacious means of obtaining better results from slave labor. Humanitarian reasons, even in the case of their illegitimate children, although present, were not the dominant reasons for the granting of voluntary manumissions. Moreover, even in tasks where positive incentives were used, violence was present. The master had absolute power over the slave and could inflict serious physical punishment. As Taunay argued, the masters who were planters should exercise their powers like "heads of small kingdoms, in which they should govern despotically, and take upon themselves the attributes of legislator, magistrate, captain, judge, and sometimes even executioner."[5]

Janeiro: Zahar, 1988); Jacob Gorender, *O escravismo colonial* (3rd ed.; São Paulo: Ática, 1980).

[4] Stefano Fenoaltea, "Slavery and Supervision in Comparative Perspective: A Model," *Journal of Economic History*, 44, no. 3. (September 1984), pp. 635–68. Also using this model is Flávio Rabelo Versiani, "Escravidão 'suave' no Brasil: Gilberto Freyre tinha razão?" *Revista de Economia Política*, 27, no. 2 (Abril–Junho 2007).

[5] "...chefe de um pequeno reinado, no qual, por governar despoticamente, e acumular as atribuições de legislador, magistrado, comandante, juiz e algumas vezes de verdugo," Taunay, *Manual do agricultor brasileiro*, pp. 48–9.

The master controlled the freedom of the slave and of the slave's child if he or she was born of a slave mother. Often a slave obtained his or her freedom, but not the freedom of his or her spouse, children, or parents. Violence was also implicit in the system that allowed families to be separated by the sale of its members. Thus, even with positive incentives, it is not possible to talk of slavery without recognizing its inherit violence.

We could give an example that clearly illustrated the two types of labor, even in the same occupation. The extraction of gold and diamonds occurred in Minas Gerais in the first half of the eighteenth century. However tight and vigilant was the supervision of the slaves, it was still necessary to count on their responsibility and initiative in the areas of both gold and diamonds. For this reason, the miners tried to stimulate their slaves in various ways, even in the large mine works. In this respect, we can separate two phases. In this brutal phase, which demanded great physical effort, slaves were used to move soil and rocks on a large scale to open up the veins of gold and diamonds. This task demanded control and supervision but not intense attention on the part of slave drivers. The other aspect, the panning for gold and diamonds, also demanded control, but this more violent method was not sufficient. It needed the interest, care, and attention of the slave workers themselves. The extraordinary watercolor paintings and lithographs of Rugendas and Carlos Julião show the rigor of control in this phase, with each slave having his or her own controller. This unusual one-on-one supervision guaranteed that slaves could not steal the gold or diamonds, but did not prevent them from throwing away valuable minerals. In this final phase of mining, it was normal for slave owners to offer all types of rewards, especially in the extraction of diamonds. Finding a precious stone could be worth even manumission. In the case of miners with few slaves and little capital, a whole range of incentives and arrangements were worked out between the master and his or her slaves. It was usual, for example, for the slave *faiscador* (itinerant miner) to be given total autonomy in his prospecting and to pay a daily fixed wage in gold *oitavas* to his or her owner.[6]

---

[6] Francisco Vidal Luna, "Economia e Sociedade em Minas Gerais (Período Colonial)," *Revista do Instituto de Estudos Brasileiros*, vol. 24 (1982), pp. 43–6. This pay arrangement was also organized for itinerant slave diamond miners in Mato Grosso in the early nineteenth century. Lucia Helena Gaeta Aleixo, "Mato Grosso: Trabalho escravo e trabalho livre (1850–1880)" (Dissertação de mestrado: PUC-SP, 1984), pp. 32–3.

By saying that most forms of slave labor were based on positive incentives and not on direct physical violence, we are not saying that violence was not one of the basic characteristics of modern slave labor that developed in Brazil. Clearly violence was behind the original capture of free persons in Africa and bringing them against their will to America. The violence of the capture, the Middle Passage, and the forced abandonment of families and friends were endogenous to the whole system. Recent studies have shown the many indications of this violence and the individual and collective manifestations in terms of revolt and aggression. But the society that was formed in Brazil was sufficiently complex to generate another type of violence similar to persons born free: violence of a personal nature, the fruit of social relations that were established there. This is seen in violence between slaves themselves and against free persons who were not their masters. Like violence in any human society, these reflected social conflicts or human passions. Sometimes it is difficult to separate these two types of violence in a slave society, but they should be separated. Clearly, the violence directed against the slave to extract labor and the violence expressed by the slave against the system and his or her master is one pattern of violence, and the daily conflicts among equals is another. But it is also crucial to realize that there were positive incentives that made total economic sense, especially in those tasks demanded by the slave owners in which violence would have been counterproductive and economically costly.

This discussion of positive and negative incentives was a fundamental part of the argument of economists Robert Fogel and Stanley Engerman in their analysis of North American slavery.[7] However, their stress was on a supposed uniform level of positive incentives with a minimum of violence across all slave activities. For this, they were criticized by a large number of scholars who showed just how important close supervision and violence were in the productivity of southern U.S. slave labor.[8] What is important about the Fenoltea model is that it recognizes, on the basis of studying numerous slave systems, that different types of slave labor can be quite different in terms of productivity on the basis of either positive and negative incentives. Clearly recognizing these differences goes a long way toward explaining the surprising variations to be found in Brazilian

[7] Robert W. Fogel and Stanley L. Engerman, *Time on the Cross: The Economics of American Negro Slavery* (Boston: Norton, 1974).
[8] Paul A. David et al., *Reckoning with Slavery: A Critical Study in the Quantitative History of American Negro Slavery* (New York: Oxford University Press, 1976).

slavery, and even the very early and very rapid expansion of the free colored class long before the final abolition of slavery in 1888.

Another factor worth considering in analyzing the economic structure of Brazilian slavery is the surprising distribution of slaves among all classes and groups of individuals, from elite white planters to poor free colored women. This is a pattern distinctly different from that which developed in the United States despite the fact that these slave systems look alike in relative importance of the slaves and slave owners within each society and the relatively modest size of slaveholdings compared to the West Indies. But as the economist Gavin Wright has suggested, there was a sharp difference in the United States among agricultural producers in terms of slaveholdings.[9] Slavery was almost exclusively associated with a high level of commercial production, whereas the less commercial farming sector usually did not have slaves. Among small producers, the tendency was toward subsistence production of foodstuffs, with a modest placing of surplus production on the local market. The long-term high risk associated with full-time market production and the high costs of entry into this sector kept these farmers out of the export sector. For Wright, this division based on long-term risk marked the distinction between slaveholders and nonslaveholders. The former were primarily associated with the export market, and the latter were primary into local foodstuff production. He thus stresses the association between high market risk and adoption of slave labor.

Although there is no question that the export sector within Brazil absorbed a large and growing part of the slave labor force over time, there was a surprising distribution of slave ownership among food producers and even some primary subsistence farmers and a high level of slave ownership among artisans. Clearly, there was a long-term risk associated with export agriculture and mining, even when attempts were made to reduce that risk for producers. Thus, the division between mill owners and cane farmers in the early sugar industry of the northeastern region was an attempt to reduce risk. The mill owners took the greatest risks and had the highest capital investment, whereas the cane producers did not have the capital costs associated with the costly milling process. But even for the independent cane producers, there was a high level of risk based on prices in the international market, especially given the long cycle of

[9] Gavin Wright, *The Political Economy of the Cotton South* (New York: Norton, 1978), chapter 3, pp. 43–89.

production of sugar cane. In the second half of the nineteenth century, the great *fazendeiros* of coffee presented a similar risk. From the beginnings of the nineteenth century, when native gold mining was replaced by foreign capital, it too used slave labor and also involved long-term market risk due to both market and geological factors that were present for the entire period of their operations. Investments in prospecting were immense and not always compensated.

But this model of risk and slavery does not hold quite as well for Brazil in relationship to low-risk production. For four centuries, slaves were involved in both export and local market production and in all aspects of agricultural production including foodstuffs and subsistence, along with a host of artisanal services. Although slaves were part of the rural labor force, including the gangs utilized in the plantation, a large part of the slave population was allocated to domestic service subsistence agriculture, manufacturing, and artisanal services for the local market. There were also small family farmers who produced some surplus for the external market who sometimes owned slaves. Initially, this was the case in coffee and early alluvial gold mining in Minas Gerais. Moreover, despite the major development of the slave plantation model in Brazil, as in sugar for the northeast and then for Rio de Janeiro and São Paulo and in coffee in the nineteenth century in Rio de Janeiro, São Paulo, and Minas Gerais, its importance in terms of slaves assigned to its control was limited, accounting for no more than 20 percent of the resident slave population.[10] Even at the height of the mining boom, the slaves involved in the large-scale *lavras* were only a minor part of the slave population in the mining regions. The Brazilian case shows a diversity of use of slaves well beyond the plantation. Moreover, we find nonslave-owning producers in all types of activities except in sugar milling. This diversity of slaves and nonslave producers is the principal characteristic of slavery in Brazil.

---

[10] Among the 75,000 slaves listed in the population census of São Paulo in 1829, at a time when sugar was becoming a predominant activity in the Oeste Paulista and coffee in the Val do Paraíba, 81 percent of the slaves belonged to masters who were agriculturalists, although only half resided in households that produced coffee or sugar. Thus, only 40 percent of these slaves in 1829 were involved in export agriculture. Most probably, the greater part of the slave labor force was not directly involved in export production, some being outside the market (infants and the aged) and others involved in everything from domestic service to subsistence agriculture. Luna and Klein, *Slavery and the Economy of São Paulo, 1750–1850* (2003), chapter 1.

Given the lack of a positive defense of slavery in colonial and nineteenth-century Brazil,[11] there never emerged a school of thought that defended the institution on noneconomic grounds. The assumption in most of the historical literature has been on the economic rationality of slaveholdings. The Marxist historiographical tradition (as exemplified by the work of Cardoso, Ianni, Caio Prado, and most recently Jacob Gorender) has taken the classical liberal position on the inefficiency of slave labor and its supposed incompatibility with modern capitalism but has not questioned its economic basis.[12] Because of this tradition, there have been relatively few detailed studies of the economics of the institution. The best such studies, which grew out of the classic work of Conrad and Meyer,[13] have been those of Pedro Carvalho de Mello,[14] Flávio Versiani,[15] Antonio Barros de Castro,[16] Iraci del Nero da Costa,[17] and Roberto Monasterio.[18] All have found that the patterns of capital investment in slave labor for coffee or sugar or even the jerked beef industry

[11] See Barbara Weinstein, "Slavery, Citizenship, and National Identity in Brazil and the United States South," in Don Doyle and Marco Antonio Pamplona, eds., *Nationalism in the New World* (Athens: University of Georgia Press, 2006), pp. 248–71.

[12] See, for example, Cardoso, *Capitalismo e escravidão no Brasil meridional*; Octavio Ianni, *As metamorphoses do escravo: Apogeu e crise da escravatura no Brasil meridional*, no. 7 (São Paulo: Difusão Européia do Livro, 1962); and Caio Prado, Jr., *Formação do Brasil contemporâneo* (3rd ed.; São Paulo: Editora Brasiliense, 1948). A more sophisticated re-restatement of aspects of this view is found in Gorender, *O escravismo colonial*, and *A escravidão reabilitada* (São Paulo: Ática, 1990).

[13] Alfred H. Conrad and John R. Meyer, "The Economics of Slavery in the Ante Bellum South," *The Journal of Political Economy*, 66, no. 2 (April 1958), pp. 95–130.

[14] Pedro Carvalho de Mello, "Aspectos Econômicos da Organização do Trabalho da Economia Cafeeira do Rio de Janeiro, 1858–88," *Revista Brasileira de Economia*, 32, no. 1 (Jan./Mar. 1978), pp. 19–68; also see Pedro Carvalho de Mello and Robert W. Slenes, "Análise Econômica da Escravidão no Brasil," in P. Neuhaus, ed., *Economia Brasileira: Uma Visão Histórica* (Rio de Janeiro: Campus, 1980); and "Estimativa da longevidade de escravos no Brasil na segunda metade do século XIX," *Estudos Econômicos*, 13, no. 1 (Jan.–Abr. 1983), pp. 151–79; and his Chicago doctoral thesis.

[15] Flávio Versiani, "Brazilian Slavery: Toward an Economic Analysis," *Revista Brasileira de Economia*, 48, no. 4 (Dezembro 1994), pp. 463–78.

[16] Antonio Barros de Castro, "Escravos e senhores nos engenhos do Brasil. Um estudo sobre os trabalhos do açúcar e a política econômica dos senhores" (Tese de doutorado; São Paulo: UNICAMP, 1976).

[17] Iraci del Nero da Costa, "Repensando o modelo interpretativo de Caio Prado Jr." São Paulo, NEHD-FEA/USP, 1995, 45 p., (Cadernos NEHD, n. 3).

[18] Leonardo M. Monasterio, "FHC errou? A economia da escravidão no Brasil meridional," *História e Economia Revista Interdisciplinar*, 1, no. 1 (2° semestre 2005), pp. 13–28.

in Rio Grande do Sul were economically rational and that the relative efficiency of slave labor was competitive with free labor in the types of agricultural activity in which slaves were employed. Moreover, recent research has shown an increasing interest in economic rationality in the use of slave labor, both in Brazil and in the other nineteenth-century American slave societies, among the administrators of slave labor. Using models from free labor control and administration, slave supervisors and overseers tried to apply these techniques to their slave workers. In Brazil, these ideas first evolved in the first half of the nineteenth century,[19] but achieved greater importance in the second half of the century with the great expansion of coffee plantations and especially given the scarce and increasing cost of labor. These ideas represented a modern view of labor administration and reflected a new rationality that was appearing in the capitalist world.[20]

Although the debates on the modes of production model still find an echo in some historical schools in Brazil, there is another aspect to this debate aside from the classic Marxian formulation. This is the issue of whether the usage of slave labor inhibited or limited the technological development in the Brazilian economy. This question is difficult to answer given the lack of studies on the subject in terms of the Brazilian experience. It is undeniable that sugar production in the sixteenth and seventeenth centuries represented the latest in advanced technology of the period. The relative decline of the Brazilian sugar industry was due to the rise of newer centers with better technology, but these new centers also used slave labor. This was especially the case in Jamaica and Cuba, which saw a revolution in sugar technology in the nineteenth century even while employing slave labor. It is true that more specialized jobs in sugar technology were usually reserved for free labor, but there was nothing to impede the planter class from using such labor on their estates, and many did so. Moreover, some of these same tasks and skills were to be found among slave workers. The economic backwardness of the Brazilian mining industry, much discussed in the literature, was not due to slave labor, but to the lack of experience among the free Portuguese and Brazilian miners. Moreover, when the

---

[19] In this category, see the manual by Taunay, *Manual do agricultor brasileiro*.
[20] Marquese is one of the authors who has written interesting studies in this new line of research in Brazil. See Rafael de Bivar Marquese, *Feitores do corpo, missionários da mente* (São Paulo: Cia. das Letras, 2004), and his study *Administração & Escravidão. Idéias sobre a gestão da agricultura escravista brasileira* (São Paulo: Hucitec, 1999).

latest technology was introduced by English miners in the nineteenth
century in Minas, these foreign companies employed slave labor just like
all other enterprises in Brazil.[21] In the textile mills, mines, and plantations
of Brazil, there were no constraints on the use of free and slave labor at
the same time, although the more rudimentary and unskilled parts of
this work were usually confined to slaves. Free and slave workers were
used together and sometime slave workers were given as highly skilled a
task as were free workers.[22] The use of positive incentives in some of the
more skilled tasks in the service area or in production often left the slave
workers (in terms of remuneration) in a similar position as free salaried
workers. Many slaves were able to obtain their freedom in return for labor
or by purchasing their freedom using the salaries they obtained in these
types of jobs. Assembly-style factory labor with its careful division of tasks
was probably difficult to maintain with slave labor, although slaves could
be found in all the early textile and other factories that were established in
the nineteenth century. It is not difficult to imagine that slaves could
have been used in this industrial labor force given the early period of
industrialization in the nineteenth century when the labor force consisted
of child and women laborers, poor working conditions, long hours, and
the use of physical violence. It would thus appear that the use of slave
labor was not an impediment to technological development, which was
probably more influenced by capital and market conditions than by the
availability of free-wage workers.

There has recently been considerable work done on the market for
slaves and most particularly on the changing price structure of this market. All such price studies have also shown that the price structure of
slaves represents a positive view of investors in the future of the institution, with the price of adult woman in the ages of fertility including a
premium for the potential to create slave children – the so-called "positive
price for unborn children."[23] They have also shown the slow and steady
evolution of a common national market for slaves in a convergence of

---

[21] See, for example, Douglas Cole Libby, *Trabalho escravo e capital estrangeiro no Brasil:*
     O caso de Morro Velho (Belo Horizonte: Itatiaia, 1984).
[22] For a good discussion of the compatibility of free and slave labor in industry, see Sérgio
     de Oliveira Birchal, "O mercado de trabalho mineiro no século XIX" (Belo Horizonte:
     Ibmec, Working Paper no. 12, 2007); Douglas Cole Libby, "Proto-Industrialisation in a
     Slave Society: The Case of Minas Gerais," *Journal of Latin American Studies*, 23, no. 1
     (February 1991), pp. 1–35; and Mário Danieli Neto, "Escravidão e Indústria: Um estudo
     sobre a Fábrica de Ferro São João de Ipanema – Sorocaba (SP) – 1765–1895"(Tese de
     doutorado: Economia/UNICAMP, 2006).
[23] Fogel and Engerman, *Time on the Cross*, pp. 73–5.

slave prices over time. The largest such studies have been the work of Bergad on Minas Gerais,[24] Carvalho de Mello on Rio de Janeiro,[25] Katia Mattoso on Bahia,[26] and Versiani and Vergolino on Pernambuco.[27] There have also been shorter term or more local price series generated for occupations, ages, and sex by a host of other scholars.[28] All such studies have found the slave market to be rational and have shown that by the nineteenth century, there was a coherent national market for slaves and that slave prices moved in similar fashion in every region in Brazil, from the coastal and interior areas of Pernambuco to the coffee regions of São Paulo and the interior towns of Minas Gerais.

The maintenance of a modern slave system for four centuries required a complex organization in terms of a market for slaves, which in essence was Brazil's basic labor market. Slave prices were not fixed, but reflected variations in market conditions and varied over time and by region. Because buying a slave represented a future purchase of labor, the slave owner has to take into consideration the market conditions of his products. But what were the factors that determined the supply and demand of slaves and, consequently, of their labor? First, we should point out the conditions of the offering of slaves in the principal slave markets and the organization of the slave trade. As noted in the previous chapters, the conditions of supply

[24] Laird W. Bergad, *Slavery and the Demographic and Economic History of Minas Gerais, Brazil, 1720–1888* (Cambridge: Cambridge University Press, 1999).

[25] Pedro Carvalho de Mello, *A economia da escravidão nas fazendas de café: 1850–1888* (Rio de Janeiro: PNPE/ANPEC, 1984).

[26] Katia M. de Queirós Mattoso, Herbert S. Klein, and Stanley L. Engerman, "Trends and Patterns in the Prices of Manumitted Slaves: Bahia, 1819–1888," *Slavery & Abolition*, 7, no. 1 (May 1986), pp. 59–67; reprinted in João José Reis, ed., *Escravidão e invenção da liberdade: Estudos sobre o negro no Brasil* (São Paulo: Editora Brasiliense, 1988), pp. 60–72.

[27] Flávio Rabelo Versiani and José Raimundo Oliveira Vergolino, "Preços de Escravos em Pernambuco no Século XIX" (Texto para Discussão no. 252; Universidade de Brasília, Departamento de Economia, Brasília, Outubro de 2002).

[28] See Renato Leite Marcondes and José Flávio Motta, "Duas fontes documentais para o estudo dos preços dos escravos no Vale do Paraíba paulista," *Revista Brasileira de História*, 21, no. 42 (2001), p. 495–512; Maria Luíza Marcílio et al., "Considerações sobre o preço do escravo no período imperial: Uma análise quantitativa (baseada nos registro de escritura de compra e venda de escravos na Bahia)," *Anais de História*, no. 5 (1973), pp. 179–94; Luiz Paulo Ferreira Nogueról, "Sabará e Porto Alegre na formação do mercado nacional no século XIX" (Tese de doutorado, Campinas: UNICAMP, Economia, 2003), chapter 4; Carlos A. M. Lima, "Escravos Artesãos: Preço e família (Rio de Janeiro, 1789–1839)," *Estudos Econômicos*, 30, no. 3 (Julho–Setembro 2000), pp. 447–84; Afonso de Alencastro Graça Filho, "As flutuações dos preços e as fazendas escravistas de São João del Rei no século XIX," *IX Seminário sobre a Economia Mineira*, pp. 147–78.

were influenced by the traffic itself. Internal conflicts in the African areas furnishing slaves changed over time, along with the permanent disputes between the principal nations involved in the control of slave supplies and in their movement to America. Despite the progressive expansion of an internal market of slaves born in Brazil, the Atlantic slave trade was the determining element in the fixing of prices until 1850, particularly in the regions where the plantation export crops predominated. As we have noted, slaves were used in the most varied activities, but probably the most important economic activities and their profitability determined the demand conditions, particularly for slaves most apt for the labor needed by such activities: adults in good physical condition who also had some type of desirable specialization. Besides, as the slave market represented the future purchase and sale of labor, the conditions of credit and the rates of interest in the local market would have a great importance in determining the price structure for slaves. Given the conditions of supply and demand in the predominant activities, it was to be expected that a structure of prices was created that rewarded physical vigor, sex, age, and skills that involve slaves of all ages, including children and the elderly. Prices reflected these supply and demand conditions and the skills of the slaves, such as the varied jobs that needed to be done, slave assignments, and the different levels of health.

It is also clear that even in Brazil there was a possibility of internal reproduction of the slave labor force. Studies have shown that in some periods and regions, there was a positive natural growth of the slave labor force. But even when this did not occur, there was a process of reproduction that amplified the participation of slaves born in Brazil and thus increased their importance in the supply of the slave labor market. The supply of slaves born in Brazil altered the general supply conditions because it created a source of slaves relatively independent of the Atlantic slave trade. It also created a labor supply completely different from the Atlantic slave trade. Instead of adults, preferably male, who were offered by the Atlantic slave trade, the internal supply offered a far more ample range of opportunities, with equality of sexes and a range of ages. This expanded the opportunities of the slave market, as much for the buyers as for the sellers of slaves. For a specialized producer needing slaves, like a miner who was uninterested in sustaining his labor force and had a slaveholding strongly concentrated in adult males, investing in the reproduction of slaves was less interesting a proposition than for a farmer dedicated to multiple crops, who may have wanted a great number of both male and female slaves equally balanced. The care of slave children, as many studies have shown, was in fact a specialized task in the larger slave units. We find that in the large slaveholdings in agriculture, there are a greater proportion of married slaves and children. Thus, as exemplified in these two extreme cases, each slave owner or potential slave owners was offered varied alternatives in terms of the age and sex composition of their slaves, depending on the work to be developed by these slaves. A slave owner could readily sell an adult ready for work for a price sufficient to acquire two young slaves, who then gradually reached maturity in physical terms, experience, and possibly of price. Others could be attended by a young child or by a woman of an advanced age, but that depended on the needs and possibilities of the buyer. These various demands and the possibility of work for the slaves permitted the elaboration of a price structure that reflected the particular demand conditions and the varied labor capabilities of the slaves.

The market for slaves was also influenced by different types of taxes imposed on slaves, from the original taxes charged by various governments in Africa or America during the transport phase to those charged in the local market. During some years, the government even charged a special head tax on slaves to their owners, as for example in the case of Minas Gerais during the early mining period. It was a way for the Crown to appropriate part of the rents being generated in the region. In some periods, the royalty taxes charged by the Crown on gold production, called the *Quinto*[29] for its value, was levied indirectly on the slaves owned, which represented the potential production capacity of each miner. Taxation was also used to limit the interprovincial slave trade after the abolition of the Atlantic slave trade. This was due to the attraction of slaves to those activities with the greatest profit, which in that period was coffee production. The only way to maintain their slave force in regions without coffee and with less profitable enterprises was through a tax on the final price of slaves in the purchasing region. This clearly prejudiced the owners of the slaves in the exporting regions, but maintained the viability of economic activity in the original slave-exporting regions. The maintenance of slave activities in the other regions was fundamental for the preservation of slavery in the third quarter of the nineteenth century when the abolitionist movement intensified. No region was denuded of slaves and all would face losses should slavery be abolished.

Numerous studies of Brazilian income and wealth in the preemancipation period have shown that slaves represented a significant part of

---

[29] The Crown taxed a fifth of gold produced, which was called the *Quinto*.

individual wealth. Although there is variation depending on time and place, the results of these wealth studies suggest that slaves normally made up about 30 percent of the individual patrimony of wealthy persons in Brazil. Even more important was the liquidity of this share of an individual's wealth, superior in fact to the value of lands and equipment.[30] Besides, part of the transactions with slaves was realized via credit, which was made possible because of the great liquidity that slaves represented, especially compared to other nonfinancial assets, and for the relative stability of their price, shown in numerous studies that have analyzed slave prices. It is also important to understand the relation between land and slave ownership. Land was obtained in large part through the land grants known as *sesmarias* until well into the nineteenth century. These were great areas of land conceded by the Crown with the condition of effective exploitation of these grants. When one compares the average size of these land grants with the structure of slave ownership, in which small- and median-size slaveholdings predominated (few greater than 40 slaves and rarely in the hundreds), one notes an incompatibility between the size of the landed property and its potential to be economically exploited, given the size of the slave labor force employed. Even with the significant increase of the poor free population that was continually used in the Brazilian economy, its utilization was not very important in the labor force contracted for the large estates. How then could these large estates, which were minimally exploited, be maintained over generations? It would appear that between squatters and servants, most of the great property owners could defend their large estates from exploitation by allowing their lands to be settled by subsistence farmers until such time as they could begin serious commercial activity, at which time all these poor workers were expelled from the large estates and replaced by slaves.[31]

It is fundamental to understand that the extraordinary extension of slave labor in Brazil was reflected in the other forms of labor. Although during the four centuries of slavery in Brazil there occurred a great expansion of the free population, the majority of whom were free persons of color, a free, salaried labor market was never organized that would have permitted the replacement of slaves for free labor in the most important economic activities, those that were primarily directed toward the

---

[30] See Table 4.5 and Chapter 4, note 44.
[31] For an analysis of this moving frontier and its impact on class structure and slave use, see Alida C. Metcalf, *Family and Frontier in Colonial Brazil: Santana de Parnaíba, 1580–1822* (Berkeley: University of California Press, 1992).

international market, like sugar and later coffee. Free labor existed, but usually in dispersed activity, not in the more complex forms of agricultural production, such as the labor gangs on the plantations or in mine production. The free worker was situated in the two pools of labor organization – either as skilled and specialized workers or those dedicated to tasks supplementary to the great exporting centers (in opening roads, clearing virgin forests, repairing fences, and so on). In addition, the persistence of slavery inhibited the use of immigrant labor, despite the vast supply of European workers in the nineteenth century. As long as slavery existed, it was not possible to effectively introduce immigrant workers into Brazil. Once slavery was eliminated, massive foreign immigration occurred in the leading coffee sectors of the Southeast, above all in São Paulo. Such was the abundant international supply of such labor that despite the abrupt emancipation of the slaves, there was no serious loss of manpower in the core Brazilian coffee fields. Immediately, black slaves were replaced by an intense influx of immigrations who effectively supplied the local labor market with workers, while elsewhere in the rural areas a complex arrangement of free labor based on the ex-slave labor force evolved that maintained local and export production in traditional crops.

How can one explain the existence of a large contingent of free persons, in large part *mestiços* and nonslave owners, who dedicated themselves to subsistence or lived as dependents (*a favor*) or servants (*agregados*) on the lands of others and could not be organized into a free labor market capable of substituting or even complementing slave labor? Even after the closing of the Atlantic slave trade and the increasing pressures of the international community made the ending of slavery a distinct and clear possibility, why was this substitution of slave labor impossible to achieve? From the beginning, it was patently difficult to attract free-wage workers with the characteristics of Brazil: a hostile tropical country, but more particularly one with abundant lands and a powerful oligarchy unwilling to allow open competition with free smallhold farmers. There was no system of control capable of preventing wage workers from gradually turning themselves into such small free farmers (either with lands officially purchased or as squatters) without some type of restriction on their freedom of labor. In the classic phrase of Edward Gibbon Wakefield:

What was the sole cause of the revival of slavery by Christians, but the discovery of waste [empty] countries, and the disproportion which has ever since existed to those countries between the demand and supply of labour? And what is it that increases the number of slaves to Christian masters, but the increase of Christian capitalists wanting labourers, by the spreading of Christian people over regions heretofore waste?[32]

As the modern economist Evsey Domar noted, of the three elements – "free land, free peasants, and nonworking landowners – any two elements but *never all three can exist simultaneously*. The combination to be found in reality will depend on the behavior of political factors – government measures...."[33] Clearly, in the Brazilian context with abundant free lands and a landowning class promoted by the Crown, the turn toward forced labor was inevitable. One has only to recall that late into the nineteenth century, the maps of the province of São Paulo showed that half the territory of the province was still classified as "lands occupied by Indian savages."[34]

What determined if a land was free or occupied was in truth its viability for economic exploitation, not a simple land title. This viability was in large part determined by the transport system. As long as the system of long-distance transport was exclusively based on mules, it was impossible to grow products that could be exported to the distant coast. This factor, for example, limited the potential expansion of sugar. It did not limit the extraction of gold and diamonds because of their high relative prices. However, it did limit the expansion of bulk products such as coffee, which only expanded into the interior of São Paulo via the railroad. Thus, there was always free land in abundance, either on the frontier or in previously exploited and abandoned areas – a common feature of Brazilian agriculture. The effective economic occupation of Brazil did not go beyond a few hundred kilometers from the coast until the second half of the nineteenth century. This factor explains the abundance of free nonslaveholding workers in subsistence farming and the lack of a large free labor wage market in Brazil. This was only created with the abolition of slavery and the massive immigration of free European workers at the end of the nineteenth century. It is also worth noting that the very existence of slavery, as an alternative labor force itself, inhibited the development of a free labor market. This created a prejudice against manual labor. The integration of free Brazilian workers into the labor

---

[32] Edward Gibbon Wakefield, "A Letter from Sydney" [1829], in Lloyd Pritchard, ed., *The Collected Works of Edward Gibbon Wakefield* (Glasgow: Colllins, 1968), pp. 112–13.

[33] Evsey D. Domar, "The Causes of Slavery or Serfdom: A Hypothesis," *Journal of Economic History*, 30, no. 1 (March 1970), p. 21.

[34] See for example the 1868 map of São Paulo produced by Candido Mendes in his *Atlas do Imperio do Brasil* and available at http://www.novomilenio.inf.br/santos/mapa23g.htm.

market was a slow process that extended into the second half of the twentieth century. There are well-known cases of attempts to integrate slaves and immigrants in coffee production. But this led to strikes and conflicts within the *fazendas* and in turn resulted in several European countries prohibiting labor recruitment of workers for Brazilian *fazendas*.

Based on the very extensive studies that deal with slavery in the various regions and during different time periods, what can be said about the general organization of that labor system in Brazil? We can say that it reproduced the essential characteristics found in other regions, but there are also unique features to the Brazilian development of African slavery in America that should be emphasized. These features resulted from the special historical process of the evolution of this implanted labor system in the evolving structure of Brazilian society and economy. In turn, this labor system lasted for such a long a time that it fundamentally influenced the structure of the society and economy of Brazil until the second half of the nineteenth century.

African slave labor was initially introduced in the northeastern regions, essentially in the production of sugar, which was gradually extended throughout the sixteenth and seventeenth centuries. Probably in this period, such labor was limited to the areas influenced by sugar production, with little utilization in other areas of the colony. Other regions could marginally utilize the slaves of African origin, but essentially used native Brazilians who were available everywhere. Through forms of cooptation or compulsion, they became the basic labor force in many regions. The Paulistas, for example, true pioneers of the Brazilian backlands, were primarily based on Indian labor in all of their many and varied activities, but generally integrated them as forced laborers. By the third century of colonization, only a limited part of the present Brazilian territory was economically exploited. Settlements were spread along the coast, with little integration between them, because there was little economic reason to do so. The only part of the colony that was well integrated were the sugar-exporting regions, which in turn were based primarily on African slave labor after 1600. Although Indians had been utilized in sugar in the colony's early stages of development, they were soon replaced by a steady supply of Africans brought across the Atlantic. Indian laborers were then used outside the sugar zones to support the export activities of the sugar plantations, zones that as yet were not heavily based on the more expensive African laborers.

The discovery of gold and diamonds in Minas Gerais, Goiás, and Mato Grosso at the beginning of the eighteenth century profoundly altered the structure of territorial settlement, with colonists and their slaves and dependent workers moving westward into the interior and southward along the coast and consequently expanding Portuguese settlement. With the new mining regions at the center, the colony became far more economically integrated, with the development of a mule-producing industry in the far south and with foodstuffs and meat animals being raised in the Paulista highlands and Rio de Janeiro to supply the growing population of the interior. Roads were opened to the three mining provinces, and the mule trains that became the common form of transport on these roads led to supporting settlements along the routes to furnish the interior markets and to provide food and support for the muleteers and their mule trains. In the eighteenth century, African slave labor was being introduced in all the regions, no matter what their economic activity. São Paulo, whose labor force was once almost totally based on Indian labor, rapidly adopted African slave labor. In other areas, this probably occurred at the same time, although perhaps in a less intense way. All the recent studies show that no matter what the region of Brazil or what its local economy produced – whether exporting sugar, coffee, precious metals, jerked beef, or foodstuff production for the local market; fishing; local craft production; or professional service activities – African slaves were found to be an important presence in all areas. In the case of export crops, they represented the labor force base. In activities directed toward the internal market, in many cases they worked alongside family laborers or as assistants and journeymen for artisans and professions. They were also found in all aspects of domestic labor.

In each region, the predominant local economy determined the demand for slaves and the appropriate local price structure, whether directed toward the external or internal markets. This constant demand generated a supply of Africans slaves, not only from Africa, but from other regions of the colony as well. Although there should have been a relatively homogeneous price structure throughout Brazil determined by African supply conditions and by the slave trade, the peculiarities of the local market, particularly those some distance from the coast, initially created local variations in these prices.

This homogeneity in the national market was also affected by the geographic mobility of the masters and their slaves. As in all such expanding frontier American slave societies, slave owners were able to constantly move themselves and their slaves to newly opened economic regions. Brazil was well-known for a moving economic and settlement frontier. Exhausting the soil or looking for new economic opportunities, farmers, ranchers, and planters moved to virgin areas, temporarily occupied them, and often moved on again to another virgin area, and this frontier remained an open one well beyond the end of slavery. Labor followed these frontiersmen, and the migrating masters brought their slaves with them. There was no static labor market that inhibited the movement of slaves to these new regions or even to new types of work. Slaves followed their masters and new slaves could be bought in local or even distant markets.

Local economic conditions also had an impact on the demography of the slave population, at least in the initial periods. Traditionally, it has been thought that the activities of greatest economic intensity, usually related to exportations and the plantation model, led to an extreme exploitation of labor, leading to a low life expectancy and an inability of the slaves to reproduce themselves through natural growth. Recent studies have shown that the determining factor in the capacity of slaves to naturally reproduce is the demographic structure of the slave population itself, primarily in terms of their age and sex distribution. In the major export crop regions, there was a high demand for adult male slaves, which led to a distorted age and sex structure. A population heavily weighted toward adult males was not ideal for self-reproduction. The latest research has shown that in those regions where these export activities were less intense or declining, or in areas little influenced by them, as in Minas Gerais in the nineteenth century or São Paulo in the period prior to the rise of sugar and coffee production or in Paraná before the impact of coffee when small-scale farming and ranching predominated, natural reproduction became possible because of the better balance of age and sex of the resident slaves, in turn determined by different demand and supply conditions.

There was a generalized use of slaves in all regions and all activities from the beginning of the eighteenth century until the middle of the nineteenth century. Only after 1850, with the end of the slave trade, were slaves once again primarily concentrated in the zones of greatest economic development. During this century and a half – the period of the most intense activity of the Atlantic slave trade – slaves were well distributed throughout the colony and empire and were utilized by their masters in the most varied economic activities. It is undeniable that the masters, who utilized their slaves in these multiple activities, had a clear notion of the economic viability of their businesses and of the potential alternatives to such slave labor. To acquire a slave represented a purchase of anticipated labor, requiring the purchaser to determine the maximum price he or she could pay based on the future value of work produced, taking into account factors such as the cost of capital, the expenses for the maintenance of the slaves, expectations on the life of the slave and his or her long-term productive capacity, as well as the conditions of the market for the goods produced with slave labor. The conditions of the local market for slaves were amply known and, in function of the potential profit of each business, became viable through the acquisition of slaves most adapted to the type of activity being developed. The market supplied men and women of all ages, physical conditions, and learned or native aptitudes. Given the liquidity of this market, the farmer, artisan, or person offering services had a gamut of alternatives to exchange, sell, rent, or buy new slaves. There are even cases of sales or inheritances that involved only a share of ownership of an individual slave. In activities of low profit, they probably utilized slaves of lesser price, such as children, older persons, or adults with limited work capacity. Slaves were also extensively used in domestic labor in practically all of the activities exercised in this area. The majority of such domestic slaves were women, but women were also used in most other activities, including agriculture.

Rather unique to Brazilian slavery was the large number of slaves who hired themselves out – the so-called *escravos de ganho*. Although masters who rented their slaves to others for all types of labor existed in Brazil as in most American slave societies, the *escravos de ganho* were relatively unique to Brazil and some of the other Latin American slave societies. Slaves rented by masters were simply given to an institution, an entrepreneur, an artisan, a farmer, or other private person and received from the renter a fixed amount, usually paid monthly, with the renter typically paying for the maintenance and well-being of the slave. In this arrangement, the slave had no autonomy whatsoever, and this type of rental arrangement was as common in Brazil as in all other slave societies.[35] In contrast to this system, the self-renting slaves, or *escravos de ganho*, were given total autonomy to carry out business arrangements

[35] For example, a survey of advertisements related to slaves in the Rio de Janeiro newspaper *Jornal do Comercio* in the month of January 1848 showed that rented slaves were offered almost every day in the newspapers, and these slaves were everything from skilled craftsmen to cooks, ironers, washerwomen, and even wet nurses who were rented out directly by their masters. Typical of such ads was that which appeared on January 18, 1846, p. 4, which offered "to rent a preta slave who knows how to wash, starch, and iron and cook for 12$000 réis per month – advanced payment ("Aluga-se uma preta que sabe lavar, engomar e cocihnar por 12$ adelantados." On January 6, 1847, p. 4, in the same newspaper, a slave wet nurse who had given birth just two months before to her first child was offered for 20$000 per month ("aluga-se uma preta ama de leite do primero parto, parida ha dois mezes por 20$ mensaid pagos adelantados").

as long as they themselves, not some third party, paid their rental fee to their master. The essential difference, then, is that such self-rental slaves made legal contracts, worked on their own, and paid their masters a fixed fee as a daily or weekly "rental" and often paid for their own maintenance if they lived outside the home of their master. Finally, many of them, especially those who worked in the streets, were licensed by the city councils. They were thus recognized to have their own *peculium* independent of their masters once their fixed rentals and whatever maintenance costs they had to undertake were paid. Such *escravos de ganho* could live at the home of the master – and thus would have maintenance paid for them by the master, or they could live outside their master's home and then could have either arrangement – either paying their own maintenance or having the master pay it for them. If they were living in a workshop (*taller*) of a master craftsmen, either a journeymen (*oficial*) or master (*mestrer*), then that artisan who was training them paid maintenance, and if they worked in a factory, the same usually would have occurred with the factory owner. The maintenance of a slave has been variously estimated. One master of urban slaves in Salvador de Bahia in 1839 estimated that maintenance costs for ten slaves were $640 réis per week per slave, a rate of 91 réis per slave per day. Another estimated that his household domestic slave cost him more than double that rate, or 200 réis per day.[36] Assuming the higher number, it would seem that a slave who paid for his or her own maintenance would have to make at least 600 réis per day to break even, if his rental payment might be as high as 400 réis per day and his maintenance could go as high as 200 réis per diem. Some commentators suggest that after the rental fee and the maintenance costs were paid (if the slave paid them), the self-rental slave had relatively little left over in savings. But because this group often purchased their freedom, it can be assumed that some savings, however small, were an essential part of the system; otherwise there would have been no incentives for the slave to work under this arrangement. At the same time, these were the classic slave occupations for which the masters had to offer positive incentives in order to obtain good economic results.

In the court city of Rio de Janeiro between 1851 and 1879, some 2,868 slaves (only 45 of whom were women) were granted license to work in the streets as *escravos do ganho na rua*, which, though the most common

---

[36] Maria José de Souza Andrade, *A mão de obra escrava em Salvador 1811–1860* (São Paulo: Corrupio, 1988), pp. 134–5.

activity, was not the only one for such slaves. Although the majority (or 95 percent) were simply described as street workers, the largest single-defined category for men was fishmongers, and for women, products of the sea, with bread and cake sellers an important second group.[37] In terms of origin, 2,195 (or 77 percent) of these *escravos de ganho na rua* were Africans.[38] These licenses seem to have been the norm in other centers. In Salvador de Bahia, such a registration law was passed by the municipal council in 1835, and the one for Rio was issued in 1838.[39]

These slaves usually paid their master a previously determined sum on a daily or weekly basis and, less frequently, on a monthly account. The majority of such street slaves were either itinerant peddlers of products or porters who carried cargo either alone or in groups, on carts, on hand-pulled wagons, on their shoulders, or even on their heads in baskets.[40] Most elite persons moved through the city on litters typically carried by slave porters who were *escravos de ganho*. These numerous slave vendors and porters were a common sight in all the cities of Brazil and appear in innumerable paintings by Europeans depicting typical daily scenes in colonial and imperial Brazilian cities. But they were also such self-rental slaves who did not ply their trade on the streets, which included fishermen, sailors, skilled or semi-skilled artisans, and even greengrocers working in stores. They were barbers and barber surgeons and stevedores formally registered with the Customs (*Alfândega*) and exclusively used to unload ships. One of the more common practices was for owners to send their slaves to learn industrial skills and then, after a period of apprenticeship, to allow them to practice their new trades in shops of free persons or even to become assembly-line workers in industries. In this case, the industrialists or artisans paid the slaves a wage less maintenance costs, a part of which was then given to their owners. Such self-rental slaves

---

[37] Luiz Carlos Soares, *O 'Povo de Cam'na capital do Brasil: A escravidão urbana no Rio de Janeiro do século XIX*, (Rio de Janeiro: Faperj, Letras, 2007), tabela XLVIII, p. 421.

[38] The single-largest group, numbering more than a thousand, came from West Central Africa; half that number came from West Africa; and 294 from East Africa. There were 347 whose African nation was not listed. Soares, *O 'Povo de Cam'na capital do Brasil*, p. 128.

[39] Such a license was also required of free workers who sold their services or goods on the street. For these two laws, see Paulo Cruz Terra, "Tudo que transporta e carrega é negro? Carregadores, cocheiros e carroceiros no Rio de Janeiro (1824–1870)" (Diss. de mestrado: UFF, Niteroi, 2007), pp. 34–5.

[40] One of the few porter occupations exclusively identified with slaves was *gasnho com cesto* – that is, carrying baskets filled with all types of goods on their heads. Terra, "Tudo que transporta," p. 40.

even practiced begging and prostitution, again paying their owners a fixed daily or weekly income.[41]

There exist a few postmortem inventories that indicate how financially important these rental incomes from their slaves were. One from Salvador in 1847 noted that the average *escravos de ganho* (who were litter bearers – *carregador de cadeira*) were paying this master 400 milréis per day and had been doing so for 934 days, to date accumulating 373$600 réis gross income, which was a significant 83 to 62 percent of the price of a male slave in good health in the prime age group. These same slaves were evaluated at 450$000 to 600$000 depending on age, health, and skills. Thus, it took 1,500 days for the slave to pay back his original 600$000 purchase price. This same owner had four such adult litter bearers, plus one who was a journeyman shoemaker who also paid the standard 400 milréis per day. He had two other male litter bearers, still young (*moços*), who only paid 320 milréis per day, and Raquel, the only female self-rental slave, who was a washerwoman who starched clothes and paid him 240 milréis per day. All of these eight *escravos de ganho* lived outside the home of the master and paid their own maintenance. He also had one regular household domestic, Francisca Nagô, whose maintenance cost him 200 réis per day – his only slave maintenance costs. Because he showed no other major property, these *ganho* slaves (plus the young domestic slave) represented almost a third of the total value of his estate.[42]

---

[41] One of the best detailed studies of these *ganho* slaves, also known as *ganhadores*, is found in Soares, *O 'Povo de Cam'na capital do Brasil*, chapter 5. Professional prostitutes were mostly free-colored Creoles or Portuguese women in the first half of the nineteenth century in Rio and they were eventually replaced by women from central and eastern Europe. Slave women practiced more part-time and hidden forms of prostitution, although masters did put their women to street solicitations, even after curfew hours, and arranged with them to work as *escravos de ganho* to encourage their activity. Luiz Carlos Soares, *Rameiras, Ilhoas, Polacas... A prostituição no Rio de Janeiro do século XIX* (São Paulo: Editora Ática, 1992), especially chapter V. A set of cases on slave prostitution in the 1870s suggests that poor owners, often women, put up their slaves for prostitution, but usually in secondary brothels, as street solicitation was too dangerous for slaves. In fact, it would seem that slaves doing street solicitation were *escravos de ganho*. Sandra Lauderdale Graham, "Slavery's Impasse: Slave Prostitutes, Small-Time Mistresses, and the Brazilian Law of 1871," *Comparative Studies in Society and History*, 33, no. 4 (October 1991), pp. 670, 673.

[42] On the relative prices of skilled and unskilled slaves by age and sex, see Lima, "Escravos Artesãoes," tabelas 4 and 5, and graficos 1–5, pp. 478–9, 482–4. What is interesting to note is that prices for skilled workers remained at the same high plateau, from 20 to 40 years of age, whereas those for unskilled workers of both sexes dropped significantly after peaking in their 20s.

What is interesting is that his eight slaves paid him an impressive sum of 2:689$920 réis in 934 days – which was more than half the current total value of his slaves and 17 percent of his total patrimony.[43]

Aside from data available from postmortem inventories, such *escravos de ganho* were also listed for sale in the daily newspapers. Thus, in 1846 a master in Rio de Janeiro offered to sell his skilled stonemason "who gains 1$000 réis daily," which was obviously at the high end of the salary scale because of his training and skills,[44] although another listed a boy (*moleuqe*) who was a skilled artisan, craft not given, and claimed he produced a daily rent of 1$000.[45] A skilled slave leather belt/strap maker was listed for sale who earned 800 réis per day, and a slave farm worker (*preto de roça*) was offered for sale who made 480 réis per day.[46] Surprisingly, a "robust preto" with no specific skills listed was claimed to make 640 réis per day,[47] whereas a healthy middle-aged *preto de ganho*, again with no skills listed, was said to make 480 réis per day.[48]

There is little data for poorer workers listing ganho incomes, but the rental by owners of such workers was fairly common and from these monthly rental fees we can get a rough idea of what they would have earned if they were *escravos de ganho*. Wet nurses (*amas de leite*) were at the high end of the scale and probably could have rented for 645 réis per diem if the 20$000 rental fee per month asked for by one owner was the norm.[49] Children and adult domestics who were rented out by their

---

43 Andrade, *A mão de obra escrava em Salvador 1811–1860*, pp. 133–4.

44 "Vende-se... um pedeiro que ganha 1$000 diarios..." *Jornal do Comercio*, January 18, 1846, p. 4; and January 12, 1846, p. 3, for the leather workers.

45 "Vende-se... um moleque perfeito oficial, que ganha 1$000 diarios..." *Jornal do Comercio*, January 7, 1846, p. 4.

46 "Vende-se... um preto de nação, oficial de correeiro, que da de jornal 800 rs, e su precio de 600$ rs." *Jornal do Comercio*, January 12, 1846, p. 4. "Vende-se... um preto de roça, que ao ganho da 480..." *Jornal do Comercio*, January 7, 1846, p. 4.

47 "Vende-se por muita crecisão um reforçado preto, que ganho 640 réis por dia..." *Jornal do Comercio*, February 6, 1846, p. 3.

48 "Vende-se... um preto de media idade, que ao ganho da 480 rs." *Jornal do Comercio*, February 9, 1846, p. 3.

49 "Aluga-se uma preta, ama de leite do primero parto, parida ha dous mezes por 20$ mensaid pagos adelantados." *Jornal do Comercio*, January 6, 1846, p. 4. For an analysis of numerous other advertisements of rentals and sales of wet nurses in Rio de Janeiro in 1848 in the *Jornal do Comercio*, see the unpublished essay by Bárbara Canedo Ruiz Martins, "Meninas e mulheres: As imagens das amas-de-leite no mercado de trabalho doméstico urbano do Rio de Janeiro (1830–1888)," and for later periods, see her thesis, "Amas-de-leite e mercado de trabalho feminino: Descortinando práticas e sujeitos (Rio de Janeiro, 1830–1890)" (Dissertação de mestrado: Universidade Federal do Rio de Janeiro–UFRJ, 2006).

owners as household workers and pages earned on average between 322 to 419 réis per diem, given the average 10$000 to 13$000 réis per month rental fees.[50]

Those slaves who lived outside of their master's home often lived in tenements (*cortiços*), and these existed in abundance in all the major cities. In 1868, for example, in the city of Rio de Janeiro there were an estimated 642 such tenements or rooming houses for the poor, with a total of 9,671 rooms housing some 21,029 persons in ten of the eleven parishes of the city.[51] Cheap housing for the poor was common everywhere and many of the criminal records show that there was little discrimination against slaves in the popular bars of the city. Thus, such *escravos de ganho* found a whole range of residential and leisure options open to them. It is thus not strange, although it would seem to be quite unusual, for slaves to even own shops and rent other slaves. This is the unusual case of Henrique, an *escravo de ganho* who owned his own small "angu" (a store that sold a traditional African drink made of corn) and who himself had enough funds left over after his paying his daily or weekly sum to his master to be able to rent the services of the slave Mariana from another master and use her as an assistant in his food shop. It turned out that Mariana was also his lover.[52]

It is evident from all sources that urban slavery declined after the end of the Atlantic slave trade in 1850, and more and more of the traditional slave occupations were replaced by free persons. Such self-employed slaves survived in many occupations but tended to move toward the lower end of the skill scale. Thus, slaves remained important as porters and litter bearers in Rio de Janeiro until the abolition of slavery,[53] but the higher end skill of coachmen seemed to have been taken over by free persons before the end of slavery.[54]

This ample and varied use of slaves in the rural and urban areas and throughout most of the settled areas created various forms of autonomy,

---

[50] See, for example, rental offers for five *pretas* at 12$ and 13$ milreis and another for a *preta* "que sabe lavar, engomar e cozinhar por 12$," *Jornal do Comercio*, January 18, 1846, p. 4.

[51] Marilene Rosa Nogueira da Silva, *Negro na rua, a nova face da escravidão* (São Paulo: Editora Hucitec, 1988), tabela 13, p. 126.

[52] Soares, O 'Povo de Cam'na capital do Brasil, pp. 140–1.

[53] Soares, O 'Povo de Cam'na capital do Brasil, p. 128.

[54] On free labor in some subspecialities, such as coachmen for horsedrawn carriages, see Ana Maria da Silva Moura, *Cocheiros e carroceiros, homens livres no Rio de senhores e escravos* (São Paulo: Editora Hucitec, 1988).

control, stimulation, penalties, and relationship of slaves with their owners and with other free persons as well with other slaves. In some activities,
as already noted, the intensity of labor was imposed through tight control and physical violence. In other activities, without eliminating either
control or the potential for violence, incentives and prizes, material and
immaterial, were crucial. In domestic labor, services, crafts, and small
family farms, perhaps positive incentives predominated. In the plantation
form of slave labor, physical force and structured work predominated;
perhaps violence and other negative incentives were more important.
These later relations of work and coexistence generated atypical situations in the Brazilian slave society. Significant ratios of manumission,
many bought by the slaves themselves, amplified the free population of
African origins, which in turn grew not only from manumissions but
from a generalized process of miscegenation that occurred between free
persons and between free persons and slaves. The form in which slavery
was organized in Brazil permitted ample socialization of the slave population and the formation of families, some of which were maintained
for generations. This is a subject that has become a major area of new
research. Marriages, families, and kinship are themes that have recently
proliferated in the research from the most varied regions of the country.
These studies demonstrate that it was usual for these slave families to
produce part of their food needs, working principally on Sundays, the
day normally dedicated to rest. Any surplus of these products could be
sold in the local market, representing a potential income for the slave. It
represented an opportunity for the slave and at the same time reduced
the maintenance costs of the slave owners.

The structure of the distribution of the slaves also reflects the economic
and social conditions that we have discussed. There are differences, but
usually the slaves were present in 20 to 30 percent of the households
in the period under discussion. Slaves represented a similar percentage
of the total population. Among masters, slave ownership was well distributed. Great were the number of small slave owners and few were the
great planters with large numbers of slaves. Masters who owned five or
fewer slaves usually represented half of the slave owners and controlled
about a quarter of the slaves. In the plantation export sector, we do find
planters with fifty or even several hundred slaves. And these slaves in
larger holdings were an expressive percentage of the local slave population. In the opposite case of a predominance of small slaveholders, those
holding forty or more slaves were relatively insignificant in terms of the

total slave labor force. The average slaveholding fluctuated between five and eight slaves in most regions and rarely passed this value. This of course was in the period prior to 1850. After the closing of the slave trade, there was a tendency for slaves to be concentrated in the activities of highest profit, especially in the coffee regions where slaves were held in large concentration, usually in coffee estates with more than one hundred slaves.

In comparison with most of the major slave societies in the Americas, Brazil prior to 1850 looked more like the United States than any Caribbean society. It had roughly the same ratio of slave owners among the free population and the same ratio of slaves to total population. But even within this framework, the average slaveholdings in this period in Brazil were smaller than in the United States, and until 1850, it had fewer owners of very large holdings of slaves. Whereas the United States in 1790 looked like Minas and São Paulo – all with 6 to 7 percent of the owners holding twenty or more slaves – by the 1850s, the United States was moving toward a higher ratio of such owners, reaching 11 percent of all owners by 1850 and 12 percent by 1860. In contrast, Jamaica already had 20 percent of its owners who held twenty or more slaves by 1833 (see Table 5.1).

In the eighteenth century, the general pattern, at least for Minas Gerais and most of the *municípios* of São Paulo, was for a predominance of owners in the five and fewer slaves category, with a quarter or more of slaves in these smaller holdings and a relatively small share of owners in the twenty or more slaves group, and with the distribution of slaves in general being equal to the ratio in the five and under category, or fewer than half of all slaves (see Table 5.2). Although few comparative data exist for the other regions, it can be assumed from later developments that these zones of slave activity were not that dissimilar in their distribution patterns from what occurred in São Paulo and Minas in the same century.[55]

But this pattern not only differed across regions, it obviously differed by type of industry and was leading to increasing levels of concentration of slaves in the larger units (holdings of twenty-one and more slaves) over time. Moreover, as can be seen in Table 5.3, even controlling for

[55] At one extreme would be the ranching communities of Paraná, which in 1818 were those owning twenty or more slaves and holding only 17 percent of the slave labor force, and the average slaveholding had just under 5 slaves (for 483 slave owners and 2,345 slaves). Horácio Gutiérrez, "Terras e gado no Paraná tradicional" (Tese de doutorado: USP, 1996), tabela 4, p. 65.

TABLE 5.1. *Distribution of Owners by Size of Slaveholding for Various Regions and Nations, 1790–1860*

Size of Slaveholding	São Paulo		Minas Gerais		United States				Jamaica	
	1829	%	1833	%	1790	%	1850	%	1832*	%
1	2,669	24.5	5,003	24.5	14,262	30.3	68,060	19.7	6,649	53.4
2–4	3,828	35.1	7,281	35.7	15,402	32.8	105,144	30.4	1,954	15.7
5–9	2,333	21.4	4,489	22.0	9,459	20.1	80,629	23.3	1,394	11.2
10–19	1,261	11.6	2,368	11.6	4,990	10.6	54,556	15.8	945	7.6
20–49	630	5.8	1,085	5.3	2,275	4.8	29,731	8.6	580	4.7
50–99	144	1.3	161	0.8	471	1.0	6,195	1.8	538	4.3
100–199	19	0.2	23	0.1	123	0.3	1,479	0.4	274	2.2
200–299	19	0.2	3	0.0	26	0.1	187	0.1	119	1.0
300+		0.0	3	0.0	7	0.0	67	0.0		
TOTAL	10,903	100.0	20,416	100.0	47,015	100.0	346,048	100.0	12,453	100.0
Number of slaves	75,783		135,951		694,207		3,200,600		310,817	
Mean	7		7		15		9		25	

Notes: * In the Jamaican data, slave owners with just one slave were not broken out of the 1–5 slave owner category. We have tried to recalculate Higman's breakdowns to be as close to possible to the other regions.

Sources: B. W. Higman, *Slave Population and Economy in Jamaica 1807–1834* (Cambridge: Cambridge University Press, 1976), pp. 274–5; U.S. Census of 1790 and 1850; for São Paulo and Minas, Luna and Klein, *Slavery and the Economy* (2003).

TABLE 5.2. *Distribution of Slave Owners and Slaves by Size of Slaveholding, Minas Gerais and São Paulo, 1718/1792 (districts with more than 100 slaves)*

District	Year	Plantel 1–5		Plantel 21+	
		Owners	Slaves	Owners	Slaves
Vila de Pitanguy	1723	69.6	29.8	5.9	30.4
Serro Frio	1738	78.4	34.8	3.7	27.0
Congonhas do Sabará	1771	68.4	29.0	1.1	21.5
Sepurihu	1789	60.0	38.8	10.0	14.6
São Domingos	1789	59.5	23.3	10.8	49.9
Agua Suja	1789	71.1	24.3	3.4	30.4
Congonhas do Sabará	1790	75.0	34.7	0.0	17.3
Santa Luzia	1790	71.6	25.3	7.3	45.8
São João Barra Longa	1792	69.1	19.5	5.1	42.1
Inficionado	1792	0.0	27.0	8.9	41.2
Santa Luzia	1790	74.7	25.3	5.6	45.8
São João Barra Longa	1792	58.9	19.5	9.1	42.1
Inficionado	1792	74.9	27.0	5.7	41.2
São Paulo/Various districts	1777–78	70.2	30.7	3.1	21.5

Source: Arquivo Público do Estado de São Paulo, Listas Nominativas (mapas).

industrial activity of slaves, concentration was increasing even before the end of the slave trade. More owners and more slaves in each of the major agricultural activities in the province of São Paulo increased their share in the larger units between 1804 and 1829.

TABLE 5.3. *Economic Activities of Owners by the Size of Their Slaveholdings in São Paulo, 1804–1829*

% Owners	1804		1829	
	1–5	21+	1–5	21+
Sugar	23%	30%	5%	57%
Aguardente	49%	7%	34%	13%
Coffee	63%	4%	53%	11%
Food crops	75%	2%	72%	2%
Ranching	45%	11%	43%	10%
% Slaves				
Sugar	4%	63%	1%	83%
Aguardente	16%	29%	9%	38%
Coffee	26%	21%	14%	46%
Food crops	38%	13%	35%	15%
Ranching	13%	36%	12%	37%

Source: Luna and Klein, *Slavery and the Economy* (2003).

This trend was evident in Minas and other regions that already showed increasing concentration at the other end. However, it also should be stressed that this trend was not uniform across all regions. Census data from the 1870s show wide variation among regions and districts, depending on local economic conditions (see Table 5.4), but in general the trends seemed to be on the rise in the centers of export agriculture. Studies of two districts in Piauí in 1875 and another in Minas Gerais in the 1860s, although based on alternative postmortem inventories, also showed rates of distribution that differed little from the *mineiro* districts of the eighteenth century.[56] But more common was the pattern of increasing concentration – as measured in the GINI index of distribution – as we can see in Table 5.4. In contrast to the 40s and mid-50s found in most eighteenth- and early nineteenth-century districts, those of the second half of the nineteenth century were to be found in the upper 50s and 60s.

Finally, there is little question that the late nineteenth-century coffee estates were the most concentrated slaveholdings Brazil had ever seen, on a par with the largest sugar districts in the Northeast and those of the Caribbean in the nineteenth century. The average coffee *fazendas* in the most advanced coffee regions contained forty-three slaves (see Graph 5.1), and these averages suggest, based on a study of one coffee district in Minas Gerais in this period, that more than half the coffee planters owned twenty-one or more slaves and that an extraordinary 90 percent of the slaves working these coffee estates were working on these larger units.[57]

---

[56] Renato Leite Marcondes and Miridan Britto Knox Falci, "Escravidão e reprodução no Piauí: Oeiras e Teresina (1875)" (Texto para Discussão, Série Economia, TD-E/26, USP-FEAC-Ribeirão Preto, 2001), tabelas 4 and 5; both these districts had GINIs in the mid-50s. One of the highest GINIs recorded (.076) was for Bananal in São Paulo in 1873; José Flávio, Motta, Nelson Hideiki Nozoe, and Iraci del Nero da Costa, "Às Vésperas da Abolição: Um Estudo sobre a Estrutura da Posse de Escravos em São Cristóvão (RJ), 1870," *Estudios Econômicos*, 34, no. 1 (Jan.–Mar. 2004), tabela 12, p. 191. For the Minas study, see Deborah Oliveira Martins dos Reis, "Araxá, 1816–1888: Posse de escravos, atividades produtivas, riqueza," *XIV Encontro Nacional de Estudos Populacionais*, ABEP (2004), tabela 4, panels 1866–68.

[57] A separate study of just the coffee producers in the Minas Gerais município de Santo Antônio do Paraibuna from 1851–1870 based on postmortem wills also showed an average of 43 slaves per *fazendas* (108 owners and 4,683 slaves). Some 90 percent of the slaves resided on estates that had twenty-one or more slaves and 53 percent of the masters owned these estates. The average for these more than twenty slave estates was a very high seventy-four slaves per unit. Mônica Ribeiro de Oliveira, "Cafeicultura mineira: Formação e consolidação 1809–1870," *IX Seminário sobre a Economia Mineira*, Quadro 4, p. 70.

TABLE 5.4. *Number of Slaves and Slave Owners and GINI Index of Inequality of Slave Ownership, Selected Districts by Province, Early 1870s*

	Owners	Slaves	GINI
Paraná	2,514	7,940	0.484
Pernambuco	1,434	8,980	0.619
Paraíba	630	1,567	0.428
Maranhão	1,690	5,325	0.488
Pará	594	2,895	0.505
Piauí	3,435	13,120	0.539
Espírito Santo	554	2,963	0.564
Minas Gerais	3,579	1,311	0.510
Rio de Janeiro (Parati)	350	1,497	0.555
São Paulo	5,090	33,736	0.660
Bahia	556	2,796	0.612
Sergipe	1,687	6,570	0.575
Goiás	2,213	7,299	0.477
Rio Grande do Sul	1,270	4,942	0.469

Source: Marcondes, "Desigualidades regionais brasileiras" (2005), tabelas 3.4, 4.4, 5.4, 6.4, 7.4, and 8.4.

At the same time that we find slaves everywhere, we find also a complex organization of foodstuff production that involved both slave owners and those who owned no slaves. Both sold products in the market. The nonslave owners and the small farmers sold the surplus of their production above subsistence in the local market. This activity, well

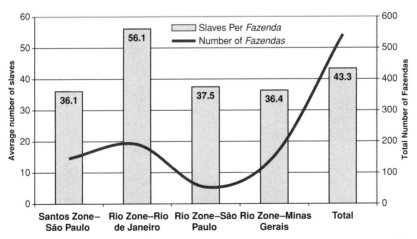

GRAPH 5.1. Number of *fazendas* and average number of slaves in the major coffee districts of Brazil, 1881–1888 (no slaves = 23,553). *Source:* C. F. Van Delden Laerne, *Brazil and Java* (1885), pp. 222–3.

revealed in the contemporary documents, was particularly evident in Minas Gerais, São Paulo, and Paraná, but also throughout the Northeast as well, all indicating the complexity of colonial and imperial Brazilian society and showing how important was the local and regional internal market – whose complexity and importance have only recently been understood.

PART TWO

BRAZILIAN SLAVE SOCIETY

6

Life, Death, and Migration in Afro-Brazilian Slave Society

The expansion of the export sector in Brazil during four centuries of its evolution was the driving force behind the forced migration of African laborers to the shores of Brazil. Portuguese merchants made this migration possible by opening up the African Atlantic markets and organizing a slave-trading fleet. At the same time, the subsequent growth or decline of these African slaves and their descendants in Brazil was determined by classic demographic factors, such as their birth and death rates, as well as their rates of internal migration and manumission. These are themes that will be explored in this chapter as we summarize the latest studies relating to the population history of these several million forced migrants who arrived in Brazil in the period to 1850.

To transport these estimated 5.5 million workers shipped from Africa across the Atlantic Ocean to Brazil, there emerged a sophisticated and complex system of the purchase of African slaves with goods demanded by the African markets, which in turn linked the economies of Asia, America, and Europe to the evolving market economy in Africa. There is little question that Brazil was the single most important arrival place for African slaves in America. Of the estimated 10.7 million Africans who safely crossed the Atlantic from the late fifteenth century until the late nineteenth century, an estimated 4.8 million survived the crossing and landed in Brazil.[1] The intensity of this forced migration of African

---

[1] The figures presented here are still quite tentative and are estimates based on the voyage collection of the Atlantic slave trade. This is an ongoing project developed under the aegis of David Eltis at Emory University and is constantly being updating and changing its overall estimates of the volume of the trade. The biggest change since the publication of

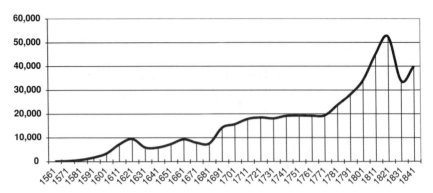

GRAPH 6.1. Estimated average annual slave arrivals to all Brazilian ports, 1651–1850, by decade. *Source*: Data accessed in August 18, 2008; http://www. slavevoyages.org/tast/assessment/estimates.

slaves was highly correlated with the growth of Brazilian exports and the expansion of the local economy. Just as the largest expansion of Brazilian production occurred in the late eighteenth and nineteenth centuries, so too the most important period of this four-century slave trade was in the late eighteenth and nineteenth centuries (see Graph 6.1).

There were also significant shifts in the relative importance of receiving regions within Brazil. In the sixteenth and seventeenth centuries, the bulk of the slaves were arriving in the ports of the Northeast, except for the period of the Dutch occupation of Pernambuco. By the late eighteenth century, however, the southeastern port of Rio de Janeiro had achieved dominance and would continue to outdistance its northeastern rivals for the entire nineteenth century (see Graph 6.2). By the mid-eighteenth

the first data set (see David Eltis, Stephen D. Behrendt, David Richardson, and Herbert S. Klein, *The Transatlantic Slave Trade, 1562–1867: A Database* [New York, Cambridge: Cambridge University Press, 2000]) has been the almost doubling of the estimate of the Brazilian slave trade. This trade is now recognized as both the longest and the largest of the Atlantic slave trades, and it is thought to have transported an estimated 5.5 million Africans from Africa. Of this number, an estimated 4.8 million survived the crossing (all estimates cited here and in the text were generated from data in the Voyages database in mid-August 2008). Given the fact that only about 10 percent of the known slave ships have data on the actual numbers of slaves carried, the total estimates are in a state of flux as new ships are found and new estimates for missing data are provided. The current iteration of the database (which I accessed on August 18, 2008) can be found at http://www.slavevoyages.org/tast/index.faces. It should be noted that although all of the volume estimates of the slave trade, the relative importance of different time periods, and the rates of national participation have changed over the last quarter-century, the overall numbers of the slave trade are still well within the total limits established by Philip Curtin, *The Atlantic Slave Trade: A Census* (Madison: University of Wisconsin Press, 1969).

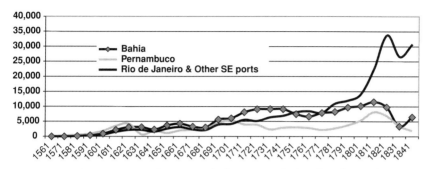

GRAPH 6.2. Average annual estimated slave arrivals by decade in the principal ports of Brazil, 1561–1851. *Source:* Data accessed August 18, 2008; http://www.slavevoyages.org/tast/assessment/estimates.

century, Rio de Janeiro had become the single most important arrival point for Africans in Brazil and accounted for 43 percent of all immigrating African slaves, and it took in more than half of all slaves by the first decade of the nineteenth century. By the 1820s, its share rose to three-quarters of all the slave arrivals and to four-fifths of all slaves by the 1830s and 1840s. Clearly, just as the economic center of Brazil had slowly shifted southward during the course of the colonial period, so too had the arriving Africans followed the economic and political changes in the colony and empire.

Overall, the three dominant regions for the origin of African slaves to Brazil were the regions of Angola-Loanda (Central Africa), the Bight of Benin (Western Africa), and the East African region of Mozambique. Although their participation varied by time, overall these three regions accounted for an estimated 94 percent of all Africans shipped to Brazil (see Graph 6.3).[2]

What is interesting to note is that these regions of origin were quite distinct from those from which mainland North America drew its African slaves. Although a much smaller trade, the majority of Africans arriving in mainland North America came from Western Africa, and most especially the Senegambia region, which was the single most important center for this northern Atlantic trade (see Graph 6.4).

Although Brazilian slaves came mainly from southwestern ports, not all receiving ports obtained their slaves from the same African sources.

---

[2] These origin data, generated on August 10, 2008, were taken from the Estimated data set, a subset of the online Voyages data set and found at http://www.slavevoyages.org/tast/assessment/estimates.faces.

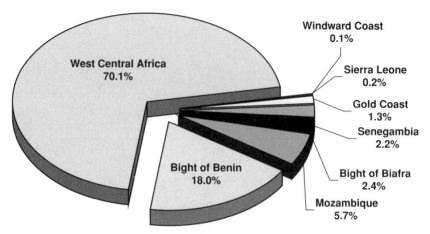

GRAPH 6.3. Estimated African regional origins of slaves shipped to Brazil, 1561–1850 (5,479,583 persons).

Even for given Brazilian ports, the origins of slaves differed over time. Although a great deal of information on given slave voyages is missing (especially for the port of Rio de Janeiro), the latest estimates suggest that the migration to Rio de Janeiro was dominated by slaves arriving from the Congo-Angola area, and the same would appear to be the case for Pernambuco. Bahia, however, was much more tied to the Bight of Benin area than any of the other ports, a pattern that persisted during all the major time periods of the slave trade (see Table 6.1). Interior zones such as Minas Gerais showed a more mixed pattern of African arrivals because they obtained slaves from both Rio de Janeiro and Bahia. Thus,

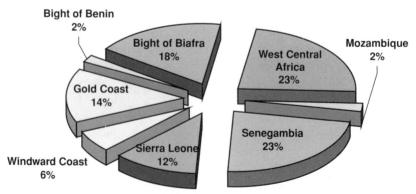

GRAPH 6.4. Estimated origin of African slaves shipped to North America, 1581–1808 (452,651).

TABLE 6.1. *Estimate of Ratio of African Slaves Arriving in Major Brazilian Ports for the 4.6 Million Whose African Region of Departure Is Known, 1581–1850*

	Senegambia, Sierra Leone, Windward Coast	Gold Coast	Bight of Benin	Bight of Biafra	West Central Africa	Southeast Africa	Totals	Number
A: Rio de Janeiro								
<1699	0.0	0.0	0.3	0.0	99.7	0.0	100.0	224,670
1700–49	0.9	0.9	5.3	0.3	92.6	0.0	100.0	280,421
1750–99	0.0	0.0	3.4	0.0	96.1	0.5	100.0	474,833
1800>	0.2	0.1	1.4	1.5	78.9	17.9	100.0	1,280,063
Totals	0.2	0.2	2.2	0.9	86.3	10.2	100.0	2,259,987
B: Bahia								
<1699	2.2	0.6	13.4	2.8	78.5	2.4	100.0	317,842
1700–49	1.2	1.9	59.9	6.0	30.8	0.2	100.0	414,291
1750–99	0.2	0.1	59.1	1.9	38.3	0.4	100.0	399,860
1800>	1.9	0.2	48.3	7.0	39.4	3.1	100.0	413,014
Totals	1.3	0.7	47.0	4.5	44.8	1.5	100.0	1,545,007
C: Pernambuco								
<1699	0.3	2.2	3.6	2.2	91.4	0.0	100.0	238,909
1700–49	0.8	21.2	28.4	0.4	47.7	0.0	100.0	184,179
1750–99	0.3	0.2	13.4	0.8	85.4	0.0	100.0	144,885
1800>	1.0	0.6	2.5	7.4	82.6	5.9	100.0	256,340
Totals	0.6	5.5	10.4	3.1	78.1	1.8	100.0	824,313
Overall Total	0.8	1.3	18.5	2.4	71.2	5.8	100.0	4,629,307

Note: This table is only a partial reconstruction of the slave arrivals to Brazil and is missing numerous voyages and contains more estimated numbers than actual registered data.

Source: New Emory estimated data set, accessed September 11, 2008.

studies of early eighteenth-century Minas show a very high participation
of African slaves from the Bight of Benin region. Thus, the north/south
dichotomy of Brazil aligned with a West-Central Western African origin
does not completely hold, as there was a far more mixed origin of slaves
in central Brazil.[3]

The Bahia-Benin connection was unusually close and involved the
movement of peoples, goods, and even ideas across the South Atlantic.
The Portuguese initially had opened up this area and constructed their
factory and fort at El Mina. When the Dutch seized this region in the
first half of the seventeenth century, there was a temporary redirection
of trade to the other areas. But the growth of an intimate trade between
Africa and northeastern Brazil prior to the Dutch takeover meant that
this connection could not be completely severed by the Dutch. African
demand for Bahian tobacco was so strong that eventually the Dutch
were forced to compromise and allow the old trade to continue. Also,
with the opening up of the *mineiro* gold fields, Brazilian and Portuguese
traders were able to further penetrate the Benin region through their
purchase of slaves with gold from America. This special relationship
between these two regions grew so powerful and existed for such a long
time that the Northeast of Brazil was probably the most concentrated
area for Ghanaian and Nigerian cultures in America. So close and recent
was the relation that even in the postemancipation period there was a
steady return of Afro-Brazilians either to settle in these regions of the
Bight of Benin or were visitors who came to re-enforce African-based
religious belief systems that were developing in late nineteenth-century
Brazil.[4]

---

[3] On the origin of the African slaves in Minas, see Francisco Vidal Luna and Iraci del Nero
da Costa, "Algumas características do contingente de cativos em Minas Gerais," *Anais
do Museu Paulista*, tomo XXIX (São Paulo: USP; 1979), pp. 79–97, and their essay "A
Presença do elemento Sudanês nas Minas Gerais," *Suplemento Cultural, O Estado de
São Paulo*, Ano II, no. 188, (26/11/1978), pp. 14–16.

[4] On the intimate relations between the two regions, see the classic study by Pierre Verger,
*Flux et reflux de la traite des négres entre le golfe de Benin et Bahia de Todos os Santos, du
dix-septième au dix-neuvieme siècle* (Paris, 1968). On the postslavery contacts, there is an
extensive literature: see Manuela Carneiro da Cunha, *Negros, Estrangeiros: Os Escravos
Libertos e a sua Volta à África* (São Paulo: Brasiliense, 1985); Manuela Carneiro da
Cunha, *Da Senzala ao Sobrado: Arquitetura Brasileira na Nigéria e na República Popular
do Benim [From Slave Quarters to Town Houses: Brazilian Architecture in Nigeria and
the People's Republic of Benin]* (São Paulo: Nobel/EDUSP, 1985); J. M. Turner, "Les
Brésiliens: The Impact of Former Brazilian Slaves upon Dahomey" (Boston: Ph.D. diss.,
Boston University, 1975); Alcione Meira Amos, "Afro-Brazilians in Togo: The Case
of the Olympio Family, 1882–1945," *Cahiers d'Études africaines*, 162, XLI-2 (2001),

The slave trade from Africa began at a relatively slow pace, and enslaved humans were just one of the major commodities exported by Africa to Europe and America in the first two and a half centuries of Atlantic contact. In fact, it was not until the early eighteenth century that slaves became Africa's largest "export."[5] It was the Portuguese who opened up the Atlantic coast of Africa for international trade, and gold and ivory were more important to early traders than slaves. Gradually this changed as Brazil developed as a major slave plantation economy. Although the Portuguese worked in all coasts, the majority of Brazil's slaves – an estimated 71 percent – came from the Congo-Angola region, part of which had been settled by Portuguese traders in the sixteenth century. The nineteenth century saw a major new development of the trade to Brazil as the ports of Mozambique were finally opened up to Portuguese slave traders. Although trading was intense from this new region, especially in the late 1830s, the ports of Mozambique still accounted for only a small share of total slave arrivals into Brazil. An estimated 85 percent of these Mozambique slaves went to Rio de Janeiro, but even in this port, they made up just an estimated 17 percent of the African slave arrivals in the nineteenth century. Thus, the Biafran and West-Central African regions together remained the prime areas of the trade at the end, with only some 6 percent of all the slaves shipped to Brazil in the nineteenth century coming from East African sources (see Table 6.1).

Unlike most of the slave trades, the trade to Brazil was an exclusive monopoly of Portuguese and Brazilian slave traders from the very beginning and remained so until its end in 1850. Portuguese and Brazilian traders also played a role in the early Spanish American slave trade and were significant players in the Cuban slave trade of the late nineteenth century.[6] Moreover, despite the traditional Anglo-Saxon bias against the

---

pp. 293–314; Alcione Meira Amos and Ebenezer Ayesu, "Sou brasileiro: História dos Tabom, afro-brasileiros em Acra, Gana," *Afro-Ásia*, no. 33 (2005), pp. 35–65; Robin Law, "The Evolution of the Brazilian Community in Ouidah," *Slavery & Abolition*, 22, no. 1 (2001), pp. 3–21; Eliseacutee Soumonni, "Some Reflections on the Brazilian Legacy in Dahomey," *Slavery & Abolition*, 22, no. 1 (2001), pp. 42–60; and Olabiyi Babalola Yai, "The Identity, Contributions, and Ideology of the Aguda (Afro-Brazilians) of the Gulf of Benin: A Reinterpretation," *Slavery & Abolition*, 22, no. 1 (2001), pp. 61–71.

5 David Eltis, "The Relative Importance of Slaves and Commodities in the Atlantic Trade of Seventeenth-Century Africa," *The Journal of African History*, 35, no. 2 (1994), pp. 237–49.

6 David Eltis, *Economic Growth and the Ending of the Transatlantic Slave Trade* (New York: Oxford University Press, 1987); and Herbert S. Klein, "The Structure of the Atlantic

Portuguese, which is reflected in the historical literature,[7] there was no major difference between the Portuguese slavers and all other European slave traders in their shipping and handling of Africans. No matter what the nationality of the traders, almost all participants carried slaves in a comparable manner, especially by the eighteenth century. All Europeans transported approximately the same number of Africans per ship in roughly the same size vessels and crossed the Atlantic in approximately the same amount of time. They housed and fed their slaves in the same manner, and, despite the usual disclaimers and prejudices, they treated their slaves with the same amount of cruelty and care. They experienced roughly the same rates of success and failure in carrying slaves across the Atlantic, and no one nation had a mortality record systematically lower than any other.[8]

Although the British may have introduced surgeons earlier than other nations, this had little measurable impact on African mortality or the incidence of diseases aboard ship. The general improvement in European knowledge about diet and the use of crude vaccinations against smallpox pervaded all the slave-trading nations by the second half of the eighteenth century, a fact that seems to account for the uniform drop in average mortality figures from approximately 20 percent in the pre-1700 period to some 5 to 8 percent by the end of the eighteenth century and beginning of the nineteenth century.[9]

Slave Trade in the 19th Century: An Assessment," *Revue Française d'Histoire d'Outre-mer*, nos. 336–7 (2éme semestre 2002), pp. 63–77.

[7] For different views on this question, see Joseph C. Miller, *Way of Death: Merchant Capitalism and the Angolan Slave Trade, 1730–1830* (Madison: University of Wisconsin Press, 1988); and Robert E. Conrad, *Tumbeiros: O tráfico de escravos para o Brasil* (São Paulo: Brasiliense, 1985).

[8] Herbert S. Klein, *The Middle Passage: Comparative Studies in the Atlantic Slave Trade* (Princeton: Princeton University Press, 1978); see also Herbert S. Klein and Stanley L. Engerman, "Slave Mortality on British Ships, 1791–1797," in Roger Anstey and P.E.H. Hair, eds., *Liverpool, the African Slave Trade, and Abolition* (Liverpool, Historical Society of Lancashire and Chesire, Occasional Papers, vol. 2, 1976), pp. 113–22; and by the same authors, "Facteurs de mortalité dans le trafic française d'esclaves au XVIIIe siècle," *Annales. Économies, Societés, Civilisations*, 31, no. 6 (1976), 1213–1223; and articles cited in notes 6 and 7.

[9] Herbert S. Klein and Stanley L. Engerman, "Long-term Trends in African Mortality in the Transatlantic Slave Trade," *Slavery & Abolition*, 18, no. 1 (April 1997), pp. 59–71; and for detailed data on mortality in the slave trade to Brazil, see Herbert S. Klein, "The Trade in African Slaves to Rio de Janeiro, 1795–1811: Estimates of Mortality and Patterns of Voyages," *Journal of African History*, X, no. 4 (1969), 533–49; and Herbert S. Klein and Stanley L. Engerman, "Shipping Patterns and Mortality in the African Slave Trade to Rio de Janeiro," *Cahiers d'études africaines*, no. 59, XV, no. 3 (1976), pp. 381–98.

It should be stressed that although mortality rates were dropping from the sixteenth century until the beginning of the nineteenth century, they were still extremely high and would have been considered of epidemic proportions had they occurred to a similarly aged population that had not been transported. Equally, these rates were high even in terms of the shipping of other persons in this period. Slaves had, on average, half the amount of room afforded convicts, emigrants, or soldiers transported in the same period, and they obviously had the most rudimentary sanitary facilities. Although the mortality suffered by these other lower-class groups was sometimes as high as the Africans', their rates eventually dropped to less than 1 percent in the late eighteenth and early nineteenth centuries, a low mortality level never achieved by the slavers.[10] Even a rate of 5 percent for a two- to three-month period for healthy young adults in the late eighteenth century – the best rate achieved by the slave traders – was very high. Such a rate in a contemporaneous nonmigrating European peasant population would have been considered of epidemic proportions; even more so because all those who were carried in the trade were healthy and in prime physical condition. Although the European traders carried out every possible health and sanitary procedure they knew about, most of these were of little utility, because the typical manner of carrying three hundred slaves on a 200-ton vessel guaranteed a disease environment from which few escaped unscathed.

Although time at sea was not usually correlated with mortality, there were some routes in which time was a factor. Simply because they were a third longer than any other route, the East African slave trade from Mozambique, which developed in the late eighteenth and nineteenth centuries, was noted for overall higher mortality than the West African routes, even though mortality per day at sea was the same or lower than on the shorter routes. Also, the simple crowding together of slaves from all types of different epidemiological zones in Africa guaranteed the transmission of a host of local endemic diseases to all those who were carried aboard. Finally, many of the sicker slaves died soon after their arrival in Brazil. It has been estimated for 1825 and 1828 that a death rate for arriving slaves varied from 2.3 percent to 4 percent of the total arriving in the port of Rio de Janeiro in these years.[11] Although any mortality that

---

[10] Herbert S. Klein, Stanley L. Engerman, Robin Haines, and Ralph Schlomowitz, "Transoceanic Mortality: The Slave Trade in Comparative Perspective," *The William & Mary Quarterly*, LVIII, no. 1 (January 2001), pp. 93–118.

[11] This is based on the total of new Africans who were buried in the special "Cementario para Pretos Novos" in Rio de Janeiro in those years compared to the estimated total

occurred on trips from the interior from the coastal ports is unknown, it was probably quite low. Many newly arrived slaves (*novos* – slaves who were unbaptized and did not speak Portuguese) were quickly moved from the port of Rio de Janeiro along with *ladino* slaves (those already residing in the country and speaking Portuguese) via mule trains in fairly large groups. A recent study has suggested an average of over 18,000 slaves per annum in the 1824–1830 period left the port for the interior parts of the provinces of Minas Gerais, Rio de Janeiro, and São Paulo, and this on average represented about half of the Africans who had just arrived in port.[12]

Although the markup of American slave prices was high relative to prices paid in Africa, the African sellers of slaves controlled the supply conditions and demanded high-cost goods for their slaves. The single largest item of European imports that paid for slaves were textiles, and these mostly came from the looms of India. In the case of the Portuguese trade, this involved shipments directly from India to Africa to pay for slaves, as well as the shipment of Brazilian-made guns, gunpowder, *aguardente* (brandy made from sugar cane, or *cachaça*), tobacco, and even gold dust as goods used to purchase slaves. All of these items, along with bar iron, added up to a considerable cost for the Europeans, and even when they used cowry shells and/or other African monetary items, these in turn had to be paid for by European goods that in turn were paid for with gold and silver.[13]

number of arrivals. This cemetery was not used by any resident *forros* or slaves, all of whom were buried by the *irmandades* in the city in their own churches or cemeteries, and thus was almost exclusively for those who had recently died upon arrival from Africa. Júlio César Medeiros da S. Pereira, "À flor da terra: O Cemitério dos Pretos Novos no Rio de Janeiro" (Dissertação de mestrado, Universidade Federal do Rio de Janeiro, 2006), pp. 120–1.

[12] Fábio W. A. Pinheiro, "Tráfico atlântico de escravos na formação dos plantéis mineiros, Zona da Mata, c. 1809 – c. 1830" (Dissertação de mestrado, UFRJ, Rio de Janeiro, 2007), tabela 13, p. 99, and tabela 7, p. 75. Over the entire period from 1809–1830, roughly a third of the newly arriving African slaves (*novos*) were sent into the interior in this period, although annual rates fluctuated quite widely and increased dramatically in the 1820s. It has been estimated for the 1770s for the port of Bahia that 22 percent of the *novo* slaves were shipped from the port to Minas Gerais and other interior regions – although again with high annual fluctuations. Alexandre Viera Ribeiro, "O comercio de escravos e a elite baiana no período colonial," in João Luis Ribeiro Fragoso, Carla Maria Carvalho de Almeida, and Antonio Carlos Juca de Sampaio, eds., *Conquistadores e negociantes. Histórias de elites no Antigo Regime nos trópicos, América lusa, séculos XVI a XVIII* (Rio de Janeiro: Civilização Brasileira, 2007), p. 317.

[13] On the economics of the trade, see the two works of Herbert S. Klein, *The Middle Passage*, especially chapters 2–4, and *The Atlantic Slave Trade* (2nd printing; Cambridge:

Unlike many of the major trades, there were no triangular voyage routes between Europe, Africa, and America.[14] The Portuguese/Brazilian trade never involved Portugal directly. It was Brazilian-originated ships that transported Brazilian goods to Africa, and they returned directly to Brazilian ports with the slaves. It was Portuguese ships that brought Asian goods to Africa to purchase slaves. Although Portuguese merchant capital was involved in all aspects of the trade, along with increasing participation of Brazilian capital, no slave ship ever returned to Portugal. Also, because the Portuguese were resident in both Mozambique and Angola, they were probably able to purchase African slaves a bit more promptly than the usual boat trading system used by the majority of Europeans. Also, Asian goods used to purchase African slaves, instead of being brought by the Brazilian traders, were usually brought directly from Asia to the African settlements, whereas the Brazilian ships concentrated on such Brazilian-produced goods as liquor, gunpowder, tobacco, and gold, which also were used to purchase slaves.[15]

Although planters often proclaimed their desires for a specific nationality or group of Africans, it is now evident that they took what they could get, and this depended exclusively on African conditions. All studies from all trades show that the Europeans, except for the Portuguese in Angola and Mozambique, had little idea of the nature of the societies they were dealing with. In most cases, Africans were simply designated by the ports that they were shipped from rather than by any truly generic ethnic or national identity. On a few occasions, such as the collapse of a large state or after a major military defeat, whole nations of well-defined and clearly delineated groups entered the slave trade and were known

Cambridge University Press, 2002), chapters 4–5; as well as Miller, *Way of Death.* Recent work on the Brazilian slave trade has included Jaime Rodrigues, *De costa a costa, escravos, marinheiros e intermediários do tráfico negreiro de Angola ao Rio de Janeiro (1780–1860)* (São Paulo: Companhia das Letras, 2005); Selma Pantoja and José Flavio Sombra Saraova (eds.), *Angola e Brasil nas rotas do Atlântico sul* (Rio de Janeiro: Bertrand Brasil, 1999); and Linda M. Heywood, ed., *Central Africans and Cultural Transformations in the American Diaspora* (New York: Cambridge University Press, 2002).

[14] In fact, the triangular trade was mostly a myth, in the sense that slave-produced American products primarily moved in regular shipping, and slave ships were only moderately used to bring these products from America to Europe. See Klein, *The Atlantic Slave Trade,* chapters 4 and 5.

[15] Manuel dos Anjos da Silva Rebelo, *Relações entre Angola e Brasil, 1808–1830* (Lisbon: Agência-Geral do Ultramar, 1970). Gold was primarily used to purchase slaves only in the ports of the Bight of Benin. See Klein, *The Atlantic Slave Trade,* chapter 5.

by their proper names in America. But this was the exception rather than the rule. While Europeans fought among themselves to protect a special section of the western African coastline, interlopers from other European and African groups went out of their way to guarantee that no monopolies were created. Although the Portuguese controlled Benguela and Luanda, for example, the French and English were getting their slaves from the same inland areas by landing further north along the Loango-Congolese coast. Attempts by any one African group to monopolize local trade often led to the opening up by their competitors of new trading routes.

Not only was the origin of all slaves largely determined by African supply conditions, but such conditions also determined the sex of the departing Africans. It has been estimated that 65 percent of all migrating Africans were males.[16] Although there was a price differential between males and females in America, this was insufficient to explain the almost two-thirds majority of males among the arriving slaves. Women performed almost all the same manual tasks as men on the plantations of America and, in fact, made up the majority of most field gangs in sugar, coffee, and cotton. African women, both free and slave, were in high demand locally, and it was this counterdemand from African markets that explains why fewer women entered the Atlantic slave trade. In some African societies, women were highly valued because they were the means of acquiring status, kinship, and family. One of the distinguishing features of western African societies was their emphasis on matrilineal and matrilocal kinship systems. Because even female slaves could be significant links in the kinship networks, their importance in the social system was enhanced. Also, slave women were cheaper to acquire than free local women in polygynous societies, making them more highly prized in societies that practiced this marriage arrangement. Even more important was the widespread Western African practice of primarily using women in agricultural labor. For all of these reasons, women had a higher price in local internal African markets than men.[17]

---

[16] The current estimate of the Emory database is that 65 percent of the slaves who were shipped from Africa were males. This was the number obtained on August 19, 2008, from the Summary Table available on the Voyage website and is based on only 12 percent of the 33,388 voyages that had actual breakdowns of the transported slaves by sex. See Summary Statistics at http://www.slavevoyages.org/tast/database/search.faces.

[17] See Herbert S. Klein, "African Women in the Atlantic Slave Trade," in Claire C. Robertson and Martin A. Klein, eds., *Women and Slavery in Africa* (Madison: University of Wisconsin Press, 1983), pp. 29–38.

Aside from the high incidence of males, the trade also exhibited a low incidence of children, with an average of 22 percent of all those transported being defined in this age category.[18] Although children suffered no higher mortality rates in crossing than any other groups of slaves, their low sale prices combined with their costs of transportation equal to that of adults discouraged slave captains from purchasing them.

All of these biases in the age and sex of the migrating Africans had a direct impact on the growth and decline of the Afro-Brazilian slave populations. The low ratio of women in each arriving ship, the fact that most of these slave women were mature adults who had already spent several of their childbearing years in Africa, and the fact that relatively few children were carried to Brazil were of fundamental importance in the subsequent history of population growth. It meant that the African slaves who arrived in America were unable to completely replace themselves through births. The African women who came to Brazil had lost several potential years of reproduction and were incapable of reproducing even the total numbers of their immigrant cohort, let alone creating a generation greater than the total number who arrived from Africa. Those Brazilian regions that experienced a heavy and constant stream of African slaves would thus find it difficult to maintain their slave populations – let alone increase their size – without resorting to more migrants. It was only in those regions where the slave trade died out or was no longer important before the end of slavery that the positive natural growth rates – which were the norm among the native-born or Creole slaves – could finally influence the growth of the entire resident slave population. The classic case of such a positive growth rate was the slave population of the United States, which unqualifiedly attained the highest level of reproduction of any slave regime in the Americas.[19] But the United States was not alone. It has been suggested by recent studies that some provinces in Brazil also achieved positive natural growth rates well before the end of the Atlantic slave trade, although none comparable to North America. Particularly singled out in this respect were the provinces of Minas Gerais, Paraná, and Piauí in the nineteenth century.[20]

---

[18] This is a current estimate provided in the "Summary Table" of the Emory data set accessed on August 18, 2008. It should be noted that only 12 percent of the 33,388 voyages listed in this source had the actual age breakdown of the transported Africans.

[19] Herbert S. Klein, *A Population History of the United States* (Cambridge: Cambridge University Press, 2004), p. 83.

[20] For a review of this issue for Minas Gerais, see Laird W. Bergad, *Slavery and the Demographic and Economic History of Minas Gerais, Brazil, 1720–1888* (Cambridge:

The impact of the biases in age and sex of the arriving slaves can be seen in a fairly complete sample of a large body of slaves, which we have separated by origin, in the provinces of São Paulo in the late 1820s (see Graph 6.5a–6.5b) and Minas Gerais in the early 1830s (see Graph 6.6a–6.6b). As can be seen in the age pyramids for the African-born slaves, males predominated and the working-age males were the most important cohorts, whereas the Creole-born slaves in both provinces showed a classic age pyramid of a pretransition population with close to a normal distribution of men and women. The final total resident slave population in both categories profoundly reflected the influence of the Africans and would of course have led to negative population growth rates (see Graph 6.5c and 6.6c). The sex ratio for the São Paulo slaves was on the order of 154 males per 100 females, and for Minas, the figure was almost identical at 155 males per 100 females.

This pattern of declining populations under the impact of the slave trade was perceived by contemporaries, most of whom assumed it was related to the treatment of the slave population. Later, commentators took up this theme and a host of claims were made for the better or worse physical treatment on the part of this or that slave regime, or one or the other type of plantation activity or crop. Claims were made for the economic logic of planters rejecting reproduction as too costly and therefore relying on "cheaper," imported African adult slaves. Recent demographic analyses show, however, none of these claims hold up. In all of the American slave regimes, the standardized birthrate among American slave women was comparable with, if not higher than, most of the contemporary European nations. Whereas the U.S. slaves in the nineteenth century achieved very high rates of fertility by any standards – in the range of 50 births per 1,000 population – the slaves of Brazil had

Cambridge University Press, 1999), pp. xix–xxi; and Clotilde Andrade Paiva and Douglas Libby, "Caminhos alternativos: Escravidão e reprodução em Minas Gerais," *Estudos Econômicos*, 25, no. 2 (Mayo–Agosto 1995), pp. 203–33. For Paraná, see Horácio Gutierréz, "A harmonia dos sexos: Elementos da estrutura demográfica da população escrava no Paraná, 1800–1830," *Anais do V Encontro Nacional de Estudos Populacionais*, ABEP (1986); "Demografia escrava numa economia não exportadora: Paraná," *Estudos Econômicos*, 17, no. 2 (1987), pp. 297–314; "Crioulos e Africanos no Paraná, 1798–1830," *Revista Brasileira de História*, 8, no. 16 (1988), pp. 161–88. On the sexual balance among the slaves and the high incidence of children in the relatively backward economy of nineteenth-century Piauí, see Renato Leite Marcondes and Miridan Britto Knox Falci, "Escravidão e reprodução no Piauí: Oeiras e Teresina (1875)" (Texto para Discussão, Série Economia, TD-E/26, USP-FEAC-Ribeirão Preto, 2001).

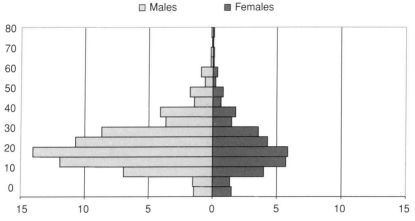

GRAPH 6.5A. Age pyramid of African-born slaves, São Paulo, 1829 (29,989).

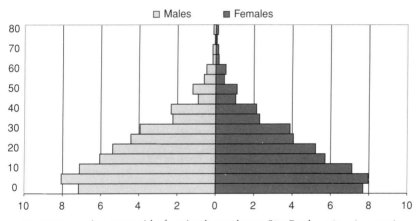

GRAPH 6.5B. Age pyramid of native-born slaves, São Paulo, 1829 (22,554).

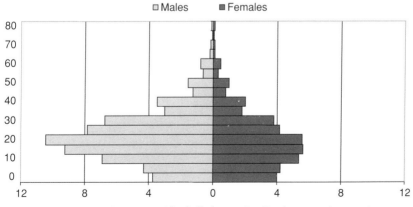

GRAPH 6.5C. Age pyramid of all slaves, São Paulo, 1829 (75,072).

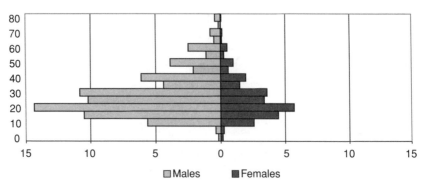

GRAPH 6.6A. Age pyramid of African-born slaves, Minas Gerais, 1829 (55,843).

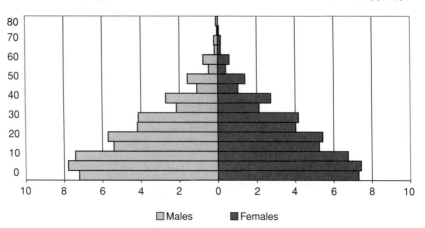

GRAPH 6.6B. Age pyramid of native-born slaves, Minas Gerais, 1829 (74,047).

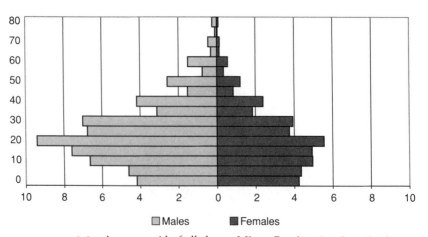

GRAPH 6.6C. Age pyramid of all slaves, Minas Gerais, 1829 (129,890).

birth rates in the upper 30s and lower 40s per 1,000, which were in fact quite high by contemporary European standards.[21]

But these high birth rates of the slave women were insufficient to maintain local populations because of both the disproportionate number of men in the arriving African slavers and the very high mortality rates suffered by slaves due to adult age bias of the arriving immigrants. In all American slave regimes with a heavy level of African immigrations, the sex ratio was in favor of men, and the average age of the slaves was higher than the free persons in the receiving societies. The fewer the number of women in the total population, the lower the overall crude birth rate (births per total population) becomes, no matter how high the birth rate of the slave women in childbearing ages. Although a crude birth rate in the range of 30 to 40 per 1,000 was high by contemporary European standards and close to that of the free populations in Brazil, it was insufficient to maintain the slave population. As Slenes noted, "in a population like that of Vassouras in the 1820s, where 77 percent of slaves were male, a female crude birth rate of 40/1000 would have corresponded to an overall rate of only about 18/1,000." Thus, the sexual imbalance of the slave population due to the slave trade, he concluded, is "the main reason why deaths exceeded births in the first half of the nineteenth century . . . under these circumstances, even high intrinsic fertility would result only in a moderate or low crude birth rate."[22]

Slaves equally experienced very high rates of mortality. Given the age of the arriving African migrants, which largely excluded children and youths, it was inevitable that the immigrant population would suffer a higher crude death rate due to their older age structure than native-born free or slaves. If Africans made up a sufficiently large part of the slave population, then their disproportionately higher death rates would influence total death rates. This in fact is what occurred. Of course, for the second generation of slaves, those born in America, the mortality rates for these Creole slaves more nearly approached those of the local native-born free populations. But slave death rates, even under the best of conditions, were invariably higher than those of the free populations in almost all areas.

[21] Pedro Carvalho de Mello, "The Economics of Labor in Brazilian Coffee Plantations, 1850–1888," (Ph.D. diss., University of Chicago, Department of Economics, 1977), and Robert W. Slenes, "The Demography and Economics of Brazilian Slavery, 1850–1888," (Ph.D. diss., Stanford University, Department of History, 1976), chapter 7. Also see the discussion on demography in Chapter 9.
[22] Slenes, "The Demography and Economics of Brazilian Slavery," pp. 273–4.

For this reason, it required crude birthrates in the upper 40s and lower 50s per 1,000 population to overcome crude death rates in the mid-40s per 1,000 range. By world standards, these were extremely high birth rates, but they were achieved in most slave regimes of America by the native-born or Creole slave women. The decline of the total slave population in slave colonies often masked a positive growth rate among the Creole slave contingent, and once the first-generation Africans died off and were not replaced, then it was common for local Creole slave populations to grow. This growth usually occurred if there were not too many manumissions of young females, which in fact was the group most often manumitted, and if there was no intra-American or internal slave trade that moved younger slaves out of the local population. This latter movement in fact occurred in the Brazilian Northeast, where a major internal slave trade after 1850 drained off the young males and females from the local populations of Bahia, Pernambuco, and other provinces, as well as from the far southern regions of Rio Grande do Sul and Santa Catarina. As a result, these regions continued to suffer declining total slave populations despite the high Creole slave birth rates and the dying out of their African-born populations.

If no outmigration occurred, and if manumissions were kept to a low level and favored older postreproductive slaves, then it was the case that the slave regimes of America would begin to grow once again approximately a generation after the end of the Atlantic slave trade. Although this seems to have been the rule for most of the American slave regimes, it is true that none of them approached the levels of growth attained by the slave population of the United States. As commentators have often pointed out, the United States and Brazil both began the nineteenth century with a slave population of 1 million each. Brazil imported some 2 million slaves in the nineteenth century and had a resident slave population of only 1.7 million in the late 1850s, whereas the United States imported a few hundred thousand slaves and ended up with a resident population of 4 million slaves on the eve of the Civil War. When one adds in the manumitted slaves and their offsprings, the difference declines greatly. There were just 4.4 million free and slave Afro-Americans in the United States at the time of the Civil War, whereas in Brazil at the time of the first census in 1872, these two groups together numbered 5.8 million persons. This would suggest that both societies saw their original African populations grow positively well beyond their initial slave trade numbers, though even so, the North American Afro-American population still grew at a more rapid rate.

It has often been suggested that slave treatment in the United States was different from elsewhere in America. This has been supported by comparing vital rates of the U.S. slave population with all other American slave groups. But such an argument has serious difficulties on several grounds. To begin with, the birth and death rates of the slaves everywhere in America reflected those of the free whites and free-colored population among whom they lived, and these rates differed between the free populations of different countries. The slave rates in Latin America were close to those of the free populations in their respective countries, just as those rates in the United States were close to those of the free population. The comparison is then not between slave groups across political boundaries but within each country between its slave and free populations. All the evidence to date suggests that although Brazilian slave mortality rates were higher than U.S. slave mortality rates, so too were the rates for whites in roughly the same proportion. This suggests that the argument that different treatment can be shown by just comparing slave death rates across colonial and national boundaries cannot be sustained by comparing only the slave populations. The vital rates of the entire society must be examined.

Next, if treatment was that different in any given slave regime we would expect to see different patterns of fertility among women. Because female fecundity is influenced by diet and treatment, one would expect that in "good treatment" regimes the ages of menarche and menopause would be lower in the former case and higher in the latter than in "bad treatment" regimes. But comparing the ages of West Indian women at the beginning and end of their reproductive cycles with those for U.S. slave women shows essentially little difference. Thus, treatment was not in and of itself sufficiently different in the American slave regimes to account for the differences in birth rates. Although this does not necessarily mean that treatment was equal in all areas, or that some work regimes were not more oppressive than others, or that some societies were more pro-natalist than others, it does suggest that the "treatment" question is a difficult one to answer, and that the detailed demographic reconstructions undertaken to date give no comfort to those who would readily identify their slave histories as "better" than others.

If it was not difference in potential fecundity that explains the differences in birth rates of Creole slave women between the United States and the other slave regimes, what then can be offered as an explanation? It has been suggested that it was a difference in the spacing between children rather than any differences in potential years of fecundity that distinguishes the U.S. slave regime from all others. Recent studies show that North American slave women had fewer months separating the births of their first and subsequent children than did those in Latin America and the Caribbean. Because no slave regimes practiced birth control, it was suggested that either abstinence or other factors explained these longer delays between children outside the United States. The evidence suggests that a sharply different pattern of breast-feeding accounts for most of the differences in spacing. Outside the United States, the norm was for breast-feeding to last on average two years, which was the West African norm of behavior. In the United States, the Creole slaves adopted the northern European pattern of one year of lactation. Because lactation reduces fertility, the extra year of on-demand breast-feeding helps explain the difference in the number and spacing of children.[23]

Although contemporaries and later commentators have speculated endlessly about the life expectancy of slaves, it is apparent that it was not that different from the free populations in the societies in which they lived. A favorite theme even in the nineteenth-century literature is of an average working life of seven years for a slave entering adulthood, or arriving in America. Even adding in the relatively high mortality suffered in the first months of a new disease environment by the recently arrived Africans (the so-called "seasoning" process), such a high mortality did not occur even for Africans, let alone Creole or American-born slaves. The average life expectancy of native-born Latin American slaves was in the low 20s. This contrasts with a U.S. slave life expectancy rate in the mid-30s. In both cases, the slave rates reflected local free population rates, with free Latin Americans having a lower life expectancy than did free North Americans. Moreover, the spread of years in life expectancy between nonslaves and slaves was much greater in the United States than in Brazil. Thus, the life expectancy of the U.S. population in 1870 was forty-two years for men and forty-three years for women,[24] whereas that of slaves resident in the United States in this same year was an estimated thirty-three years for both sexes, some ten to eleven years less than the

---

[23] See Herbert S. Klein and Stanley L. Engerman, "Fertility Differentials between Slaves in the United States and the British West Indies: A Note on Lactation Practices and their Implications," *The William & Mary Quarterly*, XXXV, no. 2 (April 1978), 357–74.

[24] Michael R. Haines, "The Use of Model Life Tables to Estimate Mortality for the United States in the Late Nineteenth Century," *Demography*, 16, no. 2 (May 1979), p. 307, table 7.

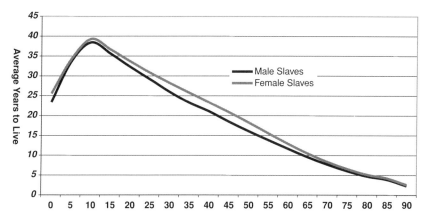

GRAPH 6.7. Estimated upper bound life expectancy of slaves (from birth and by five year cohorts). *Source:* Carvalho de Mello, "The Economics of Labor in Brazilian Coffee Plantations," p. 123.

total population.[25] In Brazil in 1872, the total population had an average life expectancy of just twenty-seven years for both sexes, which was only 3.7 years more than for male slaves in this year and just 2.3 years better than the life expectancy of female slaves.[26]

Saying that life expectancy for a male slave in Brazil was twenty-three years in this period (an upper bound estimate) does not mean that the average slave died at that age. It should be remembered that infant mortality was so high in nineteenth-century Brazil that one-third of all male children born died before the age of one, and just under half died before the age of five. For those slave male children who reached the age of one, the expectation of life was 33.6 years; for those who survived the first five years of life, the average number of years of life remaining was 38.4 years (see Graph 6.7). Thus, a male slave who survived the extremely dangerous years of infancy and early childhood stood an excellent chance

[25] Jack Ericson Eblen, "New Estimates of the Vital Rates of the United States Black Population During the Nineteenth Century," *Demography*, 11, no. 2 (May 1974), p. 609, table 6. In fact, the spread was even greater if we look only at the whites versus the slaves in the 1870s. The white rates calculated by Haines shows white men with a life expectancy at birth of 43.1 years and white women of 45.1 years. Haines, "The Use of Model Life Tables to Estimate Mortality for the United States," p. 307, table 7.

[26] Eduardo E. Arriaga, *New Life Tables for Latin American Populations in the Nineteenth and Twentieth Centuries* (Berkeley: University of California, Population Monograph Series, no. 3, 1968), table III.3, pp. 29–30; and Carvalho de Mello, "The Economics of Labor in Brazilian Coffee Plantations," table 31, p. 123.

TABLE 6.2. *Life Expectancy of Brazilian Slaves and All Brazilians at Ages 0,*
1, and 5 Years

Years of Age	Free Population	Total Population	Slave–Total Difference
0	23,4	25,5	2,2
1	33,6	34,2	0,6
5	38,4	39,3	0,9

Source: Carvalho de Mello, "The Economics of Labor in Brazilian Coffee Plantations,"
p. 123.

of reaching his 40s. For women slaves, the life expectancy was better. Only 27 percent died before the age of one and 43 percent before the age of five, which meant that life expectancy for female slaves at birth was 25.5 years, with the corresponding expectations of those who survived to one reaching 34 years and those who survived to five achieving 39 years.

Finally, the data available suggest that although slaves had a higher infant mortality rate than the total population, this difference declined significantly at ages one and five years (see Table 6.2).

Slaves who survived dysentery and other childhood diseases obviously had an average working life well over the mythical seven years. Nevertheless, it should not be forgotten that slaves were almost exclusively a working-class population and suffered more than their share from work-related accidents as well as all the infectious and dietary diseases from which the poorest elements of the population suffered.[27] Although their sanitation and housing in rural areas was probably better than the average subsistence free farm family, their food consumption was probably little better than the poorest elements of the society. Therefore, in considering their exclusive concentration in the working classes of the nation, along with their high level of work accidents and high rates of labor participation, it is no wonder that slaves suffered the worst disease and mortality rates in their individual societies. Although the general levels of disease and mortality in each individual American society may account for the different rates among the slave regimes, there is little doubt that they were at the worst levels in every society in which they lived.

---

[27] In an interesting study of fugitive slave advertisements in the leading newspaper of Rio de Janeiro in 1850, it was noted that some 40 percent of all the infirmities and diseases listed for 206 fugitives, 31 percent were work related and the majority related to conditions of poverty. Márcia Amantino, "As condições físicas e de saúde dos escravos fugitivos anunciados no Jornal do Commercio (RJ) em 1850," *História, Ciências, Saúde – Manguinhos*, 14, no. 4 (Out.–Dez. 2007), p. 1384, tabela 1.

As the Atlantic slave trade came to an end, there was still a fairly even distribution of African slaves throughout Brazil. The new coffee zones of Rio de Janeiro were growing rapidly and absorbing ever more slaves, but the northeastern sugar zones still had a fairly significant slave population, as did the far southern grazing economies. But the end of the Atlantic slave trade led to a secular rise in slave prices.[28] In turn, this made slave labor in the more marginal economies a too-costly workforce. Slowly and steadily, slaves were replaced by a free labor force, which was growing rapidly during this period. At the same time, attractive prices were now available for owners who were willing to sell their slaves, and thus there began a major internal slave trade. With some consistency, the older sugar and cattle regions began to see a steady decline in their slave labor force, while the coffee counties of the southeastern region began to expand their numbers.

Although an internal slave trade had always existed in Brazil, especially given the common reshipment of Africans arriving in the major coastal ports to smaller ports or interior countries, the post-1850 trade was far more intense.[29] Thus, even the seaborne interregional movement was not a new phenomenon in 1850, and a steady, widespread, interprovincial trade had gone on while the Atlantic slave trade was at its height. Also an important part of the internal trade, both before and after 1850, was quite local, involving the land transfer of slaves within provincial borders or between contiguous provinces, as recent studies have suggested.

---

[28] For an analysis of slave prices in the nineteenth century, see Katia M. de Queirós Mattoso, Herbert S. Klein, and Stanley L. Engerman, "Trends and Patterns in the Prices of Manumitted Slaves: Bahia, 1819–1888," *Slavery & Abolition*, 7, no. 1 (May 1986), pp. 59–67. A Portuguese version was published in João José Reis, ed., *Escravidão e invenção da liberdade: Estudos sobre o negro no Brasil* (São Paulo: Editora Brasiliense, 1988), pp. 60–72. The most recent collection and analysis of these prices is found in Bergad, *Slavery and the Demographic and Economic History of Minas Gerais*.

[29] Although there were significant fluctuations over time, by the early nineteenth century it has been estimated that only 13,168 African slaves (*novos*) were brought into Minas Gerais by coastal traders in the period from 1800–1830, along with some 561 Creole slaves (*ladinos*). Cristiano Corte Restitutti, "A circulação entre o Rio de Janeiro e o Sul de Minas Gerais, c. 1800–1830," *XVI Encontro Nacional de Estudos Populacionais, ABEP* (2008), tabela 8, p. 12. This would give an annual rate of 458 slaves, clearly far less than was the norm in the early eighteenth century, or the rates noted for the post-1850 period. In the case of Porto Alegre in Rio Grande do Sul, aside from direct African arrivals, the port has received transshipped from Rio de Janeiro some 6,958 slaves from 1809 to 1824, for an average of 435 slaves per annum. Gabriel Santos Berute, "A concentração do comércio de escravos na capitania do Rio Grande de São Pedro do Sul, c. 1790–c. 1825," *II Encontro "Escravidão e Liberdade no Brasil Meridional"* (2005), tabela 1, coluna B, p. 6.

As expected, the slaves being sold in the local markets of São Paulo in the 1860s to the 1880s were primarily of the ages fifteen to twenty-four; and in most cases males predominated, although in some markets almost as many young women were sold as young men.[30] The majority of slaves being sold in individual *municípios* came from other regions of the province, and only a minority came from northern provinces of the empire, with the majority of these northern slaves coming in the 1876–1880 period. It has been suggested that an agricultural crisis in the northeastern region in 1877–1879 was an especially active period, with specialized traders purchasing local slaves for sale outside the province.[31] Moreover, it appears that prices of slaves in the Northeast were considerably below that of prices in the southeastern region, which made such a trade profitable.[32] Nevertheless, the general sense of all these sales of slaves in local markets is that local, regional, and intraprovincial sales were more important than interprovincial ones, even in the period prior to the early 1880s.[33]

[30] José Flávio Motta, "O tráfico de escravos na Província de São Paulo: Areias, Silveiras, Guaratinguetá e Casa Branca, 1861–1887," *Anais VII Encontro Nacional de Economia Política* (Curitiba, 2002), pp. 3–5; and the same pattern was found for the 1870s in Guaratingetá in the 1870s, although in this case with a more balanced sex ratio. José Flávio Motta and Renato Leite Marcondes, "O Comércio de Escravos no Vale do Paraíba Paulista: Guaratinguetá e Silveiras na Década de 1870," *Estudos Econômicos*, 30, no. 2 (Abril–Junho 2000), table 2, p. 272.

[31] See Erivaldo Fagundes Neves, "Sampauleiros traficantes: Comércio de escravos do Alto Sertão da Bahia para o Oeste cafeeiro paulista," *Afro-Ásia*, no. 24 (2000), pp. 97–128.

[32] It would appear that on average, prices in Rio Claro São Paulo for young adult males age 15–29 were double the price paid in the same year for these young male slaves in Bahia. Neves, "Sampauleiros traficantes," tabela 5, p. 111.

[33] This is a finding encountered for all years in a whole range of *municípios* throughout São Paulo; see Motta, "O tráfico de escravos na Província de São Paulo," p. 7; José Flávio Motta, "Derradeiras transações: O comércio de escravos nos anos de 1880 (Areias, Piracicaba e Casa Branca, Província de São Paulo)," *Anais do XII Encontro Nacional de Economia Política* (São Paulo, 2007), graph 1, p. 8; in Piracicaba, he found that only 12 percent of the slaves sold whose origins were known, were from outside the province in the 1860s. In the district of Constituição between 1861–1869, interprovincial slaves accounted for a high 38 percent of local slaves; moreover, the interprovincial sales were far more male than were sales sold from any other area. José Flávio Motta, "Escravos daqui, dali e de mais além: O tráfico interno de cativos em Constituição (Piracicaba), 1861–1880," *Anais do XXXIII Encontro Nacional de Economia ANPEC* (2005), pp. 5–6, tabelas 3–4. The same findings were also noted in studies on the province of Minas Gerais. In Juiz da Fora, only 23 percent of slaves purchased in the local market in the late 1860s and early 1880s were of interprovincial origin, and here too males (who made up more than two-thirds of these interprovincial slaves) predominated, more so than any other origin group. Cláudio Heleno Machado, "O tráfico interno de escravos na região de Juiz de Fora na segunda metade do século XIX," *X Seminário de Economia Mineira*

Although the slave trade from northern ports still had some elements of an intraregional trade as it had existed in the pre-1850 period, these ports now were primarily shipping local and regional slaves to the south-central ports supplying the coffee zones of Brazil. The same was occurring in this period in the far southern ports of the empire as well. The principal destinations for these coastal traders were Rio de Janeiro and Santos, the former being the more important. In 1852, for example, Rio de Janeiro was reported to have imported more than 4,400 slaves, and its average per annum importation for the years 1852–1859 was estimated at 3,327.[34] Although no figures are available this early for Santos, its annual importation of slaves more than a decade later was in the 1,000 to 2,000 range. Thus in 1867, 904 slaves were imported, 1,229 arrived in 1868, and 2,129 in 1869.[35] Considering that these were the primary ports of

(2002), table 5, p. 17. In Mariana, the majority of slaves, both male and female, were young – the modal age being twenty to twenty-four years and only a minority were brought through the interprovincial trade; see Camila Carolina Flausino, "Negócios da escravidão: Tráfico interno de escravos em Mariana: 1861–1886" (Dissertação de mestrado em História, Universidade Federal de Juiz de Fora, 2006), tables 14 and 15, pp. 82, 87. The only scholar to date who has found very significant numbers of interprovincial slaves was Robert Slenes in his study of the Campinas Market from 1865–1879. Of some 2,684 slaves sold in the Campinas market, 68 percent came from outside São Paulo and the southeastern region in general. Slenes, "The Demography and Economics of Brazilian Slavery," table 3.3, p. 136.

34 One contemporary source reported that 26,622 slaves were imported into Rio de Janeiro between 1852–1859, which would give an annual average of 3,327 slaves. This source stated that slave imports into Rio de Janeiro were as follows:

Year	Slaves	Year	Slaves
1852	4,409	1856	5,006
1853	2,090	1857	4,211
1854	4,418	1858	1,993
1855	3,532	1859	963

Sebastão Ferreira Soares, *Notas estatisticas sobre a producão agrícola e carestia dos gêneros alimentícios no Império do Brazil* (Rio de Janeiro: J. Villeneuve, 1860), p. 1351. The British Minister to Rio de Janeiro, W. D. Christie, reported that "34,688 slaves had been imported at Rio by sea in ten years and a half, from January 1, 1852, to July 1, 1862," which would give a rate of 275 per month or 3,300 per annum. He then went on to estimate that with slaves brought by land from other regions, the estimate was 5,000 arrivals per annum in this internal slave trade. W. D. Christie, *Notes on Brazilian Questions* (London: Macmillan, 1865), p. 93.

35 For the respective importation figures, see Joaquim Saldanha Marinho, *Relatório apresentado a Assembléia Legislativa provincial de São Paulo . . . no dia 2 de fevereiro de 1868 pelo presidente da mesma província. . . .* (São Paulo: Typ. do Ypiranga, 1868), p. 15; *Relatório com que sua excelência o sr. senador Barão de Itaúna passou a administração da província ao exmo. sr. comendador Antônio Joaquim da Rosa* (São

entry for slaves transported by sea, importation may have reached as high as 5,000 to 6,000 per annum in these two decades. One contemporary Brazilian authority, in fact, estimated in 1860 that in the 1850s, some 5,500 slaves were annually being exported to the central states from the North alone.[36] Eventually, the drain on the local labor force led the "exporting" states to tax the trade in order to slow its volume, and they and the imperial government eventually killed the trade as an important source of slaves by the early 1880s.[37]

Nevertheless, even when this interprovincial movement was functioning, the overwhelming majority of the Creole slaves in the major importing provinces (Rio de Janeiro and São Paulo) of the southeastern region were born in the province in which they resided, as can be seen in the census of 1872 (see Table 6.3). This was even more the case for the exporting states of the northeast and far south and the exceptional province of Minas Gerais, whose slave population was probably growing through births of resident Creole slaves. There is only a moderate difference between men and women in terms of their birth outside their province of residence, and even for the state of São Paulo, only 10 percent of the men came from the northeastern states and only 7 percent of the women were born there. In both cases, Bahia was the most important state of origin, followed by slaves coming from Minas Gerais, and finally, by this time, African-born slaves represented just 8 percent of the slave population. In this latter case, Rio de Janeiro had more diversity compared to the other two importing provinces, because a very high 19 percent of its slave

Paulo: Typ. Americana, 1869), Annexo no. 1, Mapa no. 7; and Antonio Candido da Rocha, *Relatório apresentado à Assembléia Legislativa provincial de São Paulo pelo presidente da província*... (São Paulo: Typ. Americana, 1870), pp. 65–6. It should also be noted that slaves were exported from this same port and that the net gain for the port was 580 slaves in 1867, 780 in 1868, and 1,746 in 1869.

36 Ferreira Soares, *Notas estatísticas*, pp. 135–6. It should be noted here as well that whereas southern ports such as Santos exported as well as imported slaves, northern ports such as Salvador da Bahia also imported as well as exported. Thus, in 1855, Bahia exported 1,699 slaves and imported 471 for a net loss of 1,228. In 1856, its net loss was 1,794, with 2,388 slaves exported to other ports of the empire and 594 imported. Álvaro Tibério de Moncorvo Lima, *Falla recitada na abertura da Assembléia Legislativa da Bahia*.... (Bahia: Typ. de Antonio Olavo da França Guerra, 1856), mapa n. 48; João Lins Vieira Cansanção de Sinimbu, *Falla recitada na abertura da Assembléia Legislativa da Bahia*.... (Bahia: Typ. de Antonio Olavo da França Guerra, 1857), mapa n. 24.

37 As early as 1862, Bahia passed an export tax of 200 milréis on every slave exported from the state. Other states soon followed, and the internal interprovincial trade was definitively terminated by imperial decree in 1885 as part of the Sexagenário freedom act. Neves, "Sampauleiros traficantes," pp. 107–8.

TABLE 6.3. *Ratio of Native-Born Slaves by Birth and Current Residence by Province in 1872 (for persons whose birthplace were known)*

Province of Residence	Percentage Born in the State Province of Residence		Total Number Native-Born Slaves			Total of African-Born Slaves	Percentage of all Slaves African Born
	Men	Women	Men	Women	Total		
Minas Gerais	97%	98%	182,501	160,013	342,514	27,945	8%
Rio de Janeiro	94%	93%	109,498	126,875	236,373	56,261	19%
São Paulo	83%	86%	79,607	63,931	143,538	13,061	8%
Bahia	98%	99%	83,186	74,357	157,543	10,281	6%
Pernambuco	97%	97%	45,236	40,709	85,945	3,134	4%
Rio Grande do Sul	96%	96%	32,391	30,296	62,687	5,333	8%

Source: Data generated from CEBRAP, 1872, Quadros de Provincia, quadros 4, 5, and 6.

population was African born, a ratio not found in the other provinces studied here.[38] There is some debate in the literature about whether the end of the slave trade pushed planters toward encouraging births and marriages among slaves, or if the opposite was the case.[39] To date, there seems to be little evidence to suggest that planters themselves were more or less pro-natalist before and after 1850, and recent studies on the positive natural growth rates in Paraná and in Minas Gerais before 1850 would suggest that there was no inherent bias among slave owners against procreation of slave children and/or slave unions and marriages.[40]

Finally, the growth of the slave population was influenced not only by deaths and births and by international and interprovincial migrations, but also by the rate of manumission – or slaves leaving this status to become free. The age and sex of the manumitted slaves are now well understood from numerous manumission studies. Historians have systematically built on the pioneering work of Stuart Schwartz and Katia Mattoso that was done for Bahia. Not only has more work been done with Bahia, but we now have manumission studies for just about every region of Brazil. In fact, the analysis of these *cartas de alforria* now provides a far better national coverage than for any other single quantitative aspect of slave analysis.[41] Moreover, although there are some variations from urban and

---

[38] In total, there were some 177,000 Africans in Brazil listed in the census of 1872, of whom 22 percent (or 38,000) were free persons.

[39] For the former position, see Manolo Florentino and Cacilda Machado, "Sobre a família escrava em plantéis ausentes do mercado de cativos: Três estudos de casos (século 19)," *XI Encontro Nacional de Estudos Populacionais da ABEP* (1998), especially p. 1381. This is also the position of Gorender, who suggests that a pro-natalist attitude of slave owners could only develop after the end of the slave trade; see Jacob Gorender, *O escravismo colonial* (4th ed. rev.; São Paulo: Editora Ática, 1985), pp. 343ff. Slenes takes the opposite view, suggesting far less interest in slave fecundity and slave marriage in all the plantation areas of the Southeast after 1850; see Robert W. Slenes, *Na senzala, uma flor: Esperanças e recordações na formação da família escrava: Brasil Sudeste, século XIX* (Rio de Janeiro: Editora Nova Fronteira, 1999), p. 92. For an argument showing strong marriage ties from the earliest times, see Tarcísio Rodrigues Botelho, "Família e escravidão em uma perspectiva demográfica: Minas Gerais (Brasil), século XVIII," in Douglas Cole Libby and Júnia Ferreira Furtado, eds., *Trabalho livre, trabalho escravo, Brasil e Europa, séculos XVIII e XIX* (São Paulo: Annablume, 2006), pp. 195–222.

[40] As Carvalho de Mello has pointed out, the effect of the slave trade closure on fertility was probably minimal; because "the response of demographic behavior to changes in the economic conditions is a long-run process, it takes some time to begin and more for the effects to be significantly observed." Carvalho de Mello, "The Economics of Labor in Brazilian Coffee Plantations," p. 120.

[41] In his survey of six earlier studies of manumission in the colonial Latin American world, including Brazil, Johnson found that women predominated in all these manumission lists,

rural areas and from northeastern to southeastern regions, all studies have shown the same patterns of women and the young being overrepresented among the manumitted, that voluntary grants of manumission – both free or unhindered manumissions and onerous ones that required some postliberation obligations – were the most significant, but that self-purchase always made up a significant share of manumissions in almost all regions. There have even been some interesting attempts to relate manumission patterns to *plantel* size, and one study has shown that the smaller the slaveholding, the higher the rates of manumission.[42] It would appear that Africans and adults were more representative among the self-purchasing group than they were among the voluntary manumissions. All

and that self-purchase usually involved half the freedom acts; see Lyman L. Johnson, "Manumission in Colonial Buenos Aires, 1776–1810," *Hispanic American Historical Review*, 59, no. 2 (May 1979), p. 262, table 1. This also holds true for all the latest studies done on Brazil. See, among others, Kathleen J. Higgins, "Gender and the Manumission of Slaves in Colonial Brazil: The Prospects for Freedom in Sabará, Minas Gerais, 1710–1809," *Slavery & Abolition*, 18, no. 2 (1997); Mieko Nishida, "Manumission and Ethnicity in Urban Slavery: Salvador, Brazil 1808–1888," *Hispanic American Historical Review*, 73, no. 3 (August 1993); and Marcus J. M. de Carvalho, *Liberdade, rotinas e rupturas do escravismo, Recife, 1822–1850* (Recife: Ed. Univesitária UFPE, 1998), chapter 10. See also the older studies of Katia M. de Queirós Mattoso, "A propósito de cartas de alforria: Bahia, 1779–1850," *Anais de História*, 4 (1972), and her "A Carta de alforria como fonte complementar para o estudo de rentabilidade de mão de obra escrava urbana, 1819–1888," in Carlos Manuel Pelaez and Mircea Buescu, eds., *A moderna história econômica* (Rio de Janeiro: APE, 1976); and Stuart B. Schwartz, "The Manumission of Slaves in Colonial Brazil: Bahia, 1684–1745," *Hispanic American Historical Review*, 54, no. 4 (1974); Peter L. Eisenberg, "Ficando livre: As alforrias em Campinas no século XIX," *Estudos Econômicos*, 17, no. 2 (1987); Mary C. Karasch, *Slave Life in Rio de Janeiro, 1808–1850* (Princeton: Princeton University Press, 1987), chapter 11; and Douglas Cole Libby and Clotilde Andrade Paiva, "Manumission Practices in a Late Eighteenth-Century Brazilian Slave Parish: São José d'El Rey in 1795," *Slavery & Abolition*, 21, no. 1 (2000); Francisco Vidal Luna and Iraci del Nero da Costa, "A presença do elemento forro no conjunto dos proprietários de escravos" *Ciência e Cultura* (São Paulo: SBPC), 32, no. 7 (Julho 1980), pp. 838–41.

[42] Newer manumission studies evaluating the relative importance of the three types of voluntary and self-purchase arrangements include Manolo Florentino and José Roberto Góes, "Do que Nabuco já sabia: Mobilidade e miscigenação racial no Brasil escravista" (Congresso Internacional Brasil-Portugal Ano 2000 – Sessão de História, 2000); Antônio Henrique Duarte Lacerda, "Economia cafeeira, crescimento populacionale manumissões onerosas e gratuitas condicionais em Juiz de Fora na segunda metade do século XIX," *X Seminário sobre a Economia Mineira* (2002); and the previous cited study of Nishida on manumissions in Salvador. Unfortunately, some local scholars lump both self-purchase and post-manumission personal service as "onerous" manumissions, without distinguishing the two. This was the problem with the otherwise excellent local study of Adriano Bernardo Moraes Lima, "Trajetórias de Crioulos: Um estudo das relações comunitárias de escravos e forros no têrmo da Vila de Curitiba (c. 1760–c. 1830) (Dissertação de mestrado, UFP, Curitiba, 2001), tables 10–13, even though she

of these themes will be more completely examined in Chapter 9, but it is worth stressing here that manumission rates in nineteenth-century Brazil were extremely high by American standards and represented a steady outmigration of slaves in their fertile years.

Without question, the fastest growing part of the Brazilian population was the free colored. With young women of childbearing ages as the prime group being manumitted, it was inevitable that an important part of the growth of this class was due to migration from slave status. But given the poor quality of census materials prior to 1872, it is difficult to precisely measure the two different factors influencing free-colored growth – that is, natural growth due to births exceeding deaths and migration of manumitted slaves. Taking just a few approximate measures, one can roughly estimate the relative influence of these two factors in the growth of the free-colored population. For example, the province of Rio de Janeiro – excluding the imperial court at the city of Rio – had a free-colored population of 64,592 in 1840 and this grew to 178,960 in 1872, for a per annum growth rate of 3.2 percent. In neighboring Minas Gerais, the free-colored population also grew at 3.0 percent per annum between 1814 and 1872, as it did in Pernambuco between 1829 and 1872. São Paulo, which had one of the slower rates of growth, saw its free-colored population grow at 2.4 percent per annum between 1811 and 1872. Even the slowest growing of these populations, those of the free colored for the provinces of the far South and the West, all had rates of 2.0 percent per annum or greater (see Table 6.4). These growth rates were not achieved in most world populations until after the systematic decline of mortality – the so-called demographic transition – an event that did not occur in Brazil until the twentieth century. For this population, a very high contemporary rate of natural growth would have been 1 to 1.5 percent per annum.[43] Thus, at a minimum, half the growth of the free-colored population was probably due to the steady arrival of manumitted slaves and only half to natural rates of increase. While systematic data are

___

shows that 46 percent of the 105 emancipated slaves were listed with a family relationship, which presumably meant that some of these slaves had their freedom purchased by third parties.

[43] The growth rates of thirteen major western European countries from 1820–1870 was 0.72 percent per annum and rose to just 0.99 percent in the 1870–1913 period. At the same time, Portugal's rate was 0.56 percent and rose to 0.75 percent in the second period. Angus Maddison, *The World Economy: A Millennial Perspective* (Paris: Development Centre of the Organisation for Economic Co-operation and Development, 2001), p. 242, table B-11. On the demographic transition, see Jean-Claude Chesnair, *The Demographic Transition, 1720–1984* (Oxford: Clarendon Press, 1992).

TABLE 6.4. Slave and Free Populations in Nineteenth-Century Brazil by Color and Condition by Province, 1800–1872

Province	Year	Free Persons							Slaves
		Whites	Indians	Caboclos	Pardos	Pretos	Total Free Colored	Total Free	
Amazonas	1819							13,310	6,040
	1840	3,454	23,339	10,871	1,980		1,980	39,644	940
	1855							40,907	912
	1859							42,945	968
	1860							45,161	1,026
	1872	11,211	0	36,828	7,256	1,336	8,592	56,631	979
Pará	1819							90,901	33,000
	1849							142,811	36,896
	1872	92,634	0	44,589	93,727	16,829	110,556	247,779	27,458
Maranhão	1804	23,223	0	0	10,534	2,792	13,326	36,549	37,645
	1819							66,666	74,939
	1872	103,513	0	10,943	144,361	25,284	169,645	284,101	133,334
Piauí	1819							48,321	12,405
	1826							59,734	25,113
	1854							136,033	16,858
	1866							152,766	19,204
	1870							147,954	19,836
	1872							178,427	23,795
Ceará	1819	43,447	0	13,453	106,665	14,862	121,527	145,731	55,439
	1860							468,318	35,441
	1873	268,836	0	52,837	339,166	28,934	368,100	689,773	31,913

(continued)

TABLE 6.4 (continued)

Province	Year	Free Persons							Slaves
		Whites	Indians	Caboclos	Pardos	Pretos	Total Free Colored	Total Free	
R. G. do Norte	1819	27,638	3,103	0	33,326	6,274	39,600	61,812	9,109
	1839	48,157	6,785	0	64,770	11,207	75,977	70,341	10,189
	1845	102,465	0	11,039	84,090	23,365	107,455	130,919	18,153
	1872							220,959	13,020
Paraíba	1798	12,328	2,817	0	12,876	2,976	15,852	30,997	8,897
	1804	16,012	0	0	9,331	2,595	11,926	27,938	5,926
	1811	45,208	3,405	0	47,735	8,426	56,161	104,774	17,633
	1819							79,725	16,723
	1852							183,920	28,546
	1872	144,721	0	9,567	178,596	21,816	200,412	354,700	21,526
Pernambuco	1819							270,832	77,633
	1839	90,291	2,094	0	105,141	21,672	126,813	219,198	68,458
	1872	291,159	0	11,805	387,851	61,696	449,547	752,511	89,028
Alagoas	1819							42,879	69,094
	1847	56,199	6,733	0	92,236	12,451	104,687	167,619	39,675
	1849	56,797	6,603	0	92,134	12,442	104,576	167,976	39,790
	1855							220,104	48,123
	1857							205,269	44,418
	1870							278,194	49,336
	1872	88,798	0	6,364	200,199	16,907	217,106	312,268	35,741
Sergipe	1819							88,783	26,213
	1849	43,542	1,485	0	75,313	17,403	92,716	137,743	n.g.
	1851							166,426	56,564
	1872	49,778	0	3,087	81,583	19,172	100,755	153,620	22,623

Province	Year								
Bahia	1819							330,649	147,263
	1870							957,206	179,561
	1872	331,479	0	49,882	565,704	264,727	830,431	1,211,792	167,824
Minas Gerais	1808	106,684	0	0	129,656	47,937	177,593	284,277	148,772
	1819							463,342	168,543
	1872	830,987	0	32,322	598,813	207,154	805,967	1,669,276	370,459
Esp. Santo	1819							52,573	20,272
	1839	6,730	3,518	0	5,832	767	6,599	16,847	9,233
	1848	9,994	6,732	0	9,113	2,613	11,726	28,452	n.g.
	1856	14,311	6,051	0	13,825	2,626	16,451	36,813	12,269
	1870							37,127	15,804
	1872	26,582	0	5,529	20,529	6,838	27,367	59,478	22,659
Rio de Janeiro	1821							104,676	119,688
	1840	112,973	5,615	0	51,205	13,387	64,592	183,180	224,012
	1844	122,152	5,055	0	54,488	15,231	69,719	196,926	239,557
	1850	160,945	4,952	0	77,193	19,436	96,629	262,526	293,554
	1872	303,275	0	7,852	121,245	57,715	178,960	490,087	292,637
Corte	1799	19,578	0	0	4,227	4,585	8,812	28,390	14,986
	1821							57,605	55,090
	1838							78,525	58,553
	1848							155,864	110,602
São Paulo	1872	151,799	0	923	44,845	28,466	73,311	226,033	48,939
	1800	95,349	0	0	28,947	3,139	32,086	127,435	42,109
	1803	97,335	0	0	43,864	3,049	46,913	144,248	44,131
	1804	97,470	0	0	40,154	3,326	43,480	140,950	43,874
	1811	112,965	0	0	44,053	3,951	48,004	160,969	48,150
	1815	115,203	0	0	44,289	4,966	49,255	164,458	51,272
	1819							160,656	77,667

(continued)

TABLE 6.4 (continued)

Province	Year	Whites	Indians	Caboclos	Pardos	Pretos	Total Free Colored	Total Free	Slaves
						Free Persons			
	1822	127,888	o	o	48,860	3,960	52,820	180,708	63,697
	1824	131,330	o	o	46,299	5,269	51,568	182,898	65,006
	1836	172,879	o	o	59,454	6,811	66,265	239,144	86,933
	1854							299,418	117,731
	1872	433,432	o	39,465	151,306	56,539	207,845	680,742	156,612
Paraná	1811	18,340	o	o	8,831	929	9,760	28,100	6,840
	1819							49,251	10,191
	1836	23,895	85	o	10,135	902	11,037	35,017	7,873
	1854	33,633			n.g.	n.g.	13,030	52,069	10,189
	1866							87,491	11,596
	1872	69,698	o	9,087	30,636	6,741	37,377	116,162	10,560
Sta. Catarina	1810	23,680			n.g.	n.g.	651	24,331	7,203
	1811	23,753			n.g.	n.g.	580	24,333	7,417
	1813	24,806			n.g.	n.g.	665	25,471	7,478
	1819							34,859	9,172
	1828	37,470	839	o	969	646	1,615	39,924	12,256
	1829	38,134	855	o	1,053	721	1,774	40,763	12,620
	1833	42,017	175	o	1,872	1,021	2,893	45,085	12,657
	1836	45,065	163	o	2,070	1,092	3,162	48,390	13,019
	1838	45,596	136	o	2,375	1,861	4,236	49,968	13,658
	1841							54,638	12,580
	1844							58,432	14,382
	1849							60,743	13,942
	1852							72,391	15,057

Region	Year								
	1854							87,364	14,195
	1855							88,485	17,119
	1856							92,922	18,187
	1857							104,425	18,408
	1859							98,281	16,316
	1867							104,459	14,722
	1872	125,942	0	2,892	11,737	4,247	15,984	144,818	14,984
R. G. do Sul	1807	37,107	1,008	0	1,688	1,070	2,758	40,873	13,469
	1809	30,622	8,655		n.g.	n.g.	4,217	34,839	14,629
	1814	32,300			n.g.	n.g.	5,399	46,354	20,611
	1819							63,927	28,253
	1846							118,171	31,192
	1857							211,667	70,880
	1860							235,727	73,749
	1861							268,506	75,721
	1862							315,306	77,419
	1872	258,367	0	25,717	48,666	34,272	82,938	367,022	67,791
Goiás	1804	6,950	0	0	15,452	7,936	23,388	30,338	20,027
	1819							36,368	26,800
	1832	11,761	994	0	32,711	9,770	42,481	55,236	13,261
	1848							68,383	10,956
	1856							106,998	12,054
	1857							109,659	12,934
	1872	41,929	0	4,250	86,389	17,175	103,564	149,743	10,652
Mato Grosso	1800	4,242	1,015	0	6,348	3,321	9,669	14,926	11,910
	1815	5,813	0	0	7,908	2,656	10,564	16,377	11,985
	1817							18,853	10,948

(continued)

TABLE 6.4 (continued)

Province	Year	Whites	Indians	Caboclos	Pardos	Pretos	Total Free Colored	Total Free	Slaves
						Free Persons			
	1819			0	12,311	3,221	15,532	23,216	14,180
	1828	4,278	2,733					22,543	10,122
	1849							43,672	10,886
	1872	17,237	0	8,524	20,914	7,075	27,989	53,750	6,667
Empire	1872	3,787,289	0	386,955	3,324,278	921,150	4,245,428	8,419,672	1,510,806

Sources: Paraíba, 1798: IHGB/CU, Arq. 1–1–13, fols. 148v–149; 1804, fol. 204. São Paulo, 1800: ANRJ, cod. 808, IV, fol. 255; 1803: fol. 256; 1822: fol. 262; 1811, 1815, and 1826: Roger Bastide and Florestan Fernandes, *Brancos e negros em São Paulo* (São Paulo, 1959), p. 26. Maranhão, 1798: IHGB/CU, Arq. 1–1–6, fol. 92. Santa Catarina, 1811: ANRJ, cod. 808, 111, fol. 75; 1828, fol. 93; 1831: fol. 84; 1838: fol. 86; 1860: Cardoso and Ianni, *Côr e mobilidade social*, p. 86. Rio Grande do Sul, 1807: ANRJ, cod. 808, 111, fol. 147. Mato Grosso, 1797: *Revista do Instituto Histórico e Geográfico Brasileiro* (Rio de Janeiro), XX (1857), 281; 1815: p. 292; 1828: ANRJ, cod. 808, 111, fols. 38–9. Minas Gerais, 1814: ANRJ, cod. 808, 1, fols. 130–2. Espírito Santo, 1839: ANRJ, cod. 808, I, fol. 35. Goiás, 1824: Auguste de Saint-Hilaire, *Viagem às nascentes do Rio S. Francisco e pela província de Goyaz* (São Paulo, 1937). I, 296–7; 1832: ANRJ, cod. 808, I, fol. 96. Rio de Janeiro, 1844: ANRJ, cod. 808, 11, £01, 62. Paraná, 1854: Octávio Ianni, *As metamorfoses do escravo, apogeu e crise da escravatura no Brasil Meridional* (São Paulo, 1962), p. 104. City of Bahia, 1775: IHGB/CU, Arq. 1–1–9, fol. 230. Brazil, 1872: Directoria Geral de Estatística, *Recenseamento da população do Império do Brazil a que se procedeu no dia 1 de agosto de 1872* (21 vols.; Rio de Janeiro, 1872–6). All other census data from Joaquim Norberto de Souza e Silva, *Investigações sobre os recenseamentos da população geral do Império e de cada província de per si tentados desde os tempos coloniais até hoje* (1st ed., 1870; São Paulo: IPE-USP, 1986).

TABLE 6.5. *Decline of the Slave Population, 1872–1885*

Region/Province	1872	1874	1887	Average Annual Growth Rate	
				1872–1887	1874–1885
NORTH					
Amazonas	979	n.g.	1,183	1.3%	
Pará	27,458	19,729	10,535	−6.2%	−4.7%
Maranhão	74,939	74,939	33,446	−5.2%	−6.0%
NORTHEAST					
Piauí	23,795	25,483	8,970	−6.3%	−7.7%
Ceará	31,913	33,960	108	−31.6%	−35.7%
R. G. do Norte	13,020	13,484	3,167	−9.0%	−10.5%
Paraíba	21,526	26,025	9,448	−5.3%	−7.5%
Pernambuco	89,028	92,855	41,122	−5.0%	−6.1%
Alagoas	35,741	33,242	15,269	−5.5%	−5.8%
Sergipe	22,623	32,974	16,875	−1.9%	−5.0%
Bahia	167,824	n.g.	76,838	−5.1%	
CENTER-SOUTH					
Esp. Santo	22,659	22,738	13,381	−3.5%	−4.0%
Corte	48,939	47,260	7,488	−11.8%	−13.2%
Rio de Janeiro	292,637	304,744	162,421	−3.8%	−4.7%
Minas Gerais	370,459	n.g.	191,952	−4.3%	
São Paulo	156,612	169,964	107,085	−2.5%	−3.5%
WEST					
Goiás	10,652	10,510	4,955	−5.0%	−5.6%
Mato Grosso	6,667	7,064	3,233	−4.7%	−5.8%
SOUTH					
R. G. do Sul	67,791	10,715	3,513	−17.9%	−8.2%
Santa Catarina	14,984	10,551	4,927	−7.1%	−5.7%
Paraná	10,560	83,370	8,442	−1.5%	−16.2%
Brasil	1,510,806	1,019,607	724,358	−4.8%	

Sources: Slenes, "The Demography and Economics of Brazilian Slavery," tables B-6, B-7, and table 6.3.

difficult to obtain, one estimate suggested an overall manumission rate in the 1870s of 8.5 percent for all slaves reaching ten years of age.[44]

Had this outmigration of manumitted slaves been retained by the slave population, it is possible that the slave population after 1850 might have

---

[44] Slenes, using the *matrículas* of 1873 and 1875, has estimated an average crude manumission rate of 6.3/1,000, a figure that compares to 0.45/1,000 for the United States in the 1850s. Controlling for mortality, he estimated that any slave reaching ten years of age had a 5.1 percent change of being manumitted by age forty, and for age sixty, the overall rate was 8.4 percent. Slenes, "The Demography and Economics of Brazilian Slavery," pp. 488–93.

retained its numbers or even experienced a positive rate of growth. However, the reality was that there was a steady decline of the slave population from 1850 onward. In every province the number of slaves declined, and only in selected coffee-exporting *municípios* did their numbers remain the same or expand in this period. By the *matrícula* (census) of 1887, after the law of free womb and the sexagenarian law were passed, the total slave population had dropped to half of the 1872 figure and was declining at a rate of 4.8 percent per annum (see Table 6.5). In fact, as Carvalho de Mello has shown, prices began to reflect the declining expectation of slave owners in the survival of slavery. By 1881, prices still suggested that slavery might continue until the early twentieth century, and even in 1886, prices indicated an expectation of five more years of slavery. Only in 1887 had they declined to the point where the expectation was that it would survive only one more year.[45] Had what Carvalho de Mello calls "strong abolitionism" not occurred, it is evident that slavery – which was still profitable in the 1880s – could have continued with the post-1850 population for a very long time.[46]

[45] Carvalho de Mello, "The Economics of Labor in Brazilian Coffee Plantations," p. 209, table 41.
[46] Carvalho de Mello, "The Economics of Labor in Brazilian Coffee Plantations," chapter 5.

7

Slave Resistance and Rebellion

The growth of a sense of identity and community among Afro-Brazilian slaves was essential for their survival as a society and group. Families were established, children were educated, and beliefs were developed that gave legitimacy to their lives. Yet much of their lives were controlled by others. Their labor was defined by others and was not typically organized by households, as in the case of all other working-class persons. Even their social behavior was restricted by whites when it clashed with the needs for control or the norms of behavior found acceptable by whites. Physical violence was also inherent in chattel slavery and created a level of fear and uncertainty unmatched by any other form of class or labor relations in America. Finally, even the physical well-being of the slave and his or her family was at the whim of his or her master and could be affected by considerations outside the slave's control.

Thus, no matter how adjusted their culture and community might make them feel toward the Brazilian society in which they found themselves, slaves always felt a degree of dependency and loss of control that created basic uncertainty and hostility toward the whole system. For those who were unable to conform, incapable of restraining their individuality, or unlucky enough to find themselves with no autonomy or protection within the system, resistance, escape, and rebellion were the only viable alternatives. For others, violence against themselves or others, even of their own low status, was also an outlet for the frustrations generated by their slave experience.

Like most slave regimes in Latin America and the Caribbean, the Portuguese and Brazilian governments attempted to provide some protection for the slaves. This essential support for the humanity of the slave evolved from a set of medieval laws that were influenced by earlier Roman legal precepts. In these earlier codes, slavery was recognized as an institution that was "against natural reason," as the thirteenth-century *Siete Partidas* codes declared (Partida IV, Titulo XXI, ley I),[1] ". . . because man, who is the most noble and free creature, among all creations that God made, is placed by it in the power of another. . ." (Partida IV, Titulo V).[2] This of course did not mean that the state would not legitimate any contract of sale or ownership of slaves. It did mean that, while recognizing slavery as a necessary and historic institution, it also held that it was incumbent upon the state and its judicial institutions to guarantee certain minimal rights to the slave.

Of the three basic rights recognized in Roman law as defining a human being, that which related to personal liberty was automatically sacrificed under slavery. But the other primary rights, those involving one's security and property, need not be sacrificed for slavery to exist. A host of secondary rights also could be accepted that did not interfere with the definition of slaves as chattel; some of these held slaves accountable for their voluntary actions as human beings, whereas others guaranteed them the rights of the sacraments as Christians.

In terms of protection for personal security, the thirteenth-century *Partidas* of Alfonso X of Castile, the slave laws in the *Ordenações Manuelinas* of Portugal of the early sixteenth century, and the nineteenth-century Brazilian imperial codes provided that killing of slaves by their masters or anyone else was a crime punishable by death.[3] Although very few masters were actually executed for this crime in Brazil,[4] there were a number of cases of masters being exiled or paying major fines for such acts, and almost all killing of slaves led to formal judicial investigations, even in cases of suicide. But as Silvia Lara has pointed out, there was a delicate balance between moderate punishment and violent treatment by masters. All the laws and the society in general recognized that excessive punishment had to be controlled, if only for reasons of self-preservation

---

[1] *Los Siete Partidas del rey Alfonso el sabio, cotejadas con varios codices antiguos, por la Real Academia de la Historia* (3 vols.; Madrid: La Imprenta Real, 1807), III, p. 117.

[2] *Los Siete Partidas*, III, p. 30.

[3] *Los Siete Partidas*, III, p. 570, Partido VII, Titulo VIII, Ley IX; Agostinho Marques Perdigão Malheiro, *A escravidão no Brasil: Ensaio Histórico-Jurídico-Social* (2 vols.; Rio de Janeiro: Typografhia Nacional, 1866), I, p. 23.

[4] Apparently there were two such cases for Brazil, one in the eighteenth century and another in the mid-nineteenth century. See Luís Francisco Carvalho Filho, "Impunidade no Brasil – Colônia e Império," *Estudos Avançados* (USP), 18, no. 51 (2004), pp. 187–8.

to prevent general slave rebellions and retribution, but there was general agreement that whippings, brandings, and other physical abuses were acceptable treatment for slaves.[5] In fact, the imperial criminal code of 1830 specifically exempted all free persons from whippings, but accepted them for slaves.

In the case of personal property, the Brazilian codes granted to the slave his or her *peculium* (or personal property). If the slave owner provided land for personal use or allowed slaves to live and work outside their homes, then the resulting surplus income was considered the slave's personal property. Any surplus sold from the truck gardens granted by their owners to slaves on plantations, or income above stipulated payments going to the owners of *escravos de ganho* – that is, slaves who lived apart and paid their owners a fixed periodic income – were thus the private property of the slave. Moreover, all gifts to slaves and other compensation made to them by third parties were considered the personal property of the slave and could not be alienated by his or her owner. Thus, once owners had granted slaves use of their usufruct lands for farming or arranged stipulated income transfers, they explicitly recognized that the resulting surplus was considered the private property of the slave and was so recognized by the state.[6] This government recognition was a crucial factor in guaranteeing the right to self-purchase of freedom by Brazilian slaves.

In terms of secondary rights, the codes provided that Africans had to be baptized immediately and brought into the church, both as children and adults after instruction.[7] In fact, adult baptism, given the age of the arriving slaves, was a common experience in almost all parishes that contained slaves.[8] In turn, the Church recognized that formal marriage among slaves was equal to marriage among free persons and offered

---

[5] See her thoughtful discussion of this in Silvia Hunold Lara, *Campos da Violência: Escravos e Senhores na Capitania do Rio de Janeiro, 1750–1808* (Rio de Janeiro: Paz e Terra, 1988), chapter 2.

[6] " . . . no campo, ver entre nós cultivarem escravos para si terras nas *fazendas* dos senhores, de consentimento dêstes; fazem seus todos os frutos, que são seu pecúlio. – Mesmo nas cidades e povoados alguns permitem que os seus escravos trabalhem como livres, dando-lhes porém um certo jornal; o exceso é seu pecúlio." Perdigão Malheiro, *A escravidão no Brasil*, I, pp. 60–61.

[7] Silvia Hunold Lara, ed., *Ordenações Filipinas*, Livro V (modern edition of 1603 codes; São Paulo: Companhia das Letras, 1999), titulo 99, pp. 308–9.

[8] See, for example, Patrícia Porto de Oliveira, "Desfazendo a maldição de cam por meio dos assentos de batismo de escravos adultos da matriz do Pilar de Ouro Preto (1712–1750)," *Anais do XI Seminário sobre a Economia Mineira* (2004), which contains as well a good discussion of the entire religious background to the entire process.

special support to protect the family.[9] Slaves could also appear, with numerous restrictions, in judicial proceedings as witnesses and were given some of the basic legal rights to trials and even habeas corpus, as were free persons.[10] Like dependent children when they did have such legal rights, slaves could sometimes serve as witnesses or even make some legally binding contracts. All of these rights were usually quite limited and always took into consideration the masters' property rights over the slaves. Ultimately, those masters' rights included absolute control over the physical mobility of the slave, and of course, the undisputed right to dispose of this human property in sale or gift, which was totally supported by the state. But no Portuguese code or municipal law assumed that a slave was without some of the basic rights of humans, no matter how supportive the laws were of their chattel status and the needs of the master.

The Catholic Church, although itself an active owner of slaves, accepted Africans as having immortal souls and granted to them all the rights to the sacraments. Although the Church was slow and limited in intervening between master and slave, it did play a role in every slave society in which it operated. In the first synods of bishops in the Americas, much legislation was dedicated to proselytizing among the slaves, granting them time for worship and even determining the legitimacy of their African practices of marriage and kinship in relation to Christian doctrine, although the reality was that the spiritual conversion of the native population was given greater attention, especially in the sixteenth century. The Church emphasized that slaves should have access to the sacraments and this was to be held above all claims of the master. Moreover, as the many cases of slave protests show, this right was well-known to the slaves. Thus, the slave João who killed his master, Ignácio Mariano de Oliveiro, in Campos Grande, Paraná, in 1853 justified his act by declaring that he "was badly treated and his master obliged him to work even on Sundays and Saints days. . . ."[11]

None of the Iberian legal codes on slavery passed to the New World without modification, and in fact many of them had already been revised in the fifteenth and sixteenth centuries to take into consideration the changing composition of the slave labor force in the metropolitan

---

[9] Perdigão Malheiro, *A escravidão no Brasil*, I, pp. 56–7.
[10] Perdigão Malheiro, *A escravidão no Brasil*, I, pp. 33–6.
[11] "maus tratos, obrigando-lhe a um serviço forçado mesmo nos domingos e dias santos..." cited in Ilton César Martins, "Veredicto culpado: A pena de morte enquanto instrumento de regulação social em Castro – PR (1853–1888)" Curitiba: dissertação de mestrado, Universidade Federal de Paraná, 2005), pp. 106–7.

societies and also took into account the different religious backgrounds of the slaves coming from Africa. In translating Iberian slavery to America, the laws designed for a largely domestic slavery had to be adjusted to the new-style plantation slave regimes emerging in the Americas. In some cases, the medieval codes would be modified to support the rights of the slaves in a more concrete fashion, and at other times basic rights would be modified. Nor did all Roman law regimes provide equal access to the courts or show equal sensitivity to slave needs. Finally, many of the legal rights of slaves were suspended in times of crisis and slave rebellion, and there was even a serious attempt to close down much of the protective legislation during the generalized American elite reaction to the Haitian rebellion in the period from 1791 to about the 1830s and 1840s in all American slave societies.

Although historians have sometimes downplayed the relevance of law to slavery and its daily existence in America,[12] there is little question that the entire edifice of slavery could be constructed only with the indispensable assistance of the state. Property by its very nature is a legally based institution, and contracts are founded on the ability of the state and its courts to enforce them. Without state support, slavery would not have existed. Although the masters' rights were emphasized far more than those of the slave, the state had every right to interest itself in the "peculiar institution," as North Americans called it. It was no accident that the enslavement of Indians largely ended in the seventeenth century when the Portuguese and Spanish crowns refused to recognize legal title to such slaves. It is equally clear that abolition effectively occurred in every slave state when the governments declared such legal contracts null and void. This does not mean that the more protective and paternalistic parts of the slave code were always and everywhere enforced. Practice differed quite dramatically among nations and even by region. In most cases, the more rural and plantation-bound the slave, the less access he or she had to legal redress of grievances, especially because courts were more prominent in urban zones. But in many cases, the fundamental principles of the law were sufficiently well-known and recognized to afford some minimal rights of protection to a significant number of slaves wherever they were found.

Despite these customary and legal rights and protections, most slaves were still at the unqualified will of their masters and overseers. If legal

---

[12] See, for example, Eugene D. Genovese, *Roll Jordon Roll: The World the Slaves Made* (New York: Vintage Books, 1976).

redress proved impossible (which it did in most cases of rural slaves), then for these slaves, the only recourse open to arbitrary behavior was resistance, escape, or violence. From the very first days in all American slave societies, running away and becoming a fugitive (*fugitivo*) occurred everywhere, and as the nineteenth-century newspaper advertisements showed, it was common in Brazil as well.[13] This whole system of temporary or permanent escape from slavery was called *marronage* in French and became a common occurrence. In the majority of cases, this escape from the plantation was temporary, and most slaves remained in the neighborhood of their masters, a pattern that the French colonial society called *petit marronage*. So common was this occurrence that an elaborate arrangement of intervention was developed in all societies. Given the costs of prolonged or permanent absences, the planters and overseers were often willing to negotiate with the slaves, offering moderate punishment and some redress of grievances. In some cases, the demands of the runaways could be quite elaborate. One of the most famous such cases in the Americas occurred in Bahia in the 1789–1790 period. The majority of the three hundred slaves of the Engenho Santana in Ilhéus rebelled after killing the sugar master and escaped to the forest. The *engenho* was inactive for two years and the slaves remained at large, but finally decided to return and sent their old master a 19-point document listing the acceptable conditions for their return, which included issues of work, physical comfort, and the commercialization of their surplus production.[14]

Although *petit marronage* was a common occurrence and associated with informal arrangements for mediation, there was no guarantee that reprisals would not be taken. In such cases slaves were whipped, incarcerated, manacled, or even tortured. But in other instances, they were accepted back with little punishment. Because *petit marronage* could turn into what the French called the *grand marronage*, there were some constraints on the conduct of the masters. If no negotiations were possible, or if the terms of the negotiation were violated, then slaves left the

---

[13] The classic study on this for Brazil is Gilberto Freyre, *O escravo nos anúncios de jornais brasileiros do século XIX* (2nd ed. rev.; São Paulo: Companhia Editora Nacional, 1979).

[14] The standard study of this event is Stuart B. Schwartz, "Resistance and Accommodation in Eighteenth-Century Brazil: The Slaves' View of Slavery," *Hispanic American Historical Review*, 57, no. 1 (February 1977), pp. 69–81, which contains a translation of the original "treaty" document of the fugitive slaves; an analysis of this same movement is found in Lara, *Campos da Violência*, p. 71.

vicinity of the plantation or residence of their master and headed for permanent escape. Their ability to do this successfully depended on a variety of factors that varied regionally. The existence of dense forests or inaccessible mountains within a short distance from their homes was one crucial factor. Another was the availability in these inaccessible regions of soils and climates that allowed for local food production by which to sustain themselves independent of the slave regime. Finally, a relatively benign Indian frontier was essential if the escaped slaves were to be able to establish a permanent settlement.

Brazil, with its open and largely benign frontier, was an ideal place for this type of permanent settlements of escaped slaves. Thus, *quilombos*, or communities of runaway slaves (who were called *quilombolas* or maroons), were common and numerous in every single province of Brazil. The aims of most runaway slaves were conservative: escape from slavery and the desire to lead normal lives as free peasants. However, to establish viable communities, they needed women, tools, seeds, and other supplies. Until these factors could be obtained, such *quilombolas* often raided the settled plantation areas and otherwise found themselves in bitter and often bloody conflict with the whites and other free persons. To hide and escape was their prime aim, but it could often be achieved only by predatory activities that provoked retaliation. In the case of Brazil, these slave *quilombos* became havens for fugitives of all kinds and were thus constantly attacked by the authorities. Finally, in some rare instances, some of these settled communities joined in larger rebellious movements of either slaves or other opponents to the established order. So bitter did the conflict between the runaway communities and the masters become that Brazil, like all slave societies, employed local militia groups and even paid mercenaries, both blacks and whites, to destroy these communities and recapture the runaways. So intense were these internal wars, and so difficult the requirements for success, that the establishment of viable runaway communities was a complex and difficult task that often required a series of fortuitous developments.

Although all slave societies had runaway communities, Brazil probably had the most numerous, longest lasting, and most widespread distribution of such *quilombos* (sometimes also called *mocambos*) communities in the Americas. Such settlements were in existence for well over a century, and others would be continually founded until the end of slavery in the late nineteenth century. The reasons for the intensity of *quilombo* activity in Brazil have a great deal to do with both the size of the slave labor force introduced into the country and the open nature of the frontier in all regions of plantation or slave activity. This frontier was already inhabited by fugitives from justice and by a large and essentially *mestizo* group of frontiersmen known as *caboclos*. Until the end of slavery in the late nineteenth century, most of Brazil's commercial agriculture production and mining was confined to the coastal region or interior zones that were surrounded by frontiers. Unlike the nineteenth-century United States, the slave zones of Brazil were neither blocked by a hostile Indian frontier nor surrounded by white agricultural settlements, but rather were accessible to open frontiers everywhere just a few miles from the coast.

Quilombo activity was correlated with the distribution of slaves throughout Brazil. Although they could be as far south as Santa Catarina, most of the early and largest *quilombos* were found in the sugar region of the Northeast. The best-known of these was one of the earliest. This was the community of Palmares in the captaincy of Pernambuco, along the present-day Pernambuco-Alagoas border. The Palmares Republic was an amalgamation of several communities, all of which had passed through their earlier predatory stage and had established thriving autonomous agricultural communities. These fortified villages were organized into a tax-collecting centralized state under a king. Their agriculture and religion were a mixture of African, American, and European elements. Originating in the earliest years of the seventeenth century, these communities gained large numbers of new adherents because of the intense Dutch-Portuguese conflicts in the first half of the century. Already in the 1640s, the central town was estimated to contain some six thousand persons.[15] By the 1690s, when Palmares had reached the apogee of its power and importance, it counted some twenty thousand persons, among whom were many who had lived in their communities for three generations. Both the Dutch and the Portuguese attacked these communities from the 1630s on, but they continued to grow, and they even succeeded in establishing a state-supported army with weapons stolen or purchased from the enemy. In the 1670s, their king, Ganga-Zumba, had tried to sign a capitulation treaty with the Portuguese, but younger leaders killed the king and continued the war until extinction. After some sixty years of intermittent campaigning, a royally financed army of six thousand troops, which even

---

[15] Pedro Paulo de Abreu Funari, "A arqueologia de Palmares, sua contribuição para o conhecimento da história da cultura afro-americana," in João José Reis and Flávio dos Santos Gomes, eds., *Liberdade por um fio. História dos quilombos no Brasil* (São Paulo: Companhia das Letras, 1996), p. 31.

included men coming from São Paulo, finally succeeded in destroying the republic in 1695.[16]

In the eighteenth and nineteenth centuries, there were several important *quilombos* established in distant isolated zones such as the Amazon. More than eighty of these runaway communities were discovered in the period of 1734–1816 in the regions of Maranhão and Grão Pará, both on the frontier as well as close to the most thriving slave areas.[17] In the mining district of Minas Gerais, there were some 160 known *quilombos* in the eighteenth century.[18] They ranged in size from a few dozen inhabitants to one quilombo that had a thousand residents. This kingdom of Ambrósio, or Quilombo Grande, numbered close to one thousand slaves living in several palisaded villages (or *palenques*). After much resistance, the *quilombo* was finally destroyed in 1746.[19] Many of these communities had formal structures, and royal documents record the existence of kings, captains, and other leaders of the community. One leader captured in Minas in 1777 claimed that he was the king of the stockaded *quilombo* that had been destroyed and that he had been a *capataz* – or slave driver/foreman – on his old *fazenda*.[20] In Mato Grosso, the *quilombo* of Quariterê was probably founded in 1730 and existed sporadically for more than half a century. When it was destroyed for the first time in 1770, it contained seventy-nine fugitive slaves and thirty Indians living together under a king and queen. After being rebuilt, the *quilombo* was assaulted again in 1795, and some fifty-four fugitive slaves were taken.[21] Mato Grosso also had one of the largest *quilombos* in the nineteenth century. This Vila Maria, or the *quilombo* of Sepotuba, remained in existence for

[16] Silvia Hunold Lara, "Do singular ao plural, Palmares, capitães-do-mato e o governo dos escravos," in João José Reis and Flávio dos Santos Gomes, eds., *Liberdade por um fio: História dos quilombos no Brasil* (São Paulo: Companhia das Letras, 1996), p. 86. The standard history of the rebellion is by Décio Freitas, *Palmares, a guerra dos escravos* (5th rev. ed.; Porto Alegre: Mercado Aberto, 1984); also see his documentary collection, Décio Freitas, ed., *República de Palmares: Pesquisa e comentários em documentos históricos do século XVII* (Maceió, Alagoas: Edufal, 2004). Also see the interesting comparisons between Palmares and Angolan society in Stuart B. Schwartz, *Slaves, Peasants, and Rebels: Reconsidering Brazilian Slavery* (Urbana: University of Illinois Press, 1992), pp. 122–8.

[17] Flávio dos Santos Gomes, *A hydra e os pântanos, mocambos, quilombos e comunidades de fugitivos no Brasil (séculos XVII–XIX)* (São Paulo: Editora UNESP, 2005), p. 56.

[18] Carlos Magno Guimarães, "Mineração, quilombos e Palmares: Minas Gerais no século XVIII," in Reis and Santos Gomes, eds., *Liberdade por um fio*, p. 141.

[19] Guimarães, "Mineração, quilombos e Palmares," p. 147; and Ramos, p. 184.

[20] Guimarães, "Mineração, quilombos e Palmares," p. 147.

[21] Luiza Rios Ricci Volpato, "Quilombos em Mato Grosso: Resistência negra em área de fronteira," in Reis and Santos Gomes, eds., *Liberdade por um fio*, pp. 222–5.

at least a century, and during the 1860s it was said to contain two hundred armed ex-slaves.[22] In the Amazon river town of Trombetas to the northwest of Manaus, the *quilombo* of Pará was created, and by 1823 it had a population of two thousand runaway slaves and was unusual in its active contact with white society and intervention in the market economy. Not only did it trade with local Indians and whites, but it was also exporting cacao and other commercial crops to Dutch Guyana. Destroyed once in 1823, it was quickly re-created and lasted into the 1830s. A group from these communities even went further upriver and founded Cidade Maravilha, which in the 1850s was sending its children to the white communities to be baptized. In the nineteenth century, there even occurred *quilombo* involvement in rebellions led by free whites against the imperial government.[23] In Maranhão in the late 1830s, under the leadership of the ex-slave Cosme Bento das Chagas, the *quilombo* of Campo Grande fielded an army of three thousand ex-slaves that participated in a Liberal revolution led by the local whites.[24] An imperial army soon put down the republican revolution in Maranhão and then turned on the *quilombolas*, destroying the Campo Grande *quilombo*.[25] The inherent problems of the *quilombos*, however, were reflected in the experience of the unconquered *quilombo* Manso in Mato Grosso, which reportedly had an estimated population of 293 persons in the late 1860s. There were only twenty adult women and thirteen children in the settlement.[26] This distorted sex ratio goes a long way toward explaining the inherent instability of many these communities, as the need for women drove many *quilombolas* to raid the *fazendas* and local towns and thus provoked reactions from the slave owners. Along with sexual imbalance were the problems of obtaining food and resources to survive outside the colonial and imperial economy. In this respect, the *quilombo* of Buraco de Tatú near the city of Salvador in Bahia was typical. Destroyed in 1763, the hundred or so villagers had lived from some fishing and trading with local free farmers and even thieving in the local markets of the city. They too stole women from both the *fazendas* and local villages to incorporate into the community.[27]

[22] Volpato, "Quilombos em Mato Grosso," pp. 229–31.

[23] Eurípedes A. Funes, "'Nasci nas matas, nunca tive senhor' – História e memória dos mocambos do baixo Amazonas," in Reis and Santos Gomes, eds., *Liberdade por um fio*, pp. 467ff.

[24] Maria Januária Vilela Santos, *A Balaiada e a Insurreição de escravos no Maranhão* (São Paulo: Editora Ática, 1983), pp. 96ff.

[25] Mattias Röhrig Assunção, "Quilombos maranhenses," in Reis and Santos Gomes, eds., *Liberdade por um fio*, pp. 442ff.

[26] Volpato, "Quilombos em Mato Grosso," p. 233.

[27] Schwartz, *Slaves, Peasants, and Rebels*, pp. 112–18.

These well-known *quilombos* were mostly destroyed, but of course were the exceptions. The hundreds of *quilombos*, which left their names in the topography of all Brazil's provinces, were most often communities of a few dozen ex-slaves who sought withdrawal and anonymity as much as possible. Some of these communities blended in so well that they eventually became indistinguishable from the general *caboclo* and other subsistence-farming villages. Others were so bold that they even temporarily founded their homes close to the country's biggest cities. What is clear, however, is that they existed in all regions and at all times, and served as a viable option for runaway slaves, especially as the Brazilians rarely negotiated formal treaties with these maroon communities to close them off to fugitive slaves. Their importance was recognized by the fact that there was a separate military organization that existed everywhere in Brazil to capture runaway slaves and to destroy *quilombos*. In Minas in the eighteenth century, for example, there was established a separate Regimento dos Capitães-do-Mato whose exclusive role was to hunt runaways and destroy *quilombos*. Their pay was based on their capture rates, and some 15 percent of these troops were *forros*, or freedmen who had been born slaves. There were even cases of slave owners getting royal patents to be Capitães-do-Mato who armed their own slaves and put them into combat units, one of the few known cases of slaves being armed in large numbers. One expedition in 1769 had fifty-eight armed slaves and an accompanying slave chamber orchestra who were owned by the leader of the expedition, and who were said to entertain their master by playing minuets when they were in the field.[28]

An alternative frontier for the escaped slaves was the city or absorption within free-colored society. This was possible because Brazil contained large urban centers with many self-employed (*escravos de ganho*) slaves and freedmen. Sometimes the fugitives, especially those with a profession or living as *escravos de ganho*, claimed they were free. Sometimes *livres de cor* or other friends forged documents for them that claimed they were free persons. That friendship, or even just class consciousness, was a factor could be seen in the case of the slave Serafim who escaped from his owner in the city of Leopoldina, in the province of Minas Gerais, and headed to the city of Rio de Janeiro in 1884. He made the whole trip on foot, passing numerous *fazendas* and always seeking protection from known and unknown slaves who gave him food and

---

[28] Laura de Mello e Souza, "Violência e práticas culturais no cotidiano de uma expedição contra Quilombolas, Minas Gerais, 1769," in Reis and Santos Gomes, eds., *Liberdade por um fio*, pp. 198–200.

shelter.[29] In addition, even in the port city of Rio de Janeiro, there were enough nearby mountains and forests for some of these urban slaves to find places of refuge.[30] Alternatively, in Brazil there was also a large free-colored population living in rural areas that were especially difficult to police, and who proved to be an ideal group into which escaping slaves could disappear. Numerous were the cases and advertisements for runaway slaves who were defined as claiming they were free persons, or who even escaped by ship from their original place of enslavement. Thus, for example, Bráulio, an illiterate *pardo escuro* field-hand slave, in the 1870s fled from a coffee *fazenda* and went to live as a supposedly free person in the city of Rio de Janeiro, claiming his name was Braz and that he was a *pardo livre* and carpenter by profession. He was eventually taken when he tried to find a ship to return to his home in Bahia, from which he had originally been shipped.[31] Another fugitive slave, a middle-aged man by the name of Joaquim Benguela, apparently escaped in 1845 aboard the steamship *Venus* and was not heard from again.[32] There are even numerous cases of fugitive slaves joining the army, navy, or merchant marine to escape slavery.[33]

Whether escaping in groups to *quilombos* or losing themselves individually in towns, nearby woods, or even moving illegally to other *fazendas*, the volume of runaway slaves was impressive. It is estimated that in the province of Rio de Janeiro, the central prison (*calabouço*) in the year 1826 listed a total of 895 prisoners who were fugitive slaves, the majority of whom were taken in the interior of the province.[34] Another study of the police registers for the city of Rio de Janeiro between 1800–1830 shows a total of 5,363 recaptured fugitives, of whom 80 percent were Africans.[35]

[29] Flávio dos Santos Gomes, "Experiências negras e Brasil escravista: Questões e debates," X *Congresso Internacional da ALADAA* (Associação Latino-Americana de Estudos Africanos e Asiático), (2001), n.p.

[30] Luiz Carlos Soares, *O 'Povo de Cam'na capital do Brasil: A escravidão urbana no Rio de Janeiro do século XIX* (Rio de Janeiro: Faperj, Letras, 2007), pp. 238–46.

[31] Sidney Chalhoub, *Visões da liberdade: Uma história das últimas décadas da escravidião na Corte* (São Paulo: Companhia das Letras, 1990), pp. 54–6.

[32] *Jornal do Comercio*, January 5, 1846, p. 3.

[33] Hendrick Kraay, "'The Shelter of the Uniform': The Brazilian Army and Runaway Slaves, 1800–1888," *Journal of Social History*, 29, no. 3 (Spring 1996), pp. 637–57.

[34] Mary C. Karasch, *Slave Life in Rio de Janeiro, 1808–1850* (Princeton: Princeton University Press, 1987), p. 309, table 10.4.

[35] Flávio dos Santos Gomes, *Experiências atlânticas: Ensaios e pesquisas sobre a escravidão e o pós emancipação no Brasil* (Passo Fundo, RGS: Editora UPF, 2003), pp. 51–2.

The 2,265 slaves registered as captured fugitives residing in the city prison of Rio de Janeiro between 1810 and 1830 represented 42 percent of all slave prisoners whose crime was known. Interestingly, only 178 of these total fugitives were women.[36] A detailed study of the runaway aids in the Rio newspapers of the early nineteenth century shows that the majority of runaways in this city were male and primarily Africans. In the *Gazeta do Rio de Janeiro* between 1809 and 1821, there were notices of 337 fugitive slaves, and some 80 percent of them were males and two-thirds were Africans. Between the *Gazeta* and the *Diário do Rio de Janeiro* in the same period, some 1,258 Africans were listed as fugitives, and in general, they tended to be younger than the native-born slaves who escaped.[37] This may be due to the fact that younger Africans were only newly introduced into slavery and more rebellious, whereas Creoles were more accepting of slavery and tended to escape when they had a more sophisticated understanding of their potential ability to effect a successful flight.

Most of the fugitives probably carried out their escapes on an individual basis. But from many of the cases of recaptured slaves, it is clear that they often fled to the homes of friends or relatives and had some clear destination in mind. There are even a few documented cases that when groups of slaves escaped together, these slaves were tied together by kinship. This occurred with two groups of slaves in Rio de Janeiro. In March 1852, some thirty-two fugitives were captured near Paratí, of whom there were six married couples, including two who had children and one family containing three generations. In the same year, another plantation was denuded of slaves, and it was noted that of the sixty-two slaves who had fled, forty were related by blood, and older African males dominated the group of twenty who were not related.[38]

The ability to escape the system through running away, either for a short time or for longer periods, and hiding among urban slaves or free-colored communities or in hidden frontier communities, were all essentially safety valves for the slave system. As long as the option of escape was available, the internal pressures that normally built up in a slave regime could be handled. But often such escape was impossible, or the provocation was too immediate and too dramatic. In these cases, the slaves turned to violence. The result was isolated killings of oppressive

---

[36] Soares, *O 'Povo de Cam'na capital do Brasil*, tabelas LXXX–LXXXI, pp. 443–4.
[37] Santos Gomes, *Experiências atlânticas*, pp. 45–51.
[38] Santos Gomes, *Experiências atlânticas*, pp. 73–4.

masters and overseers or even suicide.[39] Sometimes it led to full-scale rebellion.

The slaves, like all other members of Brazilian society, committed all types of crimes: premeditated killings, crimes of passion, crimes against owners and overseers, but also crimes against free-colored persons, whites, and fellow slaves. They were victims of crimes practiced by others, free, slaves, and even their masters. They also were involved in theft and other types of violent crimes, many of which involved social relations with other slaves, *forros*, or elements of the poorest members of the society.[40] As could be expected, a unique aspect of slave crime was that slave killings of masters or overseers were relatively frequent. In Campinas in São Paulo in the period of 1831–1887, there were seventy-nine such slave assassins. What is impressive is that the slaves doing the killing were mostly Creoles (70 percent), and even more surprising, in two-thirds of the cases where their length of residence on the estate was known (in the case of thirty-eight individuals), they had resided on their *fazendas* for six or more years.[41] But slaves were also victims of homicide, not only from masters and overseers, but also from other slaves and even free persons. In the *paulista* towns of Campinas and Taubaté in this same period, there were eighty crimes against persons carried out by slaves. A very high fifty-four of these assaults were against owners and overseers, whereas 40 percent were against other slaves and the rest against free persons.[42] Equally high rates of attacks against masters and overseers were recorded in the state of Rio Grande do Sul between 1818 and 1833. There, of 104 total homicides, some 35 were slaves who killed masters

---

[39] In the nineteenth century, some forty-eight slaves committed suicide in the município of Juiz de Fora and another forty-six in the *mineira comarca* of Paraibuna. Ana Maria Faria Amoglia, "Um suspiro de liberdade: Suicídio de escravos no município de Juiz de Fora (1830–1888)," *Boletim [Núcleo de Estudos em História Demográfica, FEA USP]*, no. 18 (Novembro 1999), p. 8, tabelas 1 and 2.

[40] As Wissenbach noted, "Em linhas gerais, os crimes cometidos pelos escravos, analisados neste trabalho, incidiram em direções opostas: crimes imbricados diretamente nas questões de dominação escravista e de sua violência, e crimes plenamente integrados em vivências específicas. Tal configuração atesta que, para além da relação básica que vincava suas vidas como escravizados, uma outra dimensão se fazia tão ou mais importante: as relações intragrupos negros ou entre eles e as demais camadas socialmente desclassificadas." Maria Cristina Cortez Wissenbach, "Sonhos africanos, vivências ladinas: Escravos e forros no município de São Paulo (1850–1880)" (São Paulo: dissertação de mestrado, Departamento de História, FFCLCH, 1989), p. 19.

[41] Maria Helena P. T. Machado, *Crime e escravidão: Trabalho, luta e resistência nas lavouras paulistas, 1830–1888* (São Paulo-SP: Editora Brasiliense, 1987), p. 49.

[42] Machado, *Crime e escravidão*, quadros 2 and 3, pp. 39–40.

and 14 who killed their overseers (*capataz* or *feitor*) – or 47 percent of all murders, with only 22 slaves killing other slaves.[43] In São Paulo in the 1850s to the 1870s, there were forty-two slaves involved in violent crimes against their masters and administrators and only twenty against slaves, with seventeen made against free but poor persons – a rate of 53 percent of violent crimes of person perpetuated against their owners and their agents.[44]

In other regions, such high rates of homicide against their owners do not seem to have been the norm. Thus, in the Minas Gerais town of Juiz de Fora, in the period from 1851 to the end of slavery, there were 118 murders or attempted murders carried out by slaves against other persons, of which only 2 were against masters and 20 against overseers – or just 18 percent of these slave attacks on others. But slaves also killed or attempted homicide against fifty-one other slaves and forty-seven free persons who were not masters or plantation administrators.[45] This study found twenty-nine cases of slaves killing other slaves, one attempted homicide, and six cases of assault,[46] and noted twenty-nine cases of assault by free persons against slaves, of which twelve were ordered by masters or overseers.[47] In Bahia from 1800–1888 in the two *sertão* (backlands) districts of Caetité and Rio das Contas, there were only three slaves who were involved in crimes against masters, and four cases involved masters attacking slaves, but there were twenty slaves who attacked other slaves, and twenty-three slaves attacked either *forros* or free-colored persons (*homens livres*), and slaves in turn were attacked by fifteen *forros* and *livres*. This is in addition to slaves who participated with

[43] Solimar Oliveira Lima, *Triste Pampa: Resistência e punição de escravos em fontes judiciárias no Rio Grande do Sul, 1818–1833* (Porto Alegre, EDIPURCS, 1997), quadro 2, p. 99.

[44] Maria Cristina Cortez Wissenbach, *Sonhos africanos, vivências ladinas: Escravos e forros em São Paulo (1850–1880)* (São Paulo: Editora Hucitec, 1998), p. 49. A typical case was that of a Mozambique slave named José Antonio who killed his *feitor*. See Diego Emílio Alves Arêdes and Maria Aparecida Chaves Ribeiro Papali, "Crime de escravo em Taubaté: Assassinato de um feitor em 1852," available at www.inicepg.univap.br/INIC_2005/inic/IC7%20anais/IC7–10.pdf.

[45] Elione Silva Guimarães, *Violência entre parceiros de cativeiro: Juiz de Fora, segunda metade do século XIX* (São Paulo: Annablume, 2006), tabela 3, p. 98. Interestingly, there were only twenty-one cases of property crimes in which slaves were involved.

[46] Elione Silva Guimarães, "Criminalidade entre mancípios: A comunidade escrava no contexto de grandes fazendas cafeeiras da zona da mata mineira 1850–1881," *X Seminário sobre a Economia Mineira* (2002), tabela 1.

[47] Elione Silva Guimarães, *Criminalidade e escravidão em um município cafeeiro de Minas Gerais – Juiz de Fora, século XIX*, p. 8.

others as both victims and perpetrators of crimes against persons.[48] In contrast, in the northern *mineiro* rural district of Montes Claros in the mid- to late nineteenth century, only 7 slaves killed other slaves, whereas 36 slaves killed or attempted homicide against free persons. In turn, 24 slaves were killed or wounded by free persons – this from a total of 104 such crimes committed by all members of the community.[49] In the city of Rio de Janeiro between 1810 and 1821, some 3,682 slaves were imprisoned, with the largest category of crimes being those against public order (32 percent) and only 513 for crimes of violence, which in fact came after flight, property crimes, and even ill-defined miscellaneous crimes as the least important general category.[50] Of these crimes of violence, the majority seemed to have been against other slaves or *libertos*, and few against whites.[51]

All these statistics on violent crime committed by slaves suggest that although there were often wide regional differences in the victims, in general it can be said that slaves were probably involved almost as often in assaults against each other and other poor persons as they were against their masters and overseers and that as often, they were equally the victims as well as the aggressors. In the first set of crimes, which tended to be between known persons and were often unpremeditated attacks, the locale of the violence was often their place of residence, work, or leisure.[52] Thus, a detailed study of slaves killing other slaves in Juiz de Fora, a coffee zone in Minas Gerais, showed that twenty-eight of the thirty-six murders were between slaves of the same owner, and only eight were carried

---

[48] Maria de Fátima Novaes Pires, *O crime na cor: Escravos e forros no alto sertão da Bahia (1830–1888)* (São Paulo: Annablume, 2003), quadros 3 and 4, pp. 219–20.

[49] Alysson Luiz Freitas de Jesus, *No sertão das Minas: Escravidão, violência e liberdade (1830–1888)* (São Paulo: Annablume, 2007), quadro 3, p. 97.

[50] Leila Mezan Algranti, *O feitor ausente: Estudos sobre a escravidão urbana no Rio de Janeiro (1808–1822)* (Petrópolis: Vozes, 1988), tabela 4.1, p. 167. Of some 3,374 slave prisoners whose origin was known, an extraordinary 85 percent were African born. Algranti, *O feitor ausente*, tabela 4.8, pp. 190–1.

[51] Algranti, *O feitor ausente*, p. 173.

[52] Two killings of slaves by fellow slaves in Minas in the nineteenth century exemplified conflicts that occurred in places of work. One newly purchased slave killed another in their dormitory room while the other was sleeping, the cause seemingly due to the recent transfer of the killer and his hostility toward his new environment that he took out on an innocent fellow slave. The second case involved old conflicts between two slaves that lead to one killing the other on the way to the fields when both were members of the same work gang. See Elione Silva Guimarães, "Rixas e brigas entre companheiros de cativeiro (Juiz de Fora 1850–88)," *Revista Universidade Rural, Série Ciências Humanas*, 24, nos. 1–2 (2002), pp. 95–6.

out between slaves of different owners. Moreover, work tools or natural objects were the means used to kill other slaves.[53] Studies of female homicides, for example, suggest that the common place for these violent crimes to occur was along riverbanks where women washed clothes, in local markets where they sold goods, or in the shops (*vendas*) that were attended by both slave and *forras* women.[54] For men, it was typical to have violence erupt in moments of leisure when they were drinking or over lovers or other intimate relation questions. Thus, the *mineiro* slave Raymundo was in the house of one friend listening to music and drinking *cachaça* when he got into a drunken argument with his friend Celestino Fernandez da Costa, a free laborer, and attacked him. Brought before the court for this violent attack, he could not recall the details.[55] More complex but no less common was the crime of passion carried out by a *paulista* slave named Alvez. He murdered the *forro* Vicente in 1861 because he was sleeping with Vicente's wife, Maria do Carmo, and killed her husband in preparation for fleeing with his lover.[56]

The crimes against other slaves and poor persons thus tended to be unpremeditated, emotional, and personal and not that different from what occurred among all free persons, except when third parties such as masters were involved.[57] But the assaults between master and slave were unique to slavery and were often of longstanding conflict, even if not premeditated, and always seemed to involve great violence. The case of

[53] This was from a total of thirty-six cases in which slaves were either the aggressor or the victim. Guimarães, "Rixas e brigas entre companheiros de cativeiro, pp. 89–90.

[54] Alan Nardi de Souza, "Crime e castigo: A criminalidade em Mariana na primeira metade do século XIX" (Dissertação de mestrado em História, Universidade Federal de Juiz de Fora, 2007), pp. 80, 84. One of the few cases of a woman slave involved in killing others, rather than herself, was the case of "Thereza, preta escrava, foi presa em Mariana no dia 12 de janeiro de 1808 por ter matado um tal Simão, escravo de propriedade de seu senhor Antônio José da Cunha.... " Souza, "Crime e castigo," p. 80.

[55] Asked how the crime occurred, the victim "Respondeu que principiou por uma brincadeira de que não recorda as miudências por estar muito embriagado." He offered immediate apologies, but his friend, also drunk, attacked him. Cited in Jesus, *No sertão das Minas*, pp. 98–9.

[56] Cesar Mucio Silva, *Processos-crime: Escravidão e violência em Botucatu* (São Paulo: Alameda, 2004), pp. 76ff.

[57] Conflicts in which masters led their slaves to attack other slaves or other free persons were not uncommon. See, for example, the discussion of such conflicts in Maria Lúcia Resende Chaves Teixeira, "Lei, matriz doutrinária e escravidão: Minas Gerais, Comarca do Rio das Mortes (1800–1831)," *Anais do XII Seminário sobre a Economia Mineira* (2006), pp. 6–9.

the married slave Ana Maria in the town of Rio das Contas in 1848 may have been extreme, but was not atypical. She was accused of drowning her two young children and attempting her own suicide at the same time. When questioned by the authorities, she said that she was severely whipped by her mistress, who promised her to do it again the next day, and that she became hallucinated by the torment of the beatings and tried to escape the violence by killing herself and her two children.[58] Many are the cases of slaves defending their killing of overseers and masters because of their constant beatings by these persons and the extreme reduction in their basic rights to food and rest.

Slaves were also involved in property crimes, but usually as agents of their masters, as fugitives, or as victims. In fact, because theft from masters would be dealt with by the owners, very few such cases appear in the legal records of the government. There were numerous cases of persons illegally claiming ownership of slaves and also of masters attacking neighbors and others with their own slaves. In these cases, usually the masters were held responsible for the action of their slaves. Slaves were also the victims of theft in their own person, being robbed from their owners like all other properties.[59] There were even cases of masters hiding fugitive slaves on their estates, and one such case occurred in Macaé in 1864, where twenty-six fugitive slaves, all from the same master, were found working on the *fazenda* of Bernardo Lopes da Cruz.[60]

Given the relegation of basic discipline to the masters and the economic importance of the slaves as workers, it is not surprising that when the state dealt with slave crime, punishment was swift and public and few slaves remained in jail for a long time. Thus, only 11 percent of the 421 persons housed in the local jail in the Mariana district of Minas Gerais in the 1800–1830 period were slaves, and some of them in fact were left in the care of the prison by their masters when their masters were traveling, with the masters paying their room and board. Others were fugitive slaves being held until they could be returned to their masters. In general, slaves were executed, sent to the galleys, or whipped or otherwise sentenced for their crimes and turned over quickly to their

---

[58] She claimed she was "alucinado pelos tormentos de surras procurou aliviar-se por meio da morte assim como seus filhos." Pires, *O crime na cor*, p. 178.

[59] For example, the *preto forro* André Alves was accused in Minas Gerais in 1769 of having stolen three slaves and escaping with them. Núbia Braga Ribeiro, "Cotidiano e liberdade: Um estudo sobre os alforriados em Minas no século XVIII" (Dissertação de mestrado, FFLCH-USP, 1996), p. 176.

[60] Santos Gomes, "Experiências negras e Brasil escravista," n.p.

masters.[61] It should be recalled that the owners of the slaves always tried to defend their slaves from long-term punishment, which signified a loss of property, preferring a public and rapid whipping or short-term incarceration. The masters' response to this problem is illustrated in a case that occurred in Vassouras in 1879. Five slaves killed their overseer *(feitor)*. According to the 1835 decree, slaves killing masters, their families, or overseers required an automatic death penalty. All the witnesses in the case, despite the evidence, claimed that the person assassinated was simply passing through the estate and was not the overseer. With the help of the delegate in charge of the case, three slaves were judged innocent, and two were ordered to be flogged, but given over to their owner to do the whipping, thus preserving his property intact.[62]

Slave rebellions were of many types, from the most spontaneous to the most planned, from strictly race wars against all whites to complex attacks on selected elements of the master class. Some rebellions were hopeless from the beginning and were recognized as such by their participants, and some were successful transitions to *marronage*. However, in all cases, slave revolts were a last resort for desperate men and women who could no longer suffer the abuses of slavery. From the sixteenth century onward, there were slave rebellions in every slave society in America. Although generalizations about such a complex social process are difficult to make, certain general features can be discerned. If the slave regime was heavily African, the revolts were usually more numerous and intense than in slave communities in which the Creoles formed a majority. Because all slaves knew what the ultimate consequences of rebellion were, those with more of a commitment in the current social order tended to be more conservative. Among recently arrived Africans, where the sexual imbalance created fewer families or local ties, rebellion was more acceptable. Creoles with their family and community ties were the least likely candidates for

---

[61] Souza, "Crime e castigo," p. 84. Clearly the galleys of early Europe were no longer used for prisoners, and according to the Criminal Code of 1830, article 44, it meant confinement to prison and public works for life: "A pena de galés sujeitará os réus a andarem com calcêta no pé e corrente de ferro, juntos ou separados, e a empregar-se nos trabalhos públicos onde tiver sido cometido o delito, à disposição do govêrno...." The sentence could be for life or a fixed time, and more and more replaced executions for slaves after 1857, when the death penalty was abolished for all free persons although not for slaves. Caiuá Cardoso Al-Alam, "Questões acerca dos enforcamentos de escravos em Pelotas-RS," II Encontro "Escravidão e Liberdade no Brasil Meridional" (2003), pp. 10–11.

[62] Nilo Batista. "Pena Pública e escravismo," *Capítulo Criminológico*, 34, no. 3 (Jul.–Set. 2006), pp. 279–321.

rebellion, although even these native-born slaves were sometimes provoked beyond their endurance and conservative instincts.

In the vast majority of cases, revolt was spontaneous and involved only a few slaves. An aggrieved slave's killing of their master or overseer was probably the most common form of revolt recorded. When a group of slaves premeditated such an act, they usually tried to involve the whole plantation and also tried to plan an escape. Such revolts usually envisioned *marronage* as a final result of their violence. This seemed to have been the case with a slave uprising in a large Minas Gerais *fazenda* in 1833 in the region of Rio das Mortes. Because the leaders were killed in the rebellion itself, it appears difficult to know how much premeditation there was, although the captured members of the revolt argued that there had been some preliminary discussion. But slaves on one *fazenda* refused to join the rebellion and on another, they were armed by the *fazendeiro* and fought off the attackers. The revolt eventually involved some thirty slaves who killed several white *fazenda* families, as well as a free *pardo* and an *agregado*. Given that many of the whites were from elite families, the government's response was ferocious, and almost as many slaves were executed for this one-day movement involving just three *fazendas* as in much larger revolts. It has also been suggested that this revolt gave rise to the imperial law of 1835 that mandated the death penalty for any slave killing a master or overseer and without any jury trial provided.[63]

Clearly these ferocious and spontaneous style revolts were the norm for most of what occurred in colonial and imperial Brazil. There were, however, a few well-known cases of full-scale race and class wars in which the conspiring slaves sought to eliminate the master class and retain the lands for themselves. Sometimes these wars were directed at whites only, but sometimes they opposed elements within the servile class as well. There even exist cases of freedmen and slaves conspiring together in the hopes of forming a black and *mulato* republic. In most instances, the reaction against enslavement was instinctive and based on universal beliefs in justice and humanity. At other times, however, these rebellions evolved from alternative religious belief systems and developed an elaborate cosmology, sometimes with millenarian overtones.

Isolated mining communities were particularly prone to rebellious slave activity, whereas small family farms probably had the fewest uprisings. Anywhere slaves congregated in large numbers, slave conspiracies

---

[63] Marcos Ferreira de Andrade, "Negros rebeldes nas Minas Gerais: A revolta dos escravos de Carrancas (1833)," *Afro-Ásia*, 21–22 (1998–1999), pp. 45–82.

and rebellions were possible. In those regions with a viable frontier or a large free-colored class, the intensity of such revolts was decreased. Variation in the intensity and timing of revolts was not only related to these demographic, geographic, and structural factors, but it was also sensitive to changes over time. By the late eighteenth and early nineteenth centuries, many of the revolts began to take on a more class-conscious and ameliorative component. The French and Haitian revolutions sparked a series of conspiracies and revolts throughout America that sought slave emancipation and equality for freedmen. These revolts were usually led by free colored and poor whites, but also included slaves. Such was the case of the so-called tailors' conspiracy in Bahia in 1798. Then, in the 1820s and 1830s, as the metropolitan governments responded to liberal reformist demands for change, abolition became a general topic of debate in the colonies. The result was a maturation of slave conspiracies and plots into full-scale, class-conscious movements. As Creolized slaves got access to information about government reforms, strikes and mass-protest activities were organized demanding better working conditions, more access to provisioning grounds, or even the abolition of slavery.

The most outstanding slave revolutionary movements in Brazil were the series of Islamic rebellions in Bahia from 1808 to 1835. There was a slave conspiracy in the city of Bahia, which was repressed in 1807, and a massive attack of three hundred *quilombolas* against the interior town of Nazareth das Farinhas in 1809 that was repressed with much bloodshed. In 1810 came another such plantation uprising of Muslim slaves, followed by an uprising of coastal fishermen in 1814. Some fifty slave fishermen were killed by troops sent from Salvador, but not before many local white masters were slaughtered. Five other uprisings took place between 1816 and 1835, in both the countryside and the city. In 1830, for example, 20 armed slaves attacked an urban slave market and freed one hundred newly arrived African captives.[64] But the most important revolt was that of 1835. Well organized by mostly Muslim slaves both in the city and on the plantations, it was eventually uncovered before

---

[64] On the 1814 Hausa rebellion, see Stuart B. Schwartz, "Cantos e quilombos numa conspiração de escravos Hausás," in Reis and Santos Gomes, eds., *Liberdade por um fio*, pp. 373–406. On the other revolts, see João José Reis, *Rebelião escrava no Brasil, a história do levante dos malês (1835)* (São Paulo: Editora Brasiliense, 1986), pp. 66ff. For a quick survey of many of these rebellions, see Howard M. Prince, "Slave Rebellions in Bahia, 1807–1835" (Ph.D. diss., History, Columbia University, 1972). Also see João José Reis and Eduardo Silva, *Negociação e conflito: A resistência negra no Brasil escravista* (São Paulo: Companhia das Letras, 1989).

it could be fully developed. However, enough slaves obtained arms that deaths were numerous and destruction to property was quite extensive. More than a hundred of the Muslim slaves were executed, and the city and government were thrown into a panic, which quickly spread to other regions.[65] So violent was the repression of both slaves and free colored in the city that no other major rebellions were to occur in this region after that date.[66] Nevertheless, slave unrest was a constant in the city of Salvador, and in the midst of the Sabinada 1837–1838 independence rebellion, tensions rose when slaves abandoned their masters and joined the rebel army.[67]

Nor was Bahia the only region to suffer revolts and conspiracies. In the province of São Paulo, some thirty-two slaves were arrested for plotting to destroy *engenhos* in the area of Campinas in 1832.[68] In the major coffee district of Vassouras in 1838, some eighty slaves rose up in revolt on a major *fazenda* and then attacked another and released several hundred slaves. The aim seemed to be to set up a *quilombo* in the mountains, but the National Guard succeeded in stopping the flight and capturing the rebellious slaves.[69] In Maranhão, several thousand escaped slaves joined the provincial rebellion against the central state in the so-called *Balaiada* rebellion of 1840,[70] and this uprising of slaves or joining of rebel bands seemed to be quite common in the various regional rebellions up to the 1850s.[71] Toward the end of the slave era, there were also slave conspiracies and uprisings that included a general demand for abolition. This apparently was the case in a planned insurrection in Minas Gerais in 1874. Unusual because of its more class-conscious aspects, its long

[65] On the panicky response in the city of Rio de Janeiro, see Carlos Eugênio Líbano Soares and Flávio dos Santos Gomes, "'Com o Pé sobre um Vulcão': Africanos Minas, Identidades e a Repressão Antiafricana no Rio de Janeiro (1830–1840)," *Revista Estudos Afro-Asiáticos*, 23, no. 2 (2001), pp. 1–44.

[66] The classic study of the rebellion is by Reis, *Rebelião escrava no Brasil*. An English translation of this work appeared in 1993.

[67] Hendrik Kraay, "'As Terrifying as Unexpected'": The Bahian Sabinada, 1837–1838," *The Hispanic American Historical Review*, 72, no. 4. (November 1992), p. 502.

[68] Ricardo Figueiredo Pirola, "A conspiração escrava de Campinas, 1832: Rebelião, etni-cidade e família" (dissertação de mestrado, UNICAMP, 2005).

[69] Flávio dos Santos Gomes, *Histórias de Quilombolas: Mocambos e comunidades de senzalas no Rio de Janeiro século XIX* (Rio de Janeiro: Arquivo Nacional, 1995), chapter 2.

[70] Santos, *A Balaiada e a Insurreição de escravos no Maranhão, loc. cit.*

[71] This was the case with the *cabanagem* rebellion of the 1830s; see Mark Harris, *Rebellion on the Amazon: The Cabanagem, Race, and Popular Culture in the North of Brazil, 1798–1840* (Cambridge: Cambridge University Press, forthcoming), chapter 5.

planning, and its awareness of imperial and international developments related to abolition of slavery, was the conspiracy of slaves in the Serro and Diamantina region of Minas Gerais. It supposedly involved some four hundred slaves scattered in mines, plantations, and urban centers and was even allied with various *quilombos* in the region. In the end, it was denounced before it could be developed, and some forty or so rebel leaders were imprisoned and severely punished.[72]

Revolts, rebellions, conspiracies, and protest movements were only a small manifestation of the hostility expressed by slaves for their condition. There was also a high incidence of crimes of violence and property in which slaves were either victims or perpetrators. Slave thefts, vandalism, arson, and destruction of property were constant and clearly acts of protest against masters and their slave condition. There was also a significant level of killings of masters and their overseers by enraged slaves who had gone beyond their limits of endurance. But the poverty and oppression experienced by slaves was sometimes turned against each other. Many of these crimes came from normal interpersonal conflicts, but many were part of an uncontrolled hostility toward the system in which they were forced to live. Drunkenness, social disorder, and crime were largely urban phenomena, but no slave community even in the most isolated plantation was free of them. In a world where violence and helplessness were daily occurrences, a corresponding level of protest, coherent and random, was bound to be part of the system. As many noted, violence in all forms was a fundamental part of the system of slavery. This violence was not only against the slave, but was also a permanent part of the mentality of the owners with their constantly expressed fears of slave rebellion, especially in communities with a high ratio of slaves to free population. Thus, a basic part of the slave system was the permanent sensation of violence on the part of all members of that society.

---

[72] Isidora Moura Mota, "O 'Vulcão' negro da Chapada: Rebelião escrava nos sertões diamantinos (Minas Gerais, 1864)" (dissertação de mestrado, UNICAMP, 2005).

8

Family, Kinship, and Community

Flight, rebellion, resistance, and violence could not be the only responses possible to slavery in Brazil. The majority of Africans and their descendants tried to survive the slave experience and create as normal a life as possible in the context of this harsh regime. Thus, family and community were a fundamental part of the Afro-Brazilian experience and in turn helped to mold and define the larger society outside of slavery as well. Forced to work for others and with little control over their lives, slaves began to learn skills, form families, and create kin and friendship networks that would survive the institution of slavery. They also found solace and community in their religion and brotherhoods.

Although they spoke a multitude of different languages and came from different cultural systems and nationalities, the African slaves arriving to Brazil sometimes shared a number of commonalties that may have helped bind them together in the New World. The opening up of Atlantic trade, for instance, contributed to the development of interregional contacts within Africa by creating ever-larger market areas. Meanwhile, the fairly constant expansion and reorganization of African states and societies over time brought many different groups into contact. Although the process of cultural integration on the African continent should not be overemphasized, neither should the diversity of Africa be exaggerated. Not every ethno-linguistic group comprised a distinct culture that was totally different from others. Moreover, many Africans of the slave trade era were multilingual and at least minimally conversant in the dialects and customs of their neighbors. Significantly, the circumstances of the Atlantic slave trade did not completely disrupt this pattern. Slave ships often extracted slaves from regions where intense multinational contact had occurred, and many of the slaves whom traders purchased had also slowly migrated to the coasts where they were sold, having passed through numerous territories and interacted with a variety of populations along the way. All of this may help explain why newly arrived Africans, when setting foot in the Americas, were sometimes able to create bonds of friendship and community with slaves from different nations. Finally, the long and intense nature of the African slave trade to Brazil guaranteed that there were large groups of slaves from the same regions and even the same ethno-linguistic groups clustered within regions of Brazil, and there are numerous cases in the Brazilian documents of slaves from the same ethno-linguistic group living and working together, or even being selectively purchased by *forros* of the same African origin.[1]

Certainly, some New World masters often expressed preferences for acquiring one or another group of Africans on their estates, thinking it beneficial to cultivating a productive work environment. Others actively sought to diversify their slaveholdings, based on the belief that having too great a concentration of a particular group might foment resistance and rebellion. Yet there was no systematic attempt by slave traders to diversify their sources, and New World demand had no effect on the selection of Africans who arrived in America. Shippers purchased slaves where they could find them, and their availability for sale depended exclusively on African supply conditions and the forces of European competition. There may have been some ability for masters to selectively choose the ethnicities of the slaves they wanted within the internal slave trade that occurred in the Americas, as slaves sent directly from Africa to one colony or region were transshipped to others. Moreover, planters and masters often discovered that slaves whom they purchased had special skills in mining or agricultural tasks that they had not expected and thus tried to purchase more slaves with these skills. But overall, planters had no real ability to determine the African sources of their slaves and could only

---

[1] This idea of interethnic linguistic and cultural communities developing in the Americas has been proposed by John Thornton, *Africa and Africans in the Making of the Atlantic World, 1400–1800* (2nd ed.; Cambridge: Cambridge University Press, 1998). There is also no question of long and intimate contact between Brazil and Africa, even in both directions. There is even the case of João de Oliveira, an African-born Brazilian slave who returned to his home in the Bight of Benin in 1733 and then sent back money to Brazil to pay for his freedom. He subsequently became a major slave trader on the Slave Coast. Robin Law and Kristin Mann, "West Africa in the Atlantic Community: The Case of the Slave Coast," *The William & Mary Quarterly*, 56, no. 2 (April 1999), p. 317.

complement their Yoruba slaves, for example, by purchasing them on the internal slave market.

Specific events in Africa may have led to the clustering of some ethnic groups in the Americas. For example, a series of wars in the middle of the sixteenth century brought about the decline of the Wolof Empire in Upper Guinea, which in turn increased their availability on the slave markets of this period. Another very special case is the collapse of the Oyo Empire, which brought streams of the Yoruba into captivity in the late eighteenth century. Among arriving slaves, in cases where their ethnic identity was clearly given and recorded in the historical record, one can begin to explore the possibilities for the construction of culturally coherent slave communities based on mutually shared ethnicities. Yet such efforts must be carefully made and to some extent must remain speculative. Many slaves were simply listed as originating from the ports where they were sold rather than being assigned a more specific ethnic identity based on clan lineages and birthplace. The use of these generic port designations often makes it difficult to assert that certain groups of slaves may have definitively shared a language and culture and, consequently, could form a coherent ethnic "cluster," as some have argued.

Although many slaves recorded their actual ethnic identities with great clarity in testaments and sometimes in other official documents, not all Africans were correctly listed by origin in American registers, and relatively few left such wills and testaments.[2] It is difficult to determine the extent to which the ethnicities declared by officials and owners for their slaves formed a conscious part of everyday slave identities, and even more, it is unclear to what extent illiterate slaves actually claimed these ethnic identities recorded for them by such masters and officials. A number of slaves were either slow to assert an African ethnicity, or, if they came to the New World as children, never really grasped the meaning of their African ancestry.

Finally, there remains the question, much discussed by Brazilian historians, whether there were not hostile relations between native-born slaves (Creoles) and African ones, and even between African groups that sometimes reflected antecedent hostile contacts in Africa itself. Marriage endogamy for both Creoles and Africans suggests a preference for association with one's own group, the often-hostile role Creoles played in African-led revolts, and finally the discriminatory admission practices of

---

[2] Only Africans who were free and who held some property actually made wills, and many of them were literate. They thus form a minority of such Africans who arrived in America.

the African-based brotherhoods all suggest that there was no unified slave culture and that tensions existed along origin boundaries. At the same time, historians have shown cooperation, marriage across these boundaries, and hostility declining over time as the slave population became ever more Creole dominated. There also appear to be very wide variations by place and economy as well as by time, in these patterns of conflict or cooperation and identity.[3]

The cultural relevance of African ethnicities in the Americas was not always related to demographic strength. Within a given colony or estate, some slaves who may have been few in number originated from ethnic groups that enjoyed primacy over others – either culturally, politically, or both – or in turn were the first to arrive and define the rules of acculturation. Equally important, some aspects of African cultures were simply more transferable across the Atlantic than others or were found to be more popular among the broader slave population. Africans in the Americas had no state apparatus, no political classes, and their clan organizations were severely ruptured; thus, African beliefs associated with all these activities had difficulty crossing the Atlantic. On the contrary, those beliefs relating the individual to health and well-being, interpersonal relationships, and relation of the self to the cosmos were most likely to retain their power in the New World.

It is also clear that elements of the emerging Afro-Brazilian culture were influenced by European beliefs. Variants of European Christianity became the dominant religion among slaves, even if syncretized with large elements of African beliefs and deities, and even American Indian beliefs were found to have penetrated Afro-Brazilian rituals.[4] Second- and

---

3 Among the leading positions taken on this are those by Robert W. Slenes, *Na senzala uma flor: Esperanças e as recordações na formação da família escrava: Brasil, Sudeste, século XIX* (Rio de Janeiro: Editora Nova Fronteira, 1999), who has stressed the unity and cooperation; and Manolo Florentino and José Roberto Góes, *A paz das senzalas: Famílias escravas e tráfico atlântico, Rio de Janeiro, c. 1790 – c. 1850* (Rio de Janeiro: Civilização Brasileira, 1977); and Hebe Maria Mattos, *A Cor Inexistente: Os significados da Liberdade no Sudeste Escravista* (2nd ed.; Rio de Janeiro: Nova Fronteira, 1998), who have argued for a constant conflict among Africans arriving in Brazil and basic conflict over resources between Creoles and Africans. A thoughtful reflection on these issues and their complexity in the Brazilian context is found in Sheila de Castro Faria, "Identidade e comunidade escrava: Um ensaio," *Tempo*, 11, no. 22 (2007), p. 122–46.

4 See, for example, Seth Leacock and Ruth Leacock, *Spirits of the Deep: A Study of an Afro-Brazilian Cult* (Garden City, NY: American Museum of Natural History, 1972). For a useful review of the debate among Anglo-Saxon scholars of "creolization" versus "afrocentrism" and the possible applications of some of these ideas to the Brazilian context, see Luis Nicolau Parés, "O processo de crioulização no recôncavo baiano (1750–1800)," *Afro-Ásia*, 33 (2005), pp. 87–8.

third-generation slaves were raised speaking the language of the local master class. In their adaptation to peasant agricultural practices, Africans and their descendants, although sometimes using African technologies, were often found adopting European tools, technologies, and ways of life. The structures of social stratification within the emerging Afro-American community may also have represented an amalgam of two different worlds or even a response to the special conditions that slaves encountered under New World slavery. In some cases, differentiation in original African social status successfully made the transition across the Atlantic. In others, differences in slave status derived from struggles against the varying social positions that were assigned to slaves by their masters, which frequently did not correspond to the notions of stratification that emanated from within slave communities themselves. Consequently, although a hierarchy of status in terms of occupation and skin color was imposed on the slave population, internal slave divisions often did not necessarily replicate white standards.

Certain features of this slave culture were common to all slave societies in America, whereas others were more especially developed in the Latin American context. It is now generally accepted that in the slave periods in Cuba, Haiti, and Brazil, powerful movements of proscribed religious practices developed that were most heavily influenced by a syncretic arrangement of African religious deities. Santaria in Cuba, Vodoo in Haiti, and Candomblé in Brazil were the major manifestations of these new religions.[5] These movements came fully to light in the postabolition period in these Catholic countries, but never arose to any significant extent in the Protestant societies. These essentially non-Christian religions were among the more significant features that distinguished Brazilian Afro-American culture.

Although whites viewed all slaves as equal before the law, the differential prices paid for skilled slaves as opposed to field hands clearly suggest that whites recognized important variations in aptitudes, abilities, and other individual traits. As for the slaves themselves, there were obviously some levels of stratification within their own commonality of bondage. The traditional definitions of social status among the contemporary free persons, however, are not totally applicable when examining slave society. Positions with control over resources or other persons – highly prized

---

[5] The classic survey of these religions is Roger Bastide, *Les religions africaines au Brésil* (Paris: Presses Universitaires de France, 1960), which has been translated into Portuguese and English.

in the free community – were not necessarily those that guaranteed higher status within the community of slaves, or even those recognized by the price differentials given by whites. Autonomy and knowledge often played an equally important role. Autonomy was clearly related to independence from the control and supervision of whites, whatever the job, just as knowledge could be both of the African culture of the past or of the white culture of the present.

The life of the slaves in Latin America was primarily defined by work. With the exception of the very young and the very old, everyone spent most of their time engaged in manual labor. More than any other segment of the society, slaves were both the least sexually defined by their labor and had the highest rates of economically active employment of any class or group. For this reason, work dominated the life of the slave more than others in the society, and questions of work autonomy or dependency were of vital concern to slaves. In plantation societies, supervision of the strictest kind was the lot of the majority of slaves, but even here, relative control over one's time was available to a surprising number of them. On an average sugar or coffee plantation, gang labor involved only half of the slaves. Another third or so were craftsmen or had occupations giving them freedom from direct white or overseer supervision. In the rural slave populations that were not on plantations, there was also a distribution of jobs under close supervision on family farms as well as relatively independent families of slaves tilling lands on their own, or skilled artisans or muleteers who could escape direct white control. In the urban setting, domestics made up a large share of the labor force, came into close contact with whites, and were most tightly controlled. But all who worked on a self-hire basis or as independent craftsmen tended to have the most free time for themselves outside the normally controlled work environment.

Control over their time and labor permitted some slaves to achieve a fuller development of their talents and abilities. Short of total freedom, this was considered a highly desirable situation, and slaves who held these jobs had a higher status within the slave community. It was also no accident that many of the leaders of slave rebellions and other polit- ical and social movements came from these more autonomous slaves. Interestingly, some of these jobs were highly regarded by the whites as reflected in their prices, and some were not. Commentators on slave occu- pations noted that these jobs created an independence not found among the field hands or even the domestic slaves. In the coffee plantations in early nineteenth-century Brazil, for example, the muleteers who carried crops to market were considered a particularly lively group and were thought to be the elite of the slave force. The same could be said for the itinerant miners or even fishermen and truck garden slaves who supplied the food markets in the cities and who often worked with minimal supervision.

Knowledge was also an important granter of status within the slave community. This could be an ability to read and write the local European language, or even Arabic and a reading knowledge of the Koran, just as it could be an understanding of the dynamics of the master class and the socioeconomic realities of the free world. These types of knowledge would often be associated with skilled occupations, those possessing autonomy, or those in which contact was had on a frequent basis with the master class and other nonslave groups, such as in domestic service. It was also more commonly found in urban settings and could be discovered even at the lowest level of the occupational skills ladder. However, knowledge of African ways and customs, or even in some rare instances, of prior noble or elite status transferred directly from Africa, gave some slaves leverage in their community in contrast with their occupational status within the American economy. Thus, the leaders of the 1835 Malê rebellion in Bahia were all *alufás*, or Muslim religious leaders, but their status in the nonslave world varied from a slave water boy to a free skilled artisan.[6] The same occurred with many of the male and female Africans who were part-time religious, health, and witchcraft specialists, most of whom had a status inside the community completely unrecognized by the master class. Finally, there are even cases of lower-status slave women becoming *beatas*, or Catholic lay religious figures, who emerged with nonslave and even white followers.

Sometimes this knowledge provided leadership and status potential, and sometimes it offered a potential for power as a cultural broker. Many domestics, for example, might not be considered elites within the community but could provide the kind of brokerage knowledge or contacts of aid to slaves more isolated from the dominant society. Thus, house servants often held a special ability to mediate demands between the slave quarters and the master's house. But this role often left them with little leadership possibilities on either side. Some slave leaders did come from domestic service, but usually they had occupations outside full-time master control.

---

[6] João José Reis, *Rebelião escrava no Brasil, a história do levante dos malês (1835)* (São Paulo: Editora Brasiliense, 1986), pp. 115, 156ff.

Thus, it was no accident that urban slaves and artisan or transportation workers were usually to be found at the head of rebellions or were persons who were most likely to purchase their freedom. However, such leaders in and of themselves did not define the culture of the slave world. Afro-Brazilian culture as it emerged tended to develop in the small black villages that made up the world of the large plantations and in the common social spaces that slaves shared in cities. Thus, markets, taverns, watering spots by urban fountains, riverbanks used for washing of cloths, and even churches were sites for meeting and reinforcing relationships. Moreover, for a minority of slaves, formal religious associations were also an important component of their lives, and Catholicism for many was an accepted religion.

Whatever the effectiveness of the Church may have been in relation to protection of the slaves and their rights to celebrate the sacraments, there is no question that all slaves were baptized. Although the Church pressured the Crown to baptize all slaves in Africa or aboard the Portuguese-owned slave traders and laws were written to that effect, this was only modestly accomplished.[7] Thus, a common occurrence in all Brazilian parishes was the baptism of adults. Of the 4,775 slave baptisms for which age and type was known, which occurred in the urban Rio de Janeiro parishes of Candelária São José and Santa Rita between 1751 and 1760, some 26 percent were for adults.[8] In the São Paulo town of Mariana between 1700 and 1750 in the matriz parish, some 2,756 slaves were baptized, of whom 59 percent were adults.[9] Of some 7,217 slaves baptized in four rural parishes on the frontier of the province of Rio Grande do Sul from the mid-eighteenth century to 1835, 11 percent were adult slaves.[10] In the Vila Rica parish of Antonio Dias, of the 2,494 slave baptisms between 1759 and 1818, one-third (818) were for adults. Moreover, they were more than half of such baptisms in the earlier years when the African arrivals to Minas Gerais were heaviest. Thus, of the

---

[7] A.J.R. Russell-Wood, *The Black Man in Slavery and Freedom in Colonial Brazil* (London: Macmillan Press, 1982), pp. 130–1.

[8] Mariza Soares, *Devotos da cor: Identidade etnica, religiosidade e escravidão no Rio de Janeiro, século XVIII* (Rio de Janeiro: Civilização Brasileira, 2000), tabelas 19–21, pp. 302–3.

[9] Moacir Rodrigo de Castro Maia, "Por uma nova abordagem da solidariedade entre escravos africanos recém-chegados a América (Minas Gerais, século XVIII)," *III Encontro de Escravidao e Liberdade no Brasil Meridional* (2007), p. 4.

[10] Silmei de Sant'Ana Petizl, "Considerações sobre a família escrava da fronteira Oeste do Rio Grande de São Pedro (1750–1835)," *III Encontro de Escravidao e Liberdade no Brasil Meridional* (2007), tabela 4.

960 slave baptisms that occurred between 1759 and 1773, some 62 percent were given to adults.[11] In fact, in the internal slave trade, officials
defined "novo" slaves as those who did not have a Christian name and
did not speak Portuguese (*boçales* in the traditional literature).[12] All these
Africans were in fact baptized as soon as they arrived in their permanent
place of residence, and no records exist in Brazil of any African first names
applied to slaves – a key indication of universal baptism.

At the heart of the new black culture was the family unit. Although
masters experimented with every type of communal arrangement for their
plantation slaves, most slaves lived in family units. These households
would define the emerging Afro-Brazilian culture and would socialize
children to these beliefs and behavior. Black culture involved everything
from sexual mores and kinship arrangements to language, religion, and
the arts. It was a culture whose prime task was to create a coherent and
reproducible community that would provide a social network of resources
and support for the individual slave. Without this culture, slaves could
not have functioned, and even white planters recognized its essential
quality of providing social stability in an otherwise chaotic and hostile
world.

Although the Church played an important role in legal marriages, especially in the southeastern region of Brazil, the majority of slaves lived in
family units not formally sanctioned by the sacrament of marriage. Nevertheless, both legally sanctioned marriages and those composed of free
unions played a fundamental role in slave society, culture, and identity.
The best data currently available on slave family composition in terms
of origin come from the legal marriage data. The sex ratio among the
Africans guaranteed that initially, many males would not have access
to slave women of their own background, and they would marry out
more than the African women did. In the city of Rio de Janeiro in the
early nineteenth century, higher legal endogamy rates were noted for
African females than for African males. In three urban parishes from
1790 to 1837, African female slaves legally married African male slaves
in 96 percent of the 444 marriages in which such women were legally
married, whereas African male slaves married African women slaves in

---

[11] Iraci del Nero da Costa, *Vila Rica: População (1719–1826)* (São Paulo: IPE-USP, 1979),
    tabelas II.2 and III.2, pp. 220, 226.
[12] Fábio W. A. Pinheiro, "Tráfico atlântico de escravos na formação dos plantéis mineiros,
    Zona da Mata, c. 1809 – c. 1830" (Dissertação de mestrado, UFRJ, Rio de Janeiro,
    2007), p. 73.

only 85 percent of the 501 marriages in which they were partners.[13] In the Minas Gerais district of Barbacena between 1721–1781, some 717 Africans were married; of this number, only 68 percent married other Africans, and here, too, African males married native-born slaves far more often than African women married native-born male slaves. But it is worth noting that within all these African marriages, there was a very high degree of endogamy. In this study of Barbacena, which is one of the few such detailed and extensive studies of ethnicity currently available, it was found that among the 488 Africans who married other Africans, there was a very high rate of ethnic endogamy, with 96 percent marrying persons from the same nation, region, or language group as themselves.[14] In the legal marriages of African-born slaves in Bahia and Rio de Janeiro, there were also evident patterns of endogamy about ethnic origins. Thus, for example, in 253 legal marriages of African slaves registered in Rio de Janeiro in the first half of the eighteenth century, there was an extraordinarily high rate of men and women marrying within their own ethnic group.[15] Interestingly, the high endogamous rates among African groups were reversed in Bahia and Rio de Janeiro, which suggests that when any regional group was less well represented among the slaves, there was less endogamy. Consequently, the majority of Angolans were highly endogamous in Rio de Janeiro and far less so in Bahia, where they were a distinct minority among the Africans.[16] In the coastal district of Angra dos Reis in Rio de Janeiro, 75 percent of the slave marriages were endogamous in terms of African origin, and only a quarter involved Creoles marrying Africans.[17] In another survey of 160 marriages in the Bahian Recôncavo region in the eighteenth century, only 41 percent were shown to be endogamous marriages based on origin, but a more detailed look at origins of Africans showed that in each case, the single largest

---

[13] Based on the analysis of appendix tables 1, 1.1, and 1.2 in Janaina Christina Perrayon Lopes, "Casamentos de escravos nas freguesias da Candelária, São Francisco Xavier e Jacarepaguá: Uma contribuição aos padrões de sociabilidade matrimonial no Rio de Janeiro (c. 1800 – c. 1850)" (diss. mestrado, UFRJ, 2006), pp. 85–7.

[14] Ana Paula dos Santos Rangel, "A escolha do cônjuge: O casamento escravo no termo de Barbacena (1781–1821)," *Revista Eletrônica de História do Brasil*, 8, nos. 1–2 (Jan.– Dez. 2006), tabelas 7.

[15] Soares, *Devotos da cor*, tabela 8, p. 125.

[16] Soares, *Devotos da cor*, pp. 123–4. The significance of this finding is also discussed in Faria, "Identidade e comunidade escrava," p. 143.

[17] Marcia Cristina Roma de Vasconcellos, "Famílias escravas em Angra dos Reis, 1801– 1888" (São Paulo: tese de doutorado, USP-FFCH, 2006), tabela 40, p. 127.

grouping of their marriages were to others of their own ethno-linguistic grouping.[18]

Over time, the ratio of men to women became more balanced as the native-born slaves came to dominate the resident population, and probably the rate of adult bachelors declined and free and legal unions of two slaves with children became the norm. Almost all studies suggest that the majority of slaves lived in family units. Within Brazil, there was a wide range of family arrangements. Like most of Catholic Latin America, Brazil was unique by contemporary European standards in its extraordinarily high incidence of free unions and illegitimate births among the whites and free population in general. In few European societies prior to the nineteenth century were births among free persons close to the very high illegitimacy rates commonly found in Brazil, as in all of Latin America, and in none were the levels of free union so high. Even among the elite whites, where formal marriage played such a crucial economic and political role, the rates of illegitimacy and free unions were higher than found in any corresponding European elite, including those of Portugal. Thus, for example, an 1855 census of the city of Salvador de Bahia found that, of those couples with children, some 59 percent were not legally married.[19] In the parish of Sé of the city of Salvador between 1830 and 1874, only 38 percent of the more than nine thousand births to free persons were listed as legitimate children.[20] These urban rates of low marriages and low legitimate births seem rather special to the urban environment, especially compared to the more rural districts of the empire in the eighteenth and nineteenth centuries. Here the rates of marriage seem to have been much higher for the noncolored population of free-born persons.[21]

---

[18] Parés, "O processo de crioulização no recôncavo baiano (1750–1800)," tabela 3, p. 114.

[19] Katia de M. Queirós Mattoso, *Família e sociedade na Bahia do século XIX* (São Paulo: Corrupio, 1988), quadro IX, p. 82.

[20] Mattoso, *Família e sociedade na Bahia*, quadro XIII, p. 90. The rate of legitimate slave births in this parish is lower than any other recorded rates, being only 19 out of 3,747 births. A second study of births whose parents' origin was known in this parish from 1801 to 1888 found that 19 percent of the *liberto* children were legitimate, and only 33 percent of *livre* children were in this category. Isabel Cristina Ferreira dos Reis, "A família negra no tempo da escravidão: Bahia, 1850–1888" (tese de doutorado, História UNICAMP, 2007), quadro 1 (tabela 12), p. 105.

[21] For comparative urban and rural parish data on legitimacy of births among the free population in the eighteenth and nineteenth centuries – which shows consistently higher rates of legitimate births among rural free persons – see Sheila de Castro Faria, "Legitimidade, estratégias familiares e condição feminina no Brasil escravista," *Anais do VIII Econtro de Estudos Populacionais*, ABEP (1992), vol. I, quadro 6, p. 312. For a listing broken down by the color of the children, it is evident that whites (*brancos*) had

Given these varying patterns of legal marriage among the free population, it is rather surprising to find legally married slaves from the earliest
days of slavery in Brazil. In fact, Brazil was fairly unique among slave
societies in having a relatively important group of such couples. Moreover, these marriages were legally binding, and not only do married slaves
appear in other documents as being married or widowed, but there are
also numerous cases showing the Church and state intervening to prevent
the disruption of co-residence of married couples. But slave marriage
rates were not uniform across time and space. Although married slaves
could be found everywhere, the zones of the Southeast showed more such
legally guaranteed unions than other regions of Brazil, and some regions,
like Rio de Janeiro, saw severe declines in these marriage rates during the
nineteenth century. Other regions, however, seem to increase or at least
to maintain their high marriage rates until the last years of the slave system. Also, somewhat unexpected, it would appear that there were more
married slaves in the rural areas than in the urban centers.

The percentage of slaves who were legally married on the coffee estates
of São Paulo was higher than in any other region of the country, whether
plantation area or not. Whereas some 12 percent of the slaves were
recorded as "ever married" in Brazil in the first census of 1872, in the
coffee counties of São Paulo, some 29 percent of the adult slaves were so
designated. As was to be expected given the bias toward men among the
slaves, the ratio of slave women ages 15 and older who were married or
widowed in São Paulo in 1829 was 39 percent compared to 23 percent
of the adult slave males.[22] This difference among the sexes in marriage
rates was also found in the Minas Gerais district of Santa Luzia in 1831 –
which was a zone of relatively low marriage rates for slaves. Here, 17 percent of the males older than age 15 were married, compared to 22 percent
of the women.[23] A complete survey of the available census records for the
province of São Paulo in the late eighteenth and early nineteenth centuries

a rate of legitimacy in a series of selected southeastern parishes of 90 percent compared to slightly lower rates for *pardos livres* (in the 80–90 percent) and *forros* at
normally half of births. Sheila de Castro Faria, *A Colônia em movimento: Fortuna e
família no cotidiano colonial* (Rio de Janeiro: Nova Fronteira, 1988), quadro II.14,
p. 157.

[22] Francisco Vidal Luna and Herbert S. Klein, *Slavery and the Economy of São Paulo,
1750–1850* (Stanford: Stanford University Press, 2003), table 6.2, p. 142; and recent
postpublication calculations from our data sets.

[23] Carolina Perpétuo Corrêa, "Aspectos da demografia e vida familiar dos escravos de Santa
Luzia, Minas Gerais, 1818–1833," *XIV Encontro Nacional de Estudos Populacionais,
ABEP* (2004), tabela 8, p. 18.

TABLE 8.1. *Percentage of Slaves Age 15 and Older
Who Are Married or Widowed*

Locality	1776	1804	1829
Areias			22.9
Cunha		33.7	27.1
Curitiba		25.5	22.7
Guaratinguetá	28.8	36.4	33.8
Iguape		25.8	25.7
Itu		36.0	34.1
Jacareí		28.7	28.1
Jundiaí	30.0	22.2	33.7
Lorena		33.4	27.5
Mogi das Cruzes		28.7	27.0
São Paulo		22.2	16.3
São Sebastião		25.0	22.8
Sorocaba		42.8	37.9
Total		30.2	27.5

Source: Francisco Vidal Luna, "Observações sobre Casamento
de Escravos em Treze Localidades de São Paulo (1776, 1804 e
1829)," *Anais do Congresso sobre História da População da
América Latina, São Paulo, ABEP/SEADE* (1989), tabela 3.

shows an overall rate of 28 to 30 percent of all adult slaves being legally
married, a rate that could be considered the norm for this institution (see
Table 8.1).

As might be expected, given the problems of maintaining married
slaves in co-residence and the need for master approval, the overwhelming majority of marriages of slaves marrying other slaves were within the
confines of the same slaveholding. Thus, in the Minas Gerais district of
Catas Altas do Mato Dentro, in selected years between 1742 to 1834,
some 98 percent of the marriages were between slaves owned by the same
master, and only 2 percent involved slaves marrying nonslaves.[24] This
was the pattern found for marriages in the coastal area of Rio de Janeiro
in the nineteenth century[25] and for a frontier town in São Paulo as well.[26]
It was also common for most Rio de Janeiro slave marriages in the

---

[24] Tarcísio Rodrigues Botelho, "Família escrava em Catas Altas do Mato Dentro (MG) no
século XVIII," *Anais da V Jornada Setecentista* (2003), tabelas 4 and 5, p. 16.

[25] Vasconcellos, "Famílias escravas em Angra dos Reis, 1801–1888," p. 116.

[26] Alida C. Metcalf, *Family and Frontier in Colonial Brazil. Santana de Parnaíba, 1580–
1822* (Berkeley: University of California Press, 1992), p. 165.

seventeenth and eighteenth centuries as well.[27] All indicated that more than 90 percent of the slaves marrying other slaves were selecting their partners from within the same household. Numerous eighteenth- and nineteenth-century studies of slave plantations in Minas Gerais, Rio de Janeiro, and São Paulo also show that women on larger plantations were more likely to be living with partners than those on smaller units. Thus, to give just a few examples, in the sugar and coffee plantation region of Campinas in São Paulo in both the provincial census of 1829 and the national census of 1872, slave women living on estates with ten or more slaves were twice as likely to live in family units as were women being held on estates with fewer than ten slaves.[28] In the well-studied province of São Paulo, an analysis of some 200,000 slaves from provincial censuses stretching from 1775 to 1850 show that there was a consistent increase of married couples the larger the size of the slaveholding unit. This was more pronounced for women, for whom there was a systematic correlation between increases in the ratio of married women and the size of the slaveholding, but also showed for men, although there was a plateau reached for men for slaveholdings that exceeded ten slaves per owner. Thus, slaves who were owned by masters who had just one slave were legally married in only 6 percent of the cases for men and 4 percent for women. Meanwhile, in estates holding more than forty slaves, the ratio of married slaves was 21 percent for men and 39 percent for women.[29] Given these findings, it is not surprising to discover that in Campinas in 1872, only 29 percent of slave children under age 9 were declared legitimate on plantations holding fewer than nine slaves, compared to an 80 percent legitimacy rate for children on estates with more than ten slaves.[30]

Nevertheless, all zones recorded marriages exogenous to the slaveholding, and many that crossed the legal boundaries of the couples. In the *mineiro* town of Vila Rica in the eighteenth and early nineteenth centuries, for example, some 20 percent of the slave marriages were to nonslaves – in this case, all of them *forros*.[31] In the *paulista* frontier town of Santana de Parnaíba, there were 569 marriages of slaves in the period from 1726

---

[27] Faria, *A Colônia em movimento*, quadro V.9, p. 316.
[28] Slenes, *Na senzala, uma flor*, tabela 6, p. 104.
[29] Luna and Klein, *Slavery and the Economy of São Paulo, 1750–1850*, table 6.3, p. 148.
[30] Slenes, *Na senzala, uma flor*, table 5, p. 102.
[31] Of some 188 slave marriages whose partner's civil status was known in the period of 1727 to 1826, some 38 involved slaves marrying *forros*. Costa, *Vila Rica*, tabela 1, p. 35.

to 1820, but only 70 percent were between two slaves. There were 52 marriages between slaves and Indians and 117 between slaves and free-colored persons.[32] One of the few systematic studies of such mixed marriages was carried out for the Paraná district of São José dos Pinhais for the period 1759 to 1888. Of the total of 179 legal slave marriages, surprisingly, 79 of them involved a slave marrying either a free person or a *forro*. Some 84 percent of these mixed marriages were between slaves and free persons (color unknown) and again, a very surprising 56 percent of all of these marriages involved male slaves marrying free females. Among the few *forro*/slave marriages, in general both male and female slaves equally married *forro* partners.[33] In the Rio de Janeiro sugar zone of Campos dos Goitacases, 96 percent of the 4,507 marriages of slaves whose partner's status was known were with other slaves, but there were 60 marriages of slaves to free persons and 102 were with *forros*. Female slaves were far more likely to marry free men (72 percent of these mixed marriages), whereas male slaves were more likely to marry *forra* women (in 61 percent of these cases).[34] The Paraná and eighteenth-century Minas data seem to be quite unusual, and the norm here is more like that found in Campos, with fewer than 10 percent of slave marriage occurring between slaves and nonslaves, although even this is a significant number given the social status of the slaves.[35]

The free persons marrying slaves were almost always the poorest element among the free population and were predominantly *pardos*, *pretos*, or Indians, and very rarely whites. For free women, marriage to a slave could provide economic support from the master, who in all cases had

---

[32] Metcalf, *Family and Frontier in Colonial Brazil*, table 19, p. 167.

[33] Cacilda Machado, "Casamento & Desigualdade Jurídica: Primeiras notas de um estudo em uma área da região paulista no período colonial," *XIII Encontro da Associação Brasileira de Estudos Populacionais, ABEP* (2002), tabela 5, p. 10. There is even a well-known case of one of the leaders of the Malê rebellion of Bahia, the *liberto* storeowner and Muslim religious leader Elesbão do Carmo (Dandará) of Haussa origin who was married to a slave woman whom he did not own. Reis, *Rebelião escrava no Brasil*, p. 163.

[34] Faria, *A Colônia em movimento*, quadro II.9, II.10, pp. 143–4.

[35] Such marriages were usually 10 percent or less of all slave marriages. See, for example, Silvia Maria Jardim Brügger, *Minas patriarcal, família e sociedade São João del Rei – séculos XVIII e XIX* (São Paulo: Annablume, 2007), tabela 4.1, p. 224 (which shows a higher ratio of male slaves marrying across legal lines than female slaves); and Janaina Christina Perrayon Lopes, "Casamentos de escravos e forros nas freguesias da Candelária, São Francisco Xavier e Jacarepaguá: Uma contribuição aos padrões de sociabilidade marital no Rio de Janeiro (c. 1800 – c. 1850)," *Anais do 1 Colóquio de LAHES* (2005), tabelas 1–4.

to approve the marriage, or was the only available marriage partner if the free person had been living in a free union or had sexual relations with the slave. Such was the case of Antônia de Escobar, a *liberta*, who in 1749 appealed to the ecclesiastical authorities saying she lost her virginity to a slave – which he admitted – and as such she needed to marry him because her case was well-known in the community and no free person would marry her.[36] For males it was primarily a question of poverty. Many of them already lived and worked as *agregados* in the same households as their slave spouses or were so poor that marrying a slave permitted them to have their wife's sustenance paid for by the master as well. It would appear that free males marrying slave women was moderately more common than free women marrying slaves. Of the 125 marriages contracted between slaves and free persons that reached the ecclesiastic courts in eighteenth-century São Paulo, 60 percent were free males marrying slave women.[37] It was thus most common among slave couples, even those married with free persons, for their partners to be working for the same master.[38]

Given that master approval was required in all cases of slave marriages, it is not surprising to find that the majority of slaves were forced to select marriage partners from the same *plantel* (or slaveholding), largely for the convenience of their owners who demanded stability and control over their workers. There were thus, clear demographic constraints on available marriageable partners and thus marriage rates and the selection of partners were greatly influenced by the size of slaveholding and the available pool of marriageable-age persons.[39] This would seem to be the norm in larger slaveholdings and was obviously less common when only one or two slaves were owned by the same individual. Thus, in rural holdings, for example, the size of the marriage pool was much influenced by the size of the slaveholding. In small rural holdings and in urban settings where the average number of slaves held was much smaller than in the *fazendas*, the potential pool of partners obviously was much smaller.

---

[36] "Ficava . . . perdida e não haverá quem com ela queria casar por ter tido muita fama naquela vila. . . . " Elena María Réa Goldschmidt, *Casamentos mistos de escravos em São Paulo Colonial* (São Paulo: Annablume, 2004), p. 115.

[37] Elena María Réa Goldschmidt, "Casamentos mistos de escravos em São Paulo Colonial," (dissertação de mestrado, FFLCH-USP, 1986), tabela 6, p. 248.

[38] A major survey of Rio de Janeiro parishes in the eighteenth century of slave marriages found that more than 97 percent of them were between slaves in the same *plantel*. See Faria, "Legitimidade, estratégias familiares e condição feminina no Brasil escravista," p. 300, quadro 2; also Faria, *A Colônia em movimento*, quadro V.9, p. 316.

[39] See, for example, Machado, "Casamento & Desigualdade Jurídica."

This meant that coupling and marriage of slaves would occur across slave ownerships, and even between slaves and nonslaves in the same or other households in these smaller units. Because most slaves in fact married other slaves within their own slaveholding group, this inevitably meant that the larger the slaveholding, the more likely were slaves to find a marriageable-age partner and thus most studies that analyze marriage by size of slaveholding find that marriage rates increase with the size of the slaveholding.[40] This is the case not only of legal marriage, but of free unions as well. A study of slave families in the Rio de Janeiro district of Angra dos Reis shows that the larger the unit, the more likely the families were to be dual-parent households and the less likely they were to be matrifocal families.[41]

Finally, there is the issue of the change of marriage patterns over time. Many studies seem to suggest that during the course of the nineteenth century, the ratio of matrifocal, single-parent households increased at the expense of dual-parent households, of both legal and free union origins. This seems to have been the pattern in Lorena in São Paulo,[42] and was the case of the coastal zone of Angra dos Reis in Rio de Janeiro in which dual-parent households, already a minority of families in the early nineteenth century, dropped to half their rate by the second half of the century and accounted for only 17 percent of all families.[43] The rural zones of Rio de Janeiro also seem to have experienced this decline, with nuclear families predominating in the first half of the century and matrifocal, single-headed households dominating in the middle and later part of the century, although the trends are not consistent over time.[44] Some scholars seem to suggest that the timing of this change is related to the end of the Atlantic slave trade in 1850,[45] whereas others propose that the U.S. Civil War of the 1860s suggested to planters that the Brazilian slave system was

---

[40] See, for example, Renato Leite Marcondes and José Flávio Motta, "A família escrava em Lorena e Cruzeiro (1874)," *Anais do XII Encontro Nacional de Estudos Populacionais. ABEP* (2000), tabela 6, pp. 10–11; and Luna, "Observações sobre Casamento de Escravos em Treze Localidades de São Paulo," tabela 13, p. 14. This is the conclusion as well of Robert Slenes after reviewing numerous studies; see Slenes, *Na senzala, uma flor*, pp. 78–9.

[41] Vasconcellos, "Famílias escravas em Angra dos Reis, 1801–1888," tabela 33, p. 109.

[42] Marcondes and Motta, "A família escrava em Lorena e Cruzeiro (1874)," tabela 7, p. 13.

[43] Vasconcellos, "Famílias escravas em Angra dos Reis, 1801–1888," p. 107.

[44] Florentino and Góes, *A paz das senzalas*, pp. 141–5.

[45] Florentino and Góes, *A paz das senzalas*, pp. 141–5. This is also the position taken by Sheila Faria, who also stresses the impact of the first failed prohibition of the slave trade in 1831. See Faria, *A Colônia em movimento*, p. 339.

no longer viable and this was reflected in prices for young female slaves, no longer taking into account their reproductive potential and in turn their disinterest in promoting legal marriage.[46] Whether these or other factors can be said to exist in given regions is still questionable, given the lack of longitudinal data from enough regions to see if these trends in Rio de Janeiro and São Paulo were consistent across all slave regions in Brazil. Moreover, it would be useful to see if these patterns were also found in nonslave marriages. That these may have declined as well can be seen in the data on legitimate births in the Minas district of São João del Rei. Here the rates of legitimate births (among both the free and among the slaves) declined in the course of the nineteenth century.[47]

Whether married or not, it is clear from all recent studies that slaves lived in family units. Although formal marriage was only of significance in the eighteenth and early nineteenth centuries in Rio de Janeiro, it was always a major aspect of slave life in the province of São Paulo. However, these two provinces were the exception, and in most regions slaves lived in consensual unions unprotected by the law or the Church. In fact, it would seem that in many regions, even the majority of free persons lived in consensual unions unrecognized by the Church.[48] Almost all plantation records show that most slaves in the rural areas lived in family groups and the same appears true for urban slaves. Church records, often used in conjunction with local census *mapas*, and postmortem inventories in which all slaves are listed for a given owner, along with a few surviving plantation lists, have been used to analyze slave family structure, residence patterns, family size, and naming patterns of children across generations. Wide variation has been seen in many of these regional studies, but it is clear that the dominant pattern is dual-parent households with resident children. In a few regions, however, female-headed households or single-person residents have dominated. As Slenes has noted, many of the local studies on family structure and slave marriages have shown wide regional variation and this has made generalizations difficult until more work is done.[49]

---

[46] Slenes, *Na senzala, uma flor*, pp. 90–3.

[47] Brügger, *Minas patriarcal, família e sociedade São João del Rei*, tabelas 2.24 and 2.25, pp. 109, 116.

[48] In the census of the city of Bahia in 1855, some 52 percent of the families registered lived in consensual unions. Mattoso, *Família e sociedade na Bahia*, p. 82.

[49] Slenes, *Na senzala, uma flor*, p. 45. Along with the major study of Slenes on Campinas slave families, also see the work on Rio de Janeiro families by Florentino and Góes, *A paz das senzalas*. Other important original research in this new area of slave families and family structures include José Flávio Motta, *Corpos escravos e vontades livres: Posse*

It is difficult to estimate the fertility of the slave population based on these parish records. However, these baptismal records are crucial legal documents not only for free persons and their births, marriages, and deaths, but also for slaves. These registers were the only way for owners to legally record the progeny of their slaves as their own possession. Moreover, all inheritance issues for children depended on whether they were registered as legitimate or illegitimate. What is surprising in the Brazilian figures is the relatively high level of legitimate births among slaves, even compared to free persons. Given the low levels in general of legitimate births among the free population, the slave populations do not look that different. Although slaves always had the highest such rates of illegitimate births, in many regions they did not differ too much from the white population, whose rates were often quite high.[50] Given the higher rates of marriage found in the larger slaveholdings, it is not surprising that at least in one major coffee zone, that of Juiz de Fora in Minas Gerais, there was a high correlation between legitimacy of slave births and size of *plantel* in 1872, and more than half of slave births were registered as

---

de cativos e família escrava em Bananal, 1801–1829 (São Paulo: Annablume, 1999); Elena María Réa Goldschmidt, *Casamentos Mistos – Liberdade e Escravidão em São Paulo Colonial* (São Paulo: Annablume, 1999); Heloisa Maria Teixeira, "Reprodução e famílias escravas, em Mariana, 1850–1888" (Tese de doutorado, USP-FFLCH, 2001); and the previously cited work of Rômulo Andrade, "Casamento entre escravos na região cafeeira de Minas Gerais," *loc. cit.* The age of marriage for slaves is examined in Alida C. Metcalf, "Searching for the Slave Family in Colonial Brazil: A Reconstruction from São Paulo," *Journal of Family History*, 16, no. 3 (1991). A recent attempt to look at slave marriages in terms of origin between native and African born is found in Parés, "O processo de criulização no recôncavo baiano (1750–1800)," pp. 87–132.

50 See for example, Rafael Ribas Galvão, "Bastardia e legitimidade na Curitiba dos Séculos XVIII e XIX," *XIII Encontro da Associação Brasileira de Estudos Populacionais, ABEP* (2002); Vanda Lúcia Praxedes, "A teia e a trama da 'fragilidade humana': Os filhos ilegítimos em Minas Gerais (1770–1840)," *Anais do XI Seminário sobre a Economia Mineira* (2004). A good overall review of illegitamacy rates for free persons is found in Maria Adenir Peraro, "O princípio da fronteira e a fronteira de princípios: Filhos ilegítimos em Cuiabá no séc. XIX," *Revista Brasileira de História*, 19, no. 38 (1999), pp. 55–80; Donald Ramos, "Single and Married Women in Vila Rica, Brazil, 1754–1838," *Journal of Family History*, 16, no. 3 (1991). Worth looking at is the attempt to measure multiple illegitimate births for the same mothers in Maria Adenir Peraro, "Mulheres de Jesus no universo dos ilegítimos," *Diálogos. Revista do Departamento de História da Uem, Maringá*, 4, no. 4 (2000), pp. 51–75; and the study of parents who mentioned illegitimate children in their wills, Sonia Troitiño, "Números da bastardia: Os ilegítimos nos testamentos paulistas oitocentistas," *Anais do XII Encontro Nacional de Estudos Populacionais ABEP* (2000). A basic set of indices on the structure of families and age of married partners in this period is given in Donald Ramos, "City and Country: The Family in Minas Gerais, 1804–1838," *Journal of Family History*, 3, no. 4 (Winter 1978).

legitimate – a rather high rate.[51] But the dominant pattern for slaves was that the majority of their births were out of wedlock. Probably closer to imperial patterns was the rate of one-third of all slave births being legitimate, which was found in a survey of more than nine thousand slave births registered from 1736–1854 in the parish of Nossa Senhora do Pilar de São João del Rei, also in Minas Gerais. In contrast, the legitimacy rate for the births of free persons was 71 percent (in more than 13,000 births) and 40 percent for the 2,400 or so births to *forras* mothers.[52] Legitimacy rates in rural parishes of Rio de Janeiro in the eighteenth century show very high rates – with some 48 percent of 11,580 slave births in this category.[53] This pattern of relatively high legitimate slave births does not appear in the Bahian rural parishes or even in urban Rio de Janeiro zones in the nineteenth century – where rates varied from 10 to 33 percent.[54] However, these eighteenth-century rural *carioca* rates are quite similar to those found in Minas Gerais in the nineteenth century. In the Minas Gerais town of Santa Luzia in the early nineteenth century, an impressive 45 percent of the 1,006 slave births whose status was recorded were listed as legitimate children, this despite a relative low rate of just 19 percent of the adult population being married[55]; and in Juiz de Fora and Muriaé in 1851–1888, the rate was 47 percent for slave births in the former district and 21 percent in the later one (for an overall 37 percent rate), which compared to a legitimacy rate of 89 percent among the free non-Indian population.[56] In the *paulista* district of Franca, some

[51] Rômulo Andrade, "Ampliando estudos sobre famílias escravos no século XIX: Crianças cativas em Minas Gerais: Legitimidade, alforria e estabilidade familiar," *Revista Universidade Rural, Série Ciências Humanas*, 24, nos. 1–2 (2002), p. 103, table 2. The rates of legitimate slave births for Campinas in São Paulo in 1872 were even higher and also correlated with the size of holdings, whereas the zone of Muriaé had far lower rates and they were not correlated with the size of holdings. Ibid., p. 104, table 3.

[52] Silvia Maria Jardim Brügger, "Legitimidade, casamento e relações ditas ilícitas em São João del Rei (1730–1850)," *IX Seminário sobre a Economia Mineira* (2000), p. 45, tabela 3. This was not that different from nineteenth-century rates found in large samples of births. Thus, some 45 percent of the 4,760 slave births registered in the São Paulo district of Franca in the nineteenth century (1805–1888) were legitimate births. Maísa Faleiros da Cunha, "A legitimidade entre os cativos da Paróquia Nossa Senhora da Conceição de Franca – Século XIX," *XIV Encontro Nacional de Estudos Populacionais, ABEP* (2004), p. 7, tabela 4.

[53] Calculated from data given in Faria, *A Colônia em movimento*, quadro V.14, p. 325.

[54] Faria, *A Colônia em movimento*, quadro V.13, p. 324.

[55] Corrêa, "Aspectos da demografia e vida familiar dos escravos de Santa Luzia," tabela 9, p. 19.

[56] Andrade, "Casamento entre escravos na região cafeeira de Minas Gerais," tabela 1, p. 102.

TABLE 8.2. *Legitimate Births for Total Populations and for Slaves in Selected Districts*

	Total	Slaves
Paróquia de Sabará (MG) – 1776–1782	53.0%	40.0%
Paróquia de Raposos (MG) – 1770–1806	59.0%	49.0%
Vila Rica (MG) 1763–1773*	43.0%	16.1%
Vila Rica (MG), 1804	53.7%	
Paróquia Senhor Bom Jesus de Cuiabá (1853–1890)	56.5%	
São Cristóvão (SP), 1858–1867	66.1%	
Paróquia da Sé, (SP)	67.3%	
Curitiba (PR), 1801–1850	72.6%	
S. J. Pinhais (PR) 1776–1852	74.8%	
São Paulo (SP), 1741–1845	76.8%	
Lapa (PR), 1770–1829	77.6%	
Jacarepaguá (RJ), 2a metade séc. XVIII	81.5%	
Ubatuba (SP), 1800–1830	83.6%	

Source: Praxedes, "A teia e a trama da 'fragilidade humana'," quadros 5, 6, and 7, pp. 10–12; * for Vila Rica 1763–1773, Kátia Maria Nunes Campos, "Antônio Dias de Vila Rica: Aspectos demográficos de uma paróquia colonial (1763–1773)," *XVI Encontro Nacional de Estudos Populacionais*, ABEP (2008), tabela 3, p. 14.

45 percent of the 2,270 slave births in the first half of the nineteenth century were legitimate.[57] These *mineiro* and *paulista* patterns of high legitimate birthrates do not seem to have held for the northeast region of the empire. In Paraíba, the slave births that were considered legitimate in some three districts in the first half of the nineteenth century ranged from only 9 to 29 percent of all slave births. It is also interesting to note that the free non-*forro* population had relatively significant rates of legitimate births ranging from 64 to 79 percent in selected regions.[58] As can be seen in the summary data in Table 8.2, there is little question that legitimate slave births were consistently lower than that of the total population, and that there was considerable variation of legitimacy rates even among the free and *forro* population.

Looking at these births in more detail from the same region (see Table 8.3), we can see that, as might be expected, the *forro* population

---

[57] Cunha, "A legitimidade entre os cativos da Paróquia Nossa Senhora da Conceição de Franca," tabela 4, p. 7.

[58] Solange Pereira da Rocha, "Gente negra na Paraíba oitocentista: População, família e parentesco espiritual" (Recife: tese de doutorado, UFP, 2007), tabela 3.2, p. 205. The districts were Nossa Senhora das Neves (9 percent of 458 slave baptisms); Livramento (28 percent of 303 baptisms), and Santa Rita (29 percent legitimate of 294 baptisms).

TABLE 8.3. *Rate of Illegitimate Births in Sabará (1776–1782) and Raposos (1770–1806)*

	Sabará	Raposo
Livres	13.0	13.7
Forros	66.0	63.2
Slaves	77.7	82.7
Total	49.5	49.4
(Number of births)	(1398)	(1159)

Source: Praxedes, "A teia e a trama da 'fragilidade humana'," quadros 6 and 7, pp. 10–12.

of ex-slaves were in the middle in terms of having their children baptized as legitimate.

Moreover, as could also be expected, neither slaves nor *forros* had abandoned children (*expostos*) listed in a far more complete survey of births in the same community of Sabará. In the former case, no owner would allow a slave to be listed as *exposto*, because that would mean the child was free and he would thus have lost a slave, and in turn, the *forro* population could easily absorb all children into the household workforce and thus did not abandon their illegitimate children (see Table 8.4). Interestingly, if illegitimate children were listed as "natural," it signified that their parents, although not married, had no impediments to marry, as opposed to bastard children with one or more of whose parents was married to another person other than their parent.

Given the wide variation in legal slave marriages, it is not surprising that some regions would even show variations in legitimacy rates for slave

TABLE 8.4. *Legitimacy of Births by Legal Status of Parents, Sabará 1723–1757*

	Slaves	Free	*Forros*	Total
Legitimate	8%	86%	19%	35%
Natural	92%	13%	81%	64%
Foundling		2%		1%
Known cases	100%	100%	100%	100%
(n)	1627	1044	437	3108

Source: Ana Luiza de Castro Pereira, "A ilegitimidade nomeada e ocultada na vila de Nossa Senhora da Conceição do Sabará (1723–1757)," *Anais do XI Seminário sobre a Economia Mineira* (2004), tabela 1.

children by time. In contrast, in two different periods in the Minas mining town of Sabará, rates were much lower – just 8 percent of the 1,627 slave children born between 1723 and 1757 were declared legitimate,[59] and 22 percent for the 529 slave births were so considered in the period 1776–1882.[60] This later rate is roughly the same as reported for some 1,118 slave children born in the parish of Inhaúma in Rio de Janeiro between 1817 and 1842, only 21 percent of whom were legitimate.[61]

But high illegitimate birthrates did not mean instability or lack of familial relationships among slaves. Most studies of slave families have argued for the existence of trial marriages among slaves, with couples eventually settling down into a familial pattern after the first or second child. Moreover, the complex Church rules on legitimate births made it difficult to find the family connections among the slaves if they were not formally married. Yet all studies of plantation records find most slaves living in family units.[62] Even more surprising, these studies suggest a high rate of stability of these families even after the death of the owners. It has been argued, in fact, that the larger the slaveholding, the more likely it was that families would not be broken up through sales. It is the poorer slave owners, those with the fewest slaves, who are most likely to have slaves who are married or living with a partner outside their own *plantel*, and also most likely to suffer a breakup of the family unit because of sales.[63]

---

[59] Pereira, "A ilegitimidade nomeada e ocultada na vila de Nossa Senhora da Conceição do Sabará," tabela 1, p. 14.

[60] Praxedes, "A teia e a trama da 'fragilidade humana'," tabela 6, p. 11.

[61] José Roberto Góes, *O cativeiro imperfeito: Um estudo sobre a escravidão no Rio de Janeiro da primeira metade do século XIX* (Vitória: Lineart, 1993), tabela V, p. 59.

[62] In a study from São Paulo in the nineteenth century based on postmortem inventories, only 39 percent of the slaves whose familial relations could be identified were listed without a family tie. See Juliana Garavazo, "Relações familiares e estabilidade da família escrava: Batatais (1850–88)," *Anais de XIV Encontro Nacional de Estudos Populacionais, ABEP* (2004), tabela 1, p. 6.

[63] In a large sample of rural slaveholdings in Rio de Janeiro in the period 1790–1835, it was found that three out of four slave families remained united after the division of inheritance of the original slave owners. Florentino and Góes, *A paz das senzalas*, chapter 6. In her study of the São Paulo district of Batatais in the second half of the nineteenth century, Garavazo found that 86 percent of the slave families were together fifteen years or more. See Garavazo, "Relações familiares e estabilidade da família escrava," p. 13. Of 288 families that existed on the death of their owners in the *paulista* district of Mariana between 1850–1888 and whose fate was known on the division of the properties, some 64 percent remained together, one-third were either totally or partially broken up among the inheritors, and 4 percent were freed. Teixeira, "Reprodução e famílias escravas, em Mariana, 1850–1888" (tese de doutorado,

The majority of slaves lived in free unions that in effect were formally sanctioned and recognized family units, albeit without the powerful support of the Church. Importantly, slaves themselves recognized these units, and once such families were established, slave communities went out of their way to ensure their internal stability by using the usual mechanisms of community control. Errant spouses or nonresponsible parents were condemned by the community and were made to conform. This conformity could be enforced by normal social pressure, witchcraft, or even violence to guarantee community peace and welfare. This did not mean that the slaves kept up a Victorian-style morality, but it did mean that once a slave family was firmly established, it was given legitimacy and sanction by the community.

The dominance of organized family living can be seen, for example, in detailed studies of the coffee plantation zone of Bananal in São Paulo in the early nineteenth century, where in 1829 some 83 percent of the 2,282 slaves were found living in family units.[64] Equally important, a study of the small northeastern São Paulo town of Batatais in the period 1850–1888 showed that more than three-quarters of all slaves whose residence and family arrangements were known lived in family units, with very few children living alone.[65] A similar study of some 2,245 slaves in the São Paulo plantation towns of Lorena and Cruzeiro in 1874 showed 55 percent of the slaves living in family units.[66]

Of course, the high death rates of slaves and the impact of sales and forced separations on free unions sometimes led to serial marriages. These processes also led to the emergence of stepfamilies, as well as families with legitimate and illegitimate children. However, even in high mortality regions, on average most slave marriages, legal or otherwise, lasted for a long time. One of the few studies of marriage longevity that has been conducted for Brazilian slaves comes from the sugar and coffee plantation region of Campinas in São Paulo. In 1872, for women slaves between the ages of 35 and 44, living in units of ten or more slaves, the median length of marriage was 16 years and 8 months. Moreover, it was found that there was surprising stability of residence for these married women, with almost all breakups of families coming as a result

USP-FFLCH, 2001), tabela 50, p. 133 – based on my own calculations, which eliminated the unknowns.

[64] Motta, *Corpos escravos e vontades livres*, tabela 3.15, p. 137.

[65] Garavazo, "Relações familiares e estabilidade da família escrava," tabela 2, p. 7.

[66] Marcondes and Motta, "Família escrava em Lorena e Cruzeiro (1874)," tabela 8, p. 14.

of the death of one partner rather than sales off the plantation.[67] From the same census of Campinas, it was estimated that in six of ten marriages of young slave couples (in their mid-20s or mid-30s) in 1872, the average marriage lasted eleven years.[68] The average length of marriage in Batatais was ten years.[69] It was found that even after the division of the property of a deceased slave owner, the overwhelming majority of the slave families remained intact. Between 1850 and 1888, in the same west Paulista district of Batatais, only 5 out of 112 families whose fate was known were broken up after division of the properties of the owner.[70] A study of several hundred postmortem inventories of slaveholdings in Rio de Janeiro between 1790 and 1835 also showed that only 19 percent of the slave families whose fate was known in these lists were broken up by the death of their owners.[71] There are also numerous cases of elderly children living with their slave parents, suggesting quite stable families. Such was the case with two slave families owned by the richest slave owner in the Paulista community of Cotia in 1798. Padre Rafael Antônio de Barros owned eighty-four slaves who were distributed into six nuclear families, four matrifocal ones, and two organized around widows. The slave Agostinha, a widow of fifty-five years of age, lived with her three children ages 16 to 30 years, while Eugênia, a sixty-four year old widow lived with her six children aged 17 to 26 years of age.[72]

Although there was a moderate inverse relationship between the size of the holding and the ratio of families separated through sales, overall the data from Campinas and the study of the Batatais slave families showed that the death of the master had far less of an impact on family breakups than the death of the slaves themselves, even among smaller units of slaveholdings. Of course, these studies are for prosperous plantation zones of major slave concentrations and continued slave in-migration even after the end of the Atlantic slave trade in 1850. Thus, they were zones with limited outmigration with consequent low levels of family breakup. It might be expected that studies from the Northeast or of the

---

[67] Slenes, *Na senzala, uma flor*, tabela 3, p. 98.

[68] Slenes, *Na senzala, uma flor*, pp. 98–99

[69] Garavazo, "Relações familiares e estabilidade da família escrava," p. 13.

[70] Garavazo, "Relações familiares e estabilidade da família escrava," tabela 9, p. 14.

[71] Florentino and Góes, *A paz das senzalas*, apêndice 6, p. 237. There were a total of 128 families, of which the fate of only 12 families was unknown.

[72] Fabiana Schleumer, "Além de açoites e correntes: Cativos e libertos em Cotia colonial (1790–1810)" (dissertação de mestrado, FFCH-USP, 1999), p. 157. Of the four nuclear families, two involved a union between slave males and free women – one being a *livre* and the other a *liberta*.

southern provinces, which were subjected to an important outmigration of slaves into the internal slave trade after 1850, may show more family unit breakups through sales even prior to the death of the slave owners. Yet in general, all the current research suggests a surprising longevity of slave marriages and a relatively low incidence of separation through the death of slave owners or through sales. The overwhelming form of breakup of slave families was from the death of one of the partners.

In terms of internal marital stability, there currently exist few viable studies given the lack of major *fazenda* records over several generations with both parents being named. In studies of slave births in the United States, it was found that slave mothers began having children quite early, and it was common for them to engage in premarital intercourse rather freely. This continued until the birth of the first child. At this point, women usually settled down into a relationship that might or might not be with the child's father. Usually, except in cases of widowhood, the father of the second child was the father of all later children.[73] Unfortunately, the detailed reconstruction of births needed to evaluate this question of familial stability has only been partially carried out in the case of Brazil.[74] Until better data are provided, this theme cannot be fully explored at this time.

There is, however, a recent debate that has emerged in the literature about the impact of the end of the Atlantic slave trade on resident slave marriages, legitimate slave births, and even slave fertility. Although current studies of legal marriage and legitimate births show wide regional variation and great change over time, there seems to be no secular trends evident in the data, whereas the study of slave fertility is still a relatively recent area of concern and diachronic data are still unavailable. Yet some have argued that the end of the slave trade pushed planters toward encouraging births and marriages, whereas others have taken just the opposite position.[75] To date, there seems to be little evidence to

---

[73] Herbert G. Gutman, *The Black Family in Slavery and Freedom, 1750–1925* (New York: Vintage Books, 1976).

[74] One of the few such studies, but one still lacking crucial elements needed to answer questions of spacing and parentage, was carried out by Vasconcellos, "Famílias escravas em Angra dos Reis, 1801–1888," chapter 6.

[75] For the former position, see Manolo Florentino and Cacilda Machado, "Sobre a família escrava em plantéis ausentes do mercado de cativos: Três estudos de casos (século 19)," *XI Encontro Nacional de Estudos Populacionais da ABEP* (1998), especially p. 1381. In contrast, Slenes takes the opposite view, suggesting far less interest in slave fecundity and slave marriage in all the plantation areas of the Southeast after 1850. Slenes, *Na senzala, uma flor*, p. 92. For an argument showing strong marriage ties from the earliest times,

suggest that planters themselves were more or less pro-family or pro-natalist before and after 1850. Studies of positive natural growth rates in Paraná and Minas Gerais even before the end of the slave trade and the steady growth of their resident slave populations until the last decades of slavery would suggest that there was no inherent bias among slave owners against promoting slave children and slave marriage.

With parenthood and cohabitation came kinship arrangements. Slave families several generations deep sometimes lived in extended families. These extended families, whether cohabiting or not, in turn developed clear rules about acceptable marriage partners. These rules included such universal human taboos as sibling incest prohibitions and even discrimination about marriage partners from along collateral cousin lines. Slave families may also have observed internal rules regarding naming patterns, property inheritance, and even place of residence, as newlywed couples negotiated whether they would live alone or with the "bride's" or "groom's" parents. In Brazil, the study of the slave family is still in its early stages, and we have just a few studies that have recently been undertaken that indicate detailed kinship networks, naming patterns, and marriage organization. On the Resgate coffee plantation in Bananal (São Paulo), well-preserved records for 436 slaves in 1872, along with their baptismal records from earlier years, provide detailed evidence of kinship on this long-lasting plantation. They show that almost 90 percent of the slaves were kin to other slaves or free persons of color. Those not having kinship ties were primarily males and either older Africans or recently purchased Creole slaves born in other provinces. All but two of the mothers were legally married on the plantation. The predominant form of family organization was the nuclear family, with only one-quarter being extended families. Of the 116 married couples, only a third involved Africans marrying Creoles; the rest were endogamous for either group. Among the mixed unions, African men married Creole women. When Africans intermarried (twenty-nine couples), the age difference between partners was only four years; for couples in which both were Creoles (forty-six in number), the difference was seven years, and in the mixed African-Creole couples, it was fifteen years. These figures suggest that African women – always in the minority to African men – were able

---

see Tarcísio Rodrigues Botelho, "Família e escravidão em uma perspectiva demográfica: Minas Gerais (Brasil), século XVIII," in Douglas Cole Libby and Júnia Ferreira Furtado, eds., *Trabalho livre, trabalho escravo, Brasil e Europa, séculos XVIII e XIX* (São Paulo: Annablume, 2006), pp. 195–222.

to marry quite quickly with men close to their age, but when African men could not obtain African women, they had to be older and of more status in order to marry Creole women. Based on the baptismal records for 568 children born on this plantation from 1860 to 1872, only 67 were named for living or dead relatives.[76] This same low usage of the names of living or dead relatives was found in a study of some 130 slave families and their children in the baptismal records of several parishes in Rio de Janeiro from 1790–1830. In this case, only 5 percent of the children were named for either parent.[77] In both of the Brazilian cases, the patrilineal naming practices that were apparently the norm in the United States did not appear. The naming of children in Brazil came from both the paternal and maternal relatives. On the Resgate plantation, as in the region of Campinas, these slave marriages were quite stable and of long duration.

If we are still lacking residence patterns of families and more detailed studies of kinship in most regions of Brazil, there have been excellent recent studies on a secondary kinship system that developed among slaves in Brazil. Known as godparenthood, it was a major fictive kin system used by all classes – including slaves. Although few marriages were legally sanctioned, all births were recorded by the Church. In such Church recordings, a fictive kinship pattern of *compadrio*, or godparenthood, was established. This was a formal relationship between adults that bound them through their children. The godmother (*madrinha*) or godfather (*padrinho*) was supposed to be a close friend and one to whom the child could turn as a parent if their own parents died or even if they remained alive. The co-parent was obligated to provide for that child on all special occasions and incorporate that child into their household if the other household ceased to exist. Equally, the friendship relationship among the fictive and real parents was further cemented by these ties so that special claims could be made between them for support and services.[78]

---

[76] Manolo Florentino and José Roberto Góes, "Parentesco e família entre os escravos de Vallin," in Hebe Maria Mattos de Castro and Eduardo Schnoor, eds., *Resgate: Uma janela para o Oitocentos* (Rio de Janeiro: Topobooks, 1995), pp. 140–64.

[77] Florentino and Góes, *A paz das senzalas*, p. 88.

[78] A good discussion of the rules of *compadrio* are contained in Stephen Gudeman and Stuart B. Schwartz, "Purgando o pecado original: O compadrio e batismo de escravos na Bahia no século XVIII," in João José Reis, ed., *Escravidão e Invenção da Liberdade: Estudos sobre o negro no Brasil* (São Paulo: Brasiliense, 1988), pp. 33–59; and Stuart B. Schwartz, *Slaves, Peasants, and Rebels: Reconsidering Brazilian Slavery* (Urbana: University of Illinois Press, 1992), chapter 5.

Among the elite and for the Indians and black slaves, this institution was heavily based on friendship and respect, with either close personal friends or community-recognized elders and morally sanctioned persons as the most likely candidates for such a role. Thus, white planters had fellow white planters as their godparent relations, just as Indians and slaves had fellow Indians, slaves, or freedmen from their own communities. Free colored, *mestiços*, and other middle groups were known to have sought godparents from higher-status individuals and thus used *compadrio* as a means of establishing more formal patron–client relationships, an important but alternative development of the *compadrio* system. Slaves, too, were not beyond using *compadrio* as a tactic for solidifying such vertical ties, especially with the world of free colored. Thus, in the zona de mata Minas Gerais district of Senhor Bom Jesus do Rio Pardo, some 1,970 slaves were baptized between 1838–1887. Of this number, *padrinhos* appeared in all but 11 percent of the baptisms, and only 19 percent of the *madrinhas* were missing on these parish registers.[79] Surprisingly, only 31 percent of the *padrinhos* were fellow slaves, whereas 69 percent were free men of color. The case of godmothers was similar, with only 38 percent of them being slaves and the rest free. Despite their minority status in the slave population, Africans dominated Creoles among *padrinhos*, whereas Creole women slaves dominated the group of *madrinhas*. Moreover, even when slaves were *padrinhos* or *madrinhas* at slave births, only two-thirds of them came from the same slaveholding.[80] In the Curitiba parish of Nossa Senhora da Luz dos Pinhais in the nineteenth century in the Bahian sugar zone of Iguape in 1835, and in selected Bahian parishes of the eighteenth century, similarly high rates of free godparents assisted at the births of slaves, with very few of these being their masters.[81] This remarkable figure of having close to 60 to 70 percent of all godparents for slave children being free persons, the overwhelming majority of whom were not their masters, was also encountered in the Bahian sugar parishes of Monte e Rio Fundo in the period from 1780–1789,

---

[79] This same pattern of better representation of *padrinhos* than *madrinhas* is also found in baptisms of slaves and free colored children in several nineteenth-century northeastern parishes, and holds for both legitimate and natural-born children. Rocha, "Gente negra na Paraíba oitocentista," chapter 4.

[80] Jonis Freire, "Compadrio em uma freguesia escravista: Senhor Bom Jesus do Rio Pardo (MG) (1838–1888)," *XIV Encontro Nacional de Estudos Populacionais*, ABEP (2004), tabelas 1, 5, 6, and 7, pp. 11, 17, 19.

[81] Schwartz, *Slaves, Peasants, and Rebels*, tables 4 and 5, pp. 148, 151. Only in a sample from late nineteenth-century Paraíba do Sul did Schwartz find a majority of slaves serving as godparents.

and in the small scale slaveholdings in Cabo Frio in Rio de Janeiro in the eighteenth century.[82] However, this pattern was not consistent across all of Brazil's districts. In Rio de Janeiro, for example, in the parish of Inhaúma, between 1817 and 1842, only one-third of the 1,557 godfathers were free persons, whereas 64 percent of the slave godparents came from the same household or slaveholding as the child being baptized. Moreover, in contrast to other regions, the majority of the free persons serving as godfathers (almost three-quarters of them) were ex-slaves who had been freed within their own lifetimes (that is, they were *forros*). In the case of the godmothers, the ratio of slaves was even higher, with 78 percent of the 656 *madrinhas* being slaves and 72 percent of these slave godmothers belonging to the same master as the baptized child.[83]

Whatever the variation from parish to parish, which at this point is difficult to explain, it should be stressed that few owners were godparents to their slaves, and that in the overwhelming majority of cases even the free persons were of color, were poor, and as the case of Inhaúma suggests, they were themselves recently freed persons who may have known the child's parents when they themselves were slaves. Brazil also shows slaves acting as godparents to children born free. In the aforementioned Minas parish of Senhor Bom Jesus do Rio Pardo, roughly 35 percent of the 979 births of free children had a slave godfather, and among the 904 births of free children who had a godmother, slave women stood up for these children more than 43 percent of the time.[84] Clearly there was not a rigid barrier between poor free persons of color and slaves, and friendship routinely crossed this boundary.

Despite the importance of *compadrio* as a structuring element in the extended family networks of Brazil, the poorest elements in the society from which godparents were drawn could not always fully honor such obligations, and sometimes slaves were baptized with only a *padrinho* present. Although this was against Church practice and custom, it did reflect the weaker ties of the institution of *compadrio* at the lowest level

---

[82] For the Bahian data, see Stuart B. Schwartz, *Sugar Plantations in the Formation of Brazilian Society (Bahia, 1550–1835)* (Cambridge: Cambridge University Press, 1985), p. 409; and for the Cabo Frio materials, see Ana Maria Rios, "The politics of kinship: Compadrio among slaves in nineteenth-century Brazil," *The History of the Family*, 5, no. 3 (2000), p. 289. From a sample in the late nineteenth century from the same district, she finds an increase of the use of slave godparents that she claims is due to an increased concentration of slaves on larger slaveholdings.

[83] Góes, *O cativeiro imperfeito*, tabela III, p. 57.

[84] Freire, "Compadrio em uma freguesia escravista," tabelas 8 and 9, pp. 20, 21.

of the society. Nevertheless, all accounts seem to indicate that it was an effective support system that became an essential part of Afro-Brazilian culture, just as it was of free society. This fictive kinship system went to further the growing bonds of friendship and community among slaves, and given the status with which godparentage was held by the governing elite, it even provided white legitimacy to slave community-building efforts.

Equally important for the development of a community was the creation of a coherent belief system that would provide slaves with a sense of self, of community, and of their place in the larger cosmological order. The growth of a belief system would be a hard and slow task. One of the first areas where this evolved beyond the family level was in those practices that bound the community together. As in any peasant village, there were inevitable interpersonal conflicts among the slaves over resources. Sometimes these involved garden lands, personal effects, conflicts over potential spouses, sexual fidelity, or just personality clashes. These, plus the common problems of curing and divination, all led to the emergence of part-time specialists in witchcraft and curing. Given the importance these crafts had within Africa, it was inevitable that African influences would influence their evolution in the Western Hemisphere. It was usually older and single African males and females who provided the white or black magic that was an indispensable part of any community structure. Such individuals prepared herbs for curing and for influencing desired emotional or physical states in given subjects. They also provided recourse to a system of rough justice that guaranteed a limit to the amount of personal violence that the community could afford in fights over resources. Aggrieved adults who could not directly confront their opponents often had recourse to witchcraft to harm their rivals. This use of witchcraft and the knowledge that it was effective kept conflicts within acceptable limits within communities that had little policing powers of their own or any type of communal self-government.

Although the spiritual content embedded within the practices of these black New World ritual specialists integrated multiple non-African elements, slave beliefs began to evolve into ever-more elaborate cosmologies, and complete African-influenced religions began to develop by the late eighteenth and early nineteenth centuries. Masters were opposed to such formalized religious belief systems, which they held to be antithetical to their own Christian beliefs. All such formal cults were ruthlessly attacked, just as the less-threatening simpler forms of witchcraft were left unmolested. However, so powerful did these religious systems become that they were able to survive under the guise of alternative forms of the folk Catholicism developed under slavery, and occasionally, even influenced the practices of the dominant white society, whose members sometimes turned to the practitioners of these religious systems for guidance and assistance in their affairs. Although it often took several generations after abolition for Christian society to accept their legitimacy, the cults were finally able to establish themselves as independent religions in the twentieth century.

The most important of these cults in the era of slavery in Brazil was *Candomblé* (sometimes called *calundus* in the colonial period). It appeared in various guises throughout Brazil. A small initial group often established the basic cults that later massive migrations from entirely different areas in Africa adopted in their new environments. Even where many national *candomblés* existed – as in Bahia, for example – it was the Nago (Yoruba) *candomblé* which provided the basis for the theology, ritual, and festival activity of all other *candomblés*, even those named for Dahomean, Angolan, and Congolese tribes or nations. Thus, a process of acculturation went on among the slaves themselves, even in terms of the proscribed African cults and practices.

This process of syncretization and acculturation among the African religions in turn helps to explain why these cults found it relatively easy to accept and integrate parts of Christian religious belief and practice into the local cult activity. Initially, this integration was purely functional, providing a cover of legitimacy for religions that were severely proscribed by white masters. However, after a few generations, a real syncretism became part of the duality of belief of the slaves themselves, who soon found it possible to accommodate both religious systems. In the Catholic societies, dogma of the elite Church was not affected, but a rich tradition of folk Catholicism with its saints and local cults provided a perfect medium for syncretization of African deities. Also, the elaborate structure of lay religious societies and local community saint days was extended to the slaves and free colored by the white authorities in their desire to integrate and control slave beliefs. They also hoped these associations, many of which in the early days were based on African tribal origins, would guarantee internal divisions among the slaves and prevent the development of a coherent racial or class identity. Although moderately successful in this aim, these associations and local festival activity proved of vital importance in both legitimating and spreading African religious practices and giving blacks and mulattoes important communal organizations.

The Catholic Church was already well organized for a syncretic approach to religious conquest and conversion even before the full-scale development of American slavery. The Latin American Church had worked out most of the norms of this activity in its evangelizing of the American Indians. Local gods were to be destroyed, but sacred places were to be incorporated into the Christian cosmology through the erection of churches and shrines and the miraculous appearance of the Virgin. A brown-skinned Virgin appeared in all the traditional pre-Columbian religious centers, and her devotion took on many aspects of pre-Columbian rites and beliefs. Although the intellectual and upper-class Catholics fought the reduction of their monotheistic religion into a pantheon of virgins and saints who took on the role of local deities, they never succeeded in cleansing the Church of its folk aspects, either in Europe or America. Moreover, the Church in early colonial Latin America was unusually open to the rise of popular nonclerical religious figures, the so-called *beatas*, or lay religious individuals who developed local followings and even founded religious institutions, many of whom came from the lower classes and castes. One of the most extraordinary of such *beatas* was the mystic slave Rosa Maria Egipcíaca da Vera Cruz. Born in West Africa, she arrived in Brazil from the Gold Coast at age 6 in 1725, and was eventually forced into prostitution by her owner in Rio de Janeiro. Literate, a significant writer, and a mystic, she developed such an extraordinarily following and support, including that of the provincial of the Franciscan Order in Rio de Janeiro, that she and her final owner and confessor Padre Lopes were eventually taken prisoner by the Inquisition in 1762 and shipped to Lisbon after the Church attacked her teachings.[85] Although *beatas* had been openly tolerated in the sixteenth and seventeenth centuries, the Church became more resistant and hostile to their activities over time, and Rosa, like others in the eighteenth century, were more typically incarcerated and condemned if they developed important followings.

Into this system of syncretic absorption were implanted African belief systems. Very quickly, each of the major African deities took on an alternative saint identification. In Brazil, for instance, local Brazilian saints had a dual identity in the minds of the slaves, if not in those of the whites. Church leaders in the colony encouraged local slaves to stress the cult of Our Lady of the Rosary (*Nossa Senhora do Rosário*), which was

---

[85] Luiz Rosa Mott, *Egipcíaca: Uma santa africana no Brasil* (Rio de Janeiro: Bertrand Brasil, 1993).

reserved exclusively for the special devotion of blacks. Though all slaves were taught to accept the feasts, holidays, and saints of whites, they were also expected to celebrate their own saint days and holidays on an exclusive basis. In the urban centers this meant that slaves were to be grouped into religious brotherhoods (known as *Irmandades*) whose major purpose was to act as a mutual-aid society and prepare an annual celebration of the black-related religious figures. There were also special welfare societies (*Santa Casa*), which sometimes had black and *mulato* branches. There were even well-known dance groups or *batuques* in some of the northeast cities of Brazil that were grouped along African nationality lines.

How important these *irmandades* were in the lives of urban and rural slaves is difficult to estimate. There is no question that slaves participated in these *irmandades* everywhere. In fact, in the Rosario brotherhoods, they predominated as the major group of new or continuing members, well exceeding both the *forros* and *livres*, and sometimes making up more than half the membership (see Table 8.5).

In the brotherhood membership lists so far available that include both legal status and the sex of members, there is wide variation. Women represented two-thirds of the total slaves in Cachoeira Bahia, 51 percent in Vila Rica, and 42 percent of the slave members in São João del Rei.[86] However, they were only 23 percent of the slave members in the Rosario brotherhood of Cuiabá.[87] In a study of burials for the Antonio Dias parish of Vila Rica, of the 524 slaves buried as members of the *irmandades*, more than three-quarters were women.[88] Given these disparities and the random quality of overall female membership ratios in other *irmandades*,[89] it is difficult at this point to determine if the dominance of women among members was the norm throughout Brazil.

Although it could be expected that slaves would play a lesser role in the administration of these brotherhoods, what is impressive is that they did participate as active leaders. Thus, the executive board (*mesa*

---

[86] Lucilene Reginaldo, "Os rosários dos Angolas: Irmandades negras, experiências escravas e identidades africanas na bahia setecentista" (Tese de doutorado, UNICAMP, Campinas, 2005), p. 202; and Célia Maria Borges, *Escravos e libertos nas irmandades do Rosário: Devoção e solidariedade em Minas Gerais, séculos XVIII e XIX* (Juiz de Fora: Editora UFJF, 2005), tabelas 6 and 8, pp. 230–1.

[87] Silva, "Irmãos de fé, p. 115.

[88] Costa, *Vila Rica*, tabela 6, p. 235.

[89] For example, women represented 46 percent of all the members of the Cachoeira do Campo Rosario brotherhood, and only 36 percent of all members regardless of status in the Pilar Parish Rosario of Ouro Preto. Kiddy, *Blacks of the Rosary*, tables 4–5, p. 255.

TABLE 8.5. *Membership in Rosário Brotherhoods, Eighteenth and Nineteenth Centuries, by Legal Status*

Place	Years	Percentage Escravos	Forros	Livres	Total	Number
Cachoeira do Campo	1720–1789	43.1	10.5	46.4	100.0	717
Ouro Preto/Pilar	1724–1760	83.1	6.9	10.0	100.0	1,154
Mariana	1750–1886	48.1	12.7	39.2	100.0	1,895
Barbacena	1812–1840	40.7	12.5	46.8	100.0	513
São João del Rei	1750–1808	57.9	14.5	27.7	100.0	1,557
Mariana	1750–1804	68.9	20.9	10.2	100.0	684
Alta da Cruz/Vila Rica	1770–1808	45.9	4.1	50.0	100.0	2,484
Cuiaba	1767–1819	35.6	57.5	6.9	100.0	348
Cachoeira, Bahia*	1719–1826	84.9	15.1		100.0	2,218

Notes: * Livres not listed separately, but probably included in *forros*.
Sources: Cachoeira do Campo to Barbacena in Elizabeth W. Kiddy, *Blacks of the Rosary: Memory and History in Minas Gerais, Brazil* (University Park: Pennsylvania State University Press, 2005), tables 6–9, pp. 256–7; São João del Rei to Vila Rica, Borges, *Escravos e libertos nas irmandades do Rosário*, tabelas 6, 7, and 8, pp. 230–1; Cuiabá, Christiane dos Santos Silva, "Irmãos de fé, Iramos no poder: A irmandade de Nossa Senhora do Rosário dos Pretos na Vila Real do Senhor Bom Jesus do Cuiabá (1751–1819)" (Cuiaba: diss. de mestrado, UFMG, 2001), p. 115; Bahia, Reginaldo, "Os rosários dos Angolas," p. 202.

diretora) of the Mariana Rosário brotherhood had 303 slaves serving as officers out of 984 who served in the administration in the period 1748–1819.[90] Of course, they were underrepresented, being 71 percent of all members enrolled in this period, and only 31 percent of the board members (*mesários*), but not only were they an important minority, but the officials were overwhelmingly African born, whether free or slave. Of all the *forros* and *escravos* who served as officers of this association, those of African birth represented an impressive majority of these officials – of 723 whose origin was known, some 88 percent of them were born in Africa.[91]

Clearly then, even if only a minority of slaves in any district belonged to an *irmandades*, such organizations did play a fundamental role everywhere. There was not a region that contained slaves that did not contain

---

[90] Fernanda Aparecida Domingos Pinheiro, "Confrades do Rosário: Sociabilidade e Identidade étnica em Mariana-Minas Gerais (1745–1820)" (dissertação de mestrado, UFF, Niterói, 2006), tabela XI.
[91] Pinheiro, "Confrades do Rosário," tabela XIII.

a Rosário brotherhood, and these existed throughout the slave period of Brazilian history. Burials and festivities were their prime activity, but they also supported African identity elements as much as possible in this hostile environment. Many of the brotherhoods were predominantly of one ethnic origin, status, or color and had exclusive membership.[92] Others denied access to Brazilian-born colored.[93] Therefore, in many ways they helped perpetuate conflict among slave groups and often among Africans and Creoles and slaves and free persons of color. However, with their increasing admission of *crioulos* over time and the fact that all of them contained increasing numbers of *forros* and *livres*, these data suggest that these institutions could also serve as integrative associations as well and help acculturate the Africans to their new environment.[94] Also, they were one of the few institutions legally available to them. Although many *irmandades* were based on occupations, most of these, especially of the mechanical trades, sometimes excluded slaves from membership.[95] Thus, the *irmandades* based on identity or legal status proved to be of fundamental importance to the slaves if not to the free colored, who had more options of association opened to them.

[92] In the city of Salvador de Bahia, for example, "Os mulatos se reuniam nas Irmandades de Nosso Senhor da Cruz, na igreja da Palma, na de Nosso Senhor Bom Jesus da Paciência, na igreja de São Pedro, na Irmandade de Nossa Senhora da Conceição do Boqueirão e na igreja do mesmo nome. Os negros africanos agrupavam-se por nações de origem: os angolanos e os congoleses formavam a Irmandade de Nossa Senhora do Rosário, na praça do Pelourinho; os daomeanos, a de Nosso Senhor das Necessidades e da Redenção, na capela do Corpo Santo e os Nago-Yorubás, formada por mulheres e consagrada a Nossa Senhora da Boa Morte, na pequena igreja da Barroquinha. Os negros nascidos no Brasil se reuniam na Irmandade do Senhor Bom Jesus dos Martírios e em torno da devoção a São Benedito, seja na Igreja de Nossa Senhora da Conceição da Praia, seja na de São Francisco, ou ainda na de Nossa Senhora do Rosário, como também em quase todas as igrejas da Bahia." Humberto José Fonsêca, "Vida e morte na bahia colonial: Sociabilidades festivas e rituais fúnebres (1640–1760)" (tesis de doutorado, FAFICH/UFMG, Belo Horizonte, 2006), p. 114.

[93] In the city of Rio de Janeiro, the Irmandade de Santo Elsebão e Santa Efigênia was exclusively for Minas (Western African) persons, and Central West Africans and Creoles were excluded from membership. Apparently these Angolans and *pardos* were concentrated in the Rosário brotherhoods. Soares, *Devotos da cor*, pp. 188–9.

[94] The Rosario brotherhood in Mariana in the 1870s was already 90 percent free, and half of new members to the Barbacena Rosario brotherhood in the 1850s and 1860s were free persons. They were, of course, increasingly native born as well after 1850. Kiddy, *Blacks of the Rosary*, pp. 152–3.

[95] This was the case with the Rio de Janeiro shoemaker brotherhood. Mônica de Souza Nunes Martins, "Entre a Cruz e o Capital: Mestres, aprendizes e corporações de ofícios no Rio de Janeiro (1808–1824)" (tesis de doutorado, Rio de Janeiro: U.F.R.J./I.F.C.S., 2007), p. 50.

In Brazil, these legal and state and church-recognized associations were famous from the colonial period until the end of the Empire for their annual festive activities and, equally, for their constant conflict with the white authorities. Slave and free-colored demands for brotherhood self-government and control over their own churches and cemeteries were constantly opposed by the fraternal organizations of the whites. They were often in tense relations with ecclesiastical authorities over funding, because the *irmandades* paid for masses for the dead and funeral expenses of its members as well as the costs for religious festivals, and were often chastised for sacrificing the former obligation (with its funds supporting the Church) for the latter activity.[96] Yet despite white fears of their autonomy, in the majority of cases, the black and *mulato* brotherhoods were accepting of the dominant culture and were primarily integrative in nature. They did foster both self-pride and also legitimated African religious activity. In contrast, the African cults were forced to create independent organizations to survive. In so doing, they became essentially rejective and opposed to the values of the master class. These cults which competed with, reinterpreted Christianity for a slave audience, and most aided the development of an autonomous aspect to Afro-Brazilian culture.

From the plantation villages and the colonial cities came a distinctive Afro-American culture that provided the slaves with a self-identity and community, which allowed them to survive the rigors of their forced integration into the white society. This Afro-American culture was not homogeneous. Some of its elements were integrative and merely expressive of a subculture within the Western norms established by the white society. Others, however, were unique to blacks and provided an alternative value system to that of white society. Such a pattern was almost inevitable given the very hostility and ambiguity that the white culture expressed toward them. On the one hand, white society incorporated Africans into Christianity as co-equal members of a universalistic church. Among the Latin American legal codes, there was also a basic assumption that Africans would eventually become freedmen in these same slave societies. But at the same time, these were inevitably racist societies that rejected black self-identity and self-worth and often created a second-class

---

[96] Alisson Eugênio, "Tensões entre os Visitadores Eclesiásticos e as Irmandades Negras no século XVIII mineiro," *Revista Brasileira de História*, 22, no. 43 (2002), pp. 33–46, and her unpublished essay, "Solidariedade e tensões no simbólico das festas das irmandades de escravos e libertos em Minas Gerais no século XVIII."

citizenship for those who achieved their freedom. Social ascension and mobility were possible for enough blacks to give a majority a sense of hope, but the terms were always rejection of their Afro-American cultural identity and their blackness. In such a situation, it was inevitable that the cultures that were established by the slaves in America would serve two often-conflicting purposes: that of integrating the slaves into the larger master-dominated societies while providing them with an identity and meaning that protected them from that same society's oppression and hostility.

9

Freedmen in a Slave Society

Every slave society in the Americas permitted slaves to be manumitted from the very beginning. All such regimes accepted the legitimacy of manumission, because it was the norm in Roman law and was deeply embedded in Christian piety and practice. A free colored class thus developed in every American slave society virtually from the first days of colonization. All such populations grew slowly in the sixteenth and seventeenth centuries and all faced some type of restriction on their freedom. These restrictions were uniquely applied to them because of their origin and color. From the early eighteenth century onward, however, Brazil began to distinguish itself from other slave regimes on the basis of its changing attitude toward the manumission process, which in turn caused major changes in the number and ratio of freedmen in the respective societies.

The differences in the numbers and acceptance of the free colored population in each of the American slave societies were determined by a broad spectrum of considerations, from religious and cultural to economic and social. In all cases, however, the minority of freedmen in the predominately slave societies faced hostility from their white neighbors and former masters, and in no society were both freedom and total acceptance a possibility. Racism was a part of every American system that held African slaves and did not disappear when blacks and mulattoes became free citizens and economic and social competitors.

There has been a long debate about the nature of racism and whether it preceded slavery, coincided with the institution, or was a consequence thereof.[1] In the Latin American context, slavery long antedated colonization and even the arrival of African slaves. Thus, race prejudice followed slavery, although official policies of discrimination based on origin, creed, and, to a lesser extent, color, were being applied in the new centralizing Iberian monarchies of the fifteenth century just as Africans were arriving in significant numbers. Once Africans predominated and the plantation slave regimes of America were established, racism became one of the underlying assumptions of stratification among the free population. In the Iberian context, this racism blended with racist ideologies, which had originated both in the Castilian and Portuguese conquest of Jews and Moors in the Old World and the conquest of the American Indians in the New World. The long conflict between Christians, Jews, and Moors led in Europe and America to a discriminatory policy of "blood purity," or *limpeza do sangue*. From the time of the expulsion of the Jews and Moors from Spain and Portugal in the late fifteenth and early sixteenth centuries, church and educational institutions and then the Crown began to distinguish between the so-called Old Christians, or those who were Christians from the Middle Ages, and the so-called New Christians, or those who had recently converted from Judaism or Islam. New Christians were denied the right to practice certain occupations, to be admitted to many civil and ecclesiastical offices, and in many respects were treated as second-class citizens. American Indians also were discriminated against and were denied many of the same occupations and offices as the New Christians. With such a stratification system already in place, it was inevitable that the distinction of race would also be applied to free colored persons in an invidious manner.

From the earliest days, local and metropolitan legislation began to attack the rights of the free colored and to put them on a footing with the New Christians.[2] Free colored persons were denied the right to be

---

[1] See for example, Winthrop D. Jordan, *White over Black: American Attitudes toward the Negro, 1550–1812* (Chapel Hill: The University of North Carolina Press, 1968).

[2] With the opening up of an American empire based on servile African labor, it was inevitable that the whole process of Portuguese and Iberian discrimination by origin would expand to include color. The so-called laws of "limpeza de sangue" dividing Portuguese into Old and New Christians (the latter being of Jewish or Moorish origin) were expanded to include persons of color, this by a decree of 1671 that excluded New Christians and persons of color from all government and religious offices. In reality, the restrictions on origin were more severe than on color, and there are numerous cases where wealthy or powerful individuals of color reached high office, with royal dispensation. Nevertheless, discrimination against free persons of color was a constant in colonial society. Larissa Viana, *O idioma da mestiçagem: As irmandades de pardos na América Portuguesa* (Campinas, SP: Editora UNICAMP, 2007), pp. 54ff.

government officials even at the municipal level, although this was relaxed for the mining areas.[3] Sumptuary laws denied free colored women the right to wear the clothes and jewelry worn by free white women.[4] For many years, punishments for crimes differed for whites and for free colored. Even some of the skilled occupations were officially denied to them despite their practice of such professions.[5] Although all free colored persons were organized into their own color-defined militia units from the sixteenth century onward, there was a constant battle over the free colored to be officers in these separate Negro and mulatto companies.[6]

The laws and practices of the Ibero-American societies were those of an essentially racist society in which the free blacks and mulattoes would enter as lower "caste" within a highly stratified system. The enforcement of this caste-like system depended on the willingness of the colonial authorities to prevent the market from distributing rewards on the basis of individual skills and abilities. To make such a rigid stratification system function, wealth would have to be denied the free colored, occupational mobility severely limited, and even geographic mobility constrained.

---

[3] A.J.R. Russell-Wood, *The Black Man in Slavery and Freedom in Colonial Brazil* (London: Macmillan Press, 1982), pp. 70–71. There were also numerous decrees against free and slave colored persons bearing arms, although even these draconian codes were eventually abandoned given the need of Capitães-do-Mato and colonial militia. Russell-Wood, *The Black Man in Slavery and Freedom in Colonial Brazil*, pp. 67–8.

[4] On the law of 1741 (Lei Pragmática de 1749, capítulo IX), which prohibited *forros* and *libertos* of color from wearing fine clothes or jewels, see Silvia Hunold Lara, "Sedas, Panos e Balangandãs: O traje de senhoras e escravas nas cidades do Rio de Janeiro e Salvador (século XVIII)," in Maria Beatriz Nizza da Silva, ed., *Brasil: Colonização e escravidão* (Rio de Janeiro: Nova Fronteira, 1999), pp. 177–91.

[5] Daily hostility could be expressed in a number of ways. Thus, African slaves, although universally trained in all the crafts to journeymen level and even to that of master, were prohibited from taking official exams to practice their profession, which led to a weakening of the guilds and their associated craft-based *irmandades*. Many of these *irmandades de ofícios mecânicos* demanded constraints on sale of slave-made products from non-officially recognized artisans, while in early nineteenth century Rio de Janeiro, the shoemaker *irmandade* went so far as to prohibit slaves from the brotherhood despite their training by white masters. Mônica de Souza Nunes Martins, "Entre a Cruz e o Capital: Mestres, aprendizes e corporações de ofícios no Rio de Janeiro (1808–1824)" (tesis de doutorado, U.F.R.J./I.F.C.S., 2007), pp. 48–9.

[6] From early on, Portugal, like Spain, adopted a colonial military organization based on color; in this case, whites, *pardos*, and *pretos*. But there were always tensions inherent in this, with the colored regiments wanting their own officers and the Crown ever pushing for integration and/or white officers in charge. In the end, the dependence on these military units finally forced the Crown until the end of the colonial period to rely on black and mulatto soldiers and officers. Russell-Wood, *The Black Man in Slavery and Freedom in Colonial Brazil*, pp. 84–93.

Although proclaimed as an ideal, actual practice would eventually move away from this rigid plan as the economic importance of the free colored began to be felt.

Although all American colonies were racist and placed restrictions on the freedom of the ex-slaves, the actual societies that developed differed sharply among the various slave regimes. These differences had to do with both the process of manumission itself and the acceptance of the legitimacy of the free colored within the larger social and economic order. All societies began with a fairly active level of manumission, as masters piously freed their slaves – or fathers their children – or faithful service was rewarded with freedom. In all societies, there early developed self-purchase arrangements for slaves. The major differences began to appear only after the first several generations, when the Iberians not only continued to accept and support the traditional patterns of manumission but also actively accepted and codified the route of self-purchase. This further encouraged the growing number of freedmen, who in turn gave their support to increasing levels of manumission.

Other societies began in this manner, but, as the number of free colored began to grow, so too did the fear of those freedmen. Although they had the same restrictive legislation as the Iberian societies, the whites of the Anglo-Saxon colonies became less and less trustful that these prohibitions would guard their privileges. They therefore began to attack the whole manumission process, making it more costly to both the master and the slave. Just as the Iberian regimes were legitimizing self-purchase, the North Americans were restricting it, if not prohibiting it altogether. This fundamental opposition to manumission effectively began to curtail the numbers of freedmen in these societies, which remained relatively limited until the final years of slavery.

In Brazil, the free colored population grew at an even more rapid rate during the course of four centuries of slavery. In eighteenth-century estimates, the free colored were an important element of the population everywhere, but they did not exceed the slaves. The increasing arrival of African slaves in the nineteenth century did not slow the pace of growth of the free colored. Rather, they grew even more rapidly in the first half of the century, so that by 1850, when the slave trade finally ended, the free colored had already passed the total number of slaves. This dominance of the free colored in the total colored population increased with every passing year. By the time of the first national census in 1872, there were 4.2 million free persons of color compared with 1.5 million slaves. Not only were the free colored greater in number than the 3.8 million whites, but alone they accounted for 43 percent of the 10 million Brazilians.[7] All this was more than a decade before the abolition of slavery and just before the first partial emancipation laws.

There was, of course, some variation in the regional patterns. In the Northeast, the free colored were already dominant in the first part of the nineteenth century. Pernambuco in 1839 had 127,000 free colored to half that number of slaves, and this ratio appeared to be typical of Bahia and Maranhão as well.[8] In contrast, the province of Rio de Janeiro was unique in still having more slaves than free colored in 1872, whereas both Minas Gerais and São Paulo had many more freedmen than slaves by this time. São Paulo had attained this balance quite recently, but Minas Gerais probably had more freedmen by the 1820s.[9] Although the free colored were probably most numerous in the Northeast, they were well represented everywhere. Thus, the two largest states where they resided in 1872 were Bahia with 830,000 and Minas Gerais – also the largest slave state – with 806,000 freedmen.

In contrast to the United States, the rigid class structure and the elaborate caste and color distinctions may have provided the Brazilian whites with a relative sense of security against free colored competition, which made them more willing to accept the manumission process. This relative acquiescence of the elite whites led to both public and private commitment to manumission from the beginning to the end of slavery. Recent studies have shown that manumission was a complex process that involved both voluntary and involuntary manumission on the part of the master class, and both a passive and an active intervention on the part of the slaves themselves.

Although it was initially thought that the more economically minded Iberians were simply freeing their old and infirm slaves, this was not the case. Every study done of large samples of manumission records for Brazil, and Brazil is the best-studied country on this theme, shows that overall the manumitted were primarily young, Creole-born, and, in the majority, women, with the subset of self-purchased slaves being more male and more African than those freed without remuneration.

---

[7] Diretoria Geral de Estatística. *Recenseamento Geral do Brasil de 1872.*

[8] Joaquim Norberto de Souza e Silva, *Investigações sobre os recenseamentos da população geral do Império e de cada província de per si tentados desde os tempos coloniais até hoje.* (1st ed. 1870; São Paulo, IPE-USP, 1986), pp. 56–7.

[9] As early as the census of 1829/30, free colored represented 43 percent of the total colored population and 21 percent of the total population estimated at 128,000 persons. Herbert S. Klein and Francisco Vidal Luna, "Free Colored in a Slave Society: São Paulo and Minas Gerais in the Early Nineteenth Century," *Hispanic American Historical Review,* 80, no. 4 (November 2000), table 1, p. 7.

The data available for most regions of Brazil show a high incidence of children and young adults and a correspondingly low incidence of the elderly. Although there is wide variation by region and period, overall, children under 15 represented between one-fifth and two-fifths of all persons manumitted. Among the few studies giving average age, that of Porto Alegre in Rio Grande do Sul in the period 1858–1872 gives an average age of the manumitted slaves of 21 years.[10] The average for manumitted slaves in the port city of Santos, between 1811–1877, was estimated at 20 years for men and at 22 years for women.[11] All these results in terms of age of manumitted slaves would seem to be in conformity with what has been found for most regions, even in Spanish America (see Table 9.1).[12]

[10] Paulo Roberto Staudt Moreira, *Faces da liberdade, máscaras do cativeiro. Experiências de liberdade e escravidão precebidas através das cartas de alforria – Porto Alegre (1858–1888)* (Porto Alegre: EDIPUCRS, 1996), tabela anexo 6, p. 91. To control for the possible distortions caused by the various laws of free birth and aged, we selected only the period 1885–1872.

[11] Ian William Olivo Read, "Unequally bound: The conditions of slave life and treatment in Santos county, Brazil, 1822–1888" (Ph.D. diss., history, Stanford: Stanford University, 2006), table 8.5.

[12] For the data provided in Table 9.1, see the following sources: For Paraty, James P. Kiernan, "Baptism and Manumission in Brazil: Paraty, 1789–1822," *Social Science History*, 3, no. 1. (Autumn 1978), table 6; for the city of Rio de Janeiro, James H. Sweet, "Manumission in Rio de Janeiro, 1749–54: An African Perspective," *Slavery & Abolition*, 24, no. 1 (April 2003), table 3; for the city of Rio de Janeiro (only Creoles), Mary C. Karasch, *Slave Life in Rio de Janeiro, 1808–1850* (Princeton: Princeton University Press, 1987), table 11.5; for Porto Feliz, São Paulo, Roberto Guedes Ferreira, "Pardos: Trabalho, família, aliança e mobilidade social, Porto Feliz, São Paulo, c. 1798 – c. 1850" (Tese de doutorado, história, Universidade Federal do Rio de Janeiro, 2005), quadro 4.6; for Curitiba, São Paulo [Paraná], Adriano Bernardo Moraes Lima, "Trajetórias de Crioulos: Um estudo das relações comunitárias de escravos e forros no têrmo da Vila de Curitiba (c. 1760 – c. 1830)" (Dissertação de mestrado, Universidade Federal do Paraná, Curitiba, 2001), tabela 9; for Rio de Janeiro 1840–1850, Manolo Florentino and José Roberto Góes, "Do que Nabuco já sabia: Mobilidade e miscigenação racial no Brasil escravista" (Congresso Internacional Brasil-Portugal Ano 2000 – Sessão de História, 2000), tabela 2; for Porto Alegre RGS between 1858 and 1872, Moreira, *Faces da liberdade, máscaras do cativeiro*, tabela anexo 6; for Sabará MG 1710–1819, Kathleen J. Higgins, *"Licentious Liberty" in a Brazilian Gold-Mining Region: Slavery, Gender, and Social Control in Eighteenth-Century Sabará, Minas Gerais* (University Park: Pennsylvania State University Press, 1999), table 5.1; for Juiz de Fora, Antônio Henrique Duarte Lacerda, *Os padrões das alforrias em um município cafeeiro em expansão: Juiz de Fora, Zona da Mata de Minas Gerais, 1844–88* (São Paulo: Annablume, 2006), tabela 16; for Salvador da Bahia 1684–1745, Stuart B. Schwartz, "The Manumission of Slaves in Colonial Brazil: Bahia, 1684–1745," *Hispanic American Historical Review*, 54, no. 4 (1974), table V; for Salvador da Bahia 1779/1850, see Katia M. de Queirós Mattoso, "A propósito de cartas de alforria: Bahia, 1779–1850," *Anais de História*, 4 (1972), tabela VII; for Salvador da Bahia 1808–1888, Mieko Nishida, "Manumission and Ethnicity in Urban Slavery: Salvador, Brazil 1808–1888," *Hispanic American Historical Review*, 73, no. 3 (1993), table 4; for Campinas in São Paulo 1789–1874, see

TABLE 9.1. *Ratio of Crianças (Children) among Alforrias in Selected Districts, 17th–19th Centuries*

Place/Dates	% Crianças	Definition of Age	Number of Cases Where Age Is Known
Paraty (RJ) 1789–1822	45.9	<14	268
Rio de Janeiro (city) 1749–1754	28.9	n.g.	605
Rio de Janeiro (city) 1807–1831 (only Creoles)	24.0	n.g	732
Porto Feliz (SP) 1798–1850	40.1	n.g.	217
Curitiba (SP) 1790–1825	27.1	n.g.	107
Rio de Janeiro 1840–1850	48.5	<16	668
Porto Alegre (RGS) 1858–1872	22.0	<15	1,666
Sabará (MG) 1710–1819♦	32.9	<14	1,005
Juiz de Fora (MG) 1840–1888*	22.7	<15	207
Salvador de Bahia 1684–1745	44.8	<14	763
Salvador de Bahia 1779/1850**	12.0	<13	6,305
Salvador de Bahia 1808–1888***	32.7	<15	2,138
Campinas (SP) 1789–1874	33.7	<10	287
Santos (SP) 1811–1872	53.4	n.g.	262
Montes Claros (MG) 1830–1888	28.1	<16	210
Buenos Aires 1776–1810	21.7	<14	937
Lima 1580–1650	51.9	<14	214
Mexico City 1580–1650	53.8	<14	107

Notes:
♦ Total summed from columns in table and differs from her total.
* Women only and then ages exist for only 207 out of 329.
** Only 15 years selected in this period.
*** Totals given in Nishida (1993, table 8).
Sources: See note 12.

Conversely, there were relatively few elderly persons manumitted in Brazil. Despite the claims of some historians that masters abandoned old and infirm slaves,[13] all studies that provide data on age show that there were, in general, far fewer elderly than children among the persons being freed and that the majority of slaves were in the working-age categories.

Peter L. Eisenberg, "Ficando livre: As alforrias em Campinas no século XIX," *Estudos Econômicos*, 17, no. 2 (1987), tablea 6; for Montes Claros, Minas Gerais in 1830–1888, Alysson Luiz Freitas de Jesus, *No sertão das Minas: Escravidão, violência e liberdade (1830–1888)* (São Paulo: Annablume, 2007), quadro 12; and for the Spanish American cities, see Lyman L. Johnson, "Manumission in Colonial Buenos Aires, 1776–1810," *Hispanic American Historical Review*, 59 no. 2 (May 1979), table 1.

[13] See Jacob Gorender, *O escravismo colonial* (4th ed. rev.; São Paulo: Editora Ática, 1985), p. 355.

TABLE 9.2. *Ratio of Elderly among Alforrias in Selected Districts,
17th–19th Centuries*

Place/Dates	% Elderly	Definition of Age	Number of Cases Where Age Is Known
Paraty (RJ) 1789–1822	14.9	45+	268
Porto Feliz (SP) 1798–1850	15.7	idosos	217
Curitiba (SP) 1790–1825	9.3	45+	150
Rio de Janeiro 1840–1850	19.8	40+	668
Porto Alegre (RGS) 1858–1872	14.5	40+	1,666
Sabará (MG) 1710–1819**	0.8	46+	1,005
Salvador de Bahia 1684–1745	2.9	40+	763
Rio de Contas, Bahia 1870–1879	15.5	idosos	291
Juiz de Fora (MG) 1840–1888*	9.2	51+	207
Santos (SP) 1811–1872	14.5	n.g.	262
Campinas (SP) 1789–1874	18.4	50+	267
Montes Claros (MG) 1830–1888	17.1	46+	210
Buenos Aires 1776–1810	11.3	46+	937
Lima 1580–1650	12.6	46+	214
Mexico City 1580–1650	12.3	46+	107

Notes: * Women only and ages exist for only 207 out of 329.
** Total summed from columns in table and differs from Higgins' total.
Sources: Same as Table 9.1, with the addition of Rio de Contas by Pires (2006, tabela 2).

In fact, older the elderly, usually defined as 40 years of age or older, tended to be a tenth of the total persons being freed (see Table 9.2).

Almost all studies of manumission also show a much higher ratio of females than males among the manumitted slaves (see Table 9.3). Of the two exceptions, one is based on postmortem inventories rather than formal *cartas de alforria* and so is not totally comparable, and that of Sabará may be due to some type of recording error, because all other studies show a surprising consistency. The dominance of women in the letters of freedom (*cartas de alforria*) records is also reflected in census reports of the free colored population. Thus, in the Minas Gerais parish of São José d'El Rey in 1795, the sex ratio among the 1,411 resident *alforrias* (or manumitted) was 84 males per 100 females.[14]

[14] Douglas Cole Libby and Clotilde Andrade Paiva, "Alforrias e forros em uma freguesia mineira: São José d'El Rey em 1795," *Revista Brasileira de Estudos de População*, 17, nos. 1/2 (Jan./Dez. 2000), tabela 1, p. 22. It has been suggested that if children were removed from the *forro* class the female domination would be even greater (personal communication of Stuart B. Schwartz, November 4, 2008).

TABLE 9.3. *Sex Ratio among Alforrias in Selected Districts, 17th–19th Centuries*

Place/Dates	Sex Ratio (males per 100 females)	Number of Cases Where Sex Is Known
Paraty (RJ) 1789–1822	53	320
Rio de Janeiro (city) 1749–1754	50	425
Rio de Janeiro (city) 1807–1831	57	1,319
Rio de Janeiro 1840–1850	73	4,609
Rio de Janeiro 1600s–1850	65	7,739
Porto Feliz (SP) 1798–1850 (T)	113	493
Curitiba (SP) 1790–1825	109	222
Porto Alegre (RGS) 1800–1835	69	662
Porto Alegre (RGS) 1858–1872	88	3,427
Sabará (MG) 1710–1819***	58	1,005
São João del Rei (MG) 1774–1848	79	1,437
Juiz de Fora (MG) 1840–1888	87	615
Salvador de Bahia 1684–1745	50	1,160
Salvador de Bahia 1779/1850*	74	6,305
Salvador de Bahia & Santo Amaro 1813–1853	49	686
Salvador de Bahia 1808–1888**	76	3,783
Rio de Contas, Bahia 1870–1879	81	407
São Paulo 1800–1888	72	1,338
Santos (SP) 1811–1872	104	379
Campinas (SP) 1789–1884	72	1,264
Montes Claros (MG) 1830–1888	73	210
Buenos Aires 1776–1810	70	1,482
Lima 1580–1650	48	294
Mexico City 1580–1650	63	104

Notes: * Only 15 years selected in this period.
** We have used the totals given in Nishida (1993), tables 7 and 8.
*** Total summed from columns in table and differs from Higgins' total.
(T) Based on *testamentos* and not *cartas de alforria*.

Sources: Same as Table 9.1, except, Schwartz, "Manumission of Slaves," (table III); Juiz de Fora, Lacerda, *Os padrões* (tabela 23); Porto Alegre 1800–1825, Gabriel Aladrén, "Liberdades negras nas paragens do Sul: Alforria e inserção social de libertos em Porto Alegre, 1800–1835" (Dissertação de mestrado, História, Universidade Federal Fluminense, Niterói, 2008) (tabela 1.1); Porto Alegre 1858–1872, Paulo Roberto Staudt Moreira, *Os cativos e os homens de bem: Experiências negras no espaço urbano, Porto Alegre 1858–1888* (Porto Alegre: EST edições, 2003), (p. 194); Salvador, Mattoso, "A propósito de cartas," (tabela IV); Nishida, "Manumission and Ethnicity," (table 4); São Paulo, Enidelce Bertin, *Alforrias na São Paulo do século XIX: Liberdade e dominação* (São Paulo: Humanitas FFFCH/USP, 2004) (tabela 17), Read (table 8.3); for Santos, Eisenberg, "Ficando livre," (tabela 3); with post-1884 eliminated, Arnold Kessler, "Bahian Manumission Practices in the Early 19th Century," paper delivered at the American Historical Association, December 29, 1973, (table II, p. 17); Rio de Janeiro 1600s–1850; and São João del Rei, see Sheila de Castro Faria, "Aspectos demográficos da alforria no Rio de Janeiro e em São João Del Rey entre 1700 e 1850," *XVI Encontro Nacional de Estudos Populacionais*, ABEP (2008), (cuadro 1–2, pp. 2–3).

This pattern of emphasis on females in the emancipation process helps explain why in the census of 1872 for the province of São Paulo, for example, the sex ratio for the 355,745 freed persons of color was 79 men per 100 women. This compared to a sex ratio of 125 men per 100 women among the slaves and 99 men per 100 women among the whites. In the empire as a whole, with a population of free colored of longer duration and size than in São Paulo, the sex ratio among the 4.2 million free colored was more balanced, but even so, the free colored had the lowest ratio of men of any group in the society, with 102 males per 100 females compared to 109 males per 100 females for the whites and 115 males per 100 females for the slaves.[15]

As could be expected, native-born slaves were more likely to obtain their freedom than African-born slaves, although there was great variation by time and region, as can be seen in Table 9.4. Of course, many of these figures would be influenced by the origin of the resident slave population, which differed considerably across Brazil, and by the time selected, with Africans progressively declining over time. It would seem that on average, with a few unusual exceptions, about 33 percent to 40 percent of the slaves being freed were of African origin. Moreover, not only would the importance of Africans differ by time and place, but there would be major differences by the type of manumissions that occurred.

There were three major types of manumission: voluntary without condition (*grátis*), in which the slave was immediately freed and had no obligations whatsoever to his master; voluntary with conditions (which might involve continued service, special work, or even formal acts of respect and piety), which was given the general term of *oneroso*; and self-purchase, which also often appears in the documents as *oneroso*, because the slave had to pay for his or her freedom. This has led some historians to assume that the last two types were identical.[16] But in fact, self-purchase was the only one of the three types of manumission initiated by the slave, and once agreed upon by the master and the courts, involved a fundamental change in status. *Coartado* slaves, as they were called, paid off their purchase price in installments that could vary from months to years, they could hold funds on their own, make contracts, and could not be sold without their permission. All legal documents recognized their special status and carefully named any slaves who held this status.

[15] Diretoria Geral de Estatística. *Recenseamento Geral do Brazil de 1872.*
[16] Lima, "Trajetórias de Crioulos," tabelas 10 and 11.

TABLE 9.4. *Percentage of Africans among Alforrias in Selected Districts,*
17th–19th Centuries

Place/Dates	% of Africans among Alforrias	Number of Cases Where Origin Is Known
Paraty (RJ) 1789–1822	15	469
Rio de Janeiro (city) 1749–1754	30	605
Rio de Janeiro (city) 1807–1831	41	1,236
Rio de Janeiro 1840–1850	57	4,609
Rio de Janeiro 1600s–1850	46	7,739
Rios das Velhas & Mortes (MG) 1716–1789 (T)	39	868
Campos (RJ) 1704–1830 (T)	29	440
Porto Feliz (SP) 1798–1850 (T)	20	280
Curitiba (SP) 1790–1825	8	155
Porto Alegre (RGS) 1800–1835	34	662
Porto Alegre (RGS) 1858–1872	43	2,228
Sabará (MG) 1710–1819***	39	1,005
São João del Rei (MG) 1774–1848	33	1,437
Juiz de Fora (MG) 1840–1888	20	615
Salvador de Bahia 1684–1745	31	950
Salvador de Bahia 1808–1888**	47	3,283
Salvador de Bahia & Santo Amaro 1813–1853	48	657
São Paulo 1800–1888	31	550
Santos (SP) 1811–1872	28	262
Montes Claros (MG) 1830–1888	19	357

Notes: (T) Based on *testamentos postmortem.*
Sources: Same as Tables 9.1 and 9.3, plus Soares, "A remissão do cativeiro" (2006, quadro IV.12, p. 173).

Although there was a surprising constituency in terms of age and sex among the manumitted slaves across all regions and in both urban and rural settings, the same was not the case with types of manumission that varied quite considerably (see Table 9.5). In some regions, self-purchase was dominant, in others it was voluntary and unconditional manumissions, and in others it was voluntary and conditional. In general, the voluntary manumissions dominated in most regions, and in only a few did self-purchase represent a majority.

There was some variation by origin of slaves. Creoles, or native-born slaves, tended to be more important in voluntary manumissions of whatever type, and African-born slaves tended to be more important among

TABLE 9.5. *Type of Manumission for Alforrias in Selected Districts, 17th–19th Centuries*

Place/Dates	% Voluntary & Unconditional	% Voluntary & Conditional	Subtotal of Voluntary Manumissions	% Self-Purchased	Number of Known Cases
Paraty (RJ) 1789–1822	n.g.	n.g.	67.6	32.4	448
Campos (RJ) 1735–1832*	29.6	42.7	72.3	27.8	389
Rio de Janeiro (city) 1807–1831	20.3	39.9	60.2	39.8	895
Rio de Janeiro 1840–1869	52.9	19.4	72.3	27.7	16,729
Rio de Janeiro 1600s–1850	n.g.	n.g.	61.4	38.6	6,439
São João del Rei (MG) 1774–1848	n.g.	n.g.	53.4	46.6	1,306
Juiz de Fora (MG) 1844–1880 (T)	51.6	34.7	86.3	13.7	562
Porto Feliz (SP) 1798–1850 (T)	17.9	72.1	90.0	10.0	341
Porto Alegre (RGS) 1800–1835	31.4	24.1	55.5	44.5	771
Porto Alegre (RGS) 1858–1872	20.9	33.6	54.5	45.5	3,101
Rio das Velhas (MG) 1720–1784 (T)	n.g.	n.g.	61.5	38.5	723
Rio das Mortes (MG) 1716–1789 (T)	n.g.	n.g.	70.3	29.7	209
Sabará (MG) 1750–1810 ***	28.3	15.4	43.7	56.3	513
Juiz de Fora (MG) 1840–1880	43.0	45.4	88.4	11.6	991
Salvador de Bahia 1684–1745	n.g.	n.g.	42.1	57.9	1,160
Salvador de Bahia 1808–1888*	45.5	14.8	60.3	39.6	3,783
Salvador & Santo Amaro 1813–1853	30.7	23.1	53.8	46.2	648
Rio de Contas, Bahia 1870–1879	28.0	39.1	67.1	32.9	410
Campinas (SP) 1879–1888	49.8	32.8	82.6	17.4	2,277
Santos (SP) 1811–1872	38.3	20.6	58.9	41.2	379
São Paulo 1800–1888	28.1	41.0	69.1	30.9	1,338

(*continued*)

TABLE 9.5 (continued)

Place/Dates	% Voluntary & Unconditional	% Voluntary & Conditional	Subtotal of Voluntary Manumissions	% Self-Purchased	Number of Known Cases
Buenos Aires 1776–1810	29.3	10.9	40.2	59.8	1,356
Lima 1580–1650	33.8	18.4	52.2	47.8	299
Mexico City 1580–1650	39.3	24.3	63.6	36.4	107

Notes: * Only cartas de alforria considered for this analysis. Only 15 years selected in this period.
** We used totals given in Nishida (1993), table 8.
*** Total summed from columns in table and differs from Higgins' total.
**** Total summed from their tabela 2, which differs from their tabela 3.
(T) Based on testamentos and not cartas de alforria.

Sources: Same as Table 9.1, except, Kiernan (1978, table 4); Campos, Soares (2006), Eduardo França Paiva, Escravidão e universo cultural na colônia, Minas Gerais, 1716–1789 (Belo Horizonte: UFMG, 2001), (quadros 27 & 28); for Rio das Velhas & Mortes (MG); Juiz de Fora, Lacerda (2006), our calculations from tabelas 8 & 9); Porto Alegre 1800–1835, Aladrén (2008, tabela 1.2); Porto Alegre 1858–1872, Moreira, Os cativos (p. 194), Mattoso, "A propósito de cartas" (tabela IV), Nishida (1993, table 4); São Paulo, Bertin (2004, tabela 7); and for Sahara 1750–1810, Dantos (2003, table 4.3); Manolo Florentino, "Sobre minas, crioulos e a liberdade costumeira no Rio de Janeiro, 1789–1871," in Manolo Florentino, ed., Tráfico, cativeiro e liberdade Rio de Janeiro, séculos XVII–XIX (Rio de Janeiro: Civilização Brasileira, 2005), (tabela 2); for RJ and its hinterland 1840–1869, Read (2006, table 8.1), Eisenberg, (tabela 8); we added the 1.9% slaves purchased to replace other slaves as part of the self-purchase group for Salvador and Santo Amaro; and for Rio 1660s–1850 and São João del Rei, Faria (2008, cuadros 5 and 7, pp. 10, 12).

the self-purchasing slaves.[17] Because of their higher representation among self-purchased slaves,[18] African-born slaves were represented among the *livres* and *forros* in roughly the same ratio as in the total slave population. Thus, in a very large sample of 16,729 manumissions in Rio, Africans made up 47 percent of all slaves emancipated, but they were 50 percent of the self-purchasers and made up only 36 percent of the conditional voluntary grants.[19] One of the few studies giving the occupations of *alforrias* showed that males being freed had a far higher ratio of skilled occupations than did the slave population in general, and that women being freed were far more likely to be in domestic service than the general female slave population.[20]

Finally, it is worth noting a subset of contracts that historians have found among the self-purchasing slave manumissions. A minority of these sales involved purchases by third parties. In the region of São Paulo, for example, samples from the nineteenth century show 31 percent of 1,338 slaves manumitted were self-purchased, of whom a minority

[17] A recent study of manumissions in São João del Rei for 1774–1848, found that 58 percent of the Creoles freed (881) were given their freedom unconditionally compared to only 43 percent of the Africans (431) who were gratuitously freed. Faria, "Aspectos demográficos da alforria no Rio de Janeiro e em São João Del Rey entre 1700 e 1850," cuadro 4, p. 10.

[18] One major survey of manumissions concluded that Africans were overrepresented among the self-purchased and underrepresented among the voluntary manumissions. See Paiva, *Escravidão e universo cultural na colônia, Minas Gerais, 1716–1789*, p. 181. A smaller sample from the Bahian towns of Salvador da Bahia and Santo Amaro in the nineteenth century also found this same pattern of African overrepresentation among the self-purchased *libertos*, with *pardos* being overrepresented among the unconditional *alforrias*. See Kessler, "Bahian Manumission Practices in the Early 19th Century," table IX, pp. 19–20.

[19] Florentino, "Sobre minas, crioulos e a liberdade costumeira no Rio de Janeiro, 1789–1871," tabela 2, p. 349. Using the Florentino data set, which now includes 17,201 manumissions from Rio de Janeiro from 1840 to 1871, one recent study has concluded that the volume and timing of self-purchased slaves was exclusively based on the ability of slave families, and especially women, to accumulate funds and is in no way related to external developments such as the end of the slave trade. See Carlos Eduardo Valencia Villa, "Produzindo alforrias no Rio de Janeiro no século XIX" (Dissertação de mestrado, Universidade Federal do Rio de Janeiro, 2008). He also shows that slaves consistently paid higher real prices for their freedom than masters paid for such slaves on the open market, and that the rising real prices paid for manumission over time (which correlated with the rise in slave prices in general) had no impact on reducing the volume of self-purchases. Valencia Villa, "Produzindo alforrias no Rio de Janeiro," pp. 58–62.

[20] Eisenberg, "Ficando livre," tabela 7, p. 195.

were purchased by a relative of the slave (called *pagantes na família*),[21] whereas in the district of Porto Alegre and its hinterland, some 44 percent of the *cartas de alforria* registered between 1800 and 1834 involved self-purchase, of which 16 percent involved purchases by third parties. Of the total of self-purchase contracts available from Rio de Janeiro in the mid-nineteenth century, only 22 percent of the self-purchase contracts were paid for by third parties.[22] In the Minas town of Juiz de Fora between 1844 and 1888, there were some 992 manumissions, only 12 percent of which were self-purchased. Of these purchased freedoms, 60 percent were done by the slave being freed, 10 percent were paid for by family members, and 30 percent by third parties.[23] In the southern town of Porto Alegre of some 3,101 slaves whose manner of liberation was known between 1858 and 1887, 45 percent purchased their freedom, and of these self-purchase, third parties paid for 25 percent of sales, a figure quite similar to that found in the Rio de Janeiro sample. Of these third parties, 66 percent were parents, 14 percent were free union spouses (*amasios*), and 10 percent were godparents.[24] It is interesting to note that when the self-purchased by third parties is broken down by origin, there is an important shift in importance from Africans to native-born. Fifty-four percent of the Africans who were freed did it through self-purchase, compared to only 25 percent of the Creole slaves who did so. But when adding in third-party purchases of freedom, Creoles predominated and accounted for 92 percent of the 53 third-party purchases. Thus, 30 percent of the 164 Creole purchase agreements involved third parties paying the price, whereas just 3 percent of the 124 African purchase agreements involved third parties.[25]

As noted earlier, masters were willing to negotiate self-purchase arrangements with their slaves who were working in skilled occupations

---

[21] Bertin, *Alforrias na São Paulo do século XIX*, tabelas 1, 11, & 18, pp. 69, 97, 116. According to Bertin, some 23 percent of all manumissions were paid for by family members.

[22] Florentino and Góes, "Do que Nabuco já sabia," tabela 1.

[23] Antônio Henrique Duarte Lacerda, "Economia cafeeira, crescimento populacional, manumissões onerosas e gratuitas condicionais em Juiz de Fora na segunda metade do século XIX," *X Seminário sobre a Economia Mineira* (2002), tabelas 2 & 4, pp. 11, 16.

[24] Moreira, *Os cativos e os homens de bem*, pp. 187, 259, 272. In these calculations we have assumed that if self-purchased did not list a source (não consta) that it was the individual slave who made the purchase – thus reaching the individual self-purchase figure of 1,060.

[25] Aladrén, "Liberdades negras nas paragens do Sul, tabelas 1.2 to 1.4, pp. 43, 48, 55.

where force alone could not produce any viable economic returns. Moreover, the self-purchase process was not an uneconomic one as far as the masters were concerned. For the manumitted who paid for their own freedom or had someone buy their freedom, the price paid was usually the current market price, not the original price of purchase. This was especially irksome to the skilled and to slaves whose original price was considerably less than their freedom price would have been. The freedmen and slaves constantly fought in the courts to have the price set at what was declared a "just price," which for them meant the original purchase price or, if raised in slavery, the average adult slave price. Occasionally the courts ruled in their favor, but in most cases the current evaluation was the price used. Thus, masters were receiving the full funds for replacement and could reenter the market for new slaves with the funds they received.

The self-purchase schemes often were done in installments, with usually one-third to one-half down, and a stipulated number of years then set for complete payment. During this period of *coartação*, a *coartado* slave could not be sold to another master without his or her permission, and other restrictions applied that protected their rights. The *coartado* slave also received an official document, called in Portuguese a *Carta de Corte*, which legally allowed some physical mobility away from the master and the right of the *coartado* slave to make contracts in order to obtain funds for their self-purchase. The master in turn continued to receive the earnings of the *coartado* slave and paid for their maintenance until such time as the final installment was paid. A good example of this process was that of the slave tailor Gonçalo, who was brought to Rio de Janeiro in the 1750s. His price as an adult was estimated at 142,500 réis and he was allowed to purchase his freedom at 134,400 réis. The discounted sale price was due to the shift of daily maintenance costs to the slave. He was to pay this price in daily amounts for 840 days (or 2 years, 5 months, and 11 days), but he was now to pay for his own sustenance, a cost which his owner had previously provided.[26]

Aside from freeing their slaves in public acts notarized by officials, the master class in Brazil also manumitted slaves at baptism. This was the usual route for fathers recognizing their bastard offspring and it required just the declaration of the parents and godparents to set a child free. Also, all foundling children were declared free, no matter what their color.

---

[26] Silvia Hunold Lara, *Campos da Violência: Escravos e senhores na Capitania do Rio de Janeiro, 1750–1808* (Rio de Janeiro: Paz e Terra, 1988), pp. 252–4.

An analysis of the parish registers of Paraty, a sugar – and *aguardente* – producing coastal region of Rio de Janeiro in the early nineteenth century, revealed that one percent of the total local births were slave children being freed. These children were not later registered with formal *cartas de alforria* (certificates of manumission), which were the usual records used for all other manumissions. These seemingly few births out of all births added 16 percent to the total number of manumitted in the five-year period under consideration.[27] Interestingly, in a recent study of the 14,949 slave births registered in the Minas town of São João del Rei between 1770 and 1850, some 318 (or 2.1%) of the newborn slaves were manumitted at the baptismal font;[28] none indicated that the father was freeing their children, even though subsequent wills and testaments showed that several of these children were fathered by their masters.[29] These children were also about 55 percent female, further strengthening the female predominance among the freed slaves.[30] Of some 2,471 slave baptisms in the *mineira* districts of Muriaé and Juiz de Fora from 1851–1888, 2 percent of these births involved the freeing of the newborn slave,[31] whereas in the parish of Nossa Senhora de Pilar in Ouro Preto between 1801 and 1840, some 34 (or 3%) of 1,236 slave children baptized were freed on birth.[32] If these ratios are typical for the rest of Brazil, it would have the effect of further reducing the age of the new entrants into the free colored class and further encouraging positive rates of growth.

There is little question that manumission more frequently occurred in the urban than the rural setting and that skilled slaves more readily

---

[27] Kiernan, "Baptism and Manumission in Brazil," pp. 61–5.

[28] See Cristiano Lima da Silva, "As alforrias nos registros de batismos da matriz de Nossa Senhora do Pilar de São João del Rei: Uma análise demográfica (1751–1850)," *Anais do 2° seminário regional do CEO – Centro de Estudos do oitocentos* (Juiz de Fora: Clio Edições Eletrônicas, 2005), tabela 1.

[29] Cristiano Lima da Silva, "Senhores e pais: Reconhecimento de paternidade dos alfor-riados na pia batismal na Freguesia de Nossa Senhora do Pilar de São João del Rei (1770–1850)," *Anais do I Colóquio dos LAHES (Laboratório de Historia Econômica e Social)*, Juiz de Fora, 2005, n.p.

[30] The sex ratio for the 315 births whose sex was known was 82 males per 100 females. Silva, "As alforrias nos registros de batismos da matriz de Nossa Senhora do Pilar de São João del Rei," tabela 3.

[31] Rômulo Andrade, "Ampliando estudos sobre famílias escravos no século XIX: Crianças cativas em Minas Gerias: Legitimidade, alforria e estabilidade familia" *Revista Univer-sidade Rural, Série Ciências Humanas*, 24, nos. 1–2 (2002), tabela 7, p. 107.

[32] Mirian Moura Lott, "A lista nominativa de 1838, características demográficas, econômicas e sociais de Ouro Preto," *Anais do XIII Seminário sobre a Economia Mineira* (2008), quadro 1. In the same parish in this period, there were 429 adult slave baptisms, or 26 percent of all slave baptisms (1,665).

purchased their freedom than the unskilled ones. Urban slaves had more opportunity to gain income than rural slaves and were more cognizant of their rights than the more isolated plantation slaves. But even in rural areas, manumission was possible and it was practiced with some frequency. Even self-purchased freedom was possible for rural slaves through the funds accumulated from the sales of foodstuffs produced on their individual slave *roças*, or provisioning grounds, and there are even occasional references of rural slaves being paid for extraordinary work done on Sundays or rest days. One study has tried to calculate the chances of essentially rural slaves throughout Brazil being freed in the second half of the nineteenth century. Using data from the 1870s, an overall crude manumission rate of 6 percent of all slaves were freed each year. It was then estimated that of a cohort of 10-year-old slave children who survived to the age of 40, some 16 percent would be manumitted by that age, and that 26 percent would be manumitted for those who survived to 60 years of age. This model assumed a high death rate and a constant manumission rate across all age groups.[33]

Finally, slaves could petition to the courts for their freedom, usually arguing that masters had promised them their freedom and heirs were rejecting their claims, or that the processes of self-purchase were not being carried out. This voluntary act of slaves often resulted in positive results. Thus, in Rio de Janeiro, the *Corte de Apelação*, the highest court in the empire, heard 381 such cases demanding freedom in the nineteenth century. In the 351 cases in which a decision had been rendered, slaves gained unconditional freedom in 158 cases, and conditional freedom (which allowed self-purchases and work obligations for limited times) for another 28, which meant that 53 percent of the cases decided supported the claim of liberation of the slaves.[34] It should also be noted that when slaves did win their court cases, they were usually charged for the judicial fees and costs involved.[35]

The relative importance of recently manumitted slaves within the free colored population is little studied, and the few data available suggest quite wide variations. Clearly, in the early colonial period, most of the free

---

[33] Robert W. Slenes, "The Demography and Economics of Brazilian Slavery, 1850–1888" (Ph.D. diss., Department of History, Stanford University, 1976), pp. 489–93, and especially table 10.2, p. 491, which summarizes his complex discussion.

[34] Keila Grinberg, *Liberata, a lei da ambigüidade: As ações de liberdade da Corte de Apelação do Rio de Janeiro no século XIX* (Rio de Janeiro: Relume Dumará, 1994), p. 27. The period covered seems to be 1806–1888 (see gráfico 1, p. 109).

[35] Lara, *Campos da Violência*, pp. 256–7.

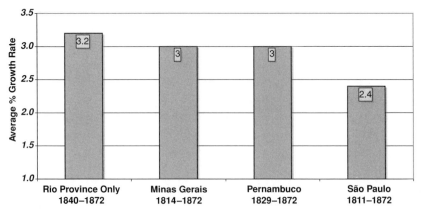

GRAPH 9.1. Average Annual Growth Rate of the Free Colored Population in Selected Provinces in the 19th Century. *Source:* Same as Table 6.3.

colored class were *forros* or persons manumitted in their own lifetimes. But as their numbers grew from generation to generation, the ratio of *forros* declined and the number of persons of color born free increased. In the few studies available that give the ratio of persons born in slavery versus those born free among the free colored class, the *forros* were usually in the order of 10 percent of the free colored class. In the *mineiro* town of São João del Rei in 1795, *forros* represented an extraordinarily high 57 percent of the free colored class, thus still reflecting the earlier colonial patterns. The sex ratio of the *pardos* and *pretos livres* (blacks and mulattoes born free) was almost equal at 97 men per 100 women, but among the *forros* population, as expected, it was just 87 men per 100 women.[36] It is probable, given the dramatic population growth of the free colored class in the nineteenth century, that the ratio of *forros* to total resident free colored was much lower after 1800 than the rate found in this *mineiro* town. But that *forros* remained an important part of the free colored population and were a major element in its growth can be seen from the crude estimates of population growth of the free colored class in the nineteenth century (see Graph 9.1).

Given the high mortality of the free population, which differed only moderately from the slave population (see Graph 9.2 and Table 6.2), it would be surprising if the natural growth rate of the free colored population was above the nineteenth century West European norm of 1

[36] Libby and Paiva, "Alforrias e forros em uma freguesia mineira," tabelas 1 & 2, pp. 22, 24.

GRAPH 9.2. Estimated Upper Bound Life Expectancy of Slaves and All Brazilians in 1872 (at 0 & 5 year cohorts). *Sources:* Pedro Carvalho de Mello, "The Economics of Labor in Brazilian Coffee Plantations, 1850–1888," (Ph.D. diss., Department of Economics, University of Chicago, 1977), p. 123 and Eduardo E. Arriaga, *New Life Tables for Latin American Populations in the Nineteenth and Twentieth Centuries* (Berkeley: University of California, Population Monograph Series, no. 3, 1968), pp. 29–30.

percent to 1.3 percent natural growth per annum.[37] The 2 percent to more than 3 percent annual growth rates estimated for the various provinces in Brazil in the nineteenth century had to have been greatly influenced by the steady migration into this class of newly freed ex-slaves.

Finally, in examining the age cohorts of the free population by color and sex for 16 *municípios* in Minas Gerais in the census years of 1831–1832, it is evident that the free colored had a steady overrepresentation of women compared to the whites ages 10 years and above, and that this is reflected in the overall sex ratio of the free colored being 91 males per 100 females compared to a balanced ratio of 100 males to 100 females among the whites. Assuming that the white population had relatively low in-migration or an immigration that was not biased by age, it can be assumed that the free colored would have had this same pattern of male and female distribution were it not for a fairly steady in-migration of woman who were born slaves into the free colored class (see Graphs 9.3a–9.3c).

---

[37] Angus Maddison, *The World Economy: A Millennial Perspective* (Paris: Development Centre of the OECD, 2001), table A-1d, p. 186. Portugal did not grow more than 1 percent per annum until the twentieth century and the 12 major West European countries grew by 1 percent in 1820–1870 and 1.3 percent per annum in 1870–1913.

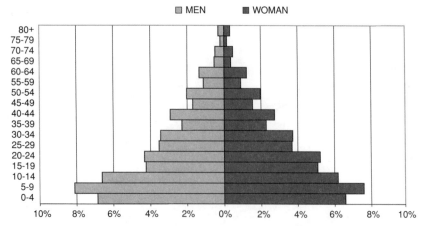

GRAPH 9.3A. Age Pyramid of Whites, Minas Gerais, 1831–1832 (113,951).

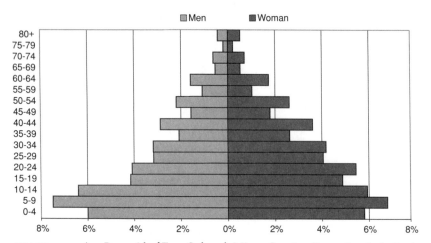

GRAPH 9.3B. Age Pyramid of Free Colored, Minas Gerais, 1831–1832 (162,895).

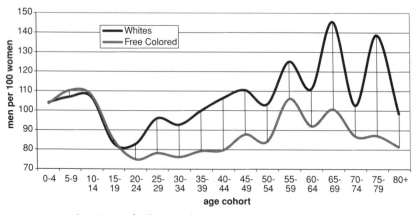

GRAPH 9.3C. Sex Ratio of Whites and Free Colored by Age Cohort, Minas Gerais, 1831–1832.

These age and sex biases among the manumitted slaves meant that the free colored class was receiving a dynamic element into their midst that was more heavily female and relatively young. The reproductive rates among the free colored population were thus consistently higher than among the slaves. Not only were the Creole freedmen reproducing themselves at a positive rate of growth, but they were receiving from the slave class a steady stream of entrants who were also prone to high reproductive rates – that is, younger and fertile women – which helps to explain their unusually high annual growth rates.

Once freed, the ex-slaves entered at the lowest stratum of the society. Even skilled slaves came into the free population with their savings exhausted in the self-purchase act. It was usually these same persons who then purchased their spouses and children in order to free them and in turn mortgaged future savings in this manumission process. In only rare cases did masters grant their ex-slave offspring any income and support in their life of freedom. It is for this reason of pervasive poverty that the free colored in Brazil, as was typical in all American slave societies, had the highest mortality and disease rates among the free populations.

Available evidence suggests that the free colored had a much higher fertility rate than the native-born whites. In Minas Gerais, which had Brazil's second-largest free colored population, the crude birth rate of the free colored in 1814 was 42 per 1,000 and its death rate was 34 per 1,000. In contrast, the white population had a birth rate of 37 per 1,000 and a death rate of 27 per 1,000.[38] Several other estimates support the idea that the free colored had intrinsically higher fertility ratios than any other population group in their respective societies.

Because of their high fertility and the constant flow of more women than men into their ranks through manumission, the free colored had the highest ratio of women and were, on average, the youngest of the three population groups that made up most of the slave societies. In terms of marriage, family, and kinship, however, they differed little from the free society around them. In a census of the captaincy of São Paulo in 1800, for example, married persons made up 30 percent of the whites, about 25 percent of the free colored, and 18 percent among the slaves. In a census of the São Paulo plantation region of Campinas in 1829, there was little difference in the ratio of female-headed households, married-couple households, and widows with children households, between whites and

---

[38] Herbert S. Klein, "Os homens livres de côr na sociedade escravista brasileria," *Dados* (Rio de Janeiro), no. 17 (1978), tabela 2.

free colored.[39] For the entire population of Brazil in the census of 1872, married whites were 30 percent of their respective population group; 26 percent of all free colored were in this category, and only 8 percent of slaves were married.

Although the free colored class tended to have very high rates of marriage endogamy, they did sometimes cross lines of status and even of color. Free colored sometimes married slaves and occasionally even married whites. In the Bahia district of Cachoeira in the eighteenth century, of the 100 marriages recorded to *forros* between 1765 and 1785, some 24 involved *forros* marrying slaves.[40] In the mining town of Vila Rica in Minas Gerais in the period 1727 to 1826, some 832 marriages were listed in which at least one partner was a *forro*. Fifty of these *forros* married slaves, or 6 percent of these marriages. In this case, liberated males married slave women in just 3 percent of all marriages listing male *forros*, whereas liberated females had a higher tendency to marry such slaves; in this case 9 percent of their marriages were to male slaves.[41] There are instances of even higher rates, even in the eighteenth century. In the prime sugar region of Campos dos Goitacases in Rio de Janeiro in the second half of the eighteenth century, 35 percent of 300 *forros* marriages involved *forros* marrying a slave. Among the 3,171 *livres* marriages, however, slave partners represented only 2 percent of the marriages.[42] Although one would expect this pattern of *forros* being more willing to marry slaves than the free colored born in freedom, this was not the case for the 2,916 marriages taking place in the *paulista* town of São José dos Pinhais between 1759 and 1888 in which at least one partner was free. Only 80 involved a slave partner, but 66 involved *livres* and only 14 involved *forros*. Interestingly, the tendency seems to be for slave women to marry into the two free colored groups more often than slave men. In São José dos Pinhais, 37 slave women married *livre* men compared to only 29 *livre* men who married slave women. The same balance occurred with slave women

[39] Data generated from the Listas Nominativas (*or mapas*) in Arquivo Público do Estado de São Paulo, Mapas de População, lata 27a.

[40] Luis Nicolau Parés, "O processo de criolização no Recôncavo Baiano (1750–1800)," *Afro-Ásia*, 33 (2005), tabela 5.

[41] Iraci del Nero da Costa, "Ocupação, Povoamento e Dinâmica Populacional," in Iraci del Nero da Costa and Francisco Vidal Luna, *Minas Colonial: Economia e Sociedade* (São Paulo: Pioneira, 1982), tabelas 1 & 2.

[42] Sheila de Castro Faria, *A Colônia em movimento: Fortuna e família no cotidiano colonial* (Rio de Janeiro: Nova Fronteira, 1988), quadro II.9 & II.10, pp. 143, 144.

marrying *forro* men in 8 out of 14 such marriages.[43] Of the 1,501 marriages recorded in the Minas Gerais town of Barbacena between 1721 and 1821 in which the legal status of the person was known, slaves appeared as spouses of free persons in only 11 instances.[44] Of the 184 marriages involving slaves that occurred in the two *mineiro* districts of Muriaé and Juiz de Fora in 1872, 10 percent involved slaves marrying free persons.[45] The scattered nineteenth-century marriage data would seem to suggest that marriage between the free colored class and the slave population was not that common an event as the experience of eighteenth-century samples would seem to suggest. When free persons married slaves, they were often *jornaleiros* or *agregados* workers on the same estate of their slave spouses and they often agreed to remain on the state as long as they were married and their spouses were slaves.

Crossing the color line for marriage among free persons seems to have occurred, but with even less frequency than across the legal boundaries. In the interior Minas Gerais town of Catas Altas do Mato Dentro, in the 115 marriages carried out between 1816 and 1850 in which the color of the partners was known, there were only 8 marriages involving whites and free colored. White men tended to marry *parda* women more than white women married *pardos*.[46]

But in one area, there was very close contact between the free colored and the slaves, and this appears in the whole process of godparenthood relations or *compadrio*. Free colored and *forros* appeared with great frequency as godfathers (*padrinhos*) and godmothers (*madrinhas*) at slave births. In a study of the town of Livramento in Paraíba in the nineteenth century, of the 447 slave births that occurred between 1814 and 1884, *livres* were *padrinhos* in 95 percent of the slave births and *livres* were *madrinhas* in 54 percent of these births. Surprisingly, there were only 2 percent of such births where a *padrinhos* did not appear, but an

---

[43] Cacilda Machado, "Casamento & Desigualdade Jurídica: Primeiras notas de um estudo em uma área da região paulista no período colonial," *XIII Encontro da Associação Brasileira de Estudos Populacionais ABEP* (2002), tabela 5, p. 10.

[44] Rangel, "Nos Limites da Escolha Matrimônio e Família entre Escravos e Forros Termo de Barbacena – 1781–1821," tabela 6.

[45] Rômulo Andrade, "Casamento entre escravos na região cafeeira de Minas Gerais," *Revista da Universidade Federal Rural, Série Ciências Humanas*, 22, no. 2 (Jul./Dez. 2000), tabela 9.

[46] Tarcísio Rodrigues Botelho, "Estratégias matrimoniais entre a população livre de Minas Gerais: Catas Altas do Mato Dentro, 1815–1850," *XIV Encontro Nacional de Estudos Populacionais, ABEP* (2004), tabela 3, p. 6.

extraordinary 43 percent of such births in which a *madrinhas* was absent from the baptismal records.[47] This same pattern could also be discerned in the nineteenth-century *mineira* town of Senhor Bom Jesus do Rio Pardo between 1838 and 1888. Of the 715 slave births, 76 percent of the *padrinhos* were free persons and 72 percent of the *madrinhas* were free persons.[48] In one of the largest studies of godparenthood and slave births, that of the Minas town of São João do Rei in the period 1736 to 1850, in some 13,473 births to slave mothers, 72 percent of the *padrinhos* were *livres* and 5 percent were *forros*. Of the total of free and *forro padrinhos* (10,391), only some 150 were the owners of the slave mothers.[49] Of the *madrinhas* in these births, 60 percent were *livres* and 5 percent were *forros*.[50] Thus, there seems to be relatively close contact with slaves on the part of the free colored population in terms of serving as godparents to slave children, a role that they seemingly dominated. Equally we often find godparents purchasing the freedom of their slave godchildren, or free colored relatives doing the same. When third parties were involved in purchases of slaves, it was often the free colored who provided the funds. Of the 74 parents and family members who purchased the freedom of slaves in eighteenth-century Bahia, 57 percent were free persons of color.[51]

Given the still incomplete nature of the study of the free colored class in Brazil, it is difficult to assess how color influences the integration of ex-slaves into both the working class as well as into the society in general. In detailed studies of plebian interactions in Mexico City, for example, it is evident that there was a great confusion about color and that colored persons in court cases and in various commercial transactions would be given different color definitions each time they were referred to by

---

[47] Solange Pereira da Rocha, "Gente negra na Paraíba oitocentista: População, família e parentesco espiritual" (Tese de doutorado, Universidade Federal de Pernambuco, 2007), tabela 4.2.

[48] Jonis Freire, "Compadrio em uma freguesia escravista: Senhor Bom Jesus do Rio Pardo (MG) (1838–1888)," *XIV Encontro Nacional de Estudos Populacionais, ABEP* (2004), tabelas 8 & 9.

[49] Silvia Maria Jardim Brügger, *Minas patriarcal, família e sociedade São João del Rei – séculos XVIII e XIX* (São Paulo: Annablume, 2007), p. 286, and table 5.1, p. 287.

[50] Silvia Maria Jardim Brügger, "Compadrio e Escravidão: Uma análise do apadrinhamento de cativos em São João del Rei, 1730–1850," *XIV Encontro Nacional de Estudos Populacionais, ABEP* (2004), tabelas 1 & 2. The data in her tables in this essay are more complete than those in the book because they include absent and *cortado padrinhos* and *madrinhos*.

[51] Schwartz, "The Manumission of Slaves," table IX.

witnesses or officials.[52] This may have been the pattern in Brazil as well given the tripartite color scheme and the traditional Brazilian overlap of class and color definitions for marking an individual's position as *pardos* or *pretos* in the society, which often resulted in a lack of agreement on the color designation of individuals. Another area that has yet to be explored in any detail is the housing of free colored. It has been noted in nineteenth-century Puerto Rico that blacks and whites lived in the same buildings and often rented rooms to each other.[53] The lack of racial ghettos and the intense and complex economic and social relationships among free persons of color and even poor whites and slaves has suggested to some scholars that the lower classes infrequently and often indifferently used color terminology and defined individuals more by their residence, sex, age, legal status, and occupation than by their color. Such fluidity may not have existed in all regions and at all times and may be more of an urban than rural phenomenon. Whereas color prejudice was clearly evident at all levels of society, for the free colored class, color discrimination probably became increasingly important as they moved up the social ladder but had less impact in dealing with their poorer compatriots.

As could be expected from such a predominantly working-class and poor people, the free colored had the highest rates of female-headed households and relatively low rates of household heads who were married compared to the white population. In the Minas Census of the early 1830s, female-headed households, which accounted for only 7 percent of the 25,000 or so white households, made up 19 percent of the some 37,000 of free colored households. Moreover, the free colored had much lower marriage rates, with the hierarchy of color being correlated with these rates. Thus, *pardos* did far better than *pretos*, with the only surprise being the Africans, who ranked higher than the *pretos* (see Table 9.6). Not only were more free colored heads of households unmarried and probably living in consensual unions, they also had higher births outside of marriage than the whites. This in itself did not mean a greater degree of instability in family life but indicated a level of poverty in which church weddings were too costly an item to be worth their performance. On the other hand, all free colored baptized their children and, unlike the slaves, usually had both a godfather and a godmother at the christening.

---

[52] See R. Douglas Cope, *The Limits of Racial Domination, Plebian Society in Colonial Mexico City, 1660–1720* (Madison: University of Wisconsin Press, 1994).

[53] Jay Kinsbruner, *Not of Pure Blood: The Free People of Color and Racial Prejudice in Nineteenth-Century Puerto Rico* (Durham: Duke University Press, 1996).

TABLE 9.6. *Civil Status of Free Adult Heads of Household*
by Color, Minas Gerais, 1831–1832

Color	Single	Married+ Widowed	Total	(n)
Brancos	16%	84%	100%	25,150
Pardos	25%	75%	100%	29,011
Africanos	36%	64%	100%	1,629
Pretos	42%	58%	100%	6,569
Total	23%	77%	100%	62,359

Whatever the relative stability of marriage and illegitimacy of births may have been among the free colored, they did build a powerful set of cohesive institutions that strengthened their internal cohesion as Afro-Americans. This development of a community identity was aided by a continuing prejudice against blacks and mulattoes on the part of whites, of legal impediments that constantly reminded them of their partial rights, and by a government and church that often insisted that they organize themselves strictly into color-based voluntary associations.

The most important of such political associations was the militia. Neither Spain nor Portugal maintained a standing royal army in America. All defense was essentially in the hands of a small group of professional officers and a mass of civilian militiamen. Military service was required of all able-bodied freedmen, and the more numerous the free colored, the greater the number of militia companies of blacks and mulattoes organized in their communities. It is probably no exaggeration to say that the vast majority of able-bodied freedmen did service at some time in their lives in the colonial military establishment. In times of peace, or in isolated regions with few settlers, such militias rarely intruded on the daily life of the population. They were mostly ceremonial and had few obligations. Often, however, these military units required enormous amounts of time and costly effort. For the free colored in the ranks, there were only modest rewards for militia duty. For black and mulatto officers, there was access to military courts of law and other privileges. Thus, the wealthiest artisans were usually quite anxious to obtain these ranks, because they could often be protected even in their commercial activities by appeal to military justice, whereas the non-officers attempted to evade obligations. Moreover, after the replacement of the colored militias with the non-colored–based national guard in the mid-nineteenth century, it was rare for *livres de côr* to achieve high rank. Although the free colored served in the police, the army, and the navy, they rarely ascended to the ranks of the officer class.[54]

Typical was the experience of Francisco Joaquim de Santana, resident of the west *paulista* sugar district of Itu, who in 1820 asked to be exempted from militia service. He had already served in the auxiliary forces (called *Ordenanças*), and in his petition he noted that he had obtained his freedom only recently and was still in debt for his self-purchase. He worked as a master tailor and sustained his family with his work, and he also thought his age too advanced to serve in the militia.[55] In another set of cases, the head of the regional militia, the Capitão Mor of the town of Porto Feliz, wrote to the governor of São Paulo asking for three exemptions for military service for three other *forros*. One was Antonio Pedroso de Campos, a soldier of the militia regiment of Sorocaba, stationed in the town of Porto Feliz. Pedroso was a skilled carpenter and a master of *engenhos* and was needed to repair most of the local *engenho* machines. The Capitão Mor also asked for exemptions for two musicians, Inácio Máximo de Faria and Jesuíno Francisco de Paula, who also were tailors and who worked in a local shop. All had served long and well, with the musicians being particularly active in all church and festive occasions; all were still burdened with debts from their obtaining their freedom, and all were needed for full-time familial and general societal needs.[56] Apparently, Jesuíno Francisco de Paula, the tailor musician, had

---

54 Luiz Carlos Soares, O 'Povo de Cam'na capital do Brasil: A escravidão urbana no Rio de Janeiro do século XIX (Rio de Janeiro: Faperj, Letras, 2007), p. 301.

55 "[S]endo de pouco tempo liberto, e isento pelo favor de sua senhora, D. Josefa Maria de Góes Pacheco, ainda se acha o Suplicante devedor do restante para o inteiro cumprimento de sua liberdade, para cujo [fim], efetivamente trabalha pelo seu ofício de Alfaiate, do qual é mestre, e sustenta sua mulher e família, apesar de seus avançados anos." Cited in Roberto Guedes Ferreira, "Trabalho, família, aliança e mobilidade social: Estratégias de forros e seus descendentes – Vila de Porto Feliz, São Paulo, século XIX," V Congresso Brasileiro de História Econômica (2003), p. 4.

56 "Antonio Pedroso de Campos é soldado Miliciano do Regimento de Sorocaba, aquartelado nesta vila de Porto Feliz, em quem concorre o atributo de bom carpinteiro, e hábil mestre de engenhos, o que se faz muito necessário a esta vila. Assim tão bem Inácio Máximo de Faria e Jesuíno Francisco de Paula, ambos músicos e bons oficiais de alfaiate, que trabalham com tenda aberta; os que pela sua arte têm servido pronta e gratuitamente todas as funções reais e eclesiásticas, fazendo-se por isso, e por seus ofícios, dignos de todo o acolhimento e conservação e utilidade ao País, como verão V. Exa. dos documentos juntos; pois é verdade que os ditos, há muitos anos, que têm servido constantemente em praça de soldados do regimento. Motivos estes, que me movem a recorrer a muita sábia proteção de V. Exa., para que, atendendo ao exposto, se digne mandar que se lhes dê a sua baixa, providenciando, outrossim, que jamais se assente praça a músicos desta vila pela grande falta e necessidade que deles há. E porque tenha sido vexado

been in the militia since 1815 and was still listed in the local town census (*listas nominativas*) as a "*miliciano soldado*" and tailor in 1824 when he was 30 years old.[57]

The church, for its part, also encouraged the free colored to form their own *irmandades*, especially as many of the white ones refused to admit them into coequal membership. These fraternal and religious societies then became a major source for maintaining Afro-American religious cults, acted as mutual-aid societies, and cemented class and color friendships through ritual ceremonial activity. Although created for racist reasons and supported by a white society bent on maintaining a social order that was more separate than equal, these voluntary religious organizations became pillars of the community and gave the free colored a sense of worth and identity, which, like their militia units, provided them with crucial support in highly racist societies. Although these brotherhoods were important for slaves, as detailed in Chapter 8, they appear to have been far more important for the free persons of color. These black brotherhoods existed in every city and town that had a substantial population of blacks and mulattoes. Because most such confraternities did admit slaves, these organizations tended to maintain important ties between the two classes and counterbalanced the antagonism that inevitably developed between those who had a firm stake in the status quo and those who inherently opposed it. However, everywhere it was the free persons who dominated. They elected the majority of officials, and given the membership fees, it was they who were the primary support for the brotherhoods.

Such brotherhoods collected their own funds, acted as burial societies, and sponsored parades and other festivals.[58] They were even a source of funds for slaves purchasing their freedom.[59] Although most of the

---

pelas justiças, e Ordenanças, para caminhar com cartas, e diligências, fazendo-se dificultoso os pagamentos de sua liberdade por inteiro cumprimento dela; Pelo que (...) mandar seja isento," cited in Ferreira, "Trabalho, família, aliança e mobilidade social," p. 5.

[57] Ferreira, "Trabalho, família, aliança e mobilidade social," p. 6.

[58] On the role of the black brotherhoods in burials of members, see João José Reis, *Death Is a Festival: Funeral Rites and Rebellion in Nineteenth-Century Brazil* (Chapel Hill: University of North Carolina Press, 2003), pp. 127–8.

[59] As one detailed study concluded, "most of the black brotherhoods advanced loans to needy slaves and offered help in lawsuits over the slaves' freedom. Usually the brotherhood asked for security or a guarantee that the loans would be repaid. It was not possible to borrow from the treasury of the brotherhoods without the expressed permission of the king or the *cabildo*." Patricia A. Mulvey, "Slave Confraternities in Brazil: Their Role in Colonial Society," *The Americas*, 39, no. 1 (July 1982), p.51. The role of these organizations in holding slave funds is also noted by Roger Bastide,

research on these brotherhoods has been focused on the colonial period, there is no question that they remained a vital part of the social life of freedmen throughout the nineteenth century. Put under provincial control with the creation of the independent nation and still required to use local priests, they continued to carry out festivals and name annual "Congo Kings" and elect *mesas administrativas,* or governing boards, despite constant periods of government repression alternating with periods of liberalization.[60] In Salvador after 1850, the official government repression eased considerably as the brotherhoods became an accepted part of the social scene, but membership seems to have declined as the Church became less receptive to these organization in the late nineteenth century.[61] But in other regions, such confraternities remained quite powerful. In 1871, for example, the local colored *Irmandades de Nossa Senhora do Rosário* of Porto Alegre organized and sponsored the first annual "*festa dos Navegantes,*" which became a major local event tied to carnival

The African Religions of Brazil (Baltimore: Johns Hopkins University Press, 1978), p. 116. Among the few studies giving membership and status for these brotherhoods was one for the Rosario of Alta Cruz brotherhood in Vila Rica of Minas Gerais in the late eighteenth century, which found that of the 4,097 members of the confraternity, 42 percent were slaves, and the overall sex ratio was 65 men per 100 women. Célia Maria Borges, *Escravos e libertos nas irmandades do Rosário: Devoção e solidariedade em Minas Gerais, séculos XVIII e XIX* (Juiz de Fora: Editora UFJF, 2005), p. 231, tabela 8. The *irmandade* Nossa Senhora do Rosário in Mariana (MG) between 1750 and 1819 had 850 *pretos* enrolled whose status was known. Of this number, slaves represented 62 percent of the total membership. Interestingly, the sex ratio among the slaves was heavily biased toward males on the order of two and a half men for every woman. Among the *forros,* the ratio was 63 males per 100 females, and the overall ratio was 166 males per 100 females. Fernanda Aparecida Domingos Pinheiro, "Confrades do Rosário: Sociabilidade e identidade étnica em Mariana – Minas Gerais (1745–1820)," (Dissertação de mestrado, Universidade Federal Fluminense, Niterói, 2006), tabelas II and III.

[60] For an earlier period, a detailed analysis of these executive committees and their budgets is found in Antonia Aparecida Quintão, *Lá vem o meu parente, as irmandades de pretos e pardos no Rio de Janeiro em Pernambuco (século XVIII)* (São Paulo: Annablume, 2002).

[61] Elizabeth W. Kiddy, *Blacks of the Rosary: Memory and History in Minas Gerais, Brazil* (University Park: Pennsylvania State University Press, 2005), chapter 5. A study of the wills of free colored persons in Bahia in the nineteenth century found that these persons belonged to some 38 different colored-based confraternities in Salvador. There appears to be a progressive decline over time, with almost everyone belonging to an *irmandade* in the early part of the century, and only a fifth or fewer registering membership in the post-1850 period. This was due to the attack on these types of organizations by the more romanized clergy who gained control over the Church in the second half of the century and who progressively attacked the social aspects of these organizations and tried to replace them with more orthodox-based organizations. Maria Inês Côrtes de Oliveira, *O liberto: O seu mundo e os outros, Salvador, 1790–1890* (São Paulo: Corrupio, 1988), pp. 84–5.

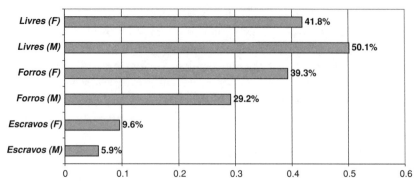

GRAPH 9.4. Percentage of Buried Persons Who Were *Irmandade* Members, by Legal Status and Sex, Paróquia de N. S. da Conceição de Antônio Dias, Vila Rica (1719–1818) (n=12,436). *Source:* Iraci del Nero da Costa, *Vila Rica: População (1719–1826)* (São Paulo: IPE-USP, 1979), tabela 6, p. 235.

in the following years. This popular festival continues to be celebrated today and has outlasted the *Rosário irmandade*, which only disappeared in the last quarter of the twentieth century.[62]

It has been claimed that most free colored persons in Brazil belonged to such brotherhoods and were far more likely to be members than were slaves. One estimate of membership, taken from a study of burials that occurred in one parish in the town of Vila Rica, Minas Gerais, in the eighteenth and early nineteenth centuries, provides an estimate of membership to total population. As shown in Graph 9.4, the roughly 2,200 free persons buried were the most likely to be members (some 48% for both sexes), followed by 35 percent of the 2,000 *forros* who died. In contrast, only 6 percent of the 8,200 slave burials were *irmandade* members. Interestingly, slave and *forro* women were more likely to be members than their male counterparts, but the opposite was true for *livres*. If anything, these rates for free colored were probably underrepresentative for the rest of Brazil because, of the two local parishes in Vila Rica, that of Pilar and Antônio Dias, this was the poorer one.[63] Of 155 wills of *libertos* registered

---

[62] Liane Susan Müller, "O negro e suas devoções: A importância da Irmandade do Rosário e da Festa dos Navegantes para a formação de uma classe média negra porto-alegrense," *II Encontro "Escravidão e Liberdade no Brasil Meridional"* (2005).

[63] According to Professor Costa, "Os dados referem-se a pessoas adultas (em termos genéricos com 7 ou mais anos de idade) que vieram a falecer entre 1719 e 1818 e cujo óbito foi registrado na Paróquia de Nossa Senhora da Conceição de Antônio Dias. Em Vila Rica havia duas Paróquias, a que concentrava pessoas relativamente mais ricas era a do Pilar, os moradores de Antônio Dias eram relativamente menos abonados. O

in the city of Salvador de Bahia between 1790 and 1830, 80 percent of the persons making such wills were members of an *irmandade*, with women having a somewhat higher participation rate than men (82% to 78%).[64] In another sample of 416 wills from the parish of Sé in Rio de Janeiro in the period 1776 to 1797, some three-quarters of the *testators* were *irmandades* members.[65] However, these were clearly the wealthiest free colored, because landless and those without income did not leave wills, and it is difficult to know how many of the poorest belonged. The burial data (see Graph 9.4) suggests that class influenced *forro* participation rates.

Such confraternities saw to the spiritual and physical needs of their members, and were especially important as burial societies. In most of Spanish and Portuguese America, these brotherhoods were relatively poor and usually shared an altar in a church. In a minority of cases, they accumulated large amounts of real estate and had their own separate chapels and cemeteries. Some of these brotherhoods were open to all persons, no matter what their color or status. In other cases, they were divided by both. There were also cases in which brotherhoods were based on unique ethnic origins.[66] In eighteenth-century Salvador, one brotherhood was based on African birth in Dahomey and another was exclusively maintained for Nago-Yoruba peoples of the Ketu nation. Angolans were the first in Bahia to create the brotherhood of *Nossa Senhora do Rosário*. Eventually, many of these confraternities allowed native-born and others to enter their ranks, but usually reserved offices to the original African founding groups.[67] Similar African-based *irmandades* were established

---

fato de o indivíduo falecido pertencer ao não a uma irmandade foi colhido no registro de óbito e não em livros pertencentes a Irmandades.... Também acredito que deve ter havido diferença entre as duas Paróquias no que diz respeito ao fato de o falecido ter pertencido ou não a alguma Irmandade, mas, infelizmente, não tenho idéia de qual seria tal diferença." Letter dated September 10, 2008.

[64] Oliveira, *O liberto*, pp. 83–4. It should be noted that this ratio progressively declined over the course of the nineteenth century as all groups reduced their participation in such organizations.

[65] There were 38 *forros* in this sample, and among them were 27 persons born in Africa, with those from the Costa da Mina predominating. Viana, *O idioma da mestiçagem*, quadros 1, 2 & 3, pp. 184, 186, 187.

[66] On the varying patterns of inclusion or exclusion by the numerous brotherhoods, see A.J.R. Russell-Wood, "Black and Mulatto Brotherhoods in Colonial Brazil: A Study in Collective Behavior," *The Hispanic American Historical Review*, 54, no. 4 (November 1974), pp. 579–81.

[67] In the wills of well-to-do African born-free persons in Bahia in the nineteenth century, it is evident that the ethnic purity of individual confraternities had broken down and Africans of quite different origin were found in the same *irmandades*, even those that accepted only *mulatos*. Oliveira, *O liberto*, p. 81.

in eighteenth- and nineteenth-century Rio de Janeiro.[68] As noted earlier, black brotherhoods devoted to *Nossa Senhora do Rosário* were established in all the towns in Minas and it was the single largest social organization, accounting for 62 out of 322 *irmandades* scattered throughout colonial Minas Gerais.[69] In Bahia in the colonial period, 86 out of 165 confraternities were black organizations dedicated to the Rosary.[70] There was even a brotherhood of the "Good Death," which was founded in 1820 by sexagenarian black women who were Catholic and also initiated in *Candomble*.[71] The city of Salvador at this time had 16 primarily black or mulatto brotherhoods, with many more mixed ones open to them. The great period of development of these brotherhoods was during the eighteenth and early nineteenth centuries, but many survived into the twentieth century as expressions of the black community. After abolition, some of these traditional *irmandades* became the source of the Afro-Brazilian cults that came to prominence in the contemporary period.[72]

Although allowed to elect their own officers, there were usual provisos that slaves or illiterates could not become secretaries, presidents, or treasurers. The Church also went out of its way to control these associations. All were given white clergymen as guardians, and sometimes the government even forced these associations to accept whites to control their finances. In most cases they played a subordinate role in local religious activity, but in some regions they became major economic and political powers. Outstanding in this respect were the *irmandades* in the city of Bahia in the eighteenth and early nineteenth centuries and those scattered throughout the major mining communities of Minas Gerais in the same period. It was these black brotherhoods, as well as many white ones, that funded major artistic activity of mulattoes and blacks. This was

---

[68] João José Reis, "Identidade e diversidade étnicas nas Irmandades negras no tempo da escravidão," *Tempo* (Rio de Janeiro), 2, no. 3 (1996), pp. 7–33. Also see Mariza Soares, *Devotos da cor: Identidade étnica, religiosidade e escravidão no Rio de Janeiro, século XVIII* (Rio de Janeiro: Civilização Brasileira, 2000).

[69] Caio César Boschi, *Os Leigos e o Poder (Irmandade Leigas e Política Colonizadora e Minas Gerais)* (São Paulo: Editora Ática, 1986), pp. 187–8. Also see Kiddy, *Blacks of the Rosary*; Borges, *Escravos e libertos nas irmandades do Rosário*; and Julita Scarano, *Devoção e escravidão – A Irmandade de Nossa Senhora do Rosário dos Pretos no Distrito Diamantino no século XVIII* (São Paulo: Editora Nacional, 1976).

[70] Patricia A. Mulvey, "Black Brothers and Sisters: Membership in the Black Lay Brotherhoods of Colonial Brazil," *Luso-Brazilian Review*, 17, no. 2 (Winter 1980), p. 256.

[71] "A Irmandade da Boa Morte é formada por senhoras sexagenárias, negras e que têm fé católica e iniciação no candomblé." Carolina L. G. Braga, "Tenha uma Boa Morte," *Científico*, IV, no. 2 (2004), n.p.

[72] On the rise of the Afro-Brazilian cults and their association with the *irmandades*, see Roger Bastide, *The African Religions of Brazil*, chapters 5 and 6.

especially the case in Minas Gerais, as noted earlier. These exceptional artists of regional, and even international, stature were a small fraction of a mass of free colored musicians, writers, and artists who produced works both for the popular masses and the elite of their respective societies.

Free colored were also to be found in all the other professions of Brazilian society. Sometimes they were forced to form their own separate craft corporations, but often they were members of the regular guilds. More common as apprentices and journeymen than as master craftsmen, they nevertheless could be found in every skilled occupation in these societies. Sometimes they were even masters of occupations legally denied to them. There were also entire occupations traditionally dominated by both free colored and slave artisans. The most important of such occupations was that of the barber surgeon, who often performed most of the major medical functions in the community.[73] That the free colored served an important role in all skilled crafts, and even dominated a few crucial ones, does not mean that their color did not always affect their economic lives. The colonial and nineteenth-century records are filled with complaints by white artisans against their free colored compatriots. For every free colored who made it to the top of his profession, there were always others who were prevented from the free exercise of their profession by whites who used color barriers to keep them from competing. Constant attempts were made by whites to force blacks and mulattoes to form their own craft corporations, make them take more extensive examinations for master's certification, or even deny them their right to carry out their craft on any level. But the government usually accepted their right to existence on the most pragmatic grounds of need and proof of success. Prejudice was current everywhere, but so was some social mobility and economic integration.

One of the few studies on free colored artisans comes from the Minas Gerais town of Vila Rica in the eighteenth century. There, traditional examinations before craft judges were presented to and officially endorsed and registered by the town council. Of 529 successful examinations in skilled occupations carried out in this community in the eighteenth century, 64 of the successful candidates were free colored (20 *forros* and 44 *negros livres*) and 23 more were slaves. Together, these skilled colored craftsmen represented 16 percent of the total.[74] The fact that slaves were

[73] Zephyr L. Frank, *Dutra's World: Wealth and Family in Nineteenth-Century Rio de Janeiro* (Albuquerque: University of New Mexico Press, 2004).

[74] Geraldo Silva Filho, "O oficialato mecânico em Vila Rica no século dezoito e a participação do escravo e do negro" (Dissertação de mestrado, FFLCH-USP, 1996), p. 81.

officially examined and registered meant that these slaves could carry their official status across legal boundaries should they become free, thus guaranteeing their maintenance within the ranks of the working class elite.

In less skilled occupations, there was little opposition because whites were less numerous and less interested in competing. In domestic service, vending, stevedoring, and seafaring the free colored and slaves were dominant. These were occupations, however, that offered less income and less mobility for the ex-slaves and their offspring. They were also petty merchants. For example, two different *forros* in late-eighteenth-century Sabará owned small stores (*vendas*). Bernard Correa, a *forro* from the Costa de Mina, owned three slaves – two from Angola and one from the Mina area. These were two small boys and an adult male slave named Luis. Another free person was the Creole Ignacía Ribeira, who purchased her own freedom for 300$000 réis. She owned a dry goods store (*vendas de secos e molhados*) and at the time of her death owned a Mina slave named Ventura, who was already involved in a self-purchase arrangement with her master.[75] Moreover, some free colored may have been engaged in labor at the margin of legality. This may have been the extraordinary case of the Bahia-born Bárbara de Oliveira, a *parda crioula* and *forra* of Sabará in the 1760s who was unmarried but had children and grandchildren, and who owned lots of expensive clothing and jewelry, as well as some 22 slaves. Most of these slaves were women, and when she died she noted that 18 were *coartados* and the rest should be sold. She even left several of the women expensive clothing and other gifts. Given her lack of lands, stores, or occupational designation and the large number of women who worked for her, it is assumed she ran a house of prostitution.[76] Such houses of prostitution run by free colored women seem to have been relatively common throughout eighteenth-century Minas.[77] Although several free women were accused of being witches, in Minas it was more common to have African or Creole *forros* attacked for practicing this craft. Most were poor, African-born *forros* and sometimes slaves, although there is the case of the *mulato forro* Antonio Julião, a master shoemaker (*mestre sapateiro*) separated from his wife

[75] Paiva, *Escravidão e universo cultural na colônia, Minas Gerais, 1716–1789*, pp. 128–9.

[76] Paiva, *Escravidão e universo cultural na colônia, Minas Gerais, 1716–1789*, pp. 151–3.

[77] See Laura de Mello e Souza, *Desclassificados do Ouro: A Pobreza Mineira No Século XVIII* (4th ed.; Rio de Janeiro: Graal, 2004), pp. 257–8.

who was accused of using witchcraft to make the *mulata* prostitutes of Sabará love him and using them to add to his income.[78]

It was not uncommon for the more successful *livres de côr* and *forros* to organize small shops. In the Rio de Janeiro parish of Santa Rita, a commercial census of 1841 found 40 out of 603 establishments were owned by colored *livres* – of which 33 were small grocery stores selling food and vegetables (*quitandas de verdura e comida*) and 7 were barbershops. More common an occupation for newly freed slaves was that of itinerant peddlers who worked throughout the city. In 1855, the African (Mina) Ignácio José Antonio petitioned the *municipal* government of the city of Rio de Janeiro (*Camara Municipal da Corte*) to allow his slave, of the same nation, to sell fish in the city. In another case, the African (Nagô) Antonio Delfino de Miranda wanted permission for his two slaves, Augusto and Andre, also Nagos, to work as *escravos de ganho* in the streets of the city.[79]

Finally, in a few cases, even *forros* were able to make it to the top ranks of the society. Some got there through inheritance. Two-year-old *forro* João Batista, born of a slave mother in 1814, inherited a 200-slave plantation from his father, Coronel João Antônio de Barcelos Coutinho. His older *parda* half sisters, born of different slave women who had illicit relations with his father, were also freed and given legal recognition. Two sisters, Carolina Leopoldina and Joana Batista, were formally recognized with the title of Dona in documents of the 1820s, and on the marriage of one sister, her birth was listed as legitimate and no reference was made in her formal marriage declarations as to her color (*parda*) or the fact that her mother was a slave and her birth was outside of wedlock. Moreover, despite constant attacks of the Colonel's other relatives, João Batista de Barcelos Coutinho was able to retain his father's impressive sugar estate, one of the largest in the Campos region of Rio de Janeiro.[80] The case of Joaquim Barbosa showed that mobility could occur through individual skill and luck. It is likely he was born of a slave mother in the late 1770s in Itu in the province of São Paulo and freed in his early childhood. By 1813, this illegitimate *parda forro* owned two slaves, was married, was a militia soldier, and a peddler of dry goods (*mascote de fazendas seca*). By 1815, he obtained a license from the municipal council of Porto Feliz (São Paulo)

---

[78] Mello e Souza, *Desclassificados do Ouro*, pp. 261–2.

[79] Soares, O *'Povo de Cam'na capital do Brasil*, p. 301.

[80] Márcio de Sousa Soares "De pai para filho: Legitimação de escravos, herança e ascensão social de forros nos Campos dos Goitacases, c. 1750 – c. 1830," *V Congresso Brasileiro de História Econômica* (2003), pp. 10–15.

to open a dry goods store and had been elevated to the position of a junior officer or *alferes* in the militia. By then he had three adult slaves and two *pardo agregados* working for him. He continued working in his store but slowly accumulated more slaves and began purchasing land, and although never giving up his commercial activities, he became a landowner and sugar producer with forty-one slaves. He also loaned capital to numerous local planters and had active commercial ties with traders in Santos and Rio de Janeiro. Whereas he served as godparent to several free persons of both color and white status, he did not do so for any of his slaves at their marriage or birth of their children, although all his children had important white government and church leaders as godparents.[81]

There are also cases of *forros* who obtained occupations that were officially denied them. The *mulato forro* Bernardo Gonçalves Bahia who was the illegitimate son of Bartolomeu and his slave Maria Gonçalves Bahia, and who was freed by his unmarried father shortly after his birth in Sabará in Minas Gerais, was listed in his father's 1752 will as a priest (*padre*), a condition that should have been denied him as both a natural child and a *mulato*.[82]

But these cases of unusual success were few, at least for the *forros*, and even for persons of color born free they were rare, and such socioeconomic mobility usually occurred only after two or three generations of freedom. Usually recent *forros* and the first generation of persons of color born free were found in the lower classes. Free colored could be found among *agregados* in Brazil in the households of many middling- and upper-class persons. In the sugar district of Itu in the province of São Paulo in 1829, there were 343 *agregados* (or 9% of total free population), of whom just under half were free persons of color, mostly women.[83] This ratio of free colored was probably lower than normal given the high

[81] Roberto Guedes, "De ex-escravo a elite escravista: A trajetória de ascensão social do pardo alferes Joaquim Barbosa Neves (Porto Feliz, São Pulo, século XIX)," in João Luis Ribeiro Fragoso, Carla Maria Carvalho de Almeida, and Antonio Carlos Juca de Sampaio, eds., *Conquistadores e negociantes: Histórias de elites no Antigo Regime nos trópicos, América lusa, séculos XVI a XVIII* (Rio de Janeiro: Civilização Brasileira, 2007), pp. 355–73.

[82] Ana Luiza de Castro Pereira, "O Sangue, a palavra e a lei: Ilegitimidade e transmissão da herança no Mundo Atlântico Português no século XVIII," paper presented at the Familia y organización social en Europa y América siglos XV–XX Murcia-Albacete 12–14 Diciembre 2007, and published in *Nuevomundo* 28-IV-2008, p. 5 (available at http://nuevomundo.revues.org/index30893.html).

[83] Eni de Mesquita Samara, *Lavoura Canavieira, trabalho livre e cotidiano, Itu 1780–1830* (São Paulo: EDUSP, 2005), tabela 6, p. 121.

concentration of slaves in this region. In the same district in 1854, the *agregados* made up 11 percent of the combined slave and *agregado* labor force, and accounted for 29 percent of the workers on the 532 cattle ranches but only 4 percent of the workers on the 664 sugar estates. In fact, *agregados* in Itu in 1829 were mainly found in urban rather than rural households.[84] As household retainers, there are cases of free colored *agregados* who moved long distances among the various households of their patron. This was the case of the *mulata forra* Cândida Izabel da Conceição, 18 years of age, who was born in Campina Grande, Paraíba do Norte in the northeast of Brazil. She was freed by her master, Joaquim José Henriques, in 1856 and two years later gave birth to a daughter, also a free colored. In 1861, she and her daughter were residing in the house of her former owner in the southern Brazilian city of Lages in Santa Catarina, and both registered themselves as free persons in the local Santa Catarina registers. Clearly she was employed as a servant to her former master.[85] Equally landless *agregados* worked on the usufruct lands of their patrons and otherwise formed part of the agricultural labor force, which was often an extension of household labor.

Aside from working as domestics, farm, and ranch hands on the estates of others, the free colored were also an important part of the independent small farmer population. On the frontiers, in the mountains, on the lands surrounding the towns and cities, and in the lands abandoned by the plantations, the majority of ex-slaves built their lives as free farmers. In most cases they remained squatters or were *agregados* on the lands of the *fazendeiros*, with few possessing full title to their lands.[86] They were a major part of the truck-farming industry near all the major urban centers and formed the bulk of the subsistence farming population, even in areas where slavery was the dominant institution.

Nor was it surprising that these poor workers were to be found among the criminal elements of the society. Eight hundred and ninety-three *livres de côr* were imprisoned in Rio de Janeiro between 1810 and 1821.

---

[84] Eni de Mesquita Samara, "O papel do agregado na região de Itu, 1780–1830," *Anais do Museu Paulista* (Série histórica), vol. 6 (1977), pp. 43–4.

[85] Nilsen C. Oliveira Borges, "Meio livre, meio liberto," *II Encontro "Escravidão e Liberdade no Brasil Meridional"* (2005), p. 7.

[86] Although the term *agregados* could include everything from free household servants to artisans or even professional full-time bandits, the majority of them were poor farmers who worked on the lands of the large *fazendeiros*. On their role in the Goiás frontier, see David McCreery, *Frontier Goiás, 1822–1889* (Stanford: Stanford University Press, 2006), pp. 198–201.

Whereas 34 were imprisoned for showing solidarity with groups of slaves (*solidariedade a grupos de escravos*), 267 were involved in thefts and 263 in acts of violence. As might be expected from their class position, many of these crimes of violence and robbery were against other poor persons, many of whom were either slaves or fellow free colored.[87] There were also the usual conflicts over work and women and even of theft of slaves. Although stealing slaves was not uncommon for whites and *livres de côr*, sometimes these involved friends or lovers. Thus, the *homem livre* José Ferreira was imprisoned in the coastal town of Parati in 1813 for having run away with a slave from Rio de Janeiro who was his lover and who gave birth to their child on her return to her owner.[88]

Given their entrance into the lowest classes of society, their lack of education and even of capital, the climb up the social ladder was slow and painful for the manumitted slaves and freedmen, but it did progress. But fundamental to all free colored was the right to physical mobility. In only a few regions and during only limited periods did the colonial or imperial governments restrict the movement of the free colored population. This was in contrast to North America, where passports and other restrictions tried to tie the freedmen to their original communities. The right of internal migration was crucial for the ability of free colored persons to respond to market incentives and to negotiate better work conditions. Physical mobility was not an automatic guarantee of economic mobility, as the experience of Brazilian frontier squatters who were forced off their lands and became urban poor suggests,[89] but it was a fundamental right that allowed freedmen to escape more oppressive exploitation by the elite.

Our detailed study of 41 *municípios* in the province of São Paulo in the 1829–1831 period found that the 9,288 free colored households were principally dedicated to farming (some 52% of the total). Next in importance were artisans, and together farmers and artisans accounted for two-thirds of these slave-owning free colored households whose occupation was known. Evidently the free colored, although found everywhere and participating in all occupations, were nevertheless at the lower end of the social and economic scale in their majority, as a quarter of these households listed the head as either a *jornaleiro* (day laborer) or a poor

---

[87] Leila Mezan Algranti, *O feitor austente: Estudos sobre a escravidão urbana no Rio de Janeiro, 1808–1822* (Petrópolis: Vozes, 1988), pp. 126–9.

[88] Algranti, *O feitor austente*, pp. 135–6.

[89] For this process of expulsion of squatters and their subsequent reduction in income and status as urban poor, see Alida C. Metcalf, *Family and Frontier in Colonial Brazil, Santana de Parnaíba, 1580–1822* (Berkeley: University of California Press, 1992).

person or even a beggar. This was to be expected given their slave origins and ultimately poorer background, more limited education, and lack of capital. These free colored, however poor, were not alone at the bottom of the social system, as the very significant participation of whites in the poor and day laboring categories indicated (some 10% of the 28,099 white heads of households surveyed in the province). Free colored also could be found everywhere in the province and in sometimes surprisingly significant numbers in more elite occupations.

In the late 1820s in São Paulo, the free colored made up a quarter of the households, but only 20 percent of farming homes. They were, of course, overrepresented among the poor and day laborers. But they did well among artisans and seamen (some 36% and 37% of all heads of household dedicated to these occupations). Unfortunately, they also represented 48 percent of the *jornaleiros* and 42 percent of the poor and beggars and just 15 percent of the liberal professions, only 12 percent of the merchant households, and 14 percent of all soldiers. When examined in terms of their own internal divisions, farmers made up just over half of the total of such free colored classes, followed by artisans and the poor as the next most numerous occupations. Thus, if one were to summarize their occupational position it would be to say that the free colored were mostly working as farmers, but could be found in almost all manual occupations and were overrepresented among the poorer occupations and underrepresented among the elite positions, a not surprising finding given their origin.[90]

That some free colored succeeded in the market economy can be seen from their role as slaveholders. In numerous studies it has been found that the free colored owned slaves.[91] Their slaveholdings were usually

---

[90] Francisco Vidal Luna and Herbert S. Klein, *Slavery and the Economy of São Paulo, 1750–1850* (Stanford: Stanford University Press, 2003), table 7.5, pp. 171–2.

[91] For recent studies showing the relative importance of free colored persons as slave owners in various *municípios* of Brazil, see, for the province of São Paulo, the two studies by Francisco Vidal Luna, *Minas Gerais: Escravos e senhores* (São Paulo: FEA-USP, 1980) and "São Paulo: População, atividades e posse de escravos em vinte e cinco localidades (1777–1829)," *Estudos Econômicos*, 28, no. 1 (1998); and Francisco Vidal Luna and Herbert S. Klein, "Slaves and Masters in Early Nineteenth-Century Brazil: São Paulo," *Journal of Interdisciplinary History*, 21, no. 4 (1991), and most recently Luna and Klein, *Slavery and the Economy of São Paulo, 1750–1850*. For Minas Gerais, see Herbert S. Klein and Clotilde Andrade Paiva, "Free Persons in a Slave Economy, Minas Gerais in 1831," *Journal of Social History*, 29, no. 4 (1996); Clotilde Andrade Paiva and Herbert S. Klein, "Slave and Free in Nineteenth-Century Minas Gerais: Campanha in 1831," *Slavery & Abolition*, 15, no. 1 (1994); and a comparison of both provinces in Luna and Klein, "Free Colored in a Slave Economy." For studies on two *municípios* in Bahia, see

much smaller than those of the white elite, however, and women were better represented among free colored slave owners than they were among whites. In the Minas census of 1831–1832, 49 percent of the 25,286 white households held slaves, whereas just 11 percent of the 37,501 free colored households were slave owning. White slave owners accounted for 71 percent of all slave-owning households. White female slave owners made up just 19 percent of all white masters, but free colored women made up 30 percent of all free colored masters. Of the slave owners, whites in general had almost eight slaves per owner, whereas the free colored had fewer than half that rate, or just over three slaves per owner. Although less important as a group, in the newer regions of São Paulo province, here too in the late 1820s, some free colored owned slaves. The *paulista* free colored slave owners made up just 6 percent of all slave-owning households, compared to the 29 percent of similar households in Minas Gerais in the same period, but like Minas, the free colored women were more important than white women as slave owners, making up a third of all free colored households owning slaves, whereas the white women slave owners accounted for only 20 percent of all white slave owners. On average, the free colored in São Paulo held roughly the same number of slaves as they did in Minas. Finally, it is worth noting that the mean number of slaves held by the free colored for both provinces had a far lower standard deviation than the mean for white owners, which suggests that two-thirds of the free colored owners held close to the three-slave average.[92]

In terms of occupations, the free colored slave owners tended to be far less involved in farming than the white slave owners were and had much greater participation in the trades. Usually the pattern was for free colored artisans of one kind or another to hold slaves or rent slaves who worked in their workshops. Moreover, there was a sharp difference

B. J. Barickman, "As cores do escravismo: Escravistas 'pretos', 'pardos' e 'cabras' no Recôncavo Baiano, 1835," *População e Família*, 2, no. 2 (1999). A detailed study of free colored testaments for nineteenth-century Bahia shows that there is a high correlation between wealth and slave ownership – with virtually all the wealthier *libertos* owning slaves and the greater number of slaves the wealthier they were. Oliveira, *O liberto*, p. 38.

[92] Based on calculations of the Minas Gerais 1831–32 census, with data provided by Clotilde Paiva from the Arquivo Público Mineiro, Seção Provincial, Mapas de População. The mean slaveholdings were 7.6 for whites and 3.4 slaves for free colored. In São Paulo the means were almost the same, with 6.8 slaves for whites who owned slaves and 3.5 slaves for free colored who owned slaves – based on unpublished *mapas* found in Arquivo Público do Estado de São Paulo.

by sex. Free colored, female-headed, slave-owning households were only modestly engaged in farming (29%) compared to their free colored, male, slave-owning peers (of whom 59% were farmers). Thirty-one percent of these female householders were listed as artisans (compared to just 10% of the free colored males who owned slaves). But even including the slave-owning households, it was evident that in both slave- and non-slave-owning households in São Paulo, the free colored were overrepresented among the poor and day laborers. Even in Minas Gerais, being a *jornaleiro* was a very common occupation for the free colored in non-slave-owning households and was not even unknown among the slave owners.[93]

That exceptional individuals emerged out of this essentially poor class is evident when we look at the Brazilian elite. Despite being overwhelmingly white, a free *pardos* and *pretos* did make it into high status positions. In Brazil, individual leaders among the free colored even played major political roles, both identifying with their fellow freedmen and slaves and as often as not playing independent or even hostile roles. This complex relationship, especially in nineteenth-century Brazilian society, had more to do with their greater acceptance and the less effective racist oppositions in their own societies. Their political activities involved everything from being part of elected officialdom and holding appointive administrative and military posts, to the leadership of illegal revolutionary armies. The Rebouças family in Brazil, whose black founding father was a lawyer and elected representative in the Bahian provincial legislature, and whose sons were engineers and administrators at the imperial court, represents one type of behavior. In the Brazilian abolitionist movement were Luis Gama and José de Patrocínio of the free colored class, whereas the mulatto viscount Francisco de Soles Torres, a former minister and head of the Bank of Brazil, was a supporter of slavery.

Finally, it should be stressed that the imperial government accepted the free colored as citizens. The constitution of 1824, which lasted to the end of the empire, declared that free colored were citizens equal to all others (Titulo 2, art. 6, no. I). They had the right to vote and hold office. The complex indirect voting under the empire was based on property qualifications, as was office holding. But with the correct property, the free

---

[93] Francisco Vidal Luna and Herbert S. Klein, "Slave Economy & Society in Minas Gerais and São Paulo, Brazil in 1830," *Journal of Latin American Studies*, vol. 36 (February 2004), table 8, p. 20; and Luna and Klein, *Slavery and the Economy of São Paulo, 1750–1850*, pp. 172–3.

colored could fully participate in imperial politics. The only qualification made was the distinction between *livres* and *libertos*, with the latter, who were born in slavery, being prevented from holding office, but allowed to vote in the first round of elections (Titulo 4, Capitulo VI, art. 94, no. II).[94]

Although attacked, despised, rejected, and feared as a class of potential competitors, the free colored class in Brazil grew rapidly under the slave regime that created it. They proved able to forge a community of freedmen capable of integrating themselves into the free market economy. They fought bitterly and sometimes successfully for the right to social and economic mobility and for the legal rights of full citizenship. This was the most difficult struggle of all and one that would go on long after the death of slavery. But it was this never-ending struggle of the freedmen for acceptance that ultimately prepared the way for the slaves to enter more successfully into free society after abolition was granted to all Africans and Afro-Americans.

[94] Available at http://www.planalto.gov.br/ccivil_03/Constituicao/Constitui%C3%A7a024 .htm.

PART THREE

END OF SLAVERY

10

Transition from Slavery to Freedom

Two events marked the transition from slavery to freedom in Brazil. The first was the definitive ending of the Atlantic slave trade in 1850. The second was the rise of abolitionism in Europe and America, which eventually doomed the institution in every Western society. The ending of the slave trade had an immediate impact on Brazil in that it marked the peak of the slave population and heralded its progressive decline. The overall negative growth rate of the imperial slave population continued unabated, and although it would not have led to the disappearance of the slave labor force, it did reduce it systematically from its 1850 peak. From the census of 1872 to slave *matrícula* of 1887, the total population of slaves had declined by 780,000 persons or 52 percent compared to its 1.5 million size in 1872.[1] Even in the prosperous Southeastern coffee zones, the slave population declined by a quarter from 1872, whereas in the Northeastern region and the far Southern provinces the decline was even more dramatic (see Table 10.1).

In turn, the secular increase in slave prices led to a slow reorientation of slave population distribution. As can be seen both in a longer term series of nominal prime slave prices in Minas Gerais and in a comparison with Rio de Janeiro slave prices in the post-1850 period, there was both a high correlation between prices in these two zones and a secular rise in slave prices during this period as an immediate response to the ending of the trade. Prices reached their peak in the decade of the 1860s, with a more than 80 percent increase when compared to the averages of the decades

---

[1] If the rate of decline noted for the period 1872 and 1887 had continued, the slave population would have declined to approximately half of the 1887 total by 1901.

TABLE 10.1. *Decline of the Slave Population by Province,*
1872–1887

ZONE/PROVINCIAS	1872	1887	% Decline
NORTH			
Pará	27,458	10,535	−62
Maranhão	74,939	33,446	−55
NORTHEAST			
Piauí	23,795	8,970	−62
Ceará	31,913	108	−100
R. G. do Norte	13,020	3,167	−76
Paraíba	21,526	9,448	−56
Pernambuco	89,028	41,122	−54
Alagoas	35,741	15,269	−57
Sergipe	22,623	16,875	−25
Bahia	167,824	76,838	−54
CENTER-SOUTH			
Esp. Santo	22,659	13,381	−41
Corte	48,939	7,488	−85
Rio de Janeiro	292,637	162,421	−44
Minas Gerais	370,459	191,952	−48
São Paulo	156,612	107,085	−32
WEST			
Goiás	10,652	4,955	−53
Mato Grosso	6,667	3,233	−52
SOUTH			
R. G. do Sul	67,791	3,513	−95
Sta. Catarina	14,984	4,927	−67
Paraná	10,560	8,442	−20
BRASIL	1,509,827	723,175	−52

Notes: The slave population of Amazonas is not included.
Source: Census 1872; Matrícula 1887 in Robert W. Slenes, "The Demography and Economics of Brazilian Slavery, 1850–1888" (Ph.D. diss., Department of History, Stanford University, 1976), pp. 697–8, table B-7.

of the 1840s and 1850s. After a significant fall, they showed relative stability until the middle of the 1870s. In this decade, as coffee production increased, there occurred a marked reduction in the slave population, especially after the Law of Free Womb (*Lei do Ventre Livre*) of 1871. This law not only turned a large number of slave children into apprentices, but also greatly expanded self-purchase, third-party interventions to free slaves, and an active legal intervention of the slaves themselves to obtain freedom. Thus, the 1871 law accentuated the gradual reduction of the slave population, which had been occurring since the end of the slave trade in 1850. This increased demand for slaves, combined with a declining number of slaves, caused slave prices to increase until the early 1880s. At this point, the accommodation with the abolitionist movement that had been achieved with the promulgation of the *Lei do Ventre Livre* came to an end and abolitionist pressure increased dramatically. From then on, despite the scarcity of slaves and the ongoing expansion of coffee, it was clear that the extinction of slavery was only a question of time. Although there was a generalized expectation that abolition would involve some form of compensation to the slave owners who would lose their slaves, the abolition movement clearly increased the risk associated with capital invested in slaves (see Graph 10.1a and 10.1b).[2]

More and more the slaves were concentrated in the Southeastern districts and less and less were the Northern and Southern elites dependent on slave labor. The relative importance of various regions changed moderately between 1872 and 1887, but the biggest decline came in the far Southern provinces, which were most affected by the internal slave trade, whereas the Northeast still retained a large share of the imperial slave population despite an active internal slave trade in this period (see Graph 10.2a and 10.2b). The shift in relative importance of slaves in different geographic zones strengthened slavery in the most dynamic part of the national economy, but weakened its hold on the rest of the country. Eventually, the local and imperial governments were forced to close the internal slave trade to prevent the total loss of slave labor in the Northern and far Southern provinces to maintain general popular support for the institution among the elite. It is interesting to observe the differences that occurred in the various areas where coffee production was concentrated. In Rio de Janeiro, in the western zone of the Paraíba Valley in the districts of Vassouras and Valença, there already was an absolute decline in the number of slaves, as occurred in the part of the Paraíba Valley that was located in the province of São Paulo. In the Oeste Paulista region, there was a 15-percent increase in the number of slaves between 1874 and 1883. By this year, the number of slaves resident in the Oeste Paulista region already surpassed the slaves found in the *paulista* region of the Vale do Paraíba.[3]

Brazil was, of course, profoundly influenced in the nineteenth century by changing world attitudes toward slavery after 1789. The first

---

[2] Pedro Carvalho de Mello has argued that the fall in prices in these last two decades of slavery was primarily correlated with the rise of the abolitionist movement. Pedro Carvalho de Mello, "The Economics of Labor in Brazilian Coffee Plantations, 1850–1888," (Ph.D. diss., economics, University of Chicago, 1977), chapter 5.

[3] Carvalho de Mello, "The Economics of Labor," tables 21 & 22, pp. 76–7.

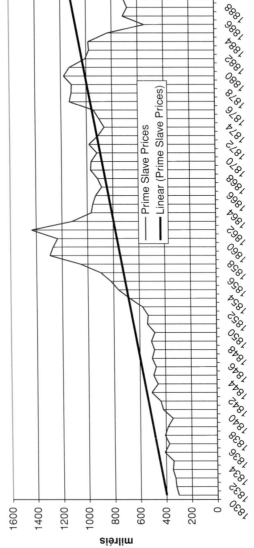

GRAPH 10.1A. Nominal Prices of Prime Age Slaves in Minas Gerais, 1830–1888. *Source:* Bergad data set.

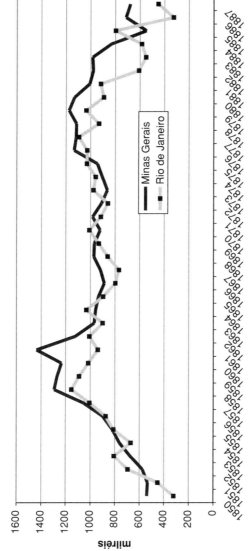

GRAPH 10.1B. Nominal Prices of Prime Age Slaves in Minas Gerais and Rio de Janeiro, 1850–1888. *Sources:* Bergad data set; Carvalho de Mello, "The Economics of Labor," table 16, p. 50.

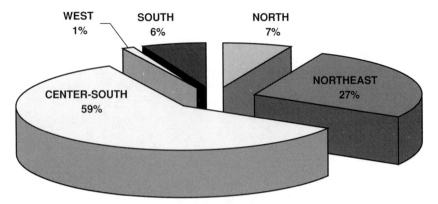

GRAPH 10.2A. Distribution of Slave Population by Region, 1872.

massive liberation of slaves dates from the French Revolution, which directly confronted the contradiction of the enslavement of humans in an egalitarian society. From 1789 to 1793, the constant conflict between planter and free colored in Saint Domingue and the subsequent rebellion of the slaves increasingly radicalized French opinion, which led in late 1793 and early 1794 to the temporary abolition of slavery in the French colonies and, even more importantly, to the Haitian rebellion. But the events of the French Revolution only moderately affected abolitionist sentiments in other American societies. Mid-eighteenth century European writers from Montesquieu to Adam Smith began systematically to attack the very concept of human enslavement, a theme picked up by Quakers and other Protestant groups in the last quarter of the century.

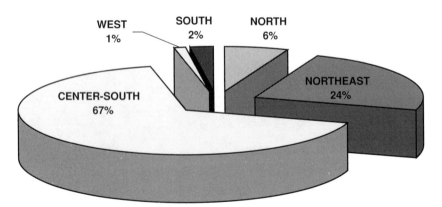

GRAPH 10.2B. Distribution of Slave Population by Region, 1887.

Finally, at the end of the century, several continental powers began to attack and eventually abolish slavery in their metropolitan centers.

This new vision of an egalitarian society in which all men were free found some response in small protests or conspiracies in most Spanish American colonies and with the *Alfaiate* rebellion in Bahia in 1798.[4] But given the effective resistance of entrenched planter elites and their influence on the Crown and local governments, it would take more than a consensus of European radicals and English protestant evangelicals to destroy the institution.

But there also began at this time a campaign of mass mobilization within Europe against one key aspect of slavery, and this would indeed have a profound effect on Brazil. This campaign concentrated on the most vulnerable part of the American slavery system, its reliance on the African slave trade. This proved a more inviting target for reformers because there was a widespread belief that trading in slaves was morally reprehensible. In 1787, a Society for the Abolition of the Slave Trade was formed in England, which mounted a successful public opinion campaign against the trade. As early as 1788 it forced through amelioration legislation, establishing a limit on the number of slaves carried by tonnage of ship for British ships engaged in the slave trade, which was strengthened in a new act of amelioration in 1799. Finally, popular pressure in England forced the total abolition of the trade in 1808 and included as well a prohibition of intercolonial slave trading. The anti slave trade campaign quickly spread to all the nations of Europe and America. In 1787, the U.S. Congress abolished the slave trade as of 1808. In 1792, the Danes had decreed the abolition of the trade, but only terminated it as of 1802, thus being the first nation to stop its slave trade. Then, in the 1810s and 1820s, all the major new Latin American republics abolished the slave trade.[5]

The English anti slave trade movement now mounted a major effort to abolish the slave trading of all nations. They pressured the British

---

[4] See the classic study of Katia M. de Queirós Mattoso, *Presença francesa no movimento democrático baiano de 1798* (Salvador de Bahia: Editôra Itapuã, 1969); and most recently the essay of Ubiratan Castro de Araújo, "A política dos homens de cor no tempo da Independência," *Estudos Avançados*, 18, no. 50 (2004), pp. 253–69.

[5] On the rise of abolitionist movements in the European and American contexts, see David Brion Davis, *The Problem of Slavery in the Age of Revolution, 1770–1823* (Ithaca, NY: Cornell University Press, 1975). For the specific campaign that ended the British slave trade, see the classic study of Roger T. Anstey, *The Atlantic Slave Trade and British Abolition, 1760–1810* (London: Macmillan, 1975).

government to force all governments to end the trade, demanding its total abolition. By the time of the Congress of Vienna in 1815, several nations renounced the trade under British pressure. The most important trader affected was France, a major carrier of African slaves in the period before the French Revolution, which had hoped to reenter the trade in the postwar era. Britain was adamant and forced the defeated French to accept their conditions. In separate treaties in 1815 and 1817 the British also extracted promises from the Spaniards and the Portuguese to begin a gradual abolition of the trade. In 1820, the British Navy began its policy of patrolling the African coast, and the government was granted the right to search the vessels of various European powers on the high seas. By the 1840s, most of the major European naval powers had granted Britain this vital right.

From 1808 to 1850, it was only the Spaniards and the Portuguese who refused to conform to these demands. It was thus a tenet of British foreign policy in the next half-century to pressure both nations to end their slave trade. The British demanded that Spain, Portugal, and the then new nation of Brazil declare slave trading to be piracy, and by the 1830s, they had forced all these nations to accept mixed judicial commissions to condemn vessels caught in the trade.[6] Through constant prevarication, both the Spaniards and the Portuguese were able to keep their trades alive until the second half of the nineteenth century. But British naval blockades and patrols made life increasingly difficult for the slave traders. By 1850, British military and diplomatic pressure on the more sensitive Brazilian empire finally forced an effective end of the slave trade.[7] The Spaniards, whose Cuban possession remained their most important colony, refused all demands for abolition or carried out meaningless abolition decrees that did not stop the trade. Although the minor trade to Puerto Rico was effectively terminated in the 1840s, it would take the combined U.S. and

---

[6] As part of recognizing its independence, England demanded that Brazil agree to end the slave trade. To respond to this demand, on November 7, 1831 the Lei Feijó was promulgated, which prohibited the slave trade. Although initially it was thought that this would end the trade, in fact the trade continued in an even more intense fashion, as the government refused to enforce the decree. But the arrival of slave ships was no longer listed in the local newspapers, as had been the custom until that date.

[7] Given the failure of Brazil to terminate the trade despite its agreement to do so, England passed the Aberdeen Bill, which gave the British Navy the right to seize slave ships, even in Brazilian territorial waters, and to judge their captains. This action reduced, but did not stop the Brazilian slave trade. But Brazil could not resist the force of the British Navy. In 1850, under direct attack by Great Britain, Brazil passed the Lei Eusébio de Queirós, which finally extinguished the three-century-old slave trade to Brazil.

British blockade of the island in the 1860s to finally force the termination of the slave trade to Cuba. With this ending, the entire Atlantic slave trade was finally and successfully terminated.[8]

Although many abolitionists were convinced that the end of the slave trade would automatically bring about the end of American slavery, such was not the case. With the end of the slave trade, the natural decline of the slave population gradually slowed, and relatively quickly the American-born slave population began to achieve positive rates of growth in those societies where emancipation was kept to a low rate. Thus, in Europe and America from the 1810s to the 1840s, abolitionist groups began gathering their forces for a frontal attack on the institution within America. But emancipation of the slaves was a far more difficult and costly affair than the abolition of the trade. Slave owners in every major American slave society fought the emancipationists, and in every case the abolition of slavery was only achieved through political and/or military intervention. Masters bitterly fought or delayed every move toward abolition and by all their actions indicated that they hoped to maintain their slave regimes intact to the very last moment. In the French and British West Indies, the United States, Brazil, and the Spanish islands, the price of slaves remained high until the last years before abolition. This expression of faith by the slave owners in their system of control and domination made each abolitionist movement a hard-fought struggle. Even when they were forced to accept defeat, the slave owners demanded cash and labor compensation for their slaves and the right to freely use the emancipated slaves as "apprentices" for many years into the future. They thus sought to maintain control of the workforce long after official emancipation was enacted.

In the independent American slave societies, the master classes dominated local politics and thus, the movement toward emancipation went

---

[8] On the long British campaign against the trade after 1808, see Chaim D. Kaufmann and Robert A. Pape, "Explaining Costly International Moral Action: Britain's Sixty-year Campaign against the Atlantic Slave Trade," *International Organization*, 53, no. 4 (Autumn 1999), pp. 631–68; and on the financial costs, see E. Phillip LeVeen, *British Slave Trade Suppression Policies, 1821–1865* (New York: Arno, 1977). The debate about British motives in the nineteenth-century campaign is evaluated in Seymour Drescher, *Econocide: British Slavery in the Era of Abolition* (Pittsburgh: University of Pittsburgh Press, 1977). On the specific actions against Brazil and the Brazilian response, see Leslie Bethell, *The Abolition of the Brazilian Slave Trade: Britain, Brazil, and the Slave Trade Question, 1807–1869* (New York: Cambridge University Press, 1970); and on the Brazilian and Cuban slave trades in the nineteenth century and its vicissitudes, see David Eltis, *Economic Growth and the Ending of the Transatlantic Slave Trade* (New York: Oxford University Press, 1987).

304 Slavery in Brazil

at a much slower pace. Most of the Spanish-American republics initiated gradual emancipation at the time of their independence by passing so-called free womb laws, which liberated the children of all slaves. However, long-term apprenticeship periods under the old slave masters were required for these newly manumitted *libertos* or *manumissos*; at the same time no slave born prior to the 1820 decrees was freed. This meant that slavery would continue, with ever-declining numbers, well into the 1840s and 1850s in most of these states.

For Brazil, the Spanish islands of Cuba and Puerto Rico, and the United States – the only major slave powers in the second half of the nineteenth century – abolition was a long and slow process. In the case of the United States, a close tie between the English and North American antislavery movements meant a long and intense campaign, which culminated in the 1840s and 1850s with a massive popular attack on the institution. The isolation of the movement in the Northern states guaranteed that the overthrow of slavery would only occur through civil war. It was the destructiveness and violence of this civil war in the 1860s that finally convinced Cuban and Brazilian intellectuals that slavery was ultimately a doomed institution. As a result, in the 1860s, a serious abolitionist movement finally began to develop in these two societies. In the case of Cuba and Puerto Rico, the problem presented itself within a complex imperial colonial relationship, which essentially involved a struggle over control of a relatively indifferent and often changing central government. From the beginning, abolitionism was associated with the liberal movement in Spain, but it was only a minor part of that reformist position. In fact, the most influential and important of the abolitionist leaders in Spain were always Cuban or Puerto Rican Creoles. It was the North American Civil War that stimulated the creation of the first Spanish abolitionist society, which was established by a Puerto Rican in Madrid in 1864. The creation of the first Spanish republic in 1868 finally led Madrid to accept a gradualist emancipation, which it decreed in September of that year. However, the weakness of the government and the simultaneous beginning of an independence rebellion in Cuba prevented its enactment. Nevertheless, the Madrid government and all the major parties now believed that slavery was doomed, so even the conservatives supported the government decision in July 1870 to abolish slavery.[9]

---

[9] On the rise of the Cuban and Puerto Rican abolitionist movements, see Christopher Schmidt-Nowara, *Empire and Antislavery: Spain, Cuba, and Puerto Rico, 1833–1874* (Pittsburgh: University of Pittsburgh Press, 1999). For the standard work on the

In contrast to the complex struggle between metropolis and colonies, or between regions as in the United States, the abolitionist movement in Brazil was a struggle between classes within one nation. Because slavery was so embedded within Brazilian society, the attack on slavery developed much later than elsewhere in Latin America. This was especially the case given the unwillingness of the master class to argue for the positive benefits of slavery for blacks. Unlike the United States, the Brazilian elite never made a positive defense of slavery and only defended its economic necessity until alternative labor could be found. They seemed to accept the idea of emancipation in some distant future, always with the caveat that there would be financial compensation made to the slave owners.[10] This made opposition difficult to mount for those who wanted an immediate end to slavery. But the delay did not prevent it from being one of the more bitterly fought of abolitionist struggles. Until 1850, an elite group of liberal urban intellectuals had fought for the abolition of the Atlantic slave trade. The signing of a treaty with the British outlawing the trade in 1831 had little effect and pressure built up until final abolition was forced on the Empire in 1850, as much by internal popular pressure as by British military intervention in Brazilian ports. There followed a ten-year period of tranquility in which slavery remained unchallenged. But the U.S. Civil War and mounting international campaigns against Brazil finally caused a reopening of the slavery question in the 1860s. All this led the government elite to move toward a gradualist abolitionary approach as the only answer to an inevitable confrontation.

In September 1871, Brazil therefore adopted a law of free birth.[11] This was less important for an immediate change of status of any slaves,

diplomatic and naval campaign against the Cuban trade, see David R. Murray, *Odious Commerce: Britain, Spain, and the Abolition of the Cuban Slave Trade* (New York: Cambridge University Press, 1980); and for the evolution of the trade to all the Americas, see Herbert S. Klein, *The Atlantic Slave Trade* (2nd printing; Cambridge: Cambridge University Press, 2002).

[10] See Barbara Weinstein, "Slavery, Citizenship, and National Identity in Brazil and the United States South," in Don Doyle and Marco Antonio Pamplona, eds., *Nationalism in the New World* (Athens: University of Georgia Press, 2006), pp. 248–71.

[11] On the law of 1871 and its background and impact, see Martha Abreu, "Slave Mothers and Freed Children: Emancipation and Female Space in Debates on the 'Free Womb' Law, Rio de Janeiro, 1871," *Journal of Latin American Studies*, 28, no. 3 (October 1996), pp. 567–80; as well as the classic statement of its successes and failures by its lead author, Joaquim Nabuco, *O abolicionismo* (1st ed., 1883; Editora Nova Fronteira, 1999), chapter 8. How slaves used the law to bring cases for freedom is shown in Lenira Lima da Costa, "A Lei do Ventre Livre e os caminhos da liberdade em Pernambuco, 1871–1888" (Diss. de mestrado, UFP, Recife, 2007).

because those free (now called *ingenuos*) had to remain "apprenticed" to their mother's owner for twenty-one years, than it was for codifying customary law in relation to slavery and was especially positive for the rights of slaves as never before in imperial legislation. Now the *peculium* of the slave was officially recognized as independent of his or her owner. Any gift or inheritance of slaves were theirs to keep and could be directly passed on to their heirs. Only wages going to the slave's property needed formal approval of the owner.[12] It also definitely sided with the slave in self-purchasing arrangements, allowing the state to formally intervene if the owner refused to sell.[13] This changed a pre-existent imperial decree of 1853, which had specifically held that an owner's permission was needed for self-purchase to occur.[14] It also encouraged individual emancipation, and in the fourth article of the law, it was declared that slaves, with the permission of their owners, could legally contract with a third

---

[12] All these were found in article 4 and several of its paragraphs. The article itself began by declaring that "É permitido ao escravo a formação de um pecúlio com o que lhe provier de doações, legados e heranças, e com o que, por consentimento do senhor, obtiver do seu trabalho e economias. O governo providenciará nos regulamentos sobre a colocação e segurança do mesmo pecúlio." Then the following paragraphs re-enforced this position. Paragraph 1 of this article stated that "Por morte do escravo, metade do seu pecúlio pertencerá ao cônjuge sobrevivente, se o houver, e a outra metade se transmitirá aos seus herdeiros, na forma de lei civil. Na falta de herdeiros, o pecúlio será adjudicado ao fundo de emancipação de que trata o art. 3°." For a detailed discussion of the origins and debates regarding this section of the new law, which was supported by Rio Branco and Nabuco and opposed by Perdigão Malheiro, see Sydney Chalub, *Visões da liberdade: Uma história das últimas décadas da escravidão na Corte* (São Paulo: Companhia das Letras, 1990), pp. 155–8. A partial English translation of this law can be found in Sue Peabody and Keila Grinberg, *Slavery, Freedom, and the Law in the Atlantic World: A Brief History with Documents* (Boston: Bedford/St. Martins Press, 2007), pp. 158–61. Interestingly, despite the constant use of self-purchase from the earliest colonial records, this was the first formal state recognition of this customary practice. Manuela Carneiro da Cunha, "Sobre os silêncios da lei: Lei costumeira e positiva nas alforias de escravos no Brasil do século XIX," in her collection of essays, Manuela Carneiro da Cunha, *Antropologia do Brasil, mito, história, etnicidade* (São Paulo: Brasilense, 1986), pp. 123–44.

[13] Article 4, paragraph 2, declared that "O escravo que, por meio de seu pecúlio, obtiver meios para indenização de seu valor, tem direito à alforria. Se a indenização não for fixada por acordo, o será por arbitramento. Nas vendas judiciais ou nos inventários o preço da alforria será o da avaliação." Several historians recently have begun to stress this second aspect of the law and show that it provided a fundamental change in the State's commitment to slaves and to emancipation. See, for example, Maria Aparecida C. R. Papali, *Escravos, libertos e órfãos: A construção da liberdade em Taubaté (1871–1895)* (São Paulo: Annablume, 2003), pp. 21ff.

[14] Adriana Pereira Campos, "Escravidão e liberdade nas barras dos tribunais," p. 1, available at http://www.historica.arquivoestado.sp.gov.br/materias/anteriores/edica009/materia03/texto03.pdf.

party to pay for their freedom in return for future services to this third party not to exceed seven years.[15] This seems to be the impetus for the rise of a new category of indentured work arrangements that began to appear in the notary records.[16] The law declared that no tax or any other charge could be made to the slave for his freedom papers[17] and that children could not be separated from their parents for any reason.[18] It even declared that freedom could no longer be taken away from an ex-slave for ingratitude to his or her master.[19] The new law also created a state-supported emancipation fund to purchase freedom for those born before 1872.[20] Finally, the law required the registration of all slaves, and these lists (*Lista de Classificação para Emancipação*) have become a new source for the study of slavery in the last quarter of the nineteenth century.[21]

Encouraged by the basic change of attitude of the state toward slavery embodied in the 1871 code, there was now a major movement in all

---

[15] Article 4, paragraph 3: "É, outrossim, permitido ao escravo, em favor da sua liberdade, contratar com terceiro a prestação de futuros serviços por tempo que não exceda de sete anos, mediante o consentimento do senhor e aprovação do Juiz de Órfãos."

[16] In fact, this practice of four-to-seven-year services to a third party for the purchase price paid to the slave owner may have already been customary activity. Several such contracts were written in Santos in the 1860s; see Ian William Olivo Read, "Unequally bound: The conditions of slave life and treatment in Santos county, Brazil, 1822–1888" (Ph.D. diss., Stanford University, 2006), p. 265.

[17] Article 4, paragraph 6 "§6°: As alforrias, quer gratuitas, quer a título oneroso, serão isentas de quaisquer direitos, emolumentos ou despesas."

[18] Article 4, paragraph 7, held that "Em qualquer caso de alienação ou transmissão de escravos é proibido, sob pena de nulidade, separar os cônjuges, e os filhos menores de doze anos, do pai ou mãe,"and paragraph 8 declared that "Se a divisão de bens entre herdeiros ou sócios não comportar a reunião de uma família, e nenhum deles preferir conservá-la sob o seu domínio, mediante reposição da quinta parte dos outros interessados, será a mesma família vendida e o seu produto rateado."

[19] Article 4, paragraph 9 "§9°: Fica derrogada a ord. liv. 4°, tít. 63, na parte que revoga as alforrias por ingratidão."

[20] On the impact of the Fondo de Emancipação on manumission in the post-1871 period, see the recent study of Fabiano Dauwe, "Os múltiplos sentidos da liberdade: A viabilidade e as expectativas da libertação pelo fundo de emancipação de escravos," *II Encontro "Escravidão e Liberdade no Brasil Meridional"* (2003), which is a summary of his 2004 master's thesis at UFF.

[21] Article 8°: "O governo mandará proceder à matrícula especial de todos os escravos existentes no Império, com declaração de nome, sexo, estado, aptidão para o trabalho e filiação de cada um, se for conhecida." For this census material see, for example, Robson Pedrosa Costa, "Cotidiano e resistência nas últimas décadas da escravidão, Olinda, 1871–1888" (Diss. de mestrado, UFP, Recife, 2006); and Renato Leite Marcondes and José Flávio Motta, "Duas fontes documentais para o estudo dos preços dos escravos no Vale do Paraíba paulista," *Revista Brasileira de História*, 21, no. 42 (2001), pp. 495–514.

regions of lawyers bringing cases against masters for freeing their slaves. It even reached the point where the old 1831 law, which officially, although not effectively, prohibited the Atlantic slave trade, was now used to bring cases for freedom for the families of slaves brought "illegally" to Brazil between 1830 and 1850 – which involved an estimated 745,000 slaves and their descendants. The law and its enabling legislation of 1832 granted slaves the right to demand freedom from the state if they had landed after the decree went into effect.[22]

Government leaders thought they had resolved the emancipation issue with this law, and, in fact, serious abolition agitation declined in this period, so that until 1880, the planter class enjoyed relative peace and control over their slave force. This did not mean that the abolitionist movement had changed its position, as the constant pace of legal challenges to enslavement was on the rise everywhere. But it was only after 1880 that Brazil finally began to experience a popular mass abolitionist movement demanding an immediate end to the institution. Once this movement began, it quickly challenged the very foundations of slavery. Although the leadership typically came from elite families, Brazilian abolitionism was unusual in having a significant minority of mulatto and black leaders. They ranged from the engineer, André Rebouças, and the pharmacist, José de Patrocinio, to the politician, Luiz Gama, and the fugitive-slave leader, Quintano Lacerda and his 10,000 runaway slave community in the port city of Santos.[23] The movement also included large numbers of free black workers on the docks and in the railroads who refused to transport slaves and assisted runaways. In the early 1880s, the internal slave trade was finally abolished and taxes were established on local sales of slaves. But these ameliorating decrees did not stem the

---

[22] See, for example, the studies of Maria Angélica Zubaran, "Os Escravos e a Lei de 7 de Novembro de 1831 no Rio Grande do Sul (1865–1888)," *II Encontro "Escravidão e Liberdade no Brasil Meridional"* (2005) and "Escravidão e liberdade nas fronteiras do Rio Grande do Sul (1860–1880): O caso da Lei de 1831," *Estudos Ibero-Americanos* (PUCRS), 32, no. 2 (Dezembro 2006), pp. 119–32; also Argemiro Eloy Gurgel, "A Lei de 7 de novembro de 1831 e as ações cíveis de liberdade na Cidade de Valença (1870 a 1888)" (diss. de mestrado, UFRJ, 2004), chapters 3 and 4. The stress in most of these unusual cases was on the failure to properly matricaular the slaves in the various post-1871 *matriculas*, thus enabling petitions of automatic freedom to be brought on the basis of post-1831 illegal entries into Brazil.

[23] On the important and very active role of the engineer André Rebouças as an active abolitionist from 1879 to 1888, see the recent thesis of Alexandro Dantas Trindade, "André Rebouças: Da Engenharia Civil a Engenharia Social" (tesis de doutorado, sociologia, UNICAMP, 2004), pp. 281ff.

rising tide of abolitionist activity. In 1884, abolitionists succeeded in proclaiming the Northeastern state of Ceará as a free state. Immediately an active underground railroad developed with free persons helping slaves escape their owners and reach Ceará. The slave owners bitterly fought this growing disobedience, and in another set of ameliorating decrees passed in September 1885 that freed slaves over the age of 60 and provided more monies for the public Emancipation Funds, slave owners obtained a harsh vagrancy law against recently freed slaves (*libertos*) that required that they have regular certified employment.[24]

From 1885 onward, the pressures increased. With each passing year, more and more cities declared slavery to be abolished within their limits. The state of Amazonas joined the ranks of free Ceará, and most importantly, São Paulo became a center of mass mobilization. In November 1886, strikes by free workers, many of them colored, forced the city of Santos to declare itself free, and by the end of the year, 10,000 fugitives were living in the town. Although slave owners proclaimed their emancipationist sentiments and claimed that the 1871 and 1885 decrees were ending slavery, the radical abolitionists challenged these assertions. The Emancipation Fund, in operation from 1871 to 1888, freed only some 32,000 slaves. Three times that number of slaves purchased their own freedom or were granted manumission by their masters. The immediate abolitionist leaders held that the gradual decrees were having little effect on the institution.

It was this move toward confrontational politics on the part of the abolitionists in the post-1885 period that finally saw the dismantling of

---

[24] The "Lei dos Sexagenários," enacted in September 1885, immediately freed all slaves over the age of 60, although even this law granted the owners three more years of work from the elderly freed slaves and was a compromise from a more liberal proposal of immediate and noncompensatory emancipation. In article 3, paragraphs 15 and 17 of this decree, *libertos* were required to maintain their traditional residences and prove to the police that they had regular employment. If not, they were supposed to be sent to military-like agricultural colonies set up for the purpose of dealing with these *liberto* vagrants (article 4, paragraph 5). This law, as well as all the other major slave laws from 1850 to 1888, is available at the UFRJ Human Rights Center website: http://www.nepp-dh.ufrj.br/estante.html#10. For a detailed analysis of the debates and logic behind the decree, see Josefi Maria Nunes Mendoça, *Entre a mão e os anéis: A lei dos sexeganários e os caminhos da abolição no Brasil* (Campinas: UNICAMP, 1999); and to see the law in the context of the earlier decrees, see Adriane Eunice de Paula Roos, "A escravidão negra sob a perspectiva do direito no Brasil Imperial," Trabalho de Conclusão do Curso de Direito, PUC-RS (Porto Alegre, 2007), p. 12, available at http://www.pucrs.br/direito/graduacao/tc/tccII/2007_1.htm.

slavery. By 1887, the number of slaves had declined to 723,000 and was falling rapidly. The army and the local police now refused to return fugitives, and mass exodus from plantations was becoming common in the most advanced plantation counties of São Paulo. Almost all the major *paulista* cities were declaring slavery abolished and their territory a free zone. Fugitive slaves had little difficulty finding safe havens. The level of violence also escalated as arms were distributed to the fugitive slaves by the more radical abolitionists. Conflicts between police and armed slaves became common and the agitation was now even spreading to the most backward areas. When even members of the imperial family were converted to a radical abolitionist position, there was little hope left for the slave owners. In May 1888, the government finally decreed immediate and totally uncompensated emancipation for all slaves. Thus ended the largest remaining slave regime in America, and with its destruction, African slavery was finally brought to an end in all the Americas.[25]

But the legal ending of slavery did not end its influence on Brazilian life. The impact of emancipation brought about one of the most fundamental changes in the world economy in the nineteenth century. It was a process that reallocated large amounts of capital, and it brought about an immediate, if sometimes temporary, reduction of formerly slave-produced commercial agricultural exports to Europe and North America. The adjustment to free labor also brought about some major shifts in the centers of production, as the shock of transition often led to the collapse of older production centers.

Brazil was not immune to these changes. Here, too, abolition profoundly transformed the nature of the labor force in Brazil as slaves abandoned the coffee plantations and were replaced by new immigrant workers. Attempts at mid-century had been made to replace coffee slaves with immigrants, but this experiment failed.[26] In the South-Central coffee fields, slaves totally abandoned the *fazendas* and were immediately replaced by immigrants. Just as slave emancipation in the West Indies became the major impulse for the migration of Asian laborers to the

[25] Standard sources on this history are Robert E. Conrad, *The Destruction of Brazilian Slavery, 1850–1888* (Berkeley: University of California Press, 1972), and Robert B. Toplin, *The Abolition of Slavery in Brazil* (New York: Atheneum, 1972). On the participation of slaves in this movement and protest at the local level, see Elciene Azevedo, "O direito dos escravos: Lutas judicais e abolicionismo na província de São Paulo na segunda metade do século XIX" (tese de doutorado, UNICAMP, 2003).

[26] The best study of this failed experiment is provided by Warren Dean, *Rio Claro: A Brazilian Plantation System, 1820–1920* (Stanford: Stanford University Press, 1976).

Americas, the abandonment of the coffee fields brought millions of southern Europeans to Brazil and profoundly changed the nature of Brazilian society.[27] Brazil moved from a society in which the whites were a distinct minority, to a society in which they would become the majority. To the traditions of Portugal were now added those of Italy, Spain, and, eventually, of Japan after 1908.

Abolition led to a major reorganization in the production of coffee, Brazil's principal export. The Valley of Paraíba, which spanned both the provinces of Rio de Janeiro and São Paulo, was the original region of the great coffee *fazendas* based totally on slave labor. After the introduction of the railroads in the 1870s, coffee expanded into the virgin West Paulista plains. This new rich frontier soon challenged the Paraíba *fazendas* whose valley lands were exhausted. Abolition was thus the death blow for the Paraíba Valley economy. The loss of their slaves, and the low productivity of the old coffee fields due to the exhaustion of the local soil because of poor management, meant that the region's coffee planters could not make the transition to free labor. Abolition turned the once mighty zone into a depressed region and accelerated the dominance of coffee in the West Paulista plains, the richest zone of the state of São Paulo then and now, which became the center of the coffee industry. The West Paulista region became the principal zone of immigrant labor, which was now paid in piecework, handling a given number of coffee trees per family.[28]

The flight of ex-slaves from the coffee plantations changed the nature of coffee plantation agricultural labor itself. From being a supervised labor force, organized in groups, and employing women in all aspects of basic agricultural production, coffee plantation labor shifted to family units of production in which control over actual working conditions was given over to the individual workers themselves. Coffee production moved from systematic gang labor to family piecework farming, and eventually shifted to the smaller-size coffee-producing units.

Whereas there is little question of the slaves leaving the coffee plantations of the Southeast in a grand exodus, they did not leave the region, nor totally abandon salaried labor. Many of them became squatters and small farming landowners in the older regions of coffee production, such

[27] On the Italian immigration, see Thomas Holloway, *Immigrants on the Land: Coffee and Society in São Paulo, 1886–1934* (Ithaca, NY: Cornell University Press, 1980); and for the other major group of coffee immigrants, see Herbert S. Klein, *A imigração espanhola no Brasil* (São Paulo: FAPESP: IDESP: Editora Sumaré, 1994).

[28] Antônio Delfim Netto, *O problema do café no Brasil* (São Paulo: Instituto de Pesquisas Econômicas – USP, 1981).

as the Paraíba Valley, or in some of the newer West Paulista and Zona de Mata counties in Minas Gerais. Despite the traditional image of the immigrants replacing the native, recently free workers, internal national migration to the *paulista* frontier was in fact steady, and poor whites and colored constantly moved to take advantage of labor markets. Most of them sharecropped and supplemented their income with seasonal agricultural labor in the export agricultural zones or as unskilled laborers on the expanding rail network that was transforming national infrastructure in the last quarter of the nineteenth century.[29] They also remained as seasonal salaried workers in the old sugar regions of the Northeast. In the former area, planters often freed their slaves before final abolition, worked out sharecropping arrangements, sold land to ex-slaves, and otherwise tried to retain ex-slave workers even as the local economies shifted from coffee into cattle and other activities. In fact, in the old plantation areas, the majority of ex-slaves remained because of extensive social and kin networks, many living on the old plantations until the 1930s when the local economy collapsed and forced migration to other zones.[30] In the Northeastern sugar plantations, free labor was introduced long before the abolition of slavery, and slaves often worked alongside free workers. It would appear from the few studies available that ex-slaves may have remained on the old sugar estates in fairly significant numbers. In an original study of hospital records from the local Santa Casa in Santo Amaro, Bahia, in 1906–1913, matched against slave lists in local *engenhos* in the late 1880s, one historian found that he could match 232 ill patients

[29] Maria Lúcia Lamounier, "Agricultura e Mercado de Trabalho: Trabalhadores Brasileiros Livres nas Fazendas de Café e na Construção de Ferrovias em São Paulo, 1850–1890," *Estudos Econômicos*, 37, no. 2 (Abril–Junho 2007), pp. 363ff.

[30] The extensive work on the postabolition experience in this old coffee region is summarized in Ana Maria Rios and Hebe Maria Mattos, "O pós-abolição como problema histórico: Balanços e perspectivas," *Topoi*, 5, no. 8, (Jan.–Jun. 2004), pp. 170–98; also see the recent thesis of Carlos Eduardo C. da Costa, "Campesinato Negro no Pós-Abolição: Migração, Estabilização e os Registros Civis de Nascimentos.Vale do Paraíba e Baixada Fluminense, RJ. (1888–1940)" (dissertação de mestrado, Universidade Federal do Rio de Janeiro, 2008). A similar pattern, involving the breakup of an old *fazenda* into smaller units, the expansion of cattle raising, and eventual conflict between ex-slaves and cattlemen over lands, can be found in Elione Silva Guimarães, "Memórias históricas de movimentos rurais – Juiz de Fora na passagem do século XIX ao XX," *Tempo*, 11, no. 22 (2004), pp. 58–79. For a comparative analysis of the transition from slave to free labor in the Caribbean and the United States, see Herbert S. Klein and Stanley L. Engerman, "The Transition from Slave to Free Labor: Notes on a Comparative Economic Model," in Manuel Moreno Fraginals et al., eds., *Between Slavery and Free Labor: The Spanish Speaking Caribbean in the Nineteenth Century* (Baltimore: Johns Hopkins University Press, 1985), pp. 255–69.

who resided in *engenhos*, and of these, 189 were adult ex-slaves residing in the sugar estate in which they were born.[31] Thus, the Northeastern ex-slave zones are more comparable to the ex-slave states of the United States, which also showed a very high residence of ex-slaves on their old plantations.[32] The transition also meant an increasing sexual division of labor as women shifted out of sugar plantation field work. It even affected the rhythm of agricultural production, for the marked seasonal occupation of labor during harvesting and planting became a more pronounced aspect of sugar plantation agriculture in Brazil, as it did in the rest of the New World as the need to keep a servile labor force occupied full-time was eliminated.

This transition from slave to free labor also opened a new chapter in the struggle between ex-masters and ex-slaves for control of land and labor. The freed slaves of the rural areas wanted to own their own lands, and they wanted freedom from any type of coerced labor. Their ideal everywhere was to own land and independently produce their own crops. They would work on the old plantations for their ex-masters only if they could not get access to their own lands or if they could find no alternative employment, urban or otherwise. If given no migration opportunities or access to land, they still refused to return to the old plantation working conditions. If they worked on the old estates, they demanded immediate withdrawal of their wives and daughters from field labor, an end to gang-labor arrangements, payment in money wages for all labor, and access to usufruct land for their own cultivations. In many cases, this made their labor more costly than that of subsidized European immigrants. It was not racial prejudice that made *paulista* coffee planters turn to foreign workers, as some have argued, but the fact that such labor was ultimately cheaper than Afro-Brazilian labor. This massive immigration of surplus European and Asian labor also had an impact on the labor opportunities of the ex-slaves. It meant that the new immigrants crowded out the recently liberated slaves and many other free rural workers from the skilled and semi-skilled labor markets because they were less educated

---

[31] Walter Fraga Filho, *Encruzilhadas da liberdade, histórias de escravos e libertos na Bahia (1870–1910)* (Campinas: Editora de UNICAMP, 2006), p. 246. He also found that in an analysis of births to ex-slave parents in several local parishes in 1889–1890 in the same province of Bahia, two thirds of the parents still lived either in the parish or on the old *engenhos*, and the rest came from nearby parishes. Fraga Filho, *Encruzilhadas da liberdade*, pp. 247–8.

[32] Herbert S. Klein, *A Population History of the United States* (Cambridge: Cambridge University Press, 2004), p. 100.

than the immigrants. Thus, many ex-slaves continued to work in the
informal economy, mostly dedicating themselves to subsistence agriculture. With the end of slavery there could have developed major economic
opportunities for this newly freed population even in commercial agriculture as wage workers. But the rapid solution of the labor problem
in coffee by foreign immigration postponed their incorporation into the
formal labor market, which would only effectively occur in the second
half of the twentieth century, with urbanization, industrialization, and
the end of major foreign immigration.

In the Northeastern sugar industry, however, a slow transition to a
mixed free and slave labor force before the end of slavery and the move
toward marked seasonality of labor needs, meant that ex-slaves were
more readily available for labor on these estates, especially as many of
these liberated slaves now had access to their own lands in the off-season
periods. Part-time mestizo or *caboclo* workers were already working in
the sugar estates even before abolition. These workers, along with full- or
part-time ex-slave workers, became the staple of the post-emancipation
plantation workforce, and a relationship of compatibility developed
between both subsistence farming and part-time plantation labor in parts
of Brazil, as occurred in Cuba. Moreover, without the need for maintaining the slave labor force on a yearly basis, some post-emancipation sugar
plantations became even more pronounced seasonal operations, with a
clearly defined "dead season" in which no work was performed.

Abolition also encouraged the total reorganization of sugar production
itself in the most advanced regions. Following the earlier experiments in
new mills (called *usines*) for sugar production in Guadeloupe in the 1860s,
the Cubans, in the last quarter of nineteenth century, began to adopt the
new system of production on a major scale. This involved the creation
of large, new steam-driven and railroad-fed central factories for milling.
This process of adjustment began in the Northeast region of Brazil. First
there was the early use of free wage-labor from the abundant free colored, white, and *caboclo* (mestizo) subsistence peasant classes living near
the sugar estates in Pernambuco and Bahia. There was a crisis in production as slaves left the estates en masse to take up squatting claims on
frontier lands. But the retention of a growing national market, as well as
continued world exports, enabled the Northeast sugar producers to find
the capital to begin constructing the new mills (which Brazilians called
usinas) in the last two decades before the end of the century. The series of
severe droughts in the Northeast that began in the 1880s and the subsequent crisis in subsistence agriculture, forced many ex-slave peasants into
part-time wage-labor on their old estates. The Brazilian sugar industry

also experienced the new stress on marked seasonal production that created a symbiotic relationship between peasant agriculture – which supported the workers most of the year – and seasonal wage labor on the plantation lands in the harvest season.

In the coffee fields of São Paulo, the transition was somewhat different. Coffee, like cotton, was an American crop for which world prices remained high throughout the transition period, providing the capital to aid the planters in their shift to free labor. This was crucial, because the coffee planters found their labor crisis even more acute than those in sugar because of the wholesale abandonment of the coffee *fazendas* by the ex-slaves. With the city of São Paulo and other large urban centers expanding in the heart of the coffee zones, with an open and fairly prosperous local frontier available to them in the West, and with poor, abandoned lands in the old coffee regions of the Paraíba Valley to the north, the ex-slaves had enough land or occupational opportunities open to them so that they had no need to compromise with the planters. They simply disappeared from plantations and overnight were replaced by a white labor force.

The coffee planters had resisted the transition to the end, but in the 1870s and early 1880s, they finally began to experiment with the use of European immigrant indentured laborers. Most of these early *paulista* experiments were failures because the Europeans refused to accept the extremely restrictive labor contracts or the working conditions that were the norm for slaves. Immigrant labor strikes, the slowing of immigration, and threats of closure of emigration from European governments all put pressure on the planters to produce both a freer labor system and one with much higher returns for the workers. Even then, the immigrants found that the repayment of the original passage money put too much of a limit on their earnings, so they refused to migrate to Brazil. This was a period when the Italians who might be coming to Brazil also could consider Argentina and the United States as viable alternatives. The end result was that the planters were required to absorb all transportation costs, just as they had to accept families rather than single male workers as the base for their labor force. Given the wealth of the coffee planters due to market conditions and their power in local politics, they were able to force the government to use public revenues to subsidize the migration of Italian families. First the provincial government of São Paulo, and then the central government after the creation of the Republic in 1899, provided state subsidization for some 900,000 immigrants who came to work the coffee plantations. In the decade after abolition, some 1.3 million immigrants arrived from Europe, of whom 60 percent were Italians.

The resulting labor of Italian families on Brazilian coffee estates led to a technical reorganization of the whole coffee production process. Trees were now assigned to families, who worked individually and were paid for their planting, caring, and harvesting on a combination of sharing and piece-wage arrangements. This shift in labor and production arrangements was occurring as the coffee frontier was moving south and east. In the first phase of this process, there was a movement of coffee production to new areas that opened up in the Valley of Paraíba, which then moved westward to the frontier of the West Paulista plains. This migration of coffee was aided by the establishment of an important network of railroads that tied these productive zones to the port of Santos. Large estates still prevailed, but were now based on European immigrant labor. The city of São Paulo, which until 1890 was a small city with only some 65,000 inhabitants, became the economic center of this production and exporting coffee region, and integrated the port of Santos with the center of coffee production, and thus quickly rose to become one of the world's largest cities. With the crisis of 1929 and the slow migration of coffee to the south of the state and to the north of Paraná, there was a reduction in the scale of producing units and a relative increase in the number of immigrant owners of land who also became producers of coffee.

Thus, the dual process of emancipation and transition to free labor had resulted in profound changes in the social, economic, and even geographic organization of most of the old slave societies. It also led to varying patterns of integration and marginalization among the liberated slaves. In most cases, whether land was secured or not, ex-slaves found themselves still living in the areas of the old plantation regimes and mostly at the lowest level of their respective socioeconomic systems. Entering free society with little or no capital – often with skills only adaptive to a now declining plantation economy – and faced with continuing discrimination based on their color or former slave status, most found it difficult to rise from the working class.[33] In Brazil, ex-slaves often found themselves in the most backward economic areas even of the most dynamic of regions.

---

[33] Numerous authors point to the labor contracts law of 1879, which was pushed by Nabuco and seems to be a counterpart to the 1871 Law of Free Birth. This *Lei de locação de Serviços* was part of legislation going back to the criminal code of 1830, which was designed to force poor free whites and colored into labor contracts. But the 1879 code allowed such state enforceable contracts between landowners and workers to be just 3 years in length for immigrants, 5 years for Brasileiros (of whatever color), and 7 years for *libertos*. Lamounier, "Agricultura e Mercado de Trabalho," pp. 360–2.

For the sons and daughters of ex-slaves, only the escape from the old plantation regions provided any hope of advancement. In most cases, such migration would not occur until major changes developed in the world economy. The impact of World War I, with its new demands for labor in the industrial areas of the Western world, and the even more profound impact of World War II, finally broke the isolation of the liberated slaves and their descendants. It was only in the mid-twentieth century that massive migration of Afro-Americans began. These migrations were substantially different from earlier intraregional movements, for although they were motivated by the search for new economic opportunities as before, they often involved either very long distance migrations or permanent residence outside the traditional centers. West Indians began major migrations to North America and Europe, just as poorer Brazilians moved from the Northeast southward into the booming urban centers and major industrial areas.

But the out-migration from the poor lands and marginal regions did not end the legacy of slavery. Even for those who obtained the skills, education, and capital needed to rise above the working class, they found that mobility was not as open to them as to the poor whites. That black color was considered a negative identity, and that "whitening" of skin color was held a prerequisite for successful mobility, were part of the cognitive view of all American societies until well into the twentieth century. What distinguished Brazil was not so much the lack of prejudice as it was the subtle differentiations that prejudice would create. Class was such a powerful determinant of position that the attributes of class would often influence the definition of color, whatever the phenotypic characteristics shown by the individual. Black lawyers were often defined as mulattoes, just as mulatto ones were defined as whites. In turn, successful Afro-Brazilians, accepting the views of their racist societies, often "married up" in color, thus "whitening" their offspring, allowing them to move into the mulatto or white category. Because class had an important influence on color definitions, the role of prejudice was far more subtle and discrimination far less precise than in those societies such as the United States where color was defined solely by phenotype and origin.

Although upwardly mobile mulattoes and blacks conformed to these racist views, the black masses did not totally accept these values, for many rejected this acculturation to "white" norms and the rejection of their color and culture that this usually implied. The isolated village of ex-slaves preserving traditional ways was one response to this prejudice, but another was the elaboration of an even more vibrant alternative cultural expression. The new religion of Umbanda, along with the pre-abolition groups of Candomblé and other cults, expanded under freedom. Although bitterly attacked by the white police in Brazil as manifestations of idolatry and social disorder, the Afro-American cults publicly revealed themselves in the late nineteenth and early twentieth centuries and forced the dominant society to grant them recognition. First, isolated intellectuals, and then, important sections of the elite realized that these beliefs were too powerful to destroy, especially after the black masses began to vote in large numbers and could influence the political process itself. More and more private churches and street festivals were permitted, and by the mid-twentieth century they began to absorb mulatto and white adherents. What started as signs of protest and self-identity became, for better or worse, symbols of a diverse but integrated national culture.

Much of this slow erosion of the harsher manifestations of racial prejudice came from two different directions. The first was the growing political power of the black masses with the arrival of democratic or representative governments to all these former slave societies. By the early decades of the twentieth century this occurred in Brazil. The traditional elites were thus forced to compromise with the black masses. Blacks and mulattoes were early elected to the local provincial assemblies, but it was only in the twentieth century that they made any headway against prejudice in the central administration, which was largely controlled by Southern and Central Brazilian whites.

Along with their growing political power, there was also an increasing acceptance of the black contribution to national culture and identity. Many late-nineteenth-century Brazilian whites were influenced by the European ideas of racial ranking and were hostile to Afro-Americans and their culture. In fact, Gobineau, the author of many of these doctrines, was the French ambassador to Brazil and a friend of Dom Pedro II.[34] But the rise of cultural anthropology under the leadership of Franz Boas in Germany and then in America had a major impact among Bahian intellectuals, who created a school of Afro-Brazilian studies and argued for the positive benefits of black–white integration, and rejected racist ideas or arguments that rejected the African element of Brazilian culture and identity. The most well-known intellectual of this school, although

---

[34] On this theme, see José Luis Petruccelli, "Doutrinas francesas e o pensamento racial brasileiro, 1870–1930," *Estudos Sociedade e Agricultura*, no. 7 (Dezembro 1996), pp. 134–49; and Thomas E. Skidmore, *Black into White: Race and Nationality in Brazilian Thought* (New York: Oxford University Press, 1974).

born in Pernambuco, was of course Gilberto Freyre, who in fact studied with Boas at Columbia University in the 1920s. The pro-Africanist movement and the collapse of supposedly superior European society in World War I challenged the legitimacy of white imperialism. This too gave impetus to the growth of relativism in cultural analysis in European and North American social sciences and provided radical Brazilians with models to reevaluate their own national cultures. In the 1930s and 1940s, the rise of nativist schools that glorified the African contributions to national culture helped to systematically redefine Brazilian identity. Rather paternalistic in their initial manifestations, the new pro-Afro-American ideologies nevertheless gave legitimacy to mass opposition to the "whitening" process and helped to reduce the high social costs of integration into the dominant society.[35]

In Brazil, the degree of economic expansion, urbanization, European immigration, and Afro-American emigration would influence the relative rates of mobility of the descendants of the slaves. Enough mobility had occurred, and enough self-awareness of the legitimacy of their own cultural needs and demands existed on the part of the Afro-Americans that relatively high rates of mobility and accommodation were achieved by the second or third generation after abolition. The struggle was often bitter and costly for Afro-Americans; however, in most of Latin America by the last quarter of the twentieth century, the Afro-American presence had become an accustomed and accepted part of the culture and national self-identity. A century after the last slave was freed, the legacy of slavery is still seen in continuing poverty of many descendants of slaves and in ongoing prejudice against Afro-Brazilians and lower rates of mobility than among whites. These class rigidities and color impediments notwithstanding, the descendants of the African slaves have achieved significant levels of socioeconomic mobility, political power, and cultural integration in the society to which their forebears had been so brutally transported many years before.

---

[35] On the racism prevalent in Brazil in the late nineteenth and early twentieth centuries, see Lilia Moritz Schwartz, *O espetáculo das raças, cientistas, instituções e questão racial no Brasil, 1870–1930* (São Paulo: Companhia das Letras, 1993); Mariza Corrêa, *As ilusões da liberdade: A escola Nina Rodrigues e a antropologia no Brasil* (Bragança Paulista, UDUSF, 1998). On the origins of the northeastern school, which re-evaluated the African contribution to Brazil, see Thomas E. Skidmore, "Raízes de Gilberto Freyre," *Journal of Latin American Studies*, 34, no. 1 (February 2002), pp. 1–20. For a recent discussion of the influence of Boas and the impact of Gilberto Freyre on redefining race, see Antonio Sérgio Alfredo Guimarães, "Preconceito de cor e racismo no Brasil," *Revista de Antropologia* (São Paulo, USP), 47, no. 1 (2004), pp. 9–43.

Bibliography

Primary Sources

Arquivo da Casa dos Contos. "Serro do Frio: Escravos, Livro de Matrícula." Codice no. 1068.

Arquivo Nacional, Rio de Janeiro. "Rol das Pessoas que Confessam e Comungam na Freguesia de Congonhas do Sabará, 1771," Caixa 202, pacote único.

Arquivo Público do Estado de São Paulo, Mapas de População.

Arquivo Público Mineiro, Seção Provincial, Mapas de População.

Christie, W. D. *Notes on Brazilian Questions* (London: Macmillan, 1865).

Diretoria Geral de Estatística. *Recenseamento Geral do Brazil de 1872.*

IHGB/CU, Arq. 1-1-19. "Correspondência do Governador da Bahia, 1751–1782," folios 228v–230, 3 Julho 1775, Bahia.

Jornal do Comércio (Rio de Janeiro). Various issues 1830s and 1840s.

Laerne, C. F. Van Delden. *Brazil and Java: Report on Coffee-Culture in America, Asia, and Africa* (London, W. H. Allen, 1885).

Lara, Silvia Hunold, ed. *Ordenações Filipinas, Livro V* (modern edition of 1603 codes; São Paulo: Companhia das Letras, 1999).

Leme, Pedro Taques de Almeida Paes. *Notícias das Minas de São Paulo e dos sertões da mesma Capitania, São Paulo [1645]* (São Paulo: Prefeitura do Município de São Paulo, Biblioteca Histórica Paulista, 1954).

Lima, Álvaro Tibério de Moncorvo. *Falla recitada na abertura da Assembléia Legislativa da Bahia...* (Bahia: Typ. de Antonio Olavo da França Guerra, 1856).

Los Siete Partidas del rey Alfonso el sabio, cotejadas con varios codices antiguos, por la Real Academia de la Historia (3 vols.; Madrid: La Imprenta Real, 1807).

Marinho, Joaquim Saldanha. *Relatório apresentado a Assembléia Legislativa provincial de São Paulo... no dia 2 de fevereiro de 1868 pelo presidente da mesma província* (São Paulo: Typ. do Ypiranga, 1868).

_____. *Relatório com que sua excelência o sr. senador Barão de Itaúna passou a administração da província ao exmo. sr. comendador Antônio Joaquim da Rosa* (São Paulo: Typ. Americana, 1869).

Rocha, Antonio Candido da. *Relatório apresentado à Assembléia Legislativa provincial de São Paulo pelo presidente da província* . . . (São Paulo, Typ. Americana, 1870).

Sinimbu, João Lins Vieira Cansanção de. *Falla recitada na abertura da Assembléia Legislativa da Bahia* (Bahia: Typ. de Antonio Olavo da França Guerra, 1857).

The Trans-Atlantic Slave Trade Database, Voyages, (Emory University) available at http://www.slavevoyages.org/tast/index.faces. The "estimates" are found at http://www.slavevoyages.org/tast/assessment/estimates.faces.

Secondary Studies

Abreu, Martha. "Slave Mothers and Freed Children: Emancipation and Female Space in Debates on the 'Free Womb' Law, Rio de Janeiro, 1871," *Journal of Latin American Studies*, 28, no. 3 (October 1996), 567–580.

Aladrén, Gabriel. "Liberdades negras nas paragens do Sul: Alforria e inserção social de libertos em Porto Alegre, 1800–1835" (Dissertação de mestrado, História, Universidade Federal Fluminense, Niterói, 2008).

Al-Alam, Caiuá Cardoso. "Questões acerca dos enforcamentos de escravos em Pelotas-RS," *II Encontro "Escravidão e Liberdade no Brasil Meridional"* (2003).

Alden, Dauril. "Late Colonial Brazil, 1750–1808," in Leslie Bethell, ed., *The Cambridge History of Latin America* (11 vols.; Cambridge: Cambridge University Press, 1984), II, pp. 601–662.

———. "Yankee Sperm Whalers in Brazilian Waters, and the Decline of the Portuguese Whale Fishery (1773–1801)," *The Americas*, 20, no. 3 (January 1964), pp. 267–288.

Aleixo, Lucia Helena Gaeta. "Mato Grosso: Trabalho escravo e trabalho livre (1850–1888)" (Dissertação de mestrado, PUC–SP, 1984).

Alencastro, Luis Felipe de. *O trato dos viventes: Formação do Brasil no Atlântico Sul, séculos XVI e XVII* (São Paulo: Companhia das Letras, 2000).

Algranti, Leila Mezan. *O feitor ausente: Estudos sobre a escravidão urbana no Rio de Janeiro, 1808–1822* (Petrópolis: Vozes, 1988).

———. "Os ofícios urbanos e os escravos de ganho no Rio de Janeiro Colonial (1808–1822)," in Tamás Szmrecsányi, ed., *História Econômica do Período Colonial* (São Paulo: Ed. HUCITEC/FAPESP, 1996), pp. 195–214.

Almeida, Joseph Cesar Ferreira de. "Entre engenhos e canaviais: Senhoras do açúcar em Itu (1780–1830)" (dissertação de mestrado, FFLCH-USP, 2007).

Amantino, Márcia. "As condições físicas e de saúde dos escravos fugitivos anunciados no Jornal do Commercio (RJ) em 1850," *História, Ciências, Saúde – Manguinhos*, 14, no. 4 (out.-dez. 2007), pp. 1377–1399.

Amoglia, Ana Maria Faria. "Um suspiro de liberdade: Suicídio de escravos no município de Juiz de Fora (1830–1888)," *Boletim [Núcleo de Estudos em História Demográfica. FEA_USP]*, no. 18 (Novembro de 1999).

Amos, Alcione Meira. "Afro-Brazilians in Togo: The Case of the Olympio Family, 1882–1945," *Cahiers d'Études Africaines*, 162, XLI-2 (2001), pp. 293–314.

——— and Ebenezer Ayesu. "Sou brasileiro: História dos Tabom, afro-brasileiros em Acra, Gana," *Afro-Ásia*, no. 33 (2005), pp. 35–65.

Andrade, Marcos Ferreira de. "Negros rebeldes nas Minas Gerais: A revolta dos escravos de Carrancas (1833)," *Afro-Ásia*, 21–22 (1998–1999), pp. 45–82.

Andrade, Maria José de Souza. *A mão de obra escrava em Salvador 1811–1860* (São Paulo: Corrupio, 1988).

Andrade, Rômulo. "Ampliando estudos sobre famílias escravos no século XIX: Crianças cativas em Minas Gerias: Legitimidade, alforria e estabilidade familia," *Revista Universidade Rural, Série Ciências Humanas*, 24, nos. 1–2 (2002), pp. 101–113.

_____. "Casamento entre escravos na região cafeeira de Minas Gerais," *Revista Universidade Rural, Série Ciências Humanas*, 22, no. 2 (Jul./Dez. 2000), pp. 177–288.

_____. "Havia um mercado de famílias escravas? (A propósito de uma hipótese recente na historiografia da escravidão)," *Revista de História (Juiz de Fora)*, 4, no. 1 (1998), pp. 93–104.

Andreau, Jean and Raymond Descat. *Esclave en Grèce et à Rome* (Paris: Hachette, 2006).

Anstey, Roger T. *The Atlantic Slave Trade and British Abolition, 1760–1810* (London: Macmillan, 1975).

Antonil, André João. *Cultura e Opulência do Brasil*. Introdução e vocabulário por A. P. Canabrava (São Paulo: Ed. Nacional, s/d).

Araújo, Ubiratan Castro de. "A política dos homens de cor no tempo da Independência," *Estudos Avançados*, 18, no. 50 (2004), pp. 253–269.

Arêdes, Diego Emílio Alves and Maria Aparecida Chaves Ribeiro Papali. "Crime de escravo em Taubaté: Assassinato de um feitor em 1852," available at www.inicepg.univap.br/INIC_2005/inic/IC7%20anais/IC7-10.pdf.

Arriaga, Eduardo E. *New Life Tables for Latin American Populations in the Nineteenth and Twentieth Centuries* (Berkeley: University of California, Population Monograph Series, no. 3, 1968).

Arruda, José Jobson de Andrade. *Brasil no comércio colonial* (São Paulo: Editora Ática, 1980).

Assunção, Mattias Röhrig. "Quilombos maranhenses," in João José Reis and Flávio dos Santos Gomes, eds., *Liberdade por um fio: História dos quilombos no Brasil* (São Paulo: Companhia das Letras, 1996), pp. 433–466.

Austen, Ralph A. "The Mediterranean Islamic Slave Trade Out of Africa: A Tentative Census," *Slavery & Abolition*, XIII (1992), pp. 214–248.

_____. "The 19th Century Islamic Slave Trade from East Africa (Swahili and Red Sea Coasts): A Tentative Census," *Slavery & Abolition*, IX (1988), pp. 21–44.

_____. "The Trans-Saharan Slave Trade: A Tentative Census," in Henry A. Gemery and Jan S. Hogendorn, eds., *The Uncommon Market: Essays in the Economic History of the Atlantic Slave Trade* (New York: Academic Press, 1979), pp. 23–75.

Azevedo, Elciene. "O direito dos escravos: Lutas judicas e abolicionismo na província de São Paulo na segunda metade do século XIX," (tese de doutorado, UNICAMP, 2003).

Bacellar, Carlos Almeida Prado. *Os senhores da terra: Família e sistema sucessório entre os senhores de engenho do oeste paulista (1765–1855)* (São Paulo: UNICAMP, 1987).

Barickman, B. J. *A Bahian Counterpoint: Sugar, Tobacco, Cassava, and Slavery in the Recôncavo, 1780–1860* (Stanford: Stanford University Press, 1998).

_____. "As cores do escravismo: Escravistas 'pretos', 'pardos' e 'cabras' no Recôncavo Baiano, 1835," *População e Família*, 2, no. 2 (1999), pp. 7–59.

_____. "Revisiting the Casa-grande: Plantation and Cane-Farming Households in Early Nineteenth-Century Bahia," *Hispanic American Historical Review*, 84, no. 4 (2004), pp. 619–659.

Bastide, Roger. *Les religions africaines au Brésil* (Paris: Presses Universitaires de France, 1960).

Batista, Nilo. "Pena Pública e escravismo," *Capítulo Criminológico*, 34, no. 3 (Jul.-Set. 2006) pp. 279–321.

Bergad, Laird W. *Slavery and the Demographic and Economic History of Minas Gerais, Brazil, 1720–1888* (Cambridge: Cambridge University Press, 1999).

Bertin, Enidelce. *Alforrias na São Paulo do século XIX: Liberdade e dominação* (São Paulo: Humanitas FFFCH/USP, 2004).

Berute, Gabriel Santos. "A concentração do comércio de escravos na capitania do Rio Grande de São Pedro do Sul, c. 1790 – c. 1825," *II Encontro "Escravidão e Liberdade no Brasil Meridional"* (2005).

Bethell, Leslie. *The Abolition of the Brazilian Slave Trade: Britain, Brazil, and the Slave Trade Question, 1807–1869* (New York: Cambridge University Press, 1970).

Bethencourt, Francisco. "Political Configurations and Local Powers," in Francisco Bethencourt and Diogo Ramada Curto, *Portuguese Oceanic Expansion, 1400–1800* (Cambridge: Cambridge University Press, 2007), pp. 197–254.

Birchal, Sérgio de Oliveira. "O mercado de trabalho mineiro no século XIX," (Belo Horizonte: Ibmec, Working Paper no. 12, 2007).

Blasenheim, Peter Louis. "A regional history of the Zona da Mata in Minas Gerais, Brazil, 1870–1906," (Ph.D. dissertation, Stanford University, 1982).

Bloch, Marc. *Slavery and Serfdom in the Middle Ages, Selected Essays* (Berkeley: University of California Press, 1975).

Bonnaissie, Pierre. *From Slavery to Feudalism in South-Western Europe* (Cambridge: Cambridge University Press, 1991).

Borges, Célia Maria. *Escravos e libertos nas irmandades do Rosário: Devoção e solidariedade em Minas Gerais, séculos XVIII e XIX* (Juiz de Fora: Editora UFJF, 2005).

Borges, Nilsen C. Oliveira. "Meio livre, meio liberto," *II Encontro "Escravidão e Liberdade no Brasil Meridional* (2005).

_____. "Terra, gado e trabalho: Sociedade e economia escravista em Lages, SC (1840–1865)" (Florianópolis: Dissertação do mestrado, Universidade Federal de Santa Catarina, 2005).

Boschi, Caio César. *Os Leigos e o Poder (Irmandade Leigas e Política Colonizadora e Minas Gerais)* (São Paulo: Editora Ática, 1986).

Botelho, Tarcísio Rodrigues. "Estratégias matrimoniais entre a população livre de Minas Gerais: Catas Altas do Mato Dentro, 1815–1850," *XIV Encontro Nacional de Estudos Populacionais, ABEP* (2004).

———. "Família escrava em Catas Altas do Mato Dentro (MG) no século XVIII," *Anais da V Jornada Setecentista* (2003).

———. "Família e escravidão em uma perspectiva demográfica: Minas Gerais (Brasil), século XVIII," in Douglas Cole Libby and Júnia Ferreira Furtado, eds., *Trabalho livre, trabalho escravo, Brasil e Europa, séculos XVIII e XIX* (São Paulo: Annablume, 2006), pp. 195–222.

Bowser, Frederick P. *The African Slave in Colonial Peru, 1524–1650* (Stanford: Stanford University Press, 1974).

Boxer, Charles R. *The Dutch Seaborne Empire, 1600–1800* (New York: A. A. Knopf, 1965).

———. *The Golden Age of Brazil, 1695–1750: Growing Pains of a Colonial Society* (Berkeley: University of California Press, 1962).

———. *The Portuguese Seaborne Empire, 1415–1825* (London: Hutchinson, 1969).

Bradley, Keith. *Slavery and Society at Rome* (Cambridge: Cambridge University Press, 1994).

Braga, Carolina. L. G. "Tenha uma Boa Morte," *Científico*, IV, no. 2 (2004), n.p.

Brügger, Sílvia Maria Jardim. "Compadrio e Escravidão: Uma análise do apadrinhamento de cativos em São João del Rei, 1730–1850," *XIV Encontro Nacional de Estudos Populacionais, ABEP* (2004).

———. "Legitimidade, casamento e relações ditas ilícitas em São João del Rei (1730–1850)," *IX Seminário sobre a Economia Mineira* (2000).

———. *Minas patriarcal, família e sociedade São João del Rei – séculos XVIII e XIX* (São Paulo: Annablume, 2007).

Calógeras, João Pandiá. *As Minas do Brasil e sua legislação* (Rio de Janeiro: Imprensa Oficial, 1905).

Campolina, Alda Maria Palhares, Cláudia Alves Melo, and Mariza Guerra de Andrade. *Escravidão em Minas Gerais: Cadernos do Arquivo* (Belo Horizonte: Arquivo Público Mineiro/COPASA MG, 1988).

Campos, Adriana Pereira. "Escravidão e liberdade nas barras dos tribunais," available at http://www.historica.arquivoestado.sp.gov.br/materias/anteriores/edica009/materia03/texto03.pdf.

Campos, Kátia Maria Nunes. "Antônio Dias de Vila Rica: Aspectos demográficos de uma paróquia colonial (1763–1773)," *XVI Encontro Nacional de Estudos Populacionais, ABEP* (2008).

Canabrava, Alice P. "A grande Lavoura," in Sérgio Buarque de Holanda (org.), *História Geral da Civilização Brasileira*, vol. 6 (Rio de Janeiro: Bertrand Brasil, 1997).

———. "A repartição da terra na capitania de São Paulo, 1818," *Estudos Econômicos*, 2, no. 6 (Dez. 1972), pp. 77–129.

———. "João Antonio Andreoni e sua obra," in José João Antonil, *Cultura e Opulência do Brasil. Introdução e vocabulário por A. P. Canabrava* (São Paulo: Ed. Nacional, s/d).

———. "Uma economia de decadência: Os níveis de riqueza na Capitania de São Paulo 1765–67," *Revista Brasileira de Economia, (Rio de Janeiro)*, 26, no. 4 (Out./Dez. 1972), pp. 95–123.

Cardoso, Ciro Flamarion et al. *Escravidão e abolição no Brasil: Novas perspectivas* (Rio de Janeiro: Zahar, 1988).

———. *Escravo ou camponês? O protocampesinato negro nas Américas* (São Paulo: Brasiliense, 1987).

Cardoso, Fernando Henrique. *Capitalismo e escravidão no Brasil meridional: O negro na sociedade escravocrata do Rio Grande do Sul* (São Paulo: Difusão Européia do Livro, 1962).

——— and Octavio Ianni. *Côr e mobilidade social em Florianópolis* (São Paulo: Companhia Editora Nacional, 1960).

Carney, Judith A. "'With Grains in Her Hair': Rice in Colonial Brazil," *Slavery & Abolition*, 25, no. 1 (April 2004), pp. 1–27.

Carreira, António. *As companhias pombalinas de Grão-Pará e Maranhão e Pernambuco e Paraíba* (2nd ed.; Lisbon: Editorial Presença, 1982).

Carvalho, Filipe Nunes de. "Do descobrimento a União Ibérica," in Harold Johnson and Maria Beatriz Nizza da Silva, eds., *O império luso-brasileiro, 1500–1620* (vol. 6 of the *Nova História da Expansão Portuguesa*, edited by Joel Serrão and A. H. de Oliveira Marques; Lisbon: Editorial Estampa, 1998).

Carvalho, Marcus J. M. de. *Liberdade, rotinas e rupturas do escravismo, Recife, 1822–1850* (Recife: Ed. Univesitária UFPE, 1998).

Carvalho Filho, Luís Francisco. "Impunidade no Brasil – Colônia e Império," *Estudos Avançados* (USP), 18, no. 51 (2004), pp. 187–88.

Castro, Antonio Barros de. "Escravos e senhores nos engenhos do Brasil. Um estudo sobre os trabalhos do açúcar e a política econômica dos senhores" (São Paulo: tese de doutorado, UNICAMP, 1976).

Chalhoub, Sidney. *Visões da liberdade: Uma história das últimas décadas da escravidião na Corte* (São Paulo: Companhia das Letras, 1990).

Chaudhuri, K. N. *Trade and Civilization in the Indian Ocean: An Economic History from the Rise of Islam to 1750* (Cambridge: Cambridge University Press, 1985).

Chaves, Cláudia Maria das Graças. *Perfeitos negociantes, mercadores das minas setecentistas* (São Paulo: Annablume, 1999).

Chesnair, Jean-Claude. *The Demographic Transition, 1720–1984* (Oxford, Clarendon Press, 1992).

Conrad, Alfred H. and John R. Meyer. "The Economics of Slavery in the Ante Bellum South," *The Journal of Political Economy*, 66, no. 2 (April 1958), pp. 95–130.

Conrad, Robert E. *The Destruction of Brazilian Slavery, 1850–1888* (Berkeley: University of California Press, 1972).

———. *Tumbeiros: O tráfico de escravos para o Brasil* (São Paulo: Brasiliense, 1985).

Cook, David Nobel. *Demographic Collapse, Indian Peru 1520–1620* (Cambridge: Cambridge University Press, 1981).

Cope, R. Douglas. *The Limits of Racial Domination, Plebian Society in Colonial Mexico City, 1660–1720* (Madison: University of Wisconsin Press, 1994).

Corrêa, Carolina Perpétuo. "Aspectos da demografia e vida familiar dos escravos de Santa Luzia, Minas Gerais, 1818–1833," *XIV Encontro Nacional de Estudos Populacionais, ABEP* (2004).

Corrêa, Mariza. *As ilusões da liberdade: A escola Nina Rodrigues e a antropologia no Brasil* (Bragança Paulista, UDUSF, 1998).

Cortes Alonso, Vicenta. *La esclavitud en Valencia durante el reinado de los reyes católicos (1479–1516)* (Valencia: Ayuntamiento, 1964).

Costa, Carlos Eduardo C. da. "Campesinato Negro no Pós-Abolição: Migração, Estabilização e os Registros Civis de Nascimentos.Vale do Paraíba e Baixada Fluminense, RJ. (1888–1940)"(dissertação de mestrado, Universidade Federal do Rio de Janeiro, 2008).

Costa, Iraci del Nero da. "Ocupação, Povoamento e Dinâmica Populacional," in Iraci del Nero da Costa and Francisco Vidal Luna, *Minas Colonial: Economia e Sociedade* (São Paulo: Pioneira, 1982), pp. 1–30.

———. "Repensando o modelo interpretativo de Caio Prado Jr." (Cadernos NEHD, n. 3) (São Paulo: NEHD-FEA/USP, 1995).

———. *Vila Rica: População (1719–1826)* (São Paulo: IPE-USP, 1979).

Costa, Lenira Lima da. "A Lei do Ventre Livre e os caminhos da liberdade em Pernambuco, 1871–1888" (Recife: dissertação de mestrado, UFP, 2007).

Costa, Robson Pedrosa. "Cotidiano e resistência nas últimas décadas da escravidão, Olinda, 1871–1888" (Recife: dissertação de mestrado, UFP, 2006).

Cunha, Maísa Faleiros da. "A legitimidade entre os cativos da Paróquia Nossa Senhora da Conceição de Franca – Século XIX," *XIV Encontro Nacional de Estudos Populacionais, ABEP* (2004).

Cunha, Manuela Carneiro da. *Antropologia do Brasil, mito, história, etnicidade* (São Paulo: Brasiliense, 1986).

———. *Da Senzala ao Sobrado: Arquitetura Brasileira na Nigéria e na República Popular do Benim. [From Slave Quarters to Town Houses: Brazilian Architecture in Nigeria and the Peoples Republic of Benin]* (São Paulo: Nobel/EDUSP, 1985).

———, ed. *História dos índios no Brasil* (São Paulo: Companhia das Letras, 1992).

———. *Negros, Estrangeiros: Os Escravos Libertos e a sua Volta à África* (São Paulo: Brasiliense, 1985).

Curti, Ana Helena, ed. *Aleijadinho e seu tempo: Fé, engenho e arte* (Rio de Janeiro: Banco Central do Brasil, 2006).

Curtin, Philip. *The Atlantic Slave Trade: A Census* (Madison: University of Wisconsin Press, 1969).

Danieli Neto, Mário. "Escravidão e Indústria: Um estudo sobre a Fábrica de Ferro São João de Ipanema – Sorocaba (SP) – 1765–1895" (Tese de doutorado, Economia/UNICAMP, 2006).

Dantas, Mariana L. R. "Black Townsmen: A Comparative Study of Persons of African Origin and Descent in Slavery and Freedom: Baltimore, Maryland and Sabará, Minas Gerais, 1750–1810" (Ph.D. diss.; Baltimore: Johns Hopkins University, 2003).

Dauwe, Fabiano. "Os múltiplos sentidos da liberdade: A viabilidade e as expectativas da libertação pelo fundo de emancipação de escravos," *II Encontro Escravidão e Liberdade no Brasil Meridional* (2003).

David, Paul A. et al. *Reckoning with Slavery: A Critical Study in the Quantitative History of American Negro Slavery* (New York: Oxford University Press, 1976).

Davis, David Brion. *The Problem of Slavery in the Age of Revolution, 1770–1823* (Ithaca, NY: Cornell University Press, 1975).

Dean, Warren. "Indigenous populations of the São Paulo-Rio de Janeiro Coast: Trade aldeamento, slavery and extinction," *Revista de História*, 117 (1984), pp. 3–26.

_____. *Rio Claro: A Brazilian Plantation System, 1820–1920* (Stanford: Stanford University Press, 1976).

Debien, Gabriel. *Les esclaves aux antillais françaises (XVIIe–XVIIIe siècles)* (Basse-Terre: Société d'Historie de la Guadeloupe, 1974).

Deerr, Noel. *The History of Sugar* (2 vols.; London: Chapman and Hall, 1949–1950).

Delfim Netto, Antônio. *O problema do café no Brasil* (São Paulo: Instituto de Pesquisas Econômicas–USP, 1981).

Dias, João José Alves. "A população," in Joel Serrão and A. H. de Oliveira Marques, eds., *Nova História de Portugal* (12 vols.; Lisbon: Editorial Presença, 1998).

Díaz, Maria Elena. *The Virgin, the King and the Royal Slaves of El Cobre: Negotiating Freedom in Colonial Cuba, 1670–1780* (Stanford: Stanford University Press, 2000).

Dockès, Pierre. *Medieval Slavery and Liberation* (London: Methuen, 1982).

Domar, Evsey D. "The Causes of Slavery or Serfdom: A Hypothesis," *Journal of Economic History*, 30, no. 1 (March 1970), pp. 18–32.

Drescher, Seymour. *Econocide: British Slavery in the Era of Abolition* (Pittsburgh, PA: University of Pittsburgh Press, 1977).

Ebert, Christopher. "Dutch Trade with Brazil before the Dutch West India Company, 1587–1621," in Johannes Postma and Victor Enthoven, eds., *Riches from Atlantic Commerce: Dutch Transatlantic Trade and Shipping, 1585–1817* (Leiden: Brill, 2003), pp. 49–76.

Eblen, Jack Ericson. "New Estimates of the Vital Rates of the United States Black Population during the Nineteenth Century," *Demography*, 11, no. 2 (May 1974), pp. 301–319.

Eisenberg, Peter L. "Ficando livre: As alforrias em Campinas no século XIX," *Estudos Econômicos*, 17, no. 2 (1987), pp. 175–216.

_____. *The Sugar Industry in Pernambuco: Modernization without Change, 1840–1910* (Berkeley: University of California Press, 1974).

Elbl, Ivana. "Volume of the Early Atlantic Slave Trade, 1450–1521," *Journal of African History*, XXXVIII (1997), pp. 31–75.

Ellis Junior, Alfredo. "O Ciclo do Muar," *Revista de História*, vol. I (São Paulo, 1950).

_____. "Ouro e a Paulistania," *Boletim de História da Civilização Brasileira*, 8, (1948).

Ellis, Myriam. *A Baleia no Brasil colonial* (São Paulo: Edições Melhoramentos, EDUSP, 1969).

_____. "A economia paulista no século XVIII," *Boletim de História da Civilização Brasileira*, 11 (1950).

Eltis, David. *Economic Growth and the Ending of the Transatlantic Slave Trade* (New York: Oxford University Press, 1987).

_____. "The Relative Importance of Slaves and Commodities in the Atlantic Trade of Seventeenth-Century Africa," *The Journal of African History*, 35, no. 2. (1994), pp. 237–249.

_____. "Slavery and Freedom in the Early Modern World," in Stanley L. Engerman, ed., *Terms of Labor, Slavery, Serfdom, and Free Labor* (Stanford: Stanford University Press, 1999), pp 25–49.

_____. "The Volume and Structure of the Transatlantic Slave Trade: A Reassessment," *The William & Mary Quarterly*, 3rd series, 58, no. 1 (January 2001), pp. 17–46.

Eltis, David, Stephen D. Behrendt, David Richardson, and Herbert S. Klein. *The Transatlantic Slave Trade, 1562–1867: A Database* (New York, Cambridge: Cambridge University Press, 2000).

Eschwege, W. L. von. *Pluto Brasiliensis* ([1833]; 2 vols.; São Paulo: Ed. Nacional, 1944).

Eugênio, Alisson. "Solidariedade e tensões no simbólico das festas das irmandades de escravos e libertos em Minas Gerais no século XVIII," unpublished manuscript.

_____. "Tensões entre os Visitadores Eclesiásticos e as Irmandades Negras no século XVIII mineiro," *Revista Brasileira de História*, 22, no. 43 (2002), pp. 33–46.

Faria, Sheila de Castro. *A Colônia em movimento: Fortuna e família no cotidiano colonial* (Rio de Janeiro: Nova Fronteira, 1988).

_____. "Aspectos demográficos da alforria no Rio de Janeiro e em São João Del Rey entre 1700 e 1850," *XVI Encontro Nacional de Estudos Populacionais*, ABEP (2008).

_____. "Identidade e comunidade escrava: Um ensaio," *Tempo*, 11, no. 22 (2007), pp. 122–146.

_____. "Legitimidade, estratégias familiares e condição feminina no Brasil escravista," *Anais do VIII Encontro de Estudos Populacionais ABEP* (1992).

Fenoaltea, Stefano. "Slavery and Supervision in Comparative Perspective: A Model," *The Journal of Economic History*, 44, no. 3 (September, 1984), pp. 635–668.

Fernandéz, Ramón Vicente Garcia. "Transformações econômicas no litoral norte paulista, (1778–1836)" (Tese de doutorado, FEA, Universidade de São Paulo, 1992).

Ferreira, Roberto Guedes. "Pardos: Trabalho, família, aliança e mobilidade social, Porto Feliz, São Paulo, c. 1798 – c. 1850" (Tese de doutorado, História, Universidade Federal do Rio de Janeiro, 2005).

_____. "Trabalho, família, aliança e mobilidade social: Estratégias de forros e seus descendentes – Vila de Porto Feliz, São Paulo, século XIX," *V Congresso Brasileiro de História Econômica* (2003).

Finley, M. I. "Between Slavery and Freedom," *Comparative Studies in Society and History*, 6, no. 3 (April 1964), pp. 233–249.

———. *Classical Slavery* (London: F. Cass, 1987).

Flausino, Camila Carolina. "Negócios da escravidão: Tráfico interno de escravos em Mariana: 1861–1886" (Dissertação de mestrado, História, Universidade Federal de Juiz de Fora, 2006).

Florentino, Manolo. "Sobre minas, crioulos e a liberdade costumeira no Rio de Janeiro, 1789–1871," in Manolo Florentino, ed., *Tráfico, cativeiro e liberdade Rio de Janeiro, séculos XVII–XIX* (Rio de Janeiro: Civilização Brasileira, 2005), pp. 331–366.

Florentino, Manolo and Cacilda Machado. "Sobre a família escrava em plantéis ausentes do mercado de cativos: Três estudos de casos (século 19)," *XI Encontro Nacional de Estudos Populacionais da ABEP* (1998).

Florentino, Manolo and José Roberto Góes. *A paz das senzalas: Famílias escravas e tráfico atlântico, Rio de Janeiro, c. 1790 – c. 1850* (Rio de Janeiro: Civilização Brasileira, 1997).

———. "Do que Nabuco já sabia: Mobilidade e miscigenação racial no Brasil escravista" (Congresso Internacional Brasil-Portugal Ano 2000 – Sessão de História, 2000).

———. "Parentesco e família entre os escravos de Vallin," in Hebe Maria Mattos de Castro and Eduardo Schnoor, eds., *Resgate: Uma janela para o Oitocentos* (Rio de Janeiro: Topobooks, 1995), pp. 140–164.

Fogel, Robert W. and Stanley L. Engerman. *Time on the Cross: The Economics of American Negro Slavery* (Boston: Norton, 1974).

Fonsêca, Humberto José. "Vida e morte na bahia colonial: Sociabilidades festivas e rituais fúnebres (1640–1760)" (Belo Horizonte: tesis de doutorado, FAFICH/UFMG, 2006).

Fraga Filho, Walter. *Encruzilhadas da liberdade, histórias de escravos e libertos na Bahia (1870–1910)* (Campinas: Editora de UNICAMP, 2006).

Fraginals, Manuel Moreno. *El Ingenio: Complexo económico social cubano del azúcar* (3 vols.; Habana: Editorial de Ciencias Sociales, 1978).

Franco Silva, Alfonso. *La esclavitud en Sevilla y su tierra a fines de la edad media* (Sevilla: Diputación Provincial de Sevilla, 1979).

Frank, Zephyr. *Dutra's World: Wealth and Family in Nineteenth-Century Rio de Janeiro* (Albuquerque: University of New Mexico Press, 2004).

Freire, Jonis. "Compadrio em uma freguesia escravista: Senhor Bom Jesus do Rio Pardo (MG) (1838–1888)," *XIV Encontro Nacional de Estudos Populacionais, ABEP* (2004).

Freitas, Décio, ed. *Palmares, a guerra dos escravos* (5th rev. ed.; Porto Alegre: Mercado Aberto, 1984).

———. *República de Palmares: Pesquisa e comentários em documentos históricos do século XVII* (Maceió, Alagoas: Edufal, 2004).

Freyre, Gilberto. *The Masters and the Slaves: A Study in the Development of Brazilian Civilization* (2nd English-language ed., rev.; Berkeley: University of California Press, 1986).

———. *O escravo nos anúncios de jornais brasileiros do século XIX* (Recife: Imprensa Universitária, 1963).

Funari, Pedro Paulo de Abreu. "A arqueologia de Palmares, sua contribuição para o conhecimento da história da cultura afro-americana," in João José Reis and Flávio dos Santos Gomes, eds., *Liberdade por um fio: História dos quilombos no Brasil* (São Paulo: Companhia das Letras, 1996).

Funes, Eurípedes A. "'Nasci nas matas, nunca tive senhor' – História e memória dos mocambos do baixo Amazonas," in João José Reis and Flávio dos Santos Gomes, eds., *Liberdade por um fio: História dos quilombos no Brasil* (São Paulo: Companhia das Letras, 1996), pp. 467–497.

Galenson, David W. "The Rise and Fall of Indentured Servitude in the Americas: An Economic Analysis," *Journal of Economic History*, 44, no. 1 (March 1984), pp. 1–26.

_____. *White Servitude in Colonial America: An Economic Analysis* (Cambridge: Cambridge University Press, 1981).

_____ "White Servitude and the Growth of Black Slavery in Colonial America," *Journal of Economic History*, 41, no. 1 (March 1981), pp. 39–47.

Galloway, J. H. "The Last Years of Slavery on the Sugar Plantations of Northeastern Brazil," *Hispanic American Historical Review*, LI, no. 4 (November 1971), pp. 586–605

_____. *The Sugar Cane Industry: An Historical Geography from Its Origins to 1914* (Cambridge: Cambridge University Press, 1989).

Galvão, Rafael Ribas. "Bastardia e legitimidade na Curitiba dos Séculos XVIII e XIX," *XIII Encontro da Associação Brasileira de Estudos Populacionais, ABEP* (2002).

Garavazo, Juliana. "Relações familiares e estabilidade da família escrava: Batatais (1850–88)" *Anais de XIV Encontro Nacional de Estudos Populacionais, ABEP* (2004).

Garlan, Yvon. *Slavery in Ancient Greece* (rev. ed.; Ithaca, NY: Cornell University Press, 1982).

Genovese, Eugene D. *Roll Jordon Roll: The World the Slaves Made* (New York: Vintage Books, 1976).

Giovanini, Rafael Rangel. "Regiões em movimento: Um olhar sobre a Geografia Histórica do Sul de Minas e da Zona da Mata Mineira (1808–1897)" (Belo Horizonte: dissertação de mestrado, Geografia, UFMG, 2006).

Godinho, Vitorino Magalhães. *Os descobrimentos e a economia mundial* (2d ed. rev.; 4 vols.; Lisbon: Editorial Presença, 1981–1983).

Godoy, Marcelo Magalhães. "Espaços canavieiros regionais e mercado interno subsídios para o estudo da distribuição espacial da produção e comércio de derivados da cana-de-açúcar da província de Minas Gerais," *X Seminário sobre a Economia Mineira* (2002).

_____. "Fazendas diversificadas, escravos polivalentes, caracterização sóciodemográfica e ocupacional dos trabalhadores cativos em unidades produtivas com atividades agroaçucareiras de Minas Gerais no século XIX," *XIV Encontro Nacional de Estudos Populacionais, ABEP* (2004).

_____. "Uma província artesã: O universo social, econômico e demográfico dos artífices da Minas do oitocentos," *Anais do XII Encontro Nacional da ABEP* (2004).

————, Mario Marcos Sampaio Rodarte, and Clotilde Andrade Paiva. "Negociantes e tropeiros em um território de contrastes; o setor comercial de Minas Gerais no século XIX," *Anais do V Congresso Brasileiro de História Econômica, ABHPE* (2003).

Góes, José Roberto. *O cativeiro imperfeito: Um estudo sobre a escravidão no Rio de Janeiro da primeira metade do século XIX* (Vitória: Lineart, 1993).

Goldschmidt, Elena María Réa. "Casamentos mistos de escravos em São Paulo Colonial" (dissertação de mestrado, FFLCH-USP, 1986).

————. *Casamentos mistos de escravos em São Paulo Colonial* (São Paulo: Annablume, 2004).

Gomes, Flávio dos Santos. *A hydra e os pântanos, mocambos, quilombos e comunidades de fugitivos no Brasil (séculos XVII–XIX)* (São Paulo: Editora UNESP, 2005).

————. *Experiências atlânticas: Ensaios e pesquisas sobre a escravidão e o pós emancipação no Brasil* (Passo Fundo, RGS: Editora UPF, 2003).

————. "Experiências negras e Brasil escravista: Questões e debates," *X Congresso Internacional da ALADAA* (Associação Latino-Americana de Estudos Africanos e Asiático) (2001), n.p.

————. *Histórias de Quilombolas: Mocambos e comunidades de senzalas no Rio de Janeiro século XIX* (Rio de Janeiro: Arquivo Nacional, 1995).

Gorender, Jacob. *A escravidão reabilitada* (São Paulo: Ática, 1990).

————. *O escravismo colonial* (4th ed. rev.; São Paulo: Editora Ática, 1985).

Graça Filho, Afonso de Alencastro. "As flutuações dos preços e as fazendas escravistas de São João del Rei no século xix," *IX Seminário sobre a Economia Mineira* (2000).

Graham, Sandra Lauderdale. "Slavery's Impasse: Slave Prostitutes, Small-Time Mistresses, and the Brazilian Law of 1871," *Comparative Studies in Society and History*, 33, no. 4 (October 1991), pp. 669–694.

Green, William A. "Supply versus Demand in the Barbadian Sugar Revolution," *Journal of Interdisciplinary History*, 18, no. 3 (Winter 1988), pp. 403–418

Grinberg, Keila. *Liberata, a lei da ambigüidade: As ações de liberdade da Corte de Apelação do Rio de Janeiro no século XIX* (Rio de Janeiro: Relume Dumará, 1994).

Grubb, Farley. "The End of European Immigrant Servitude in the United States: An Economic Analysis of Market Collapse, 1772–1835," *Journal of Economic History*, 54, no. 4 (December 1994), pp. 794–824.

————. "The Transatlantic Market for British Convict Labor," *Journal of Economic History*, 60, no. 1 (March 2000), pp. 94–122.

Gudeman, Stephen and Stuart B. Schwartz. "Purgando o pecado original: O compadrio e batismo de escravos na Bahia no século XVIII," in João José Reis, ed., *Escravidão e Invenção da Liberdade: Estudos sobre o negro no Brasil* (São Paulo: Brasiliense, 1988), pp. 33–59.

Guedes, Roberto. "De ex-escravo a elite escravista: A trajetória de ascensão social do pardo alferes Joaquim Barbosa Neves (Porto Feliz, São Pulo, século XIX)," in João Luis Ribeiro Fragoso, Carla Maria Carvalho de Almeida, and Antonio Carlos Juca de Sampaio, eds., *Conquistadores e negociantes: Histórias de elites no Antigo Regime nos trópicos, América lusa, séculos XVI a XVIII* (Rio de Janeiro: Civilização Brasileira, 2007), pp. 337–376.

Guimarães, Antonio Sérgio Alfredo. "Preconceito de cor e racismo no Brasil," *Revista de Antropologia* (São Paulo, USP), 47, no. 1 (2004), pp. 9–43.

Guimarães, Carlos Magno. "Mineração, quilombos e Palmares: Minas Gerais no século XVIII," in João José Reis and Flávio dos Santos Gomes, eds., *Liberdade por um fio: História dos quilombos no Brasil* (São Paulo: Companhia das Letras, 1996).

Guimarães, Elione Silva. "Criminalidade entre mancípios: A comunidade escrava no contexto de grandes fazendas cafeeiras da zona da mata mineira 1850–1881," *X Seminário sobre a Economia Mineira* (2002).

———. "Rixas e brigas entre companheiros de cativeiro (Juiz de Fora 1850–88)," *Revista Universidade Rural, Série Ciências Humanas*, 24, nos. 1–2 (2002), pp. 89–100.

———. *Violência entre parceiros de cativeiro: Juiz de Fora, segunda metade do século XIX* (São Paulo: Annablume, 2006).

Gurgel, Argemiro Eloy. "A Lei de 7 de novembro de 1831 e as ações cíveis de liberdade na Cidade de Valença (1870 a 1888)" (dissertação de mestrado, UFRJ, 2004).

Gutierrez, Ester J. B. *Negros, Charqueadas e Olarias: Um estudo sobre o espaço pelotense* (2nd ed.; Pelotas: Editora e Gráfica Universitária – UFPel, 2001).

Gutiérrez, Horácio. "A harmonia dos sexos: Elementos da estrutura demográfica da população escrava no Paraná, 1800–1830," *Anais do V Encontro Nacional de Estudos Populacionais, ABEP* (1986).

———. "Crioulos e Africanos no Paraná, 1798–1830," *Revista Brasileira de História*, 8, no. 16 (1988), pp. 161–188.

———. "Demografia escrava numa economia não exportadora: Paraná," *Estudos Econômicos*, 17, no. 2 (1987), pp. 297–314.

———. "Donos de terras e escravos no Paraná: Padrões e hierarquias nas primeiras décadas do século XIX," *História*, 25, no. 1 (2006), pp. 100–122.

———. "Escravidão e pequena propriedade no Paraná" (unpublished manuscript).

———. "Terras e gado no Paraná tradicional" (tese de doutorado, USP, 1996).

Gutman, Herbert G. *The Black Family in Slavery and Freedom, 1750–1925* (New York: Vintage Books, 1976).

Haines, Michael R. "The Use of Model Life Tables to Estimate Mortality for the United States in the Late Nineteenth Century," *Demography*, 16, no. 2 (May 1979), pp. 289–312.

Harris, Mark. *Rebellion on the Amazon: The Cabanagem, Race, and Popular Culture in the North of Brazil, 1798–1840* (Cambridge: Cambridge University Press, forthcoming).

Herrmann, Lucila. *Evolução da estrutura social de Guaratinguetá num período de trezentos anos* (São Paulo: Ed. Facsimilada. Instituto de Pesquisas Econômicas [IPE/USP], 1986).

Heywood, Linda M., ed. *Central Africans and Cultural Transformations in the American Diaspora* (New York: Cambridge University Press, 2002).

Higgins, Kathleen J. "Gender and the Manumission of Slaves in Colonial Brazil: The Prospects for Freedom in Sabará, Minas Gerais, 1710–1809," *Slavery & Abolition*, 18, no. 2 (1997).

———. *"Licentious Liberty" in a Brazilian Gold-Mining Region: Slavery, Gender, and Social Control in Eighteenth-Century Sabará, Minas Gerais* (University Park: Pennsylvania State University Press, 1999).

Higman, B. W. *Slave Population and Economy in Jamaica, 1807–1834* (Cambridge: Cambridge University Press, 1976).

———. *Slave Populations of the British Caribbean, 1807–1834* (Baltimore: Johns Hopkins University Press, 1984).

Holanda, Sérgio Buarque de. *Caminhos e Fronteiras* (2nd ed.; São Paulo: Cia. das Letras, 1995).

———. "Metais e pedras preciosas," in Sérgio Buarque de Holanda, ed., *História geral da civilização brasileira* (10 vols.; São Paulo: Difusão Européia do Livro, 1960), tomo I, pp. 259–310.

———. *Monções* (2nd ed.; São Paulo: Alfa Omêga, 1976).

———. "Movimentos de população em São Paulo no Século XVIII," *Revista do Instituto de Estudos Brasileiros*, vol. 1 (1966), pp. 55–111.

———. *Raízes do Brasil* (Rio de Janeiro: José Olympio Editora, 1956).

———. *Visão do Paraíso* (São Paulo: Editora Brasiliense, 1994).

Holloway, Thomas. *Immigrants on the Land: Coffee and Society in São Paulo, 1886–1934* (Ithaca, NY: Cornell University Press, 1980).

Hopkins, Keith. *Conquerors and Slaves* (Cambridge: Cambridge University Press, 1978).

Ianni, Octavio. *As metamorphoses do escravo: Apogeu e crise da escravatura no Brasil meridional*, no. 7 (São Paulo: Difusão Européia do Livro, 1962).

Israel, Jonathan I. *Dutch Primacy in World Trade, 1585–1740* (Oxford: Clarendon Press, 1989).

Jesus, Alysson Luiz Freitas de. *No sertão das Minas: Escravidão, violência e liberdade (1830–1888)* (São Paulo: Annablume, 2007).

Johnson, Harold. "Desenvolvimiento e espansão da economia brasileira," in Harold Johnson and Maria Beatriz Nizza da Silva, eds., *O império luso-brasileiro, 1500–1620* (vol. 6 of the *Nova História da Expansão Portuguesa*, edited by Joel Serrão and A. H. de Oliveira Marques; Lisbon: Editorial Estampa, 1998), pp. 205–302.

———. "Portuguese Settlement, 1500–1580," in Leslie Bethell, *The Cambridge History of Latin America* (11 vols.; Cambridge: Cambridge University Press, 1984), vol. I, pp. 249–286.

Johnson, Lyman L. "Manumission in Colonial Buenos Aires, 1776–1810," *Hispanic American Historical Review*, 59, no. 2 (May 1979), pp. 258–279.

Jordan, Winthrop D. *White over Black: American Attitudes toward the Negro, 1550–1812* (Chapel Hill: The University of North Carolina Press, 1968).

Karasch, Mary C. *Slave Life in Rio de Janeiro, 1808–1850* (Princeton: Princeton University Press, 1987).

Kaufmann, Chaim D. and Robert A. Pape. "Explaining Costly International Moral Action: Britain's Sixty-year Campaign against the Atlantic Slave Trade," *International Organization*, 53, no. 4 (Autumn 1999), pp. 631–668.

Kessler, Arnold. "Bahian Manumission Practices in the Early 19th Century," paper delivered at the American Historical Association, December 29, 1973.

Kiddy, Elizabeth W. *Blacks of the Rosary: Memory and History in Minas Gerais, Brazil* (University Park: Pennsylvania State University Press, 2005).

Kiernan, James P. "Baptism and Manumission in Brazil: Paraty, 1789–1822," *Social Science History*, 3, no. 1 (Autumn 1978), pp. 56–71.

Kinsbruner, Jay. *Not of Pure Blood: The Free People of Color and Racial Prejudice in Nineteenth-Century Puerto Rico* (Durham: Duke University Press, 1996).

Klein, Herbert S. *A imigração espanhola no Brasil* (São Paulo: FAPESP: IDESP: Editora Sumaré, 1994).

_____. "African Women in the Atlantic Slave Trade," in Claire C. Robertson and Martin A. Klein, eds., *Women and Slavery in Africa* (Madison: University of Wisconsin Press, 1983), pp. 29–38.

_____. *The Atlantic Slave Trade* (2nd ed. Cambridge: Cambridge University Press, 2002).

_____. "The Demographic Structure of Mexico City in 1811," *Journal of Urban History*, 23, no. 1 (Nov. 1996), pp. 66–93.

_____. "The Internal Slave Trade in Nineteenth-Century Brazil: A Study of Slave Importations into Rio de Janeiro in 1852," *Hispanic American Historical Review*, LI, no. 4 (November 1971), pp. 567–568.

_____. *The Middle Passage: Comparative Studies in the Atlantic Slave Trade* (Princeton: Princeton University Press, 1978).

_____. "Os homens livres de côr na sociedade escravista brasileria," *Dados* (Rio de Janeiro), no. 17 (1978), pp. 3–27.

_____. *A Population History of the United States* (Cambridge: Cambridge University Press, 2004).

_____. "The Structure of the Atlantic Slave Trade in the 19th Century: An Assessment," *Revue Française d'Histoire d'Outre-mer*, nos. 336–337 (2éme semestre 2002), pp. 63–77.

_____. "The Supply of Mules to Central Brazil: The Sorocaba Market, 1825–1880," *Agricultural History*, 64, no. 4 (Fall 1990), pp. 1–25.

_____. "The Trade in African Slaves to Rio de Janeiro, 1795–1811: Estimates of Mortality and Patterns of Voyages," *Journal of African History*, X, no. 4 (1969), 533–549.

Klein, Herbert S. and Stanley L. Engerman, "Facteurs de mortalité dans le trafic française d'esclaves au XVIIIe siècle," *Annales. Économies, Societés, Civilisations*, 31, no. 6 (1976), 1213–1223.

_____. "Fertility Differentials between Slaves in the United States and the British West Indies: A Note on Lactation Practices and their Implications," *The William & Mary Quarterly*, XXXV, no. 2 (April 1978), 357–374.

_____. "Shipping Patterns and Mortality in the African Slave Trade to Rio de Janeiro," *Cahiers d'études africaines*, 59, XV, no. 3 (1976), pp. 381–398.

_____. "Slave Mortality on British Ships, 1791–1797," in Roger Anstey and P.E.H. Hair, eds., *Liverpool, the African Slave Trade, and Abolition* (Liverpool, Historical Society of Lancashire and Chesire, Occasional Papers, vol. 2, 1976), pp. 113–122.

————. "Long-term Trends in African Mortality in the Transatlantic Slave Trade," *Slavery & Abolition*, 18, no. 1 (April 1997), pp. 59–71.

————, Robin Haines, and Ralph Schlomowitz. "The Transition from Slave to Free Labor: Notes on a Comparative Economic Model," in Manuel Moreno Fraginals, et al., eds., *Between Slavery and Free Labor: The Spanish Speaking Caribbean in the Nineteenth Century* (Baltimore: Johns Hopkins University Press, 1985), pp. 255–269.

————. "Transoceanic Mortality: The Slave Trade in Comparative Perspective," *The William & Mary Quarterly*, LVIII, no. 1 (January 2001), pp. 93–118.

Klein, Herbert S. and Francisco Vidal Luna. "Free Colored in a Slave Society: São Paulo and Minas Gerais in the Early Nineteenth Century," *Hispanic American Historical Review*, 80, no. 4 (November 2000), pp. 913–941.

Klein, Herbert S. and Clotilde Andrade Paiva, "Free Persons in a Slave Economy, Minas Gerais in 1831," *Journal of Social History*, 29, no. 4 (1996), pp. 933–962.

Klein, Herbert S. and Ben Vinson III. *African Slavery in Latin America and the Caribbean* (2nd rev. ed.; New York: Oxford University Press, 2007).

Kraay, Hendrick. "'As Terrifying as Unexpected': The Bahian Sabinada, 1837–1838," *The Hispanic American Historical Review*, 72, no. 4 (November 1992), pp. 501–527.

————. "'The Shelter of the Uniform': The Brazilian Army and Runaway Slaves, 1800–1888," *Journal of Social History*, 29, no. 3 (Spring 1996), pp. 637–57.

Lacerda, Antônio Henrique Duarte. "Economia cafeeira, crescimento populacional, manumissões onerosas e gratuitas condicionais em Juiz de Fora na segunda metade do século XIX," *X Seminário sobre a Economia Mineira* (2002).

————. *Os padrões das alforrias em um município cafeeiro em expansão: Juiz de Fora, Zona da Mata de Minas Gerais, 1844–88* (São Paulo: Annablume, 2006).

Lamounier, Maria Lúcia. "Agricultura e Mercado de Trabalho: Trabalhadores Brasileiros Livres nas Fazendas de Café e na Construção de Ferrovias em São Paulo, 1850–1890," *Estudos Econômicos*, 37, no. 2 (Abril–Junho 2007), pp. 353–372.

Lang, Francisco Kurt. "A musica barroca," in Sérgio Buarque de Holanda, ed., *História geral da civilização brasileira*, vol. II, pp. 121–144.

Lara, Silvia Hunold. "Do singular ao plural, Palmares, capitães-do-mato e o governo dos escravos," in João José Reis and Flávio dos Santos Gomes, eds., *Liberdade por um fio: História dos quilombos no Brasil* (São Paulo: Companhia das Letras, 1996), pp. 81–109.

————. *Campos da Violência: Escravos e senhores na Capitania do Rio de Janeiro, 1750–1808* (Rio de Janeiro: Paz e Terra, 1988).

————. "Sedas, Panos e Balangandãs: O traje de senhoras e escravas nas cidades do Rio de Janeiro e Salvador (século XVIII)," in Maria Beatriz Nizza da Silva, ed., *Brasil: Colonização e escravidão* (Rio de Janeiro: Nova Fronteira, 1999), pp. 177–91.

Law, Robin. "The Evolution of the Brazilian Community in Ouidah," *Slavery &* *Abolition*, 22, no. 1 (2001), pp. 3–21.

Law, Robin and Kristin Mann. "West Africa in the Atlantic Community: The Case of the Slave Coast," *The William & Mary Quarterly*, 56, no. 2 (April 1999), pp. 307–334.

Leacock, Seth and Ruth Leacock. *Spirits of the Deep: A Study of an Afro-Brazilian Cult* (Garden City, NY: American Museum of Natural History, 1972).

Lestringant, Frank. *L'expérience Huguenote au nouveau monde (XVIe siècle)* (Geneva: Librairie Droz, 1996).

LeVeen, E. Phillip. *British Slave Trade Suppression Policies, 1821–1865* (New York: Arno, 1977).

Libby, Douglas Cole. "Proto-Industrialisation in a Slave Society: The Case of Minas Gerais," *Journal of Latin American Studies*, 23, no. 1 (February 1991), pp. 1–35.

———. *Trabalho escravo e capital estrangeiro no Brasil: O caso de Morro Velho* (Belo Horizonte: Itatiaia, 1984).

Libby, Douglas Cole and Clotilde Andrade Paiva. "Alforrias e forros em uma freguesia mineira: São José d'El Rey em 1795," *Revista Brasileira de Estudos de População*, 17, nos. 1/2 (Jan./Dez. 2000), pp. 17–46.

———. "Manumission Practices in a Late Eighteenth-Century Brazilian Slave Parish: São José d'El Rey in 1795," *Slavery & Abolition*, 21, no. 1 (2000), pp. 96–127.

Lima, Adriano Bernardo Moraes. "Trajetórias de Crioulos: Um estudo das relações comunitárias de escravos e forros no têrmo da Vila de Curitiba (c. 1760 – c. 1830)," (Curitiba: dissertação de mestrado, UFP, 2001).

Lima, Carlos A. M. "Escravos Artesãos: Preço e Família (Rio de Janeiro, 1789–1839)," *Estudos Econômicos*, 30, no. 3 (Julho-Setembro 2000), pp. 447–484.

Lima, Solimar Oliveira. *Triste Pampa: Resistência e punição de escravos em fontes judiciárias no Rio Grande do Sul, 1818–1833* (Porto Alegre: EDIPUCRS, 1997).

Lobo Cabrera, Manuel. *La esclavitud en las Canarias orientales en el siglo XVI (negros, moros y moriscos)* (Las Palmas: Cabildo Insular de Gran Canaria, 1982).

Lockhart, James. *Spanish Peru, 1532–1560: A Social History* (2d ed.; Madison: University of Wisconsin Press, 1994).

Loiola, Maria Lemke. "Trajetórias Atlânticas, percursos para a Liberdade: Africanos e Descendentes na Capitania dos Guayazes" (Goiânia: dissertação de mestrado, FCHF, Universidade Federal de Goiás, 2008).

Lopes, Janaina Christina Perrayon. "Casamentos de escravos e forros nas freguesias da Candelária, São Francisco Xavier e Jacarepaguá: Uma contribuição aos padrões de sociabilidade marital no Rio de Janeiro (c. 1800 – c. 1850)" *Anais do 1 Colóquio de LAHES* (2005).

———. "Casamentos de escravos nas freguesias da Candelária, São Francisco Xavier e Jacarepaguá: Uma contribuição aos padrões de sociabilidade matrimonial no Rio de Janeiro (c. 1800 – c. 1850)," (dissertação de mestrado, UFRJ, 2006).

Lott, Mirian Moura. "A lista nominativa de 1838, características demográficas, econômicas e sociais de Ouro Preto," *Anais do XIII Seminário sobre a Economia Mineira* (2008).

Lovejoy, Paul E. *Transformations in Slavery: A History of Slavery in Africa* (Cambridge: Cambridge University Press, 1983).

Luna, Francisco Vidal. "Economia e Sociedade em Minas Gerais (Período Colonial)," *Revista do Instituto de Estudos Brasileiros*, vol. 24 (1982), pp. 43–46.

————. "Estrutura da Posse de Escravos," in Francisco Vidal Luna and Iraci del Nero da Costa, *Minas Colonial: Economia e Sociedade*.

————. "Estrutura da Posse de Escravos em Minas Gerais (1718)," in A.E.M. Barreto et al., *História Econômica: Ensaios* (São Paulo: IPE/USP, 1983), pp. 25–41.

————. "Estrutura da Posse de Escravos em Minas Gerais (1804)," in Iraci del Nero da Costa, ed., *Brasil: História Econômica e Demográfica* (São Paulo: IPE/USP, 1986), pp. 157–172.

————. *Minas Gerais: Escravos e senhores. Análise da estrutura populacional e econômica de alguns núcleos mineratórios (1718–1804)* (São Paulo: FEA-USP, 1980).

————. "Mineração: Métodos extrativos e legislação," *Estudos Econômicos*, vol. 13 (1983), pp. 845–859.

————. "Observações sobre Casamento de Escravos em Treze Localidades de São Paulo (1776, 1804 e 1829)," *Anais do Congresso sobre História da População da América Latina, São Paulo, ABEP/SEADE* (1989).

————. "São Paulo: População, atividades e posse de escravos em vinte e cinco localidades (1777–1829)," *Estudos Econômicos*, 28, no. 1 (1998), pp. 99–169.

Luna, Francisco Vidal and Iraci del Nero da Costa. "A presença do elemento forro no conjunto dos proprietários de escravos," *Ciência e Cultura* (São Paulo: SBPC), 32, no. 7 (Julho 1980), pp. 838–841.

————. "Algumas características do contingente de cativos em Minas Gerais," *Anais do Museu Paulista*, tomo XXIX (1979), pp. 79–97.

————. "Demografia Histórica de Minas Gerais no Período Colonial," *Revista Brasileira de Assuntos Políticos* (Belo Horizonte, UFMG), vol. 58 (1984), pp. 15–62.

————. "Estrutura da Massa Escrava de Algumas Localidades Mineiras (1804)," *Revista do Instituto de Estudos Brasileiros* (1981), pp. 137–142.

————. *Minas Colonial: Economia e Sociedade* (São Paulo: FIPE/PIONEIRA, 1982).

Luna, Francisco Vidal and Herbert S. Klein, "Free Colored in a Slave Economy: The Case of São Paulo and Minas Gerais, 1829–1830," *Hispanic American Historical Review*, 80, no. 4 (November 2000), pp. 913–941.

————. "Slave Economy & Society in Minas Gerais and São Paulo, Brazil in 1830," *Journal of Latin American Studies*, vol. 36 (February 2004), pp. 1–28.

————. *Slavery and the Economy of São Paulo, 1750–1850* (Stanford: Stanford University Press, 2003).

————. "Slaves and Masters in Early Nineteenth-Century Brazil: São Paulo," *Journal of Interdisciplinary History*, 21, no. 4 (1991), pp. 349–379.

Luna, Francisco Vidal and Wilson Cano. "Economia escravista em Minas Gerais," *Cadernos* IFCH/UNICAMP (Outubro de 1983).

Machado, Alcântara. *Vida e Morte do Bandeirante* (São Paulo: Livraria Martins, 1965).

Machado, Cacilda. "Casamento & Desigualdade Jurídica: Primeiras notas de um estudo em uma área da região paulista no período colonial," *XIII Encontro da Associação Brasileira de Estudos Populacionais ABEP* (2002).

Machado, Cláudio Heleno. "O tráfico interno de escravos na região de Juiz de Fora na segunda metade do século XIX," *X Seminário de Economia Mineira* (2002).

Machado, Maria Helena P. T. *Crime e escravidão: Trabalho, luta e resistência nas lavouras paulistas, 1830–1888* (São Paulo: Editora Brasiliense, 1987).

Maddison, Angus. *The World Economy: A Millennial Perspective* (Paris: Development Centre of the Organisation for Economic Co-operation and Development, 2001).

Maestri Filho, Mário José. *O escravo no Rio Grande do Sul: A Chaqueada e a gênese do escravismo gaúcho* (Porto Alegre: Escola Superior de Teologia São Lourenço de Brindes, 1984).

Maia, Moacir Rodrigo de Castro. "Por uma nova abordagem da solidariedade entre escravos africanos recém-chegados a América (Minas Gerais, século XVIII)," *III Encontro de Escravidao e Liberdade no Brasil Meridional* (2007).

Malheiro, Agostinho Marques Perdigão. *A escravidão no Brasil: Ensaio Histórico-Juridico-Social* (2 vols.; Rio de Janeiro: Typografhia Nacional, 1866).

Manning, Patrick. *Slavery and African Life: Occidental, Oriental, and African Slave Trades* (Cambridge: Cambridge University Press, 1990).

Marchant, Alexander. *Do escambo à Escravidão: As relações econômicas de portugueses e índios na colonização do Brasil, 1500–1580* (São Paulo: Companhia Editora Nacional, 1980).

Marcílio, Maria Luíza. "The Population of Colonial Brazil," *The Cambridge History of Latin America*, edited by Leslie Bethell (11 vols.; Cambridge: Cambridge University Press, 1984), II, pp. 37–57.

Marcílio, Maria Luíza et al. "Considerações sobre o preço do escravo no período imperial: Uma análise quantitativa (baseada nos registro de escritura de compra e venda de escravos na Bahia)," *Anais de História* (1973), no. 5, pp. 179–194.

Marcondes, Renato Leite. *A arte de acumular na economia Cafeeira* (Lorena, São Paulo: Editora Stiliano, 1998).

_____. "Desigualidades regionais brasileiras: Comércio marítimo e posse de cativos na década de 1870" (Tese livre-docência, FEA, USP, Riberão Preto, 2005).

Marcondes, Renato Leite and José Flávio Motta. "A família escrava em Lorena e Cruzeiro (1874)," *Anais do XII Encontro Nacional de Estudos Populacionais ABEP* (2000).

_____. "Duas fontes documentais para o estudo dos preços dos escravos no Vale do Paraíba paulista," *Revista Brasileira de História*, 21, no. 42 (2001), pp. 495–514.

Marcondes, Renato Leite and Miridan Britto Knox Falci. "Escravidão e reprodução no Piauí: Oeiras e Teresina (1875)" (Texto para Discussão, Série Economia, TD-E/26, USP-FEAC-Ribeirão Preto, 2001).

Mariz, Vasco and Lucien Provençal. *Villegagnon e a França Antártica* (Rio de Janeiro: Nova Fronteira, 2000).

Marques, A. H. de Oliveira. "A expansão quatrocentista," vol. 2, *Nova História da Expansão Portuguesa*, edited by Joel Serrão and A. H. de Oliveira Marques (Lisbon: Editorial Estampa, 1998).

Martins, Bárbara Canedo Ruiz. "Amas-de-leite e mercado de trabalho feminino: Descortinando práticas e sujeitos (Rio de Janeiro, 1830–1890)" (dissertação de mestrado, Universidade Federal do Rio de Janeiro – UFRJ, 2006).

————. "Meninas e mulheres: As imagens das amas-de-leite no mercado de trabalho doméstico urbano do Rio de Janeiro (1830–1888)" (unpublished essay).

Martins, Ilton César. "Veredicto culpado: A pena de morte enquanto instrumento de regulação social em Castro – PR (1853–1888)" (Curitiba: dissertação de mestrado, Universidade Federal de Paraná, 2005).

Martins, Mônica de Souza Nunes. "Entre a Cruz e o Capital: Mestres, aprendizes e corporações de ofícios no Rio de Janeiro (1808–1824)" (tesis de doutorado, U.F.R.J./I.F.C.S., 2007).

Martins, Roberto Borges. "Growing in Silence: The Slave Economy of Nineteenth-century Minas Gerais, Brazil" (Ph.D. diss., economics, Vanderbilt University, 1980).

Martins Filho, Amílcar V. and Roberto B. Martins. "Slavery in a Non-Export Economy: Nineteenth-Century Minas Gerais Revisited," *Hispanic American Historical Review*, 63, no. 3 (1983), pp. 537–568.

Mathias, Carlos Leonardo Kelmer. "O perfil econômico da capitania de Minas Gerais na segunda década do século XVIII, notas de pesquisa – 1711–1720," *Anais do XII Seminário sobre a Economia Mineira* (2006).

Mattoso, Katia M. de Queirós. "A Carta de alforria como fonte complementar para o estudo de rentabilidade de mão de obra escrava urbana, 1819–1888," in Carlos Manuel Pelaez and Mircea Buescu, eds., *A moderna história econômica* (Rio de Janeiro: APE, 1976), pp. 149–164.

————. "A propósito de cartas de alforria: Bahia, 1779–1850," *Anais de História*, 4 (1972), pp. 23–52.

————. *Bahia, século XIX, Uma província no império* (Rio de Janeiro: Editora Nova Fronteira, 1992).

————. *Família e sociedade na Bahia do século XIX* (São Paulo: Corrupio, 1988).

————. *Presença francesa no movimento democrático baiano de 1798* (Salvador de Bahia: Editôra Itapuã, 1969).

————. "Sociedade escravista e mercado de trabalho: Salvador – Bahia, 1850 – 1868," *Bahia Análise & Dados* (Salvador), 10, no. 1 (Julho 2000), pp. 12–20.

Mattoso, Katia M. de Queirós, Herbert S. Klein, and Stanley L. Engerman. "Trends and Patterns in the Prices of Manumitted Slaves: Bahia, 1819–1888," *Slavery & Abolition*, 7, no. 1 (May 1986), pp. 59–67; reprinted in João José Reis, ed., *Escravidão e invenção da liberdade: Estudos sobre o negro no Brasil* (São Paulo: Editora Brasiliense, 1988), pp. 60–72.

Mauro, Frédéric. *Le Portugal et l'Atlantique au XVIIe siècle (1570–1670), étude économique* (Paris: SEVPEN, 1960).

McCreery, David. *Frontier Goiás, 1822–1889* (Stanford: Stanford University Press, 2006).

Meillassoux, Jean Claude. *L'Esclavage en Afrique précoloniale* (Paris: Presses Universitaires de France, 1975).

Meira, Roberta Barros. "Bangüês, Engenhos centrais e usinas: O desenvolvimento da economia açucareira em São Paulo e a sua correlação com as políticas estatais (1875–1941)" (Dissertação de mestrado, FFLCH/USP, 2007).

———. "O processo de modernização da agroindústria canavieira e os engenhos centrais na Província de São Paulo," *História e Economia Revista Interdisciplinar* (São Paulo), 3, no. 1 (2° semestre 2007), pp. 39–54.

Mello, Evaldo Cabral de. *O Negócio do Brasil: Portugal os Países Baixos e o Nordeste 1641–1669* (Rio de Janeiro: Topbooks, 1998).

Mello, José Antônio Gonçalves de. *Tempo dos Flamengos: Influência da ocupação holandesa na vida e na cultura do norte do Brasil* (3rd ed. rev.; Recife: Fundação Joaquim Nabuco, Editora Massangana, 1987).

Mello, Pedro Carvalho de. "Aspectos Econômicos da Organização do Trabalho da Economia Cafeeira do Rio de Janeiro, 1858–1888," *Revista Brasileira de Economia*, 32, no. 1 (Jan./Mar. 1978), pp. 19–68.

———. "The Economics of Labor in Brazilian Coffee Plantations, 1850–1888," (Ph.D. dissertation, Department of Economics, University of Chicago, 1977).

———. "Estimativa da longevidade de escravos no Brasil na segunda metade do século XIX," *Estudos Econômicos*, 13, no. 1 (jan.-abr. 1983), pp. 151–179.

Mello, Pedro Carvalho de and Robert W. Slenes. "Análise Econômica da Escravidão no Brasil" in P. Neuhaus, ed., *Economia Brasileira: Uma Visão Histórica* (Rio de Janeiro: Campus, 1980).

Mello, Suzy de. *Barroco mineiro* (São Paulo: Editora Brasiliense, 1985).

Mello e Souza, Laura de. *Desclassificados do Ouro: A Pobreza Mineira No Século XVIII* (4th ed.; Rio de Janeiro: Graal, 2004).

———. "Violência e práticas culturais no cotidiano de uma expedição contra Quilombolas, Minas Gerais, 1769," in João José Reis and Flávio dos Santos Gomes, eds., *Liberdade por um fio: História dos quilombos no Brasil* (São Paulo: Companhia das Letras, 1996), pp. 193–212.

Mendonça, Josefi Maria Nunes. *Entre a mão e os anéis: A Lei dos sexagenários e os caminhos da abolição no Brasil* (Campinas: UNICAMP, 1999).

Metcalf, Alida C. *Family and Frontier in Colonial Brazil, Santana de Parnaíba, 1580–1822* (Berkeley: University of California Press, 1992).

———. *Go-betweens and the Colonization of Brazil* (Austin: University of Texas Press, 2005).

———. "Searching for the Slave Family in Colonial Brazil: A Reconstruction from São Paulo," *Journal of Family History*, 16, no. 3 (1991), pp. 283–297.

Miers, Suzanne and Igor Kopytoff, eds. *Slavery in Africa: Historical and Anthropological Perspectives* (Madison: University of Wisconsin Press, 1977).

Miller, Joseph C. *Way of Death: Merchant Capitalism and the Angolan Slave Trade, 1703–1830* (Madison: University of Wisconsin Press, 1988).

Miranda, Daniela. "Músicos de Sabará: A prática musical religiosa a serviço da Câmara (1749–1822)" (Belo Horizonte: tese de doutorado, FFCH/UFMG, 2002).

Monasterio, Leonardo M. "FHC errou? A economia da escravidão no Brasil meridional," *História e Economia Revista Interdisciplinar* (São Paulo, BBS), 1, no. 1 (2° semestre 2005), pp. 13–28.

Monteiro, John Manuel. "From Indian to Slave: Forced Native Labour and Colonial Society in São Paulo during the 17th Century," *Slavery & Abolition*, 9, no. 2 (September 1988), pp. 105–127.

———. *Negros da Terra: Índios e Bandeirantes nas Origens de São Paulo* (São Paulo: Companhia das Letras, 1994).

Moreira, Paulo Roberto Staudt. *Faces da liberdade, máscaras do cativeiro: Experiências de liberdade e escravidão precebidas através das cartas de alforria – Porto Alegre (1858–1888)* (Porto Alegre: EDIPUCRS, 1996).

———. *Os cativos e os homens de bem: Experiências negras no espaço urbano, Porto Alegre 1858–1888* (Porto Alegre: EST edições, 2003).

Morel, Genaro Rodríguez. "The Sugar Economy of Española in the Sixteenth Century," in Stuart B. Schwartz, ed., *Tropical Babylons: Sugar and the Making of the Atlantic World, 1450–1680* (Chapel Hill: University of North Carolina Press, 2004), pp. 85–114.

Mota, Isidora Moura. "O 'Vulcão' negro da Chapada: Rebelião escrava nos sertões diamantinos (Minas Gerais, 1864)" (dissertação de mestrado, UNICAMP, 2005).

Mott, Luiz Rosa. *Egipcíaca: Uma santa africana no Brasil* (Rio de Janeiro: Bertrand Brasil, 1993).

Motta, José Flávio. "A família escrava e a penetração do café em Bananal (1801–1829)," *Revista Brasileira de Estudos Populacionais*, 5, no. 1 (1988), pp. 71–101.

———. *Corpos escravos e vontades livres: Posse de cativos e família escrava em Bananal, 1801–1829* (São Paulo: Annablume, 1999).

———. "Derradeiras transações: O comércio de escravos nos anos de 1880 (Areias, Piracicaba e Casa Branca, Província de São Paulo)," *Anais do XII Encontro Nacional de Economia Política* (São Paulo, 2007).

———. "Escravos daqui, dali e de mais além: O tráfico interno de cativos em Constituição (Piracicaba), 1861–1880," *Anais do XXXIII Encontro Nacional de Economia ANPEC* (2005).

———. "O tráfico de escravos na Província de São Paulo: Areias, Silveiras, Guaratinguetá e Casa Branca, 1861–1887," *Anais VII Encontro Nacional de Economia Política* (Curitiba, 2002).

———. "O tráfico de escravos na Província de São Paulo: Areias, Silveiras, Guaratinguetá e Casa Branca, 1861–1887" (Texto para Discussão. São Paulo: IPE/USP, 21, 2001);

———. "Tráfico interno de cativos: O preço das mães escravas e sua prole," *XI Encontro Nacional de Estudos Populacionais, ABEP* (1998).

Motta, José Flávio and Renato Leite Marcondes. "O Comércio de Escravos no Vale do Paraíba Paulista: Guaratinguetá e Silveiras na Década de 1870," *Estudos Econômicos*, 30, no. 2 (Abril–Junho 2000), pp. 267–299.

Motta, José Flávio and Nelson Hideiki Nozoe. "Cafeicultura e acumulação," *Estudos Econômicos*, 24, no. 2 (Maio/Ago. 1994), pp. 253–320.

Motta, José Flávio, Nelson Hideiki Nozoe, and Iraci del Nero da Costa. "Às Vésperas da Abolição: Um Estudo sobre a Estrutura da Posse de Escravos em São Cristóvão (RJ), 1870," *Estudios Econômicos*, 34, no. 1 (Jan.–Mar. 2004), pp. 157–213.

Moura, Ana Maria da Silva. *Cocheiros e carroceiros, homens livres no Rio de senhores e Escravos* (São Paulo: Editora Hucitec, 1988).

Müller, Liane Susan. "O negro e suas devoções. A importância da Irmandade do Rosário e da Festa dos Navegantes para a formação de uma classe média negra porto-alegrense," *II Encontro "Escravidão e Liberdade no Brasil Meridional"* (2005).

Mulvey, Patricia A. "Black Brothers and Sisters: Membership in the Black Lay Brotherhoods of Colonial Brazil," *Luso-Brazilian Review*, 17, no. 2 (Winter 1980), pp. 253–279.

_____. "Slave Confraternities in Brazil: Their Role in Colonial Society," *The Americas*, 39, no. 1 (July 1982), pp. 39–68.

Murray, David R. *Odious Commerce: Britain, Spain, and the Abolition of the Cuban Slave Trade* (New York: Cambridge University Press, 1980).

Nabuco, Joaquim. *O abolicionismo* (1st ed., 1883; Rio de Janeiro: Editora Nova Fronteira, 1999).

Nascimento, Álvaro Pereira do. "Do cativeiro ao mar: Escravos na Marinha de Guerra," *Estudos Afro-Asiáticos*, no. 38 (December 2000), pp. 1–25.

NEPP-Direitos Humanas, UFRJ Human Rights Center, Leis historicas do Brasil, http://www.nepp-dh.ufrj.br/estante.html#10.

Neves, Erivaldo Fagundes. "Sampauleiros traficantes: Comércio de escravos do Alto Sertão da Bahia para o Oeste cafeeiro paulista," *Afro-Ásia*, no. 24 (2000), pp. 97–128.

Nishida, Mieko. "Manumission and Ethnicity in Urban Slavery: Salvador, Brazil 1808–1888," *Hispanic American Historical Review*, 73, no. 3 (1993), pp. 361–391.

Nogueról, Luiz Paulo Ferreira. "Sabará e Porto Alegre na formação do mercado nacional no século XIX" (Campinas: tese de doutorado, UNICAMP, Economia, 2003).

Nogueról, Luiz Paulo Ferreira, Diego Rodrigues, Ezequiel Giacomolli, and Marcos Smith Dias. "Elementos Comuns e Diferenças entre os Patrimônios Registrados na Pecuária Gaúcha e na Pernambucana no Início do Século XIX," *VIII Encontro de Economia da Região Sul – ANPEC SUL* (2005).

Oliveira, Maria Inês Côrtes de. *O liberto: O seu mundo e os outros, Salvador, 1790–1890* (São Paulo: Corrupio, 1988).

Oliveira, Mônica Ribeiro de. "Cafeicultura mineira: Formação e consolidação 1809–1870," *IX Seminário sobre a Economia Mineira* (2000).

Oliveira, Myriam Andrade Robeiro de et al. *O Aleijadinho e sua oficina: Catálogo das esculturas devocionais* (São Paulo: Editora Capivara Ltda., 2002).

Oliveira, Patrícia Porto de. "Desfazendo a maldição de cam por meio dos assentos de batismo de escravos adultos da matriz do Pilar de Ouro Preto (1712–1750)," *Anais do XI Seminário sobre a Economia Mineira* (2004).

Oliveira, Vinicius Pereira de. "Sobre o convés: Marinheiros, marítimos e pescadores negros no mundo atlântico do Porto de Rio Grande/RS (século XIX)," *IX Encontro Estadual de História – ANPUH-RS* (Porto Alegre, 2008).

Otávio, Rodrigo. *Os selvagens americanos perante o direito* (São Paulo: Companhia Editora Nacional, 1946).

Paiva, Clotilde Andrade. "População e economia nas Minas Gerais do século XIX" (São Paulo: tese de doutorado, FFLCH/USP, 1996).

Paiva, Clotilde Andrade and Herbert S. Klein. "Slave and Free in Nineteenth-Century Minas Gerais: Campanha in 1831," *Slavery & Abolition*, 15, no. 1 (1994), pp. 1–21.

Paiva, Clotilde Andrade and Douglas Libby. "Caminhos alternativos: Escravidão e reprodução em Minas Gerais," *Estudos Econômicos*, 25, no. 2 (Mayo–Agosto 1995), pp. 203–233.

Paiva, Eduardo França. *Escravidão e universo cultural na colônia, Minas Gerais, 1716–1789* (Belo Horizonte: UFMG, 2001).

———. *Escravos e libertos nas Minas Gerais do século XVIII* (São Paulo: Annablume, 1995), pp. 67–78.

Pantoja, Selma and José Flavio Sombra Saraova, eds. *Angola e Brasil nas rotas do Atlântico sul* (Rio de Janeiro: Bertrand Brasil, 1999).

Papali, Maria Aparecida C. R. *Escravos, libertos e órfãos: A construção da liberdade em Taubaté (1871–1895)* (São Paulo: Annablume, 2003).

Parés, Luis Nicolau. "O processo de crioulização no recôncavo baiano (1750–1800)," *Afro-Ásia*, 33 (2005), pp. 87–132.

Patterson, Orlando. *Slavery and Social Death: A Comparative Study* (Cambridge, MA: Harvard University Press, 1982).

Peabody, Sue and Keila Grinberg. *Slavery, Freedom, and the Law in the Atlantic World: A Brief History with Documents* (Boston: Bedford/St. Martins Press, 2007).

Pedreira, Jorge M. "From Growth to Collapse: Portugal, Brazil, and the Breakdown of the Old Colonial System (1760–1830)," *Hispanic American Historical Review*, 80, no. 4 (2000), pp. 839–864.

Peraro, Maria Adenir. "Mulheres de Jesus no universo dos ilegítimos," *Diálogos. Revista do Departamento de História da Uem*, Maringá, 4, no. 4 (2000), pp. 51–75.

———. "O princípio da fronteira e a fronteira de princípios: Filhos ilegítimos em Cuiabá no séc. XIX," *Revista Brasileira de História* 19, no. 38 (1999), pp. 55–80.

Pereira, Ana Luiza de Castro. "A ilegitimidade nomeada e ocultada na vila de Nossa Senhora da Conceição do Sabará," *Anais do XI Seminário sobre a Economia Mineira* (2004).

———. "O Sangue, a palavra e a lei: Ilegitimidade e transmissão da herança no Mundo Atlântico Português no século XVIII." Paper presented at the Familia y organización social en Europa y América siglos XV–XX Murcia-Albacete 12–14 Diciembre 2007, and published in *Nuevomundo* 28-IV-2008 (available at http://nuevomundo.revues.org/index30893.html).

Pereira, Júlio César Medeiros da S. "À flor da terra: O Cemitério dos Pretos Novos no Rio de Janeiro" (dissertação de mestrado, Universidade Federal do Rio de Janeiro, 2006).

Petrone, Maria Thereza Schorer. *A lavoura canavieira em São Paulo: Expansão e declínio (1765–1851)* (São Paulo: Difusão Européia do Livro, 1968).

Petrone, Pasquale. *Aldeamentos Paulistas* (São Paulo: EDUSP, 1995).

Petruccelli, José Luis. "Doutrinas francesas e o pensamento racial brasileiro, 1870–1930," *Estudos Sociedade e Agricultura*, no. 7 (Dezembro 1996), pp. 134–149.

Petizl, Silmei de Sant'Ana. "Considerações sobre a família escrava da fronteira Oeste do Rio Grande de São Pedro (1750–1835)," *III Encontro de Escravidao e Liberdade no Brasil Meridional* (2007).

Phillips, William D. *Slavery from Roman Times to the Early Transatlantic Trade* (Minneapolis: University of Minnesota Press, 1985).

Pinheiro, Fábio W. A. "Tráfico atlântico de escravos na formação dos plantéis mineiros, Zona da Mata, c. 1809 – c. 1830," (Rio de Janeiro: dissertação de mestrado, UFRJ, 2007).

Pinheiro, Fernanda Aparecida Domingos. "Confrades do Rosário: Sociabilidade e identidade étnica em Mariana – Minas Gerais (1745–1820)" (Niterói: dissertação de mestrado, UFF, 2006).

Pinheiro, Maria Cristina Luz. "O trabalho de crianças escravas na cidade de Salvador, 1850–1888," *Afro-Ásia*, 32 (2005), pp. 159–183.

Pinto, Virgílio Noya. *O ouro brasileiro e o comércio anglo-português* (São Paulo: Companhia Editora Nacional, 1979).

Pires, Maria de Fátima Novaes. *O crime na cor: Escravos e forros no alto sertão da Bahia (1830–1888)* (São Paulo: Annablume, 2003).

Pirola, Ricardo Figueiredo. "A conspiração escrava de Campinas, 1832: Rebelião, etnicidade e família," (dissertação de mestrado, UNICAMP, 2005).

Prado, Jr., Caio. *Evolução Política do Brasil e Outros Estudos* (8th ed.; São Paulo: Brasiliense, 1972).

———. *Formação do Brasil contemporâneo* (3rd. ed.; São Paulo: Editora Brasiliense, 1948).

Praxedes, Vanda Lúcia. "A teia e a trama da 'fragilidade humana': Os filhos ilegítimos em Minas Gerais (1770–1840)," *Anais do XI Seminário sobre a Economia Mineira* (2004).

Prince, Howard M. "Slave Rebellions in Bahia, 1807–1835," (Ph.D. diss., History, Columbia University, 1972).

Queiroz, Suely Robles Reis de. "Algumas notas sobre a lavoura de açúcar em São Paulo no período colonial," *Anais do Museu Paulista*, vol. 21 (1967), pp. 109–277.

———. *Escravidão Negra em São Paulo* (Rio de Janeiro: Livraria José Olympio Editora, 1977).

Quintão, Antonia Aparecida. *Irmandades negras: Outro espaço de lua e Resistencia (São Paulo: 1870–1890)* (São Paulo: Annablume, 2002).

———. *Lá vem o meu parente, as irmandades de pretos e pardos no Rio de Janiero em Pernambuco (século XVIII)* (São Paulo: Annablume, 2002).

Ramos, Donald. "City and Country: The Family in Minas Gerais, 1804–1838," *Journal of Family History*, 3, no. 4 (Winter 1978), pp. 361–375.

———. "Single and Married Women in Vila Rica, Brazil, 1754–1838," *Journal of Family History*, 16, no. 3 (1991), pp. 261–282.

Rangel, Ana Paula dos Santos. "A escolha do cônjuge: O casamento escravo no termo de Barbacena (1781–1821)," *Revista Eletrônica de História do Brasil*, 8, nos. 1–2 (Jan.–Dez. 2006).

Rangel, Armenio de Souza. "Escravismo e riqueza – Formação da economia cafeeira no município de Taubaté – 1765/1835" (São Paulo: tese de doutorado, FEA-USP, 1990).

Read, Ian William Olivo. "Unequally bound: The conditions of slave life and treatment in Santos county, Brazil, 1822–1888" (Ph.D. diss., history, Stanford University, 2006).

Rebelo, Manuel dos Anjos da Silva. *Relações entre Angola e Brasil, 1808–1830* (Lisbon: Agência-Geral do Ultramar, 1970).

Reginaldo, Lucilene. "Os rosários dos Angolas: Irmandades negras, experiências escravas e identidades africanas na bahia setecentista" (Campinas: tese de doutorado, UNICAMP, 2005).

Reis, Arthur Cézar Ferreira. "A província do Rio de Janeiro e o Município Neutro," in Sérgio Buarque de Holanda, ed., *História geral da civilização brasileira* (11 vols.; São Paulo: Difusão Européia do Livro, 1960), tomo II, vol. 2.

Reis, Flávia Maria da Mata. "Entre faisqueiras, catas e galerias: Explorações do ouro, leis e cotidiano das Minas do Século XVIII (1702–1762)" (Belo Horizonte: dissertação de mestrado, FFCH-UFMG, 2007).

Reis, Isabel Cristina Ferreira dos. "A família negra no tempo da escravidão: Bahia, 1850–1888" (tese de doutorado, História, UNICAMP, 2007).

Reis, João José. *Death Is a Festival: Funeral Rites and Rebellion in Nineteenth-Century Brazil* (Chapel Hill: University of North Carolina Press, 2003).

———. "Identidade e diversidade étnicas nas Irmandades negras no tempo da escravidão," *Tempo* (Rio de Janeiro), 2, no. 3 (1996), pp. 7–33.

———. *Rebelião escrava no Brasil, a história do levante dos malês (1835)* (São Paulo: Editora Brasiliense, 1986).

———. "The Revolution of the Ganhadores: Urban Labour, Ethnicity, and the African Strike of 1857 in Bahia, Brazil," *Journal of Latin American Studies*, 29, no. 2 (May 1997), pp. 355–393.

Reis, João José and Eduardo Silva. *Negociação e conflito: A resistência negra no Brasil escravista* (São Paulo: Companhia das Letras, 1989).

Renault, François and Serge Daget. *Les traites négriéres en Afrique* (Paris: Karthala, 1985).

Restitutti, Cristiano Corte. "A circulação entre o Rio de Janeiro e o Sul de Minas Gerais, c. 1800–1830," *XVI Encontro Nacional de Estudos Populacionais*, *ABEP* (2008).

Rezende, Rodrigo Castro, Mariângela Porto Gonçalves, Regina Mendes Araújo, and Karina Paranhos da Mata. "Os proprietários de escravos nas Minas Gerais em 1718–1719: Um estudo comparativo dos distritos de Vila do Carmo e Vila Rica," *XIII Encontro da Associação Brasileira de Estudos Populacionais*, *ABEP* (2002).

Ribeiro, Alexandre Viera. "O comércio de escravos e a elite baiana no período colonial," in João Luis Ribeiro Fragoso, Carla Maria Carvalho de Almeida, and Antonio Carlos Juca de Sampaio, eds., *Conquistadores e negociantes: Histórias de elites no Antigo Regime nos trópicos, América lusa, séculos XVI a XVIII* (Rio de Janeiro: Civilização Brasileira, 2007), pp. 313–335.

Ribeiro, Núbia Braga. "Cotidiano e liberdade: Um estudo sobre os alforriados em Minas no século XVIII" (dissertação de mestrado, FFLCH-USP, 1996).

Ricardo, Cassiano. *Marcha para Oeste* (Rio de Janeiro: José Olympio, 1942).

Rios, Ana Maria. "The politics of kinship: Compadrio among slaves in nineteenth-century Brazil," *The History of the Family*, 5, no. 3 (2000), pp. 287–298.

Rios, Ana Maria and Hebe Maria Mattos. "O pós-abolição como problema histórico: Balanços e perspectivas," *Topoi*, 5, no. 8 (Jan.–Jun. 2004), pp. 170–198.

Robertson, Claire C. and Martin A. Klein, eds. *Women and Slavery in Africa* (Madison: University of Wisconsin Press, 1983).

Rocha, Solange Pereira da. "Gente negra na Paraíba oitocentista: População, família e parentesco espiritual" (Recife: tese de doutorado, UFP, 2007).

Rodney, Walter. *How Europe Underdeveloped Africa* (London: Bogle-L'Ouverture Publications 1972).

Rodrigues, Jaime. "Cultura marítima: Marinheiros e escravos no tráfico negreiro para o Brasil (sécs. XVIII E XIX)," *Revista Brasileira de História*, 19, no. 38 (1999), pp. 15–53.

_____. *De costa a costa, escravos, marinheiros e intermediários do tráfico negreiro de Angola ao Rio de Janeiro (1780–1860)* (São Paulo: Companhia das Letras, 2005).

Roos, Adriane Eunice de Paula. "A escravidão negra sob a perspectiva do direito no Brasil Imperial," Trabalho de Conclusão do Curso de Direito, PUC-RS (Porto Alegre) (2007), available at http://www.pucrs.br/direito/graduacao/tc/tccII/2007_1.htm.

Russell-Wood, A.J.R. "Black and Mulatto Brotherhoods in Colonial Brazil: A Study in Collective Behavior," *The Hispanic American Historical Review*, 54, no. 4 (November 1974), pp. 567–602.

_____. *The Black Man in Slavery and Freedom in Colonial Brazil* (London: Macmillan Press, 1982).

_____. "Colonial Brazil: The Gold Cycle, c. 1690–1750," in Leslie Bethell, ed., *The Cambridge History of Latin America* (11 vols.; Cambridge: Cambridge University Press, 1984), II, pp. 547–600.

Salles, Gilka V. F. *Economia e escravidão na Capitania de Goiás* (Goiânia: CEGRAF/UFG. 1992).

Samara, Eni de Mesquita. *Lavoura Canavieira, trabalho livre e cotidiano, Itu 1780–1830* (São Paulo: EDUSP, 2005).

_____. "O papel do agregado na região de Itu, 1780–1830," *Anais do Museu Paulista* (Série histórica), vol. 6 (1977), pp. 43–44.

Sánchez-Albornoz, Nicolás. *La población de América Latina: Desde los tiempos precolombinos al año 2025* (2nd rev. ed.; Madrid: Alianza Editorial, 1994).

_____. "The Population of Colonial Spanish America," in Leslie Bethell, ed., *The Cambridge History of Latin America* (Cambridge: Cambridge University Press, 1984), II, pp. 3–6.

Santos, Maria Januária Vilela. *A Balaiada e a Insurreição de escravos no Maranhão* (São Paulo: Editora Ática, 1983).

Santos, Ynaê Lopes dos. "Além da senzala: Arranjos escravos de moradia no Rio de Janeiro (1808–1850)" (São Paulo: dissertação de mestrado, USP, 2006).

Saraiva, Luiz Fernando. "Estrutura de terras e transição do trabalho em um grande centro cafeeiro, Juiz de Fora 1870–1900," *X Seminário sobre a Economia Mineira* (2002).

Saunders, A. C. de C. M. *A Social History of Black Slaves and Freedmen in Portugal, 1441–1555* (Cambridge: Cambridge University Press, 1982).

Saunders, William T. "The Population of the Central Mexican Symbiotic Region, the Basin of Mexico, and the Teotihuacan Valley in the Sixteenth Century," in William M. Denevan, ed., *The Native Population of the Americas in 1492* (Madison: University of Wisconsin Press, 1976), pp. 85–150.

Scarano, Julita. *Devoção e escravidão – A Irmandade de Nossa Senhora do Rosário dos Pretos no Distrito Diamantino no século XVIII* (São Paulo: Editora Nacional, 1976).

Scheidel, Walter. "Quantifying the Sources of Slaves in the Early Roman Empire," *The Journal of Roman Studies*, vol. 87 (1997), pp. 156–169.

Schleumer, Fabiana. "Além de açoites e correntes: Cativos e libertos em Cotia colonial (1790–1810)" (dissertação de mestrado, FFCH-USP, 1999).

Schmidt-Nowara, Christopher. *Empire and Antislavery: Spain, Cuba, and Puerto Rico, 1833–1874* (Pittsburgh: University of Pittsburgh Press, 1999).

Schwartz, Lilia Moritz. *O espetáculo das raças, cientistas, instituções e questão racial no Brasil, 1870–1930* (São Paulo: Companhia das Letras, 1993).

Schwartz, Stuart B. "Cantos e quilombos numa conspiração de escravos Hausás," in João José Reis and Flávio dos Santos Gomes, eds., *Liberdade por um fio: História dos quilombos no Brasil* (São Paulo: Companhia das Letras, 1996), pp. 373–406.

———. "A Commonwealth within Itself: The Early Brazilian Sugar Industry, 1550–1670," in Stuart B. Schwartz, ed., *Tropical Babylons: Sugar and the Making of the Atlantic World, 1450–1680* (Chapel Hill: University of North Carolina Press, 2004), pp. 158–200.

———. "Indian Labor and New World Plantations: European Demands and Indian Responses in Northeastern Brazil," *American Historical Review*, 83, no. 3 (June 1978), pp. 43–79.

———. "The Manumission of Slaves in Colonial Brazil: Bahia, 1684–1745," *Hispanic American Historical Review*, 54, no. 4 (1974), pp. 603–635.

———. "Patterns of Slaveholding in the Americas: New Evidence from Brazil," *The American Historical Review*, 87, no. 1 (February 1982), 55–86.

———. "Resistance and Accommodation in Eighteenth-Century Brazil: The Slaves' View of Slavery," *Hispanic American Historical Review*, 57, no. 1 (February 1977), pp. 69–81.

———. *Slaves, Peasants, and Rebels: Reconsidering Brazilian Slavery* (Urbana: University of Illinois Press, 1992).

———. *Sugar Plantations in the Formation of Brazilian Society (Bahia, 1550–1835)* (Cambridge: Cambridge University Press, 1985).

———. ed. *Tropical Babylons: Sugar and the Making of the Atlantic World, 1450–1680* (Chapel Hill: University of North Carolina Press, 2004).

Sharp, William F. *Slavery in the Spanish Frontier: The Colombian Chocó, 1680–1810* (Norman: University of Oklahoma Press, 1976).

Silva, Cesar Mucio. *Processos-crime: Escravidão e violência em Botucatu* (São Paulo: Alameda, 2004).

Silva, Cristiano Lima da. "As alforrias nos registros de batismos da matriz de Nossa Senhora do Pilar de São João del Rei: Uma análise demográfica (1751–1850)," *Anais do 2° seminário regional do CEO – Centro de Estudos do oitocentos* (Juiz de Fora: Clio Edições Eletrônicas, 2005).

———. "Senhores e pais: Reconhecimento de paternidade dos alforriados na pia batismal na Freguesia de Nossa Senhora do Pilar de São João del Rei (1770–1850)," *Anais do I Colóquio dos LAHES (Laboratório de História Econômica e Social)* Juiz de Fora, 13 a 16 de Junho de 2005, n.p.

Silva, Cristiane dos Santos. "Irmãos de fé, Irmãos no poder: A irmandade de Nossa Senhora do Rosário dos Pretos na Vila Real do Senhor Bom Jesus do Cuiabá (1751–1819)" (Cuiabá: dissertação de mestrado, UFMG, 2001).

Silva, Leonardo Dantas. *Holandeses em Pernambuco: 1630–1654* (Recife: Instituto Ricardo Brennand, 2005).

Silva, Marilene Rosa Nogueira da. *Negro na rua, a nova face da escravidão* (São Paulo: Editora Hucitec, 1988).

Silva Filho, Geraldo. "O oficialato mecânico em Vila Rica no século dezoito e a participação do escravo e do negro," (dissertação de mestrado, FFLCH-USP, 1996).

Simonsen, Roberto C. *História Econômica do Brasil* (São Paulo: Companhia Nacional, 1977).

Skidmore, Thomas E. *Black into White: Race and Nationality in Brazilian Thought* (New York: Oxford University Press, 1974).

———. "Raízes de Gilberto Freyre," *Journal of Latin American Studies*, 34, no. 1 (February 2002), pp. 1–20.

Slenes, Robert W. "The Demography and Economics of Brazilian Slavery, 1850–1888" (Ph.D. diss., Department of History, Stanford University, 1976).

———. *Na senzala, uma flor: Esperanças e recordações na formação da família escrava: Brasil Sudeste, século XIX* (Rio de Janeiro: Editora Nova Fronteira, 1999).

Soares, Carlos Eugênio Líbano and Flávio Gomes. "'Com o Pé sobre um Vulcão': Africanos Minas, Identidades e a Repressão Antiafricana no Rio de Janeiro (1830–1840)," *Revista Estudos Afro-Asiáticos*, 23, no. 2 (2001), pp. 1–44.

Soares, Luiz Carlos. "A escravidão industrial no Rio de Janeiro do século xix," *Anais do V Congresso Brasileiro de História Econômica ABPHE* (2003).

———. "A manufatura na sociedade escravista: O surto manufatureiro no Rio de Janeiro e nas suas circunvizinhanças (1840–1870)," in F. Mauro, ed., *La préindustrialization du Brésil* (Paris: CNRS, 1984).

———. *O 'Povo de Cam'na capital do Brasil: A escravidão urbana no Rio de Janeiro do século XIX* (Rio de Janeiro: Faperj, Letras, 2007).

———. "Os escravos de ganho no Rio de Janeiro do século XIX," *Revista Brasileira de História*, V, no. 16 (1988), pp. 107–142.

———. *Rameiras, Ilhoas, Polacas... A prostituição no Rio de Janeiro do século XIX* (São Paulo: Editora Ática, 1992).

Soares, Márcio de Sousa. "De pai para filho: Legitimação de escravos, herança e ascensão social de forros nos Campos dos Goitacases, c. 1750 – c. 1830," *V Congresso Brasileiro de História Econômica* (2003).

Soares, Mariza. *Devotos da cor: Identidade étnica, religiosidade e escravidão no Rio de Janeiro, século XVIII* (Rio de Janeiro: Civilização Brasileira, 2000).

Soares, Sebastão Ferreira. *Notas estatisticas sobre a producão agrícola e carestia dos gêneros alimentícios no Império do Brazil* (Rio de Janeiro: J. Villeneuve, 1860).

Soumonni, Eliseacutee. "Some Reflections on the Brazilian Legacy in Dahomey," *Slavery & Abolition*, 22, no. 1 (2001), pp. 42–60.

Souza, Alan Nardi de. "Crime e castigo: A criminalidade em Mariana na primeira metade do século XIX" (dissertação de mestrado em História, Universidade Federal de Juiz de Fora, 2007).

Souza e Silva, Joaquim Norberto de. *Investigações sobre os recenseamentos da população geral do Império e de cada província de per si tentados desde os tempos coloniais até hoje* ([1870]; reprint, São Paulo: Instituto de Pesquisas Econômicas, 1986).

Stein, Stanley J. *Vassouras: A Brazilian Coffee County, 1850–1900* (Cambridge, MA: Harvard University Press, 1957).

Stella, Alessandro. *Historie d'esclaves dans la peninsula Ibérique* (Paris: École des Hautes Études en Sciences Sociales, 2000).

Stuard, Susan M. "Ancillary Evidence for the Decline of Medieval Slavery," *Past & Present*, 149 (November 1995), pp. 3–28.

Sweet, James H. "Manumission in Rio de Janeiro, 1749–54: An African Perspective," *Slavery & Abolition*, 24, no. 1 (April 2003), pp. 54–70.

Taunay, Affonso de E. *História do Café no Brasil* (20 vols.; Rio de Janeiro: Departamento Nacional do Café, 1939).

Taunay, Carlos Augusto. *Manual do agricultor brasileiro* (reprint of the 1839 edition; São Paulo: Companhia das Letras, 2001).

Teixeira, Adriano Braga. "População, sistema econômico e poder na transição do século XVIII para o XIX em Minas Colonial – Barbacena – 1791/1822," (Rio de Janeiro, dissertação de mestrado – UFRJ, 2007).

Teixeira, Heloisa Maria. "Reprodução e famílias escravas, em Mariana, 1850–1888" (tese de doutorado, USP-FFLCH, 2001).

Teixeira, Luana. "Trabalho escravo na produção pecuária: São Francisco de Paula de Cima da Serra (Rio Grande de São Pedro, 1850–1871)," *III Encontro Escravidão e liberdade no Brasil Meridional* (2007).

Teixeira, Maria Lúcia Resende Chaves. "Lei, matriz doutrinária e escravidão: Minas Gerais, Comarca do Rio das Mortes (1800–1831)," *Anais do XII Seminário sobre a Economia Mineira* (2006).

Terra, Paulo Cruz. "Tudo que transporta e carrega é negro? Carregadores, cocheiros e carroceiros no Rio de Janeiro (1824–1870)" (Niteroi: dissertação de mestrado, UFF, 2007).

Thomas, Georg. *Política indigenista dos portugueses no Brasil, 1500–1640* (São Paulo: Edições Loyola, 1982).

Thornton, John. *Africa and Africans in the Making of the Atlantic World, 1400–1800* (2nd ed.; Cambridge: Cambridge University Press, 1998).

Toplin, Robert B. *The Abolition of Slavery in Brazil* (New York: Atheneum, 1972).

Trindade, Alexandro Dantas. "André Rebouças: Da Engenharia Civil a Engenharia Social" (tesis de doutorado, sociologia, UNICAMP, 2004).

Troitiño, Sonia. "Números da bastardia: Os ilegítimos nos testamentos paulistas oitocentistas," *Anais do XII Encontro Nacional de Estudos Populacionais ABEP* (2000).

Turner, J. M. "Les Brésiliens: The Impact of Former Brazilian Slaves upon Dahomey" (Boston: Ph.D. diss., Boston University, 1975).

Valencia Villa, Carlos Eduardo "Produzindo alforrias no Rio de Janeiro no século XIX" (dissertação de mestrado, UFRJ, 2008).

Valentin, Agnaldo. "Arroz no Vale do Ribeira (1800–1888)" (São Paulo: tese de doutorado, FFLCH/USP, 2006).

Vasconcellos, Marcia Cristina Roma de. "Famílias escravas em Angra dos Reis, 1801–1888" (São Paulo: Tese de doutorado, USP-FFCH, 2006).

Verger, Pierre. *Flux et reflux de la traite des négres entre le golfe de Benin et Bahia de Todos os Santos, du dix-septième au dix-neuvieme siècle* (Paris: Mouton & Co., 1968).

Verlinden, Charles. *L'esclavage dans l'Europe médiévale* (2 vols.; Brugge: De Tempel, 1955–1977).

Versiani, Flávio Rabelo. "Brazilian Slavery: Toward an Economic Analysis," *Revista Brasileira de Economia*, 48, no. 4 (Dezembro 1994), pp. 463–478.

_____. "Escravidão 'suave' no Brasil: Gilberto Freyre tinha razão?" *Revista de Economia Política*, 27, no. 2 (Abril-Junho, 2007), pp. 163–183.

Versiani, Flávio Rabelo and José Raimundo Oliveira Vergolino. "Posse de Escravos e Estrutura da Riqueza no Agreste e Sertão de Pernambuco: 1777–1887" (Universidade de Brasília, Departamento de Economia, Texto para discussão, no. 231, 2002); also published in *Estudos Econômicos*, 33, no. 2 (Abril–Junho 2003), pp. 353–393.

_____. "Preços de Escravos em Pernambuco no Século XIX" (Texto para Discussão, no. 252; Universidade de Brasília, Departamento de Economia, Brasília, Outubro de 2002).

_____. "Slave holdings in nineteenth-century Brazilian northeast: Sugar estates and the backlands." Paper presented at *XIII Congress of the International Economic History Association*, (Buenos Aires), July 2002.

Viana, Larissa. *O idioma da mestiçagem: As irmandades de pardos na América Portuguesa* (Campinas, SP: Editora UNICAMP, 2007).

Vieira, Alberto. *Os escravos no arquipélago da Madeira: séculos XV a XVII* (Funchal: Centro de Estudos de História do Atlântico, 1991).

_____. "Sugar Islands: The Sugar Economy of Madeira and the Canaries, 1450–1650," in Stuart B. Schwartz, ed., *Tropical Babylons: Sugar and the Making of the Atlantic World, 1450–1680* (Chapel Hill: University of North Carolina Press, 2004), pp. 42–84.

Vitorino, Artur José Renda. "Operários livres e cativos nas manufaturas: Rio de Janeiro, segunda metade do século XIX," *I Jornada Nacional de História do Trabalho* (Florianópolis: Laboratório de História Social do Trabalho e da Cultura, 2002).

Vogt, John L. *Portuguese Rule on the Gold Coast, 1469–1682* (Athens: University of Georgia Press, 1979).

Volpato, Luiza Rios Ricci. "Quilombos em Mato Grosso: Resistência negra em área de fronteira," in João José Reis and Flávio dos Santos Gomes, eds., *Liberdade por um fio: História dos quilombos no Brasil* (São Paulo: Companhia das Letras, 1996), pp. 222–225.

Wakefield, Edward Gibbon. "A Letter from Sydney" [1829], in Lloyd Pritchard, ed., *The Collected Works of Edward Gibbon Wakefield* (Glasgow: Colllins, 1968).

Watson, James, ed. *Asian and African Systems of Slavery* (Berkeley: University of California Press, 1980).

Weinstein, Barbara. "Slavery, Citizenship, and National Identity in Brazil and the United States South," in Don Doyle and Marco Antonio Pamplona, eds., *Nationalism in the New World* (Athens: University of Georgia Press, 2006), pp. 248–271.

Wissenbach, Maria Cristina Cortez. *Sonhos africanos, vivências ladinas: Escravos e forros em São Paulo (1850–1880)* (São Paulo: Editora Hucitec, 1998).

————. "Sonhos africanos, vivências ladinas: Escravos e forros no município de São Paulo (1850–1880)" (São Paulo: dissertação de mestrado, Departamento de História, FFCLCH, 1989).

Wright, Gavin. *The Political Economy of the Cotton South* (New York: Norton, 1978).

Yai, Olabiyi Babalola. "The Identity, Contributions, and Ideology of the Aguda (Afro-Brazilians) of the Gulf of Benin: A Reinterpretation," *Slavery & Abolition*, 22, no. 1 (2001), pp. 61–71.

Zemella, Mafalda P. *O abastecimento da Capitania das Minas Gerais no século XVIII* (São Paulo: Hucitec-Edusp, 1990).

Zubaran, Maria Angélica. "Escravidão e liberdade nas fronteiras do Rio Grande do Sul (1860–1880): O caso da Lei de 1831," *Estudos Ibero-Americanos* (PUCRS), 32, no. 2 (Dezembro 2006), pp. 119–132.

————. "Os Escravos e a Lei de 7 de Novembro de 1831 no Rio Grande do Sul (1865–1888)," *II Encontro, "Escravidão e Liberdade no Brasil Meridional"* (2005).

Index